The COLD is in her BONES

PETERNELLE van ARSDALE

SIMON & SCHUSTER

First published in Great Britain in 2019 by Simon & Schuster UK Ltd
A CBS COMPANY

First published in the USA in 2019 by Margaret K. McElderry Books,
an imprint of Simon & Schuster Children's Publishing Division

1 3 5 7 9 10 8 6 4 2

Simon & Schuster UK Ltd
1st Floor, 222 Gray's Inn Road
London WC1X 8HB

www.simonandschuster.co.uk
www.simonandschuster.com.au
www.simonandschuster.co.in

Simon & Schuster Australia, Sydney
Simon & Schuster India, New Delhi

A CIP catalogue record for this book is available from the British Library.

PB ISBN 978-1-4711-6088-2
eBook ISBN 978-1-4711-6089-9

Book design by Sonia Chaghatzbanian and Irene Metaxatos

Printed and bound by CPI Group (UK) Ltd, Croydon, CR0 4YY

Simon & Schuster UK Ltd are committed to sourcing paper that is made from wood grown
in sustainable forests and support the Forest Stewardship Council, the leading international
forest certification organisation. Our books displaying the FSC logo are printed on FSC
certified paper.

For Jan

The
COLD
is in her
BONES

PROLOGUE

THERE ONCE WAS A GIRL WITH TANGLES IN HER HAIR. She liked the tangles. She dug her fingers into them, twirled and spun them with curious, searching fingers. Her name was Hulda.

Hulda had a sister whose hair was as smooth as river water. The mother brushed the sister's hair like it was something precious. "Like spun gold," the mother said. Hulda had never seen spun gold. But if it was anything like the sister's hair, she thought it must be very beautiful.

Maybe, Hulda thought, spun gold was like snakeskin. Snakeskin shimmered like the sister's hair. Hulda wondered if the sister's hair felt like a snake's skin, too. Cool and alive. But the sister didn't let Hulda touch her hair. "Dirty hands," the sister would say, and wrinkle her pretty nose. Hulda's hands were often dirty, it was true. It was only when the sister was sleeping in the bed next to hers that Hulda could creep over and pick up a coil of the sister's hair, spread it across her arm. The hair lay there, lifeless. Not like a snake at all. Hulda let it drop to the pillow. Wrinkled her own less pretty nose.

Every evening after that, she watched with altered eyes while the mother brushed the sister's hair, the firelight turning each strand a different shade of sunshine-yellow. Hulda felt caught in a place between envy and disdain. It was a silly thing to fuss over something so dead. And yet she saw the pleasure the mother took in each stroke, the way the sister's eyes half closed like a drowsy cat's.

The mother used to brush Hulda's hair that way. That was a long time ago. Hulda was little then, years before her first bleed. She could hardly recall the feel of the mother's hands in her hair. The last time, the mother had threatened to cut it all off. "Child, if you can't keep the tangles out yourself and you cry so when I brush it, what choice do I have?" But the father had insisted no. "A woman's hair is her glory," he said. Hulda hadn't known what that meant at the time. Now she did. On her wedding night a woman was supposed to unwrap her hair and offer it to her husband like a gift, something only he was allowed to see and touch. This was why the sister, on her eighteenth birthday, had taken to braiding her hair and winding it around her head, a secret to be revealed to none other than the man she married.

Hulda was sixteen, and such things only played at the periphery of her vision, like a bird fluttering off before she could catch sight of what it was. But birds didn't interest Hulda so much anymore.

When they were little, Hulda and the sister had been always together. When the mother woke them in the morning, she'd find them curled up in the same narrow bed, legs and arms and hair intertwined. After breakfast the girls fussed over the baby animals on their parents' farm. The puffy white lambs and yellow chicks. They'd even taken to naming them. But the parents had admonished them that there was no sense naming something that they or one of their neighbors would someday be eating. The sister lost interest in the game after that, but Hulda had concluded that in the natural order of things, one didn't eat what one named. So she took to naming the creatures that weren't likely to be eaten by anyone in the village. The parents made this difficult, though. It seemed there were few living things in Hulda's world that weren't ultimately headed for someone's dinner table. Deer. Doves. Rabbits. So she turned her attention to smaller things. Ants. Beetles. Butterflies and moths. Fireflies on summer evenings. She'd catch one in her hands, whisper a name into her palms, and then let it go. "Fly, Asmund! Enjoy a nice long life!"

Years passed that way, and while the sister pinned her hair to her head and grew into a woman, Hulda christened salamanders and snacked on wild berries until her lips turned purple. She liked to think each time she named a creature was a sort of blessing, like the pastor's upraised hands at the end of Sunday service. An invocation of some magical, protective gift. She loved to lie in the field near home, the one that gently sank into marsh, and let the wind blow the long grasses softly over her in tickles and strokes. She'd lay perfectly still, her fingernails dug into the earth as if she too were dug in, while bees buzzed around her, flies landed but never bit. She named each one.

The first time a snake slithered over her, she held her breath. It wasn't fright that made her still. It was delight. The feel of snake scale on skin was so delicious it sent a tremor up her spine.

The snake was slender and green and its tiny black eyes regarded her with a calm that made her calm as well. She named it Grön, which seemed only fitting.

After that, the snakes became her special friends. They spoke to her. Not in a way that she could hear, but in a place that she could feel. They told her their secret names, the names they held within themselves. It was a presumption, Hulda realized, to have given a name to the snake she called Grön. When she found him again, she apologized. He flicked her earlobe with his gentle forked tongue and she knew she was forgiven. His name, he told her, wasn't Grön at all.

While the sister stayed at home collecting eggs and learning to churn butter, Hulda escaped immediately after breakfast and rarely returned before supper. This way she mostly avoided the mother's despairing gaze. Still, she felt the mother's eyes following her hands as she reached for bread at the table. When the mother's lips thinned with disgust, Hulda knew what would happen. Once the dishes had been cleared, the mother would take Hulda's hands in her own and scrape the dirt from under her fingernails. Hulda quietly endured the digging of the mother's file in those tender places. While the mother labored, she didn't marvel over Hulda's hands the way she did over the sister's hair. Instead the mother said, "Life is difficult enough without your daughter making it more so."

One day Hulda sat at the roots of a large tree. She was still learning all the snakes' names, concentrating hard on the task, and that was why she didn't notice the approach of the farmer boy the sister's age. He was more man than boy, really—broad in the shoulders and sprouting a new beard.

The snakes were gathered around Hulda, patiently whispering

to her, nestled among the tree roots, and maybe that was why the boy didn't see them until they were almost underfoot.

Hulda's favorite snake had woven itself into her hair like a green ribbon. She and it looked up when they sensed the boy's presence. The boy's eyes widened. He lifted his finger and started to say something. But then he saw the snakes. All the snakes. And the snakes saw him, and they all raised their heads and turned to him. If the boy had known anything about snakes he might have been calmer, but he wasn't that kind of boy. He was the kind of boy who stomped, and that was what he did then. He stomped those snakes, stomped them hard. Hulda screamed. She got to her feet and the sounds coming out of her weren't girl sounds at all, the boy would swear later. The eyes that looked back at him from her face weren't girl eyes, either. He fled.

Hulda ran her fingers over the snakes the boy had bruised with his awful boy feet. They coiled around her wrists, sought solace in the crooks of her arms. The green snake slithered more deeply into her hair.

Hours later, in the cool of dusk, she went home to the sound of crickets. She'd forgotten all about the clumsy boy. She'd learned so many names since then.

They were all there when Hulda got home. The mother and father. The sister. The boy and his mother and father. The memory of the boy's stomping feet came back to Hulda in a rush, and she nearly opened her mouth to tell them how horrible he'd been, but the words dissolved on her tongue. They were looking at Hulda with accusing eyes. The boy's mother said to Hulda's mother, "You'll do as we agreed?" Hulda's mother nodded.

Hulda was sent to bed hungry, and downstairs she heard her family talking.

"We'll keep her locked up. No more running wild," the father said.

"You can't make me sleep in the same room with her," the sister said.

"In the barn with her then," the father said.

"No, not that," the mother said. "Besides, what would the neighbors think?"

"What do the neighbors think already?" the sister said. "I wish I had no sister. She'll ruin us all. Who will want to marry me with a creature like that for a relation?"

Hulda lay in her bed listening to all of this while hot tears stung the corners of her eyes. She remembered when the sister and she had been as woven together as a single braid. She mourned the loss in a rush that emptied her heart and left nothing in its place. She'd never felt so alone.

Just then, a delicate stroke above her left ear reminded her that she wasn't alone, and never would be. The slender green snake slid down her cheek and throat, grazed her earlobe with its tongue, and then wove himself into her hair once again. Hulda fell asleep that way.

Hours later, Hulda woke to a dark room and the sister's screams. "It's crawling on me! It's crawling on me!"

Hulda's hands flew to her hair, searched her scalp. The slender green snake was gone.

The darkness was broken by lamplight and the mother and father in the doorway. "What's happened, child? What's crawling on you?"

Hulda held her breath, but the mother and father found nothing. The sister was untouched, despite her wailing to the contrary. She pointed at Hulda. "It was a snake crawling on me. She did it." The parents looked at Hulda.

"I was asleep," Hulda said. "I woke up to her screaming, same as you. I did nothing."

The sister's eyes narrowed at Hulda and then at the parents. "You believe her and not me?"

"No, child, it's not like that," the mother said.

"What's it like, then? You heard what happened. She's a monster. You'll know it when she's killed me in my bed."

"All right, child. There, there." The mother placed soothing hands on the sister's brow. Stroked her rivers of golden hair. "Nothing evil can befall you here. It was a dream, that's all."

The father said nothing, but looked at Hulda with cold eyes. Hulda lay her head down on her pillow.

The door closed and the room darkened to black again.

Minutes passed and Hulda felt the cool stroke of scales on her cheek, and the green snake nestled himself in her hair once again. Hulda let go of the breath she'd been holding in her chest since the sister first screamed.

Then the sister spoke to her soft and low from across the room. "I hate you, Hulda."

"I hate you, too," Hulda said.

It didn't happen every night. Days might go by when Hulda woke to the dawn and the snake was nestled in her hair, right where he belonged. But just often enough, the sister woke up in the night screaming, and the slender green snake was nowhere to be found. The mother always insisted these were nothing but nightmares. The trouble would pass, she said. Dreams always did. And the father always looked at Hulda with cold eyes.

In the meantime the mother kept Hulda locked inside. When Hulda wasn't helping the mother in the kitchen, or mending socks with uneven stitches, she stared longingly through the window, craving the dirt under her fingernails, the snakes whispering their names in her ears. The slender green snake was a comfort, but Hulda sensed he was ailing. Hulda felt herself sickening as well. As fall sank into winter, leaves browning and drifting, Hulda also withered and drifted. She wasn't really the girl sitting in the chair by the window, the green snake coiled in her hair. Her body was there. But the other part of her, the better part, was gone.

She longed for the voices of the snakes in her ears. They'd been silent to her for so long. The green snake spoke to her still, but his whisper was so faint she had to strain to hear it. *Call to them,* the green snake said, *tell them we're dying.*

In her bones, Hulda knew this to be true. If she didn't get out, she would die here in this chair by the window. She and the green snake.

She begged the mother to let her out for even an hour. "I could help you," Hulda said. "I could fetch father for dinner. I could sell eggs in the village for you."

But the mother always said, "You stay here."

Then one Sunday morning, Hulda woke up and the snake voices were loud and there were so many of them, all talking at once. The words hissed over each other, but Hulda felt their meaning.

Get out, they said. *Get out. He's coming.*

It was the boy the snakes were warning her about. The boy who'd stomped them.

The mother and father had invited him to dinner after church. The sister had made cake.

Sunday mornings were the only time the mother and father let Hulda place a foot on the ground outside their farmhouse, and to breathe air that wasn't still and stale. This wasn't a mercy, Hulda knew. It was because they feared what she might do if they left her alone.

Hulda carried herself like any other girl attending service with her family. Mostly. She sat with folded hands. She bowed her head. And when all the rest of the congregation whispered their prayers, Hulda whispered to the snakes, ever so quietly and under her breath. She felt them far beneath her, in their deep winter dens where they burrowed and warmed each other in the cold. The soles of her feet tickled.

In the back of the wagon on the way home from church, the sister pinched Hulda hard in the fleshy part of her arm. "Behave," she said. "They'll send you away if you don't."

"Good," Hulda said, and smiled in a way that caused the sister to shrink from her.

"There's something very wrong with you," the sister said.

Hulda didn't talk to the snakes while the boy was there that afternoon, but the snakes talked to her. *Get out*, they said. *Get out. He's here.*

Hulda was quiet while the father talked to the boy, asking him polite questions about his family's farm, their yield and horses. The sister smiled and served the boy her cake. The mother smiled and cleared the table while the boy and the sister pulled chairs up to the fire.

Hulda darned socks and rocked with the voices in her head. She felt the boy's eyes on her, and she wondered why he was looking at her. She touched her hand to her hair, making sure the green snake was where he belonged. He moved against her index finger. She stroked him and then pulled her hand away.

The sister's eyes were bright, lit by the fire and her desire for the boy's attention. "Why, I daresay Hulda's fixing her hair for you," she said to the boy.

The boy laughed and Hulda felt her cheeks burn. "I wasn't," she said.

The father laughed now, too. "There are worse things than fixing your hair for a boy, Hulda. You're old enough for braiding now." He looked over at the mother where she sat with her own mending.

The mother caught Hulda's eye and what Hulda saw when she looked back was fear. Not fear of Hulda, but rather fear for Hulda. "There's time for that," the mother said. "But not yet."

Hulda's heart filled and opened toward the mother, suddenly and painfully. It had been so long since she'd felt cared for. Her eyes widened and she almost smiled. Maybe this was why Hulda didn't notice how the sister's excitement had grown, and how the sister's hand reached for her, picking up a tangled hank of Hulda's hair.

Hulda's gasp of surprise was drowned by the sister's shriek. The green snake had reared its head and hissed at the moment the sister's hand invaded his home.

The sister fell backward. The father shot to his feet, sending his cup of tea spilling and rolling across the floor. The mother whitened and froze, her needle held midair.

The boy was more decisive. He leapt toward Hulda, grasped the green snake with his fist, and threw him into the fire.

Hulda heard the green snake screaming in her head, and

she matched his screams with her own. Then the green snake screamed no more, but Hulda couldn't stop.

Hulda felt herself being held and she couldn't have said who it was that held her. She thrashed and bucked. The scent of burnt flesh was in her nostrils, and she felt burnt herself, heated up outside and in. Too hot. Too hot. When she could scream words they were words of burning. "I'm on fire," she howled. "On fire."

The snakes in her head were all screaming at once and she could no longer make out what they were saying. Were they burning, too? Were they all burning?

Hulda felt something cold and wet on her forehead and she looked up at the mother leaning over her, resting a cloth there. Hulda was in her bed; she and the mother were alone. "Child," the mother said. "You must calm yourself. This screaming and carrying on, it'll do you no good. Nor any of us."

Hulda looked up at the mother's face, written with concern. This time the mother's concern was for herself, not for Hulda.

"Mother," she said. "If I could. If only I could." And then the snakes in her head screamed and so did Hulda. "I'm on fire," she howled. "On fire."

For three days and nights Hulda writhed, twisted, and sweat through her bed linens.

On the fourth day, a woman appeared in the doorway to Hulda's bedroom. Hulda recognized her: the midwife.

The midwife said, "She looks well enough."

"Well enough?" the mother said. "She's burning up! You can feel it yourself. She'll burn away to ash before long."

"You mistake me," the midwife said. "She looks well, but she isn't well. I believe her . . . suffering . . . is spiritual in nature."

The mother narrowed her eyes at the midwife. "How so?"

"If it were a fever she'd be weak and pliable. But look at her strength! Look how she twists and screams. And that heat. That's not fever heat. No. This is something . . . else."

The midwife stepped gingerly toward Hulda. The nearer she came, the more Hulda thrashed. She felt the midwife closing in, sensed her looming body. She tried to shrink from the midwife; she pressed down into the pillow and bed linens. In her head the snakes were still talking over each other, a jumble of voices that sounded like pain felt. Her skin burned hotter. She couldn't bear it, the heat, the fire, the terrible heat.

She leapt up from the bed and hurled herself toward the open window. She would throw herself through it, she thought. Into the cold and snow. Put out the fire. Then there would be no more burning, no voices screaming in her head. No more frightened faces staring at her from across rooms. No more sitting in chairs looking through windows at places she couldn't go. She could dig her fingers into earth once again, if only to die there.

But before she could leap through the window the father's hands were on her, and the midwife's hands were on her, and where they touched her she felt scorched, as if her flesh might pull away in their grips. She screamed in agony. To make them stop was all she wanted. But they forced her down to the floor, the father holding her arms, the midwife straddling her legs.

So she used the only weapon they'd left her with. She sank her teeth into the father's fleshy earlobe and didn't let go until she tasted blood.

Finally, she wasn't the only one screaming.

✦ ✦ ✦

Later, after Hulda's hands and feet had been tied to the bedposts, the midwife said, "I told you. It's the demon heat."

"Yes, the demon heat," the father said, cradling his ear.

The sister fled to her aunt and uncle's farm and promised she never would return so long as that monster was in the house.

The mother wept. "Why us? We've done nothing to deserve this."

"We cannot know why some are stricken," the midwife said.

"What's to be done about it?" the father said. "How can we purge ourselves of . . . " He gestured at Hulda.

The midwife said that the best way to battle a demon so fiery was to douse its flame. She would freeze the demon out of Hulda. Take her away from the farm, into the woods, and leave her there for three days, long enough for the demon to pass out of her. The third day would be a Sunday, which they all agreed was fitting. After church and praying for the Lord's mercy on her soul, they would return for the child that remained once the demon was gone.

The mother asked if she might clothe Hulda, but the midwife refused. "No, that will only give shelter to the demon."

Hulda was left alone again. When the light through the window had dimmed to afternoon, Hulda felt herself surrounded. She was untied from the bed, and though she thrashed, there were too many hands and arms upon her. They wrapped ropes around her and she could no longer move, only scream.

Her eyes cleared for a moment and she saw the mother there, hands twisted together, face drawn tight. Hulda said, "Mother?"

The mother's hands went to her mouth. Then to her eyes.

Then there was no mother anymore. No father. Only the fire inside Hulda and the screaming of the snakes.

Hulda felt the bite of the cold as she was carried out of the house and into the woods. Her wet nightshift froze to her skin.

They laid her down. Hulda looked up at the branches of an evergreen white with snow. She shook. There was no fire inside her anymore. There were no voices in her head. There was only terror. Cold like the ground she lay upon. Colder even than the snow they piled over her.

"Cover her head, too?" someone asked.

The midwife bent over Hulda, considering. Hulda looked up at her, shivered, felt the meager heat of her own breath as it curled over her lips. "I hate you," she said.

The midwife shook her head at Hulda. "Yes. The head, too." As the first scoop of snow dropped over Hulda's face she heard the midwife add, "Vile creature."

Hulda couldn't say how long it took for the cold to overtake her. Minutes or hours. Time had lost meaning for her, ever since the screaming started.

At first the cold was painful to her, but then that passed, and for a brief while, she felt almost warm. Or maybe it was a memory of warmth. Of a time when she hadn't been made of ice. When there had been warm blood in her veins, warm breath in her chest, heat in the places where her limbs met her body.

But then the cold reached her bones. The cold was in her bones. And that was when she allowed herself one last cry for help.

She didn't cry for her mother or her father.

She didn't cry for her sister.

She cried for no one who had abandoned her.

She cried for the snakes.

She called them by name.

She called to them where they huddled in their dens, warming each other. She asked them to come stroke her cheeks, to curl around her wrists, to remind her of what it had been like when she too felt warm and free to move through the grass, to feel soil on her skin.

And the snakes came. They rose from their near-slumber and worked their way up to her. They wrapped themselves around her limbs and belly. They wove themselves through her fingers. They threaded themselves into her hair. They didn't scream in her head anymore. They whispered to her, soft and sweet. *We're here,* they said. *And we will never leave you.*

The snakes didn't come to her alone, however. They brought another with them.

The morning of the third day dawned bright, clear, and cold. So cold. The mother and father met their oldest daughter at church, and the family sat together and prayed.

After the service, the congregation spilled from the church. The children turned gleeful, the adults murmured and chatted, their eyes drifting to the family with the demon child.

Stories of what happened next would be told many times and in many ways. The people saw what they saw and felt what they felt. And who's to say what they did or didn't?

This is what really happened:

Hulda came to church.

She broke through the trees, a girl made of snakes. A girl with snakes for hair, and arms, and fingers. A girl with snakes for legs. A girl with fangs.

And the people backed away from her; they fled into the church, they tried to bar the doors.

But there was no more backing away from Hulda. With her body made more of muscle than of bone, she pushed through the church doors and blocked their retreat.

Then she spoke.

Or rather, she hissed. It was hundreds of hisses together, thousands. The people felt her hisses in their own heads, and they clapped their hands to their ears, but they couldn't drown out the sound. The hissing only grew louder.

She cursed them. She cursed them all. From the oldest to the youngest. She cursed their mothers and fathers, their sisters and brothers. She cursed the babies they had yet to dream of having.

They would know this curse when it woke up in their homes. They would know this curse when it sat at their kitchen tables. They would know this curse when it reached out for the milk and bread.

The curse would grow among them, and it would spread. And they would never feel peace or contentment again.

The coldness of Hulda's curse sank into them. Babies whimpered. Adults clutched their chests. Children shivered.

And then Hulda left them. She went away where they couldn't find her, even if they'd tried. But her curse remained, and it settled in. It sat on stools in warm corners of kitchens. It fed chickens and milked cows. It cuddled in laps and braided hair. It went to church on Sunday.

The people tried to forget the curse. But the curse wouldn't be forgotten. The curse reached up to them with soft, chubby fingers. The curse held their hands.

PART
1

I

To protect your home from demons:

1. If you see a snake, kill it. Then burn it.

2. Pour salt where the air comes in—sills, thresholds, hearths.

3. Stay inside after dark. Lock tight doors and windows.

4. Pray.

2

M ILLA POURED THE SALT IN A STRAIGHT LINE, LEFT
to right. It was daytime, so the window was open and the breeze
scattered a few grains that caught in the grooves of the wooden
sill. When she was little, Milla would make drifts of the salt, like
snow, then walk her fingers through. She'd furtively lick the tips
when she was done.

But she wasn't little anymore. She was sixteen, and it had
been a long time since she'd done anything as rebellious as wasting salt.

"Don't dawdle so." Milla's mother looked over her shoulder at
Milla, a pinched expression on her face. Gitta's face was a lock,
and Milla had yet to find the key to opening it.

Gitta was already turning away, headed out to fetch some
eggs for breakfast, when Milla said, "Yes, Mamma. I'm sorry."
Milla knew that she had nothing to be sorry for. She hadn't been

dawdling. But this was the way of things, and if Milla wanted to smooth even one line from her mother's forehead, the only thing was to give in. To say: *Yes, I know, I was wrong, and I'll do better next time.* Anything less than agreement would seem like disobedience—or worse, wildness. And that was what the demons wanted; that was how they got you. Run off the path, skip your chores, carelessly leave an opening in the white line of salt around the hearth, and *whoosh* down the chimney a demon would come and make you its own. Next thing you knew, you were waking up in the morning far less you and a lot more *it*.

Milla went to the next window and poured another fresh line of salt. She'd never received a good answer for why salt kept demons away. She'd learned not to ask questions about such things. It was another sign of disobedience to ask a question that shouldn't be asked, had no answer, or that had an answer you should already know. "A question that shouldn't be asked doesn't deserve an answer." That was what her father, Jakob, said whenever she asked why they'd always done things a certain way, why they couldn't do things a different way. Milla had long ago learned that for Pappa there was simply one right way of doing things, and no argument to be made for the wrong way.

Her brother, Niklas, seemed less bothered by the rules than she was. Maybe that was because it wasn't such an effort for him to follow them. He was naturally so pleasant, so good-natured. He was the one person who had the key to their mother's face. When Niklas walked in the room, the lines on her forehead relaxed and she looked years younger, and so pretty. Pretty in a way that Milla could never hope to be. "Pretty is as pretty does," Gitta had always said to Milla. But Milla knew that couldn't be right. Milla had never done anything but behave, and still she wasn't pretty the way her mother was. If she were, she'd know it. She'd see proof of her prettiness in her mother's eyes, or her father's. Instead what she saw there was disappointment. Perhaps it wasn't true that pretty is as pretty *does*. Maybe, Milla worried, it was pretty is as pretty *thinks*. And if that was the case, then Milla was doomed. Because she could control her behavior, but she couldn't control her mind. Her mind would have its way.

It wasn't quite true that Milla had always behaved. There was one time Milla had disobeyed so horribly that it made her never want to misbehave again. This was back when she and Niklas were very young. All one summer afternoon, they'd fought together in the woods, with knobby sticks as their swords. They screamed battle cries that shook the earth and the leaves and sent the birds circling up and up, and terrified their imaginary troll enemies. Just as the sky turned a deeper blue, they walked toward home with dirt under their nails and leaves in their hair and mud smeared across their cheeks.

From the corner of her eye, Milla regarded Niklas—happy Niklas whom their mother loved. He looked so jolly. So confident that he'd be embraced upon his return, no matter how dirty he was, or how torn his clothing. Something came over Milla then, and she wanted to frighten him. Niklas was two years older then Milla, but never as brave. He was fine when the enemy was something big and oafish like a troll, but Milla's imagination traveled to darker places than his. "Oh, Niklas," Milla whispered, "I smell blood. Fresh boy blood. It must be a forest witch. There she is, see her? The blood from her last kill is dripping from her teeth. But she's still hungry. And now she's coming for you. You'd better run."

Niklas paled. "That's not funny, Milla. You shouldn't say such things. I'll tell Mamma."

Now it was Milla's turn to pale. "I'm sorry." Niklas's face was hard and scared at the same time. Then she made the mistake of trying to tease him out of his upset. "Silly. You know I was making it up."

Niklas turned on her, hands on hips. "I'm not silly, and you're a bad girl."

Milla felt his words like a slap. "I'm not. I'm a good girl."

"No. You're not. Mamma and Pappa both say so." His eyes traveled to her hair. "You're a mess. You'll never brush out all those tangles before Mamma sees you. Remember what happened the last time you went home like that."

Milla did remember. She'd cried and cried as her mother ripped the tangles from her hair with her comb, all the while berating Milla for being so rough and wild. Now Milla forgot all about forest witches, and she wanted only to be good and smooth for Mamma. "Oh, Niklas," she said. Her eyes welled with tears and some spilled over.

Niklas seemed to soften. "There, there, Milla," he said, patting her shoulder. "You can cut them out before we get home. Mamma will never know." Niklas pulled his sharp knife from his pack, the one their father had given him when he turned eight. "Here, you can use this."

"Oh no," Milla said. "I don't think I can." Milla was only six, and while she had the heart of a bear about most things, she knew her limits. "You do it, Niklas. Please?"

So, one by one, Niklas sawed the tangled clumps from her hair. He stood back now and then to survey his work. Then he sawed off some more, and some more. Milla looked down at her feet, and it seemed like an awful lot of hair was collecting there. Finally he stopped. She looked at him. "How is it now? Better?"

Niklas smiled. "Much."

As they walked home, Milla gingerly touched her head. It felt so much lighter. And there was so much air on her neck. That didn't seem like a good thing at all, but it felt kind of nice. She told herself that it must be all right, because Niklas had said so.

When they got home, Milla expected to see her mother's usual locked face, the one that opened the moment she turned to Niklas. Perhaps a part of Milla expected a little worse than that. But she wasn't expecting her mother to drop a bowl and shriek at the sight of her.

"What have you done, Milla? What in all of creation have you done?"

Milla looked at her brother, and for an instant, one corner of his mouth turned up with satisfaction. Milla knew in that moment that he'd gotten her back for having frightened him and then laughed at him. At the sight of their mother's shattered bowl, though, his half smile vanished as quickly as it had appeared.

Milla's mouth opened and closed, and her hands went to her head, searching, hoping to find more hair than she now knew there was. For the first time she allowed herself to realize that it was all gone. Her hair was back there in the woods, in a pile. Where she'd once had bark-brown ringlets that grazed the middle of her back, she was left with uneven clumps no longer than her little finger.

Gitta gripped her by the shoulders. "Why did you do that? You stupid, stupid girl."

"Mamma," Niklas said. "It's not her fault. We were playing and her hair got all tangled, and I suggested she cut it. And she wouldn't use my knife to do it, even though I said she should. I did it, Mamma, I'm the one who did it."

"Oh, Niklas," Gitta said. She shook her head at him the way she did when he spilled milk at the breakfast table. Then she looked back at Milla, her face closed again. "Why must you always be so wild? If you hadn't made such a mess of yourself, your brother wouldn't have had to try to fix you." Gitta released Milla's shoulders and turned toward the kitchen. "Pappa won't like this. Not one bit. Now go and get clean and then I'll see what sense I can make of your hair. I suppose the way you look is punishment enough, but your father may think different."

In the kitchen yard, Niklas pumped water into two pitchers and handed one to Milla. "Is my hair so very bad?" she asked him.

Niklas laughed. "Oh, Milla. It's horrible."

Milla burst into tears.

"There, there." He patted her shoulder the way he had back in the woods, only this time she sensed he meant it. "It's all right. I'll handle Mamma and Pappa." Then he took the pitcher back from her, and he had Milla hold out her hands while he helped her wash with a fresh bar of soap. When he finished rinsing her hair he said, "Well, that was quick. Maybe you should keep it this way, right?"

Then she finally stopped crying, because it was impossible to keep feeling awful with Niklas standing there smiling at her.

That was a long time ago.

Once she had laid the salt down in perfect lines along every window and doorway and arching in a perfect semicircle around the hearth, Milla went out to help Niklas finish loading the wagon. She should have stayed behind to help Mamma with breakfast. But she'd go back inside in a moment—after she'd spoken to Niklas.

In the end, she didn't say anything to him at all. He'd finished loading the wagon with strong, confident arms just as she arrived to help him. Then he looked at her and said, "I'm hungry." So they went back inside.

Don't leave me, she had wanted to say to him. But if she'd said it, her brother would only have laughed at her, the way he always did. It would be a laugh that wasn't meant to make her feel stupid, and yet it would have that effect all the same. His face would break into a smile like sunshine, if sunshine were made of teeth.

She'd said it to him many times before when he and father would go off to the market in the village, leaving her and Mamma behind. And each time he'd respond the same way. "Silly Milla." She was silly Milla, just a girl. Silly Milla, just a lonely girl. Silly Milla, just a lonely girl who must stay at home on the farm while her brother went off and had adventures.

"I'm not having adventures," Niklas always said. "I'm working with Pappa. Standing ankle-deep in manure while he haggles with the other farmers. You're lucky you don't have to go. You get to stay here where it's clean, and Mamma takes care of you, and all you have to do is sew and feed the chickens."

"But you get to see things," she'd argue. "I don't understand why I can't go. It's not fair."

Then he'd smile and laugh like always. "Silly Milla."

Milla knew better than to make such arguments to her father and mother. Pappa would ignore her. Mamma would look frightened. Of what, Milla could never figure out. But her mother's fear was always there, always hanging between Milla and Gitta like an impenetrable fog. It lifted when Niklas was at home. Gitta's face lit up then, and she laughed at Niklas's jokes and she swept his hair from his forehead and kissed him there. Niklas wrapped his arms around Gitta's waist, even when she was cooking, and she let him. If Milla had done that, Gitta would have shooed her off and told her not to hang on her so. When Gitta spoke to Milla at all, it was a word of caution. *Don't do that. Be careful there. Watch you don't get dirty. Lower your voice. Brush your hair. Put on a clean apron.* Milla couldn't remember a time when it wasn't that way, and so it didn't occur to her any longer to try to soften her mother toward her. Nor did it occur to Milla to blame Niklas. After all, she loved Niklas best, too. It was impossible not to.

That loving was from a distance these days—ever since Niklas had turned thirteen, five years ago, and Pappa had said he was man enough to learn how to run things. Running things meant packing the wagon, and saddling a horse and driving cows and goats to the village—the village where Milla wasn't allowed to go.

When she entered the kitchen, Milla felt Gitta's eyes on her, scanning her, making sure her hair was smooth, her apron tied, and her fingernails clean of grime before she set the bread in front of Pappa and took her place at the breakfast table. Milla thought it hardly mattered what she looked like, because she couldn't remember the last time her father had really noticed her. Jakob would have noticed if the bread wasn't fresh, or if the meal wasn't hot. But if all was in order, if the meal was served at the right time and his fork was to the left of his plate, Jakob would see nothing else. Milla might have traded places with a goat, she thought to herself. As long as the goat was well-behaved, Pappa would be none the wiser. Milla imagined herself as a goat, placing the big wooden bread board in front of her father with her teeth instead of her hands, and she laughed.

Gitta wrinkled her brow at Milla then. "What's funny," she said. She said it like a statement, not a question. As if she were really saying, *There's nothing funny. And we don't laugh for no reason.*

Niklas came to the rescue, as he often did. "Did you hear Trude's rooster chased Wolf right out of the kitchen yard?" Trude and Stig were their family's only neighbors, and Wolf was their elkhound. Stig worked for her father, and since Niklas was so often away now, either in the fields or traveling to the village, Milla spent as much time sitting and sewing with Trude as she did with Gitta. "That old rooster is more of a guard dog than Wolf is."

At that, Gitta laughed, and that meant that Milla could, too. Because now something was funny. "That rooster is so mean," Milla said. "Poor Wolf."

"That dog's no use if a rooster can run him off," Jakob said. "I told Stig he should put Wolf down."

"Oh, Pappa," Milla said. "No. That's awful."

Jakob stopped chewing and looked at Milla with surprise, as if he'd just that moment seen she was there. "What would you know about it? And wouldn't it be awful if a fox came and ate up all of Trude's chicks, meanwhile Wolf's asleep by the fire? You're old enough to be thinking sense about these things, Milla."

Milla felt blood rush to her cheeks. She couldn't remember the last time her father had spoken so many words to her. The ignoring she'd grown used to, but this was far worse. She looked down at her plate. She wondered if all girls were treated this way, like something to be frightened for, or ridiculed and thought ignorant if they ever did speak, or found useless if they weren't perfectly behaved all the time. How was she any better than Stig's dog? She looked up at her father's square, sun- and wind-hardened face topped by thick, sandy hair mixed with gray. She realized how rarely she looked into his opaque blue eyes. "Perhaps you should put me down, too, Pappa."

The words were out of her mouth before she could stop them, before she even knew where they were coming from.

Her father's cheeks purpled.

"*Milla.*" The expression on Gitta's face was one of horror. Like a goat really had replaced her daughter at the table. A talking goat with horns on its head and clattering teeth. Gitta's disgust was so great she couldn't even utter a *don't* or a *no* or a *take care.* Milla watched while Gitta turned her attention from Milla's disobedience to Jakob's disapproval. Her mother's most immediate job was to soothe the latter. A storm on her father's side of the table would ruin the meal. And a ruined meal was a grave failure. "Jakob," her mother said. "The child is softhearted. That's all it is. You know how she is about the animals." Gitta reached out her hand and barely grazed Jakob's cuff with her fingertips.

Niklas was struck silent. He looked from Milla to their father, then back again. Jakob stared straight at Milla, his cheeks slowly fading to red. It was Milla's turn now to make things right. She spoke softly. "I'm sorry, Pappa." That word. *Sorry.*

Her father said nothing, but stared at her one beat longer as if he wanted her to wonder what might happen next if he had a mind for something to happen next.

After breakfast, Jakob climbed into the wagon and Gitta spoke to him softly while she handed him the food she'd packed for him and Niklas. Milla walked Niklas to his horse. Once he'd mounted it, he said, "Milla, why must you worry them so?"

Milla had to restrain herself from shouting, but instead she kept her voice low enough so only he could hear. "Worry them so? What do I do all day but try not to cause them worry? Try to be sweet and clean the way Mamma wants, and obedient and . . . and invisible the way Pappa wants. I swear to you, Niklas, I thought just this morning that Pappa wouldn't notice if I were a goat. If I were a goat with horns and fur who sat at his table. So long as I set his plate down in front of him at the right time and the right way, it wouldn't matter." Milla laughed then. "Can you imagine, Niklas! I should do it. Dress up one of the goats in my apron and set it loose in the kitchen."

Niklas looked at her in a funny way then. A way that he didn't normally look at her. It was the way her mother always did. Like he was frightened for her—or of her. "You mustn't talk that way, Milla."

Milla took a step back then. "What way, Niklas? Like a bad girl?"

He shook his head. "Don't be silly, Milla." Then he smiled. "I'll bring you back something from the market. Promise not to upset Mamma while I'm away."

Then he rode off, and Milla wondered how she could avoid doing something that she had never tried to do in the first place.

Milla ate a quiet supper with her mother that evening. If it weren't always so awkward between them, Milla might have enjoyed these nights without Pappa and Niklas. There were no men to feed or clean up after. There was so much less food to make. No clumps of soil shaken from heavy boots and trailed across the floor. There was a fire to warm their toes and the pleasing shimmer of their needles in and out of their sewing. And silence. Dreadful silence.

They might have chatted amiably about which chickens were laying and which would end up in a stew. That's what Trude would have prattled on about if she were here. Trude had a way of using a lot of words to talk about very little, and it would have at least filled the air between them. Instead, the dark fog of Gitta's fear hung there, thicker than ever.

Gitta paused her needle in her sewing and looked at Milla. Milla kept her eyes on her sewing, but she felt her mother's examination like fingers on her scalp. "Milla," Gitta said. "We'll say our prayers together tonight."

Milla felt a chill inside, despite the fire. She knew what was coming next. Milla set aside her sewing, and her mother reached across and took Milla's hands in her own, then pulled her down to kneel across from her on the floor.

Gitta squeezed her eyes shut so tightly that it looked more like wincing than praying.

> *Lord, help us to stay on the path.*
> *Lord, help us to do as we should.*
> *Lord, help us to obey.*

It was a prayer that Milla knew well, but tonight it felt different. Tonight it felt like every word her mother spoke was meant for her, either to protect her or to punish her. It was blasphemous to think so, but Milla doubted there was much of a difference between the two.

> *Lord, we have spread the salt.*
> *Lord, we have locked the doors.*
> *Lord, let us not answer the knock of the stranger.*

The knock of the stranger. For as long as Milla could remember, this line in the prayer had given her a secret thrill. There'd never been a knock of a stranger on their door. There had only ever been her mother and father and Niklas, and Stig and Trude just a shout away. Faces she knew so well she would have noticed if a freckle were misplaced.

Milla wanted a stranger to knock on the door. She begged for one. Anything to break the lonely sameness of her days.

> *Lord, protect us from demons.*
> *Lord, protect us from demons.*
> *Lord, protect us from demons.*

Three times. Three times always. Three times was supposed to be the charm. Milla had often wondered what would happen if she said it only twice.

"Amen," Gitta said. Then she opened her eyes and looked hard at Milla, so hard that Milla feared she'd said aloud what she thought she'd only been thinking.

The heat from the fire licked Milla's right cheek, and a cold draft from under the door kissed her left. "Amen," she said.

Gitta held her grip on Milla's hands, and stared into Milla's eyes as if looking for something. Milla resisted the impulse to break her gaze and instead held steady, steady, steady. Soon, Milla thought to herself, soon she'd be free to go to her bed, and then what happened in the space between her ears was her own business and no one else's.

Finally her mother released her, and Milla rose to her feet.

Gitta stayed where she was, kneeling on the floor. As she turned to the stairs to go up to bed, Milla noticed a break in the stream of salt in front of the door. A small gap—but there. If Gitta noticed it, she'd want Milla to do something about it. Milla looked back at her mother and made a decision.

"Goodnight, Mamma," she said.

Milla went to bed then, and in the moments before sleep took her, she thought about a stranger knocking on their door. And then she thought about opening it.

3

SOMETHING WAS HAPPENING. THAT WAS WHAT MILLA
said to herself over and over that day. *Something is happening.*

Something was happening. Soon.

Soon her days wouldn't be the same. Soon there would be a
new face at the table—at least sometimes. A new face to discover, and a new voice to say new things. Things that might
surprise her.

Milla was so excited she spilled the salt. Gitta was too distracted to admonish her for it.

Someone was coming. A girl. A girl just a year older than
Milla. Her name was Iris.

Gitta told Milla the news right after Niklas and Jakob had
returned from their last trip to the village. The girl was Stig
and Trude's granddaughter, the only child of their daughter and

son-in-law who lived in the village. And she was coming to live with Stig and Trude now.

When Milla asked Gitta why Iris was coming, Gitta hesitated at first. Then she sighed. Her face became soft, and Milla couldn't tell if it was a happy or a sad softness. Then she thought it was both. "It will soon be time for our Niklas to think about marrying. And Iris is a good girl. Or so Stig and Trude say. So for the next few years she and Niklas will get to know each other, and if they like each other, well, they'll marry. And we'll build them a house here. And things will go on."

Niklas . . . marry? Milla turned the words over in her head. It wasn't that the thought had never occurred to her, but it had seemed so impossibly far away that either of them would have to think about it. And Niklas was her brother, a boy. A boy with a man's shoulders, but still—a boy. "Does Niklas know?"

"That Iris is coming? Of course."

"No, does he know that he's to marry her?"

Gitta looked away from Milla, through the window and at the green of the fields that rolled away from their home, and the darker green of the forest that bordered it. That view through the window was all Milla had ever known. She wondered how her mother could be content with it. With everything always going on and on, the same. She wondered what a girl like Iris—a girl raised in the village!—would think of so much quiet. So much sameness. Then she went back to thinking about her brother marrying. Marrying!

"He knows it's how we're thinking of it," Gitta said. "And he knows he can say no if he doesn't like her. But they've met, and he seems happy enough about it."

"They've met?" Milla couldn't keep the surprise from her voice.

Or the hurt. How long had Niklas known, and he hadn't told her? Once again she felt filled with resentment that his life was so much bigger than her own. His life occupied a whole other world that she hadn't even been allowed to see. And then there was the hurt that her brother, to whom she'd once been so close, now felt so far away. That he hadn't told her something so important about himself. Not to mention, he knew how lonely she was. How much she craved companionship. How could he not have told her that her wish was being granted?

Instead of ringing the bell for dinner, Milla decided to go find Niklas in the field. It was spring, and the sun was warm on her head, but the air was still chilly on her skin, so she wrapped a wool shawl around her shoulders and walked at a clip through the fields to where she knew her brother would be. She called to him the moment she saw him. He looked up, waved, and walked toward her.

When he was not less than thirty feet away, Milla said, "Just when were you planning to tell me that you're to marry?"

He walked closer before he answered her. "Mamma told you?"

"No, Wolf did. That dog talks to me more than you do."

Niklas laughed. Kept smiling. "Don't tell Pappa you're talking to that dog. He considers him a bad influence."

Milla kept her mouth in a straight line. Her eyebrows, too. Niklas would not get her to smile. He would not. "Niklas."

He sighed. "I didn't know what to say."

"How about, 'Milla, a girl named Iris is coming to live with Stig and Trude, and Mamma and Pappa think I should marry her in a few years.'"

"Well, right. I suppose I could have said that. But honestly, Milla, it's all so strange. Imagine how I feel. I've seen the girl at the market with her mother and father, but I haven't spoken to her more than twice. She seems nice enough, and I suppose I'm happy about it. You're not the only one who gets lonely, you know."

Milla looked at her tall, handsome brother. For the last five years she'd imagined him having friends in the village, charming everyone with his smile the way he charmed their mother. It hadn't occurred to her that he got lonely. She only thought about how lonely she was, and how much more exciting his life seemed.

But still. Something was wrong. There was something her brother wasn't telling her. She could see it in his eyes, that there was a closed door in there, and he was trying to distract her away from it.

"I'm mad at you," Milla said. "You should have told me."

"You're always mad, Milla. And you have less to be mad about than you think."

Milla raised an eyebrow. That closed door had just opened a crack. "What do you mean," she said.

The tiniest ripple of consternation crossed Niklas's forehead, then dissolved into a smile. "Nothing, Milla. I just mean you don't know how easy you've got it." He took one of her hands in his own and turned it over. Then he took her other hand, held one of her fingers between two of his own and ran it over the pads of her open palm. "So soft," he said.

"My hands aren't soft," she said, pulling her hands away from him. "I work plenty. Who do you think helped Mamma make the dinner you're about to eat? Who do you think is going to wash the shirt you're wearing?" She rubbed lard into her hands at night, just to soothe the painful, bloody cracks that burned every time she dipped them into soapy water.

Niklas held up his own hands, palms facing her. She touched

them. The calluses were as thick and hard as wood chips.

"Fine," she said. She turned away from him and walked toward home. He chased after her and threw an arm over her shoulder.

"Silly Milla. Let's not fight."

She crossed her arms over her chest so her elbows stuck out hard and sharp.

"Don't you want to know what Iris is like?"

"No," Milla said.

"Oh really?" Niklas said. "You're not curious? You'd cover your ears and run away if I tried to tell you?" He smiled at her, triumphant.

"I hate you," Milla said. But her own smile gave her away.

"No you don't," Niklas said. "And you never could."

Milla sighed. It was true. She couldn't. She couldn't ever.

Milla knelt to sweep up the salt she'd spilled. Stig and Trude had gone to fetch Iris two days before, and the plan was that they'd stay one day visiting with their daughter and son-in-law, and then they would come back here. Milla did calculations in her head, guessing how long it might take them to make the trip. It must be very far, Milla thought. After all, she never saw anyone from the village, so it must be hard to get from there to here. The way Mamma and Pappa talked about it, it seemed like the village was a world away.

Milla stood up, and that's when she heard wagon wheels. Stig and Trude. And Iris. They were back. Milla's hands flew to her hair to tuck away any stray strands. Iris was the first girl she was meeting in her life, and Milla had been worried for days how she might appear to her. If she might look . . . off . . . to Iris. If she dressed the same as the girls in the village. Talked the same.

Wore her hair the same way. Gitta was always so despairing of Milla that she thought she must be very clumsy and awkward. She imagined Iris must be more like Gitta. Pleasing to look at, and graceful. Always knowing what to say and how to act, even without her mother's rules to guide her.

Milla said to her mother, "Mamma, please. May I go meet them?"

"We'll go together," Gitta said. She untied her apron and hung it from a hook, then smoothed her own hair. Milla waited, even though she wanted to take off at a run and not miss even a moment of Iris's arrival.

Milla thought her mother walked slower than usual on purpose, just to teach her daughter a lesson about patience. Everything in Milla's life, it seemed, was a lesson. Milla had asked Niklas that morning if he'd stay home that day so as to be there when Iris arrived. Pappa had answered for him. "Work doesn't wait just because we have a visitor," he said. *A visitor.* That was an odd way of putting it, Milla thought. As if Iris's stay were temporary. As if, maybe, it wouldn't work out. Then it occurred to her that maybe Iris's life would also be full of lessons now, and if Milla wanted her to stay, she'd have to help her learn them very well.

When they reached Stig and Trude's small, neat cottage, Stig was unloading baskets from the wagon, but there was no sight of Trude or Iris.

"Hallo," Stig said, when he caught sight of them. "Trude's showing our granddaughter about the cottage. You wouldn't think that would take very long, but our Trude's a bit excited. I think she's presently giving her a tour of the kitchen table." He walked toward the house. "Trude. Gitta and Milla are here to meet Iris. Hurry along."

Iris emerged from the cottage, and the girl-shaped creature in front of Milla was at once strange and beautiful and familiar and ordinary. She was about the same height and width as Milla. Her hair was long about her shoulders the way Milla's was. Those were all the ordinary parts. Everything else was extraordinary.

Her face was heart shaped, starting with a V at the center of her forehead and ending at the soft point of her chin. Her cheekbones were high, and she had wide, sweeping eyebrows the color of rust, matching her hair the color of rust—if rust were also shiny and liquid. The color of her skin wasn't like Gitta's, which was milky with touches of rose on her cheeks and the tip of her nose. Nor was it like Milla's, which was more yellow, like butter. Iris's skin was more brown, like harvest wheat. And her eyes were at once bright and dark, like syrup. Milla hadn't known that eyes came in that color. She took in all this newness with thirsty eyes.

Then the most unusual thing happened. Iris rushed toward Milla and threw her arms around her. "Milla! I've heard so much about you. We're going to be better than friends. We're going to be sisters."

Milla startled and shook and then something broke inside her. Or opened. Or collapsed. Some structure that had existed inside Milla, which had given form to her world and defined what was possible, shattered and scattered and blew away. And in its place was Iris.

Milla felt Iris's arms across her back and Iris's hair in her face and it was as real and unreal as a dream. Real because it felt so natural, and unreal because it shouldn't feel so.

Stig continued unloading the wagon, completely unaware of the world-shifting event that was presently occurring inside Milla.

Gitta, for her part, seemed less interested in Iris, and more interested in being alone with Trude.

"Milla, walk Iris over to our place so she knows how to find
us. And show her the chickens while you're at it. And the garden.
Show her everything."

Her mother never gave Milla such freedom, and the idea that
she should be the one to show a stranger around their home was
as odd as suggesting that Wolf should do it. Milla saw how Gitta
had already tilted herself toward Trude's kitchen, urging Trude
along with her. She felt that tickle of suspicion again, the same
one she'd felt with Niklas. The sense that she was being distracted
away from some truth she wasn't allowed to know.

Iris linked arms with Milla and said, "Lead on." Then she
smiled.

Of all the things that were most extraordinary about Iris,
from her syrup eyes to her liquid-rust hair, what mesmerized
Milla most about her was the way that Iris made her feel. Iris
didn't make Milla feel upside down—rather she made Milla feel
as if she'd finally turned the world right side up. And oh, *this*
was how it was supposed to be. And no wonder Milla had felt
so off-kilter before.

Another thing: Iris smiled even more than Niklas, which Milla
hadn't thought possible. This opened up a world of other possibilities for Milla, who just yesterday had known only five people.
Now that she knew six, and this sixth person was so very different
from the other five . . . well, it stood to reason that the seventh—if
ever she should meet a seventh—would be as well.

She couldn't imagine that the seventh, or eighth, or one hun-
dredth person that she met would ever be as interesting to her as
Iris was, though. Milla found herself arrested by the way Iris used

her hands when she spoke, tracing lines in the air that seemed to make what she said all the more interesting and original. Iris looked at the same tree that had stood outside Milla's window her whole life, and she said, "What a funny tree! It looks like an old man scratching his head." And Milla looked at it and realized that why, yes, it did look very much like an old man scratching his head and why had she never noticed that before? Maybe it was because she'd seen so little—she had nothing to compare it to. Iris seemed full of memories, and everything reminded her of something else. Buckets and buckets of recollections spilled out of her when she noticed something. Milla showed her Gitta's jars of preserves, and that led Iris to a story about berry picking, and that led her to a story about her favorite berry, and why it was her favorite, and then she asked Milla if she could only ever eat one berry for the rest of her life, what would it be?

Milla paused to ponder while Iris waited expectantly for her answer, her syrup-eyes bright with interest. "Well," Milla said. "I haven't ever thought about that." Iris looked disappointed for a moment, and Milla felt dull and stupid. So she rushed to say more. "What I mean is that I haven't thought about it that *way*. Because I haven't been anywhere or done anything the way you have, so I'm always thinking about what more I could see or do. I don't want to think about doing even less."

It was an unusually long rush of words for Milla, not because she didn't like to talk, but because there was no one to talk to. Even Niklas only half listened when she talked to him these days, so she lost interest in making the effort, and kept her thoughts to herself. She worried Iris would find her very odd.

"Oh, Milla, of course!" Iris said. "That makes complete sense. It was a silly question anyway. Who would want to only eat one berry? Especially when you have so many berries here. We don't have nearly so many in the village." She ran a finger over one of Gitta's jars.

"Really?" Milla said. She hadn't ever thought of there being less of anything in the village. "Will you miss it there?" Milla wondered if she would miss the farm if she were sent away to live somewhere else. But she could only imagine excitement at the prospect.

Iris's face had turned thoughtful. "I'll miss Mamma and Pappa. But maybe I'll visit." She brightened then. "And you can come with me!"

For a moment Milla thought she might rise off the floor with happiness, but then she remembered. "I'm not allowed."

"Oh, Milla. Of course not. I knew that. I'm so sorry. I keep saying all the wrong things." Iris went blank again.

Milla didn't think anyone had ever said sorry to her before. She was always the one saying it. And she felt such a rush of wanting to reassure Iris the way she'd always wanted to be reassured herself, that she reached for Iris's hand. "Oh no, not at all! You're so kind to offer. And . . . maybe things will change? Maybe someday they'll let me."

Iris smiled. "We'll *make* them."

Milla laughed. "You haven't met my father."

Iris said, "Oh, but I have! He's not so bad. And anyway, we'll just leave when their backs are turned. And maybe we won't go to the village at all. Maybe we'll go somewhere else."

Milla's mind took a leap. She'd been so desperate, and for so long, to go to the village that she hadn't thought about there being other places to go. "Where?"

Iris tugged gently on one of Milla's long, dark curls. "Anywhere."

4

THAT FIRST EVENING, THEY ATE DINNER TOGETHER, ALL
seven of them. This only ever happened on holidays, and it felt
festive, like a party. Even Jakob smiled at one point, and warmed
up to tell a story about how he got the best price for a cow. It
wasn't a very good story—there was barely a beginning, not much
of a middle, and no real end. But Iris listened to it attentively
and nodded at all the right places. Milla remembered her father's
word—*visitor*—and she was glad for how well Iris seemed to be
doing at pleasing him. Gitta was harder to read, but Iris's manners
were so pretty that Milla couldn't imagine Gitta not liking what
she saw. And Iris was just right with Niklas, too. Friendly, but
not too friendly. She knew exactly how much attention to pay to
him—just enough that a beloved boy like him would feel was his
due, but not so much that he'd weary of it. Milla didn't think she
could ever grow tired of watching Iris.

After dinner, Jakob and Stig pulled out their pipes and smoked by the fire, and Niklas carved a new wooden spoon for Mamma. "Such a good boy," Trude said, and smiled at Iris. Milla held her breath for a moment. Mamma might not like this special attention paid to Niklas on Iris's behalf—Gitta had always had Niklas for her own, and maybe she would feel . . . jealous. The thought of that made Milla feel odd inside, and she wondered where this suspicion had even come from. What a strange thing to think— that her mother would be jealous of a girl. But there it was. Milla watched her mother and saw a flicker of annoyance in Gitta's otherwise still, locked face.

"It is a very beautiful spoon," Iris said. "And I noticed your others, ma'am. They're so much nicer than my mother's. And I saw that there's only one that's stained purple. Is that the spoon you use when you make preserves? That's so clever. All of my mamma's spoons are stained purple. It didn't even occur to us to keep just one aside for making preserves."

Milla watched her mother's face, and the wariness that Milla always saw there when Gitta looked at her didn't give way for Iris. It was still there. But nonetheless Mamma said, "In the summer, Iris, you'll help us with the preserving."

In the summer. That was months away. That was a kind of promise, wasn't it? Gitta was saying that Iris would still be there in the summer. Milla looked at Iris then.

Iris winked at her.

The next day, Iris was at their door directly after breakfast and just as Jakob and Niklas were headed to the fields. Milla was to teach Iris the rules.

Gitta observed closely while Milla showed Iris the right way to pour salt in a line—no breaks, but no waste, either. Once Gitta was certain Milla hadn't been careless, she left the girls to themselves and went off to see Trude again. Gitta rarely had so much to say to Trude, so this aroused another flicker of curiosity in Milla, but she was too relieved to see her go, and too happy to be alone with Iris, to wonder about it for long.

Once Gitta was out of earshot, Milla said, "I'm sorry. This must be so boring for you. I don't know why Mamma is having me teach you rules you must already know. We'll just do the hearth now, and then we're done. Do you want to do it?"

Iris shrugged. "That's all right. You can do it. I don't see much point."

"Oh," Milla said. She felt ashamed, and she wasn't sure why.

"It's just that if a demon wants you, a demon will get you. I don't think a little line of salt is going to keep it away."

"No?"

Iris shook her head. "No."

Iris seemed so certain, which made Milla think once again how much more Iris must know about the world than she did. "How do you know?"

Iris's face went blank for a moment. This had happened before with Iris, and it was the kind of blank that Milla was used to in other faces—in Pappa's and Mamma's especially. And more recently in Niklas's, too. But she could tell that Iris's face didn't want to be blank. It wasn't a normal state for Iris's face to be so empty of emotion. So shut up tight.

Once again, Milla had that feeling. That feeling that something was being held back from her. "You're not telling me something."

Iris looked at Milla, and now her face wasn't blank, it was

pleading. "I can't, Milla. Please don't make me. If you make me, they'll send me back. And I want to stay here." Then she took one of Milla's hands in her own. "I would tell you if I could."

"But I wouldn't tell anyone," Milla said. "And it's not fair. Why is everyone keeping secrets from me? Why do you get to know, but I don't? Is it something about the village? Is that why I'm not allowed to go there?"

They both heard the clatter of the chicken coop opening and closing. Gitta was back.

"Milla, listen to me," Iris said. "If I ever told you, they'd know. They'd find out and they wouldn't let me stay here anymore."

Milla wanted to protest, but Gitta came inside, and she told Iris that Trude was asking for her.

Then Milla was alone.

Every day since Iris arrived, Milla had rushed through her chores so she could spend as much time as possible with her. Milla couldn't remember ever being so happy in all her life—at least not since she was eleven, before Niklas was taken away from her.

Milla was so happy that she hadn't pestered Iris with any more questions. She decided not to worry about such things for a while. Maybe, she told herself, in this one area she could be a truly good girl. To simply do as she was told and not to ask for more than she should. Maybe in time she could learn to be as in command of herself as Iris was. Iris seemed to know how to be right with everyone. She knew how to be sweet with Stig and Trude, amiable with Niklas, and well-behaved with Mamma and Pappa.

With Milla, Iris seemed to let all that go. For Milla's part, being with Iris reminded her of those days in the forest with Niklas when they were children, fighting off trolls. Milla felt wild again during her afternoons with Iris—but without the consequences. She knew how to return home with a clean apron and an innocent face and her hair still long down her back.

When she was little, and Milla and Niklas went off for their walks in the forest, Milla had been the one making up stories. But Iris was far better at stories than Milla had ever been. Milla could conjure a witch with teeth dripping blood, but Iris would make that witch do and say such horrible things that Milla marveled at how Iris could ever have thought of them. Milla was used to Trude's simple stories about trolls and princesses and princes that turned into frogs and back again, but Iris's stories were different. Milla's favorite was the one about the snake tree.

One day, a pretty girl named Anna was walking through the woods picking berries. This girl was so pretty and so good that her parents let her walk in the woods all by herself without fear that she would ever do anything wrong, or that anything wrong would ever befall her.

As Anna reached for a particularly juicy strawberry, a gnarled hand closed over her own and Anna gasped in surprise. The gnarled hand belonged to a gnarled and ugly old woman with a wart on her nose. The wart had its own wart growing on top of it, and from that wart grew one long black hair.

The ugly old woman was dressed in rags and bent over like a question mark. She leaned on a walking stick and seemed very frail, so Anna's fear flew away and she asked the ugly old woman if she needed help reaching home, and if Anna might carry her basket for her.

The ugly old woman said, well, aren't you a dear, and you are such a dear that you deserve a reward for being so good.

Anna liked being told how good she was, and it made sense

to her that she deserved a reward. Because she *was* terribly good, wasn't she?

So Anna thanked the ugly old woman, and asked her what the reward was.

The ugly old woman said that Anna's reward was buried in a clearing in the forest that was too far to reach for such an old woman. It was a treasure, you see, an enormous treasure. And all the ugly old woman required was that Anna go and dig it up. And then Anna could keep half, and the other half she would return to the ugly old woman. Did they have a deal?

Why certainly, Anna said. Most certainly they had a deal.

Anna made her way back to the clearing in the forest. A pretty place. A very pretty place, and just as the ugly old woman had described. Anna used the little trowel her mamma had given her for foraging, and she dug up that treasure. And the moment Anna caught sight of it, her heart embraced that treasure as if it were all her own. After all, shouldn't it be? Wasn't she a pretty, good young girl? And how very old the ugly old woman was. And how very ugly the ugly old woman was, too. Too old and too ugly to need a treasure. What would she do with it, anyway?

So Anna took all the treasure. She packed it up in her basket and she went home and hid it under her bed. She didn't tell her mamma and pappa, because she wasn't sure how to explain to them how she'd dug up and stolen a treasure from an ugly old woman in the forest. That was the second time when Anna felt a little bit afraid.

Anna shook off that fear and she continued on with her life, and for a while she didn't go back to the forest. Eventually, though, her fear was so long gone that she forgot about it entirely and she went back. And just as she was reaching for the blackest, ripest blackberry she had ever seen, a gnarled hand closed over her own.

And Anna gasped.

It was the ugly old woman, and the ugly old woman asked where her half of the treasure was.

That was the third and last time Anna felt afraid.

Anna said there was no treasure. She had dug where the ugly old woman had told her to dig, but there was nothing there. Anna said that the ugly old woman was very mean for scaring her so, and really Anna should be heading for home because her mamma and pappa would be waiting for her.

Then the ugly old woman looked much less like a question mark. She stood as straight as the walking stick that she no longer seemed to need. Black smoke rose from her feet, enveloping her rags and transforming them into a cloak so black that it was blacker than the blackest blackberry. Her hair swirled around her head.

Anna knew then that the ugly old woman was a witch, and this was all a terrible trick.

The witch told Anna that she had one more chance to save her life. She held out her gnarled hand and waggled her fingers over the earth beneath their feet, and from that spot sprouted a low tree with long, skinny leaves. And from one of its branches grew a single green apple. An apple so green it glowed. It made Anna's mouth water.

The witch said that Anna had only to eat that apple, and then all would be forgiven.

Anna reached out and plucked the apple. Then she sank her teeth into it, and for just a moment, Anna thought she had never tasted anything so delicious in all her life.

But after that first bite, Anna wasn't Anna anymore. Or at least she wasn't an Anna-shaped Anna. Anna was a snake. A small, slender, perfect snake. She shimmered as she curled around the green apple where it had fallen to the ground. She wondered at her new station in life.

The witch bent over and plucked up Anna by the tail. She held Anna in the air, and looked into her snake eyes. And she said to Anna: The prettiest snake is eaten first.

Then she dropped Anna into her mouth. And as the witch chewed, enjoying the sensation of Anna fighting back a bit, only just a bit, she also enjoyed the sweetness of the apple she could taste on Anna's snake lips.

When the witch had swallowed Anna down, she waggled her fingers once again and the snake tree disappeared. Then, as the witch continued on down the path, looking for other pretty, good girls and boys, she laughed. These good children, she said. They do love their rewards. . . .

When Iris told Milla that story, she knew exactly when to pause and lower her voice, and she made Milla shiver in places and laugh in others.

One afternoon when the sky was blue and the sun was warm and the shade from the trees was the perfect degree of cool, Iris and Milla sat in a clearing that looked very much like where the witch's treasure was buried. When Iris finished telling Milla her story, she reached over and tugged on one of Milla's long brown curls. "You have beautiful hair, Milla."

"I do?"

"Of course you do. Don't you know it?"

Milla felt such hopelessness in her chest at that moment, such an awareness of the vast, uncrossable distance between what she knew and what she didn't know. "Iris, I don't know anything. And if you don't tell me, I never will."

"Your mother must tell you things."

"All Mamma tells me is how to cook what Pappa likes to eat and how to get things clean."

"Well, I suppose that's useful. And lots of mothers are like that."

"Is yours?" Milla knew Iris missed her mother.

"There's always so much work to be done. And life is . . . hard. But in the evenings, Mamma brushes my hair and we talk. And that's nice. Was nice. I thought it might be that way with Grandmamma. But she's old and she falls asleep by the fire. So mostly I sit and sew while she and Grandpappa snore. You're lucky you have Niklas."

Milla thought about that for a moment. She supposed she was lucky. She couldn't imagine life without him, with just her and Mamma and Pappa. It would be so dreary. "You don't have brothers or sisters, do you? I just realized that I never asked."

"No. It's only me."

"Your mother and father must miss you so much. I'm surprised they let you leave them." Milla knew she was treading dangerously close to asking Iris more questions, but she couldn't help herself.

"Milla," Iris said. She looked at Milla with her bright syrup eyes that seemed to take in everything so quickly.

"I know, no questions." Milla sighed. "All right. Tell me about your friends. You're the only girl I've ever met. You can at least tell me about other girls."

"Oh," Iris said. "All right. Well, I had a friend, yes."

"What is she like?" Milla had a thought. "Maybe she could come visit you?" Then Milla would get to meet someone else. A seventh person.

Iris went blank. So blank. So blank it was as if Iris weren't there anymore and only an Iris-shaped shell were left in her place.

"What's wrong?" Milla said. "What did I say?"

Iris stood up suddenly and walked away from Milla. "We should get back."

"Iris." Milla caught up with Iris, only to have Iris walk away even faster. "I'm sorry. I didn't mean to upset you. But if you'd only tell me how I upset you, then I'd know not to do it again. As it is I'm so confused that I feel like I'm wrong and I don't even know why. And I'm so very tired of feeling this way." Milla's voice cracked and she realized she was crying.

Iris stopped walking, but she didn't turn around. "My friend's name was Beata."

Was. Milla stopped crying. Wiped her eyes with the back of her hand.

"Beata and I were friends since we were babies. Always together. She taught me all the stories I tell you. You think I'm so smart, but Beata was the smart one. So quick and sharp. But then she got sick."

Iris paused. Then she turned around and looked at Milla. "And now Beata's not Beata anymore."

Beata's not Beata anymore. The line from the prayer came to Milla now. *Lord, let us not answer the knock of the stranger.* Had Beata answered the knock of the stranger? Is that why she wasn't herself anymore?

"You're my only friend, Milla. Be my friend." Iris wasn't crying, and she wasn't pleading. She was telling Milla something, and Milla knew she needed to listen. To collect all that she was being told so she could do something with it later.

"Yes, Iris," Milla said. "I'm your friend. Always."

5

Spring warmed toward summer, and Milla no
longer worried that Iris might be snatched away from her at
any moment. She and Iris had taken to doing all of their chores
together, making short work of them. Sometimes they chatted,
other times they were happy to be quietly in each other's company
while they peeled potatoes or hung the laundry to dry.

On Sundays, when Niklas, Pappa, and Stig rested from
their work in the fields and there was no market in the village,
Niklas joined Milla and Iris on their walks in the forest. Iris
was easy and friendly with Niklas, but she never made Milla
feel as if she really wished she were alone with him. Milla had
been worried about this the first time he had walked out with
them. She wondered if she might feel stupid and awkward and
childish if Niklas teased her in front of Iris. But when Niklas
called her "silly Milla," Iris always came to her rescue, teasing

Niklas back and saying that he was the silly one.

The first time they walked out together, Milla had been so eager to show Niklas how well she knew Iris, and to display Iris to Niklas in all her wonderfulness, that she begged Iris to tell him the story about the snake tree. While Iris told the story, Milla watched Niklas's face and saw that it troubled him. At the end he said, "Why would the good child get eaten? That's not the way stories are supposed to go." So Iris didn't tell any more stories when Niklas was around.

Something else Milla noticed was that whenever conversation took a turn toward the village, Niklas steered it away again. Sometimes she said something about the village just to watch him do it.

"Iris," she said once, "how would you be spending your day if you were back in the village?"

Before Iris could answer, Niklas pointed out a fox to them, a fox that magically disappeared when she and Iris tried to spot it. And then he changed the subject to hunting foxes, knowing that Milla would argue with him and tell him that he should leave the foxes alone. Milla allowed herself to be distracted, because she already had her answer: Niklas knew something she didn't. He was in on the secret, and he was trying to keep it from her.

Milla might have wished Iris could tell her whatever the secret was, but she forgave her for this; she understood Iris's reasons. Iris feared she'd be sent away. Milla felt betrayed by Niklas, though, and it closed a tiny part of her heart to him. She found herself wishing he wouldn't walk with them on Sundays—which shocked her. Not so long ago, she'd wanted so desperately for Niklas to stay with her always. But everything had changed since Iris arrived, and for the first time Milla allowed herself to think that maybe, in this one way, her life hadn't changed for the better. She didn't want to feel this way about Niklas. It made her unhappy. But there it was. The truth was out. And she couldn't put it back in.

On the first hot afternoon of the summer, when Milla and Iris had finished their chores and cleaned up after dinner, Milla told Iris that she'd take her to a spring where they hadn't been before. Without Niklas, they could take off their boots and stockings and hitch up their dresses and wade in up to their knees. It would be heaven.

Milla hadn't known Iris very long, but she'd studied her so closely that soon after they set off for the spring, Milla knew something was wrong. Iris's harvest-wheat skin looked pale on the surface, like a thin veil had been pulled tight across her.

"Are you feeling well, Iris? Are you sure you want to walk so far today?"

"Oh yes, quite well, Milla. Quite well."

Iris sounded odd to Milla, too, as if she were slightly off the beat of the world around her. After Iris spoke, she shadowed her own words, silently reforming them with her lips as if she were making sure of them, or not quite ready to let them go.

"I have a new story for you," Iris said, and she didn't wait for Milla to respond. She spilled it out in a rush of words. "Once there was a prince, who fell in love with a beautiful princess. So he asked her to marry him and she said yes. On her wedding day, white doves flew down and dressed her in a beautiful blue gown. Then they perched on her shoulders and cooed to her while bluebirds flew down and braided her hair. When the prince saw her, he said, my darling, what's that all over your shoulders? And pray tell, what is that in your hair? And the princess looked and saw that the white doves had shat all over her shoulders. And she reached up to her hair and discovered that indeed the bluebirds had shat all over her hair. So the prince beat her and then he ordered her burned as a witch because only a witch would let birds dress her and braid her hair."

"Oh," Milla said. "Oh."

Iris laughed. Then she put her hands to her face and cried. "There's something wrong with me, Milla. Something terribly wrong."

"No, no, dearest. Not at all," Milla said. "I loved that story. It was wonderful. All of your stories are wonderful." They'd reached the spring, and Milla led Iris to a flat rock where they could sit and talk.

"You don't understand," Iris said. "It's happening to me. Just like it happened to Beata."

Milla felt frightened then, because she knew she was about to hear something terrible, and for the first time she realized that perhaps she didn't want to know. Perhaps it might be better not to.

"I'm hearing it in my head, Milla."

"You're hearing what in your head?"

"The demon." Iris tapped her forehead. "It's in here."

"Oh no. No, no, no. That's not possible." Milla felt herself going blank now. She wanted to clap her hands over her ears and squeeze her eyes shut and pretend she hadn't heard any of that. "We spread the salt. We locked the doors and windows."

Iris smiled strangely, in a way that showed teeth but no happiness. "That doesn't work. I told you that. Nothing ever works. The demon gets us anyway."

Milla had a choice to make, she realized. She could tell Iris to be quiet, the way her mother would have told Milla to be quiet if she'd said something troubling. Or she could be the friend that Iris had asked her to be. "Tell me, Iris. Tell me everything."

And Iris did.

It wasn't the oldest girls who were taken by the demon. Or the youngest. Or the ones in the middle. Or rather, it was the oldest *and* the youngest *and* the ones in the middle. It was any of them, sometimes all of them. Very few families were spared entirely. Maybe they had only sons, or they had daughters who managed to escape the demon. Those families considered themselves blessed. But most families could list off sisters or aunts or cousins or daughters who were taken by the demon. And the cruelty of the demon was its randomness. There was no pattern to its grasping, so there was no way to protect against it. The most devout weren't spared, nor were the least. They were all at risk. If you were born a girl, you were fair game.

The youngest girl who'd ever been taken was twelve, and no one could recall a girl over the age of eighteen being taken. This was why Jakob and Gitta had at first insisted that Iris's mother and father wait until she was eighteen before they sent her to live with Stig and Trude to be Niklas's intended. This way Jakob and Gitta could be assured that Iris was out of danger—or rather, that Jakob and Gitta were out of danger of bringing a demon-possessed girl into their home. Trude told Iris that it was Niklas who'd convinced Jakob and Gitta that Iris should come now. After all, she was almost eighteen, and such a good girl. And Niklas said she'd be a calming influence on Milla—because they all had their worries about Milla. She was too much alone. It wasn't healthy. A girl could start hearing things under those circumstances.

That was how it started with the girls who were taken by the demon—hearing things. It was the demon talking to the girls, telling them nasty lies about their mothers and fathers, sisters and brothers. Then the girls began whispering to themselves. Then one morning they woke up seeing monsters in the faces of their families. They screamed at the sight of their own mothers.

When the first girls were taken—long before Iris was born—the village was caught unawares. But as it happened to more and more girls, the demon-possessions became a sad way of life. Fear and grief and suspicion fell over the village like a fog that the villagers continued to walk through in the hopes that one day it might lift. And what choice did they have? Leave their homes and farms and shops? And go where? And eat what?

Then it happened to Beata. Iris's dear Beata. One day Beata confided in Iris that there was a whispering in her head, a whispering that wasn't her own. She asked Iris if she thought the demon was taking her, and Iris had said, *no, no, of course not.* Iris wouldn't let herself believe it, because she couldn't bear for it to be true. Then the whispering grew louder and clearer in Beata's head. It was a voice, strong and certain. And Beata found it increasingly hard to doubt what the voice said to her. *Beata,* the voice said, *your family doesn't love you. They think you're a monster. But they're the monsters. Look at their faces. See the monsters all around you.*

Beata begged Iris to help her leave the village, and for Iris to leave with her. But Iris was afraid. Then Beata woke up one day screaming. She looked at her mother's face at the breakfast table and insisted she was trying to poison her. She looked at her father's face and said he was the devil. And by then it was too late; there was no escape for Beata. Consumed by guilt, Iris pleaded with Beata's mother and father not to let the midwife take Beata away. Iris told Beata's mother and father she could look after Beata herself. But that wasn't allowed. Possession, the midwife said, was contagious. This was why all the stricken girls were taken to The Place, where the midwife looked after them. Families were allowed to visit, and some did. But many found it too upsetting to be reminded of their loss—to look into the eyes of a daughter who sometimes knew them and at other times said terrible things. Hateful things.

Iris didn't know what The Place was, or even where it was. But she knew she didn't want to be sent there. She'd rather die. The Place had become something that mothers and fathers used to scare their misbehaving children. *If you carry on so, the midwife will come and take you to The Place.* So she made Milla promise her that no matter what happened, Milla wouldn't let them take her.

And Milla promised.

"Be my friend," Iris said to Milla.

"Yes, Iris," Milla said. "I'm your friend. Always."

Then Milla and Iris took off their boots, and they walked into the icy water together. As they went deeper, letting the cold sink into them—toes, then ankles, then knees—Iris gripped Milla's hand so tightly that it hurt.

6

MILLA SEWED WHILE WAITING FOR PAPPA TO YAWN.
When Pappa yawned, Mamma would say it was time for bed.
Then Milla could find a moment alone with Niklas.

All through dinner, Milla had looked at her family with new
eyes. Her mother's fear for her made sense now—and her father's
insistence on obedience. Of course. They were terrified that one
day they'd wake up and Milla would have become someone else in
the night. Or some*thing* else. A monster wearing their daughter's
dress.

Maybe, though, such things only happened in the village.
Maybe that was why they lived so far away, and why Milla was
forbidden to go to the village—because it truly was contagious.
She supposed that was reasonable, but why couldn't they have
told her? Why was Niklas brought in on the secret, trusted in
that way, when her life was the one most at risk? It was infuriat-

ing. She had watched her brother eating his supper, making inane small talk with Pappa, and she wanted to slap their bowls away from them. She twitched.

She pressed a hand to one of her cheeks. Was this how it started? With such violent anger? No. Iris had said it was a voice in your head that was the first sign. But what was a voice in your head? How did you know it wasn't your own voice? What did the voice sound like? Milla had spent so much time alone before Iris came that she had gotten quite used to talking to herself. Sometimes the voice in Milla's head didn't seem quite like her—it seemed sharper. Meaner.

But no, Milla sensed this wasn't what Iris was talking about. Milla remembered how Iris had looked that afternoon, like her usual self-command had been stripped from her. She seemed afraid that she was being rearranged piece by piece and all twisted. This was something different from the odd thoughts that Milla often had. Milla sometimes wondered why she thought the way she did—certainly she felt strange at times. But she felt sure, almost sure, that her thoughts were her own. They weren't anyone else's. She didn't think.

Maybe that's what the other girls thought, too.

And how would Milla ever know if no one told her? Perhaps her family thought they were protecting her by keeping her so ignorant, but they were wrong. She accepted her mother and father's disregard for her as simply the way things were. But Niklas. Her whole life she had loved him best of all. And Mamma and Pappa had loved him best of all, too, and Milla didn't even mind. All she hoped for in return was that Niklas might love her best of all. Or at least think of her sometimes. But now she knew he never had. He wanted to keep her as small and helpless as Mamma and Pappa did. He thought she was too fragile—too strange—to be trusted with the truth about the village and the workings of the demon. He didn't know her at all.

She stared at Niklas where he sat working on a wooden bowl for Mamma. She willed him to look at her, to notice how angry she was. But he blandly ignored her.

She watched Pappa. He smoked his pipe facing the fire—not so much looking at it as pointed toward it. Blank as always. Then she watched Mamma at her sewing. Occasionally Mamma looked up from her work and straight at Niklas. It was as if a thread connected Mamma to Niklas, and the only direction her attention could go was toward him.

Milla turned her gaze back toward her father. *Yawn, Pappa. Yawn.* Then, finally, he did—a face-cracking yawn that Mamma couldn't help but notice. Mamma folded up her sewing and Pappa tipped the remains of his pipe into the fire. "Bedtime," Gitta said. She followed Jakob upstairs. Milla heard their door close.

"Niklas." Milla hissed his name, and he looked up at her, seeming surprised at what he saw in her face. "I know about the village. I know about the girls, and the demon, and The Place. And I know you've been keeping it all from me."

Niklas closed his eyes and pressed his lips together. He only ever did that when he was very upset. Then he opened his eyes again. Niklas had the kind of green, brown, and amber eyes that changed color with his surroundings. Right now they were black, full of pupil. "Iris told you."

The mention of Iris's name opened up a crack in her chest that filled with cold air. Iris had told her, yes, and the reason Iris had told her was that she was afraid she was hearing the voice of the demon in her head. And if Niklas knew that, he would tell their mother and father, and then Iris would be taken away from her and sent to The Place.

She looked at her brother, registered the fury in his eyes, and thoughts streamed through her head like wheat berries through her fingers. If she tried to catch one, she not only lost it, but ten others slipped past as well.

Milla had made a terrible mistake. She knew it even before Niklas said, "You have no idea what you've done. And what Iris has done in telling you."

"I begged her to tell me. I knew you were keeping something from me. You don't know what it's like to live this way, Niklas. Feeling like there's a world out there that's so different from this one and I'm not even allowed to know how. Or why. It's maddening. Sometimes I think I can't bear it another day."

"Don't you think I know that? You don't even know what I do for you. How lucky you are. Do you think I like going to the village without you? Believe me, I don't. But Pappa made me swear I wouldn't tell you anything about it. He said it was the only way to keep you safe." He stared at Milla, blinking too hard and too fast. "This is all my fault."

Milla struggled with how differently their conversation was unfolding than she'd thought it would. She'd known only her anger a few minutes before, and that was so simple, but this was complicated. Her brother sat in front of her, and instead of hating him, she regretted causing him such anguish. That little part of her heart that she'd closed to him opened back up again, and she felt deep guilt for having closed it in the first place. She was the wrong one. She was always the wrong one. And then she felt angry again. Why was she always the wrong one? It wasn't fair. And so her thoughts went, around and around.

"It's not your fault," Milla said to Niklas. And she meant it. "It's theirs, Mamma's and Pappa's. They've done this to us. They took you away from me, and they keep me here, trapped. And they convinced you it's for my own good. But it's not." Even as Milla said all this, though, another thought streamed through her brain, and this one she caught and held onto tightly. Iris. What would Milla tell Niklas about Iris, and what Iris was afraid was happening to her? Then he answered Milla's question for her.

"I have to tell Pappa and Mamma that you know, and that Iris told you. I can't lie to them."

"Oh no, Niklas. No, you can't." The cold crack in Milla widened. "If you do they'll send her back. You don't want her to go back, do you?"

"Of course not, Milla. I'm the one who convinced Pappa to let her come here now."

"Because you think I'm strange. And you think Iris will make me less strange." Milla's anger was coming back.

Niklas put a hand to his forehead. "Everything I do for you, you turn it all around. I knew Pappa and Mamma wanted her to come eventually, and I know how lonely you've been. I know you, Milla. You may not think I do, but I do."

"If you know me, then you know I love you more than anyone else. And you know I wouldn't lie to you. If you tell Mamma and Pappa that Iris told me, and if they send her back, then I'll run away."

"I'll tell Mamma and Pappa you said that, and Mamma will never let you out of her sight. She'll lock you up. You won't be able to run away."

"If they ever did that to me I'd turn into one of those demon

girls." She almost laughed when she said it, but the words horrified her the moment they left her lips.

"You *mustn't* say such things, Milla." He grabbed her hand
and squeezed his eyes shut. "Lord protect us from demons Lord
protect us from demons Lord protect us from demons. Amen."
He looked at her. "Say it, Milla."

"Amen," she said.

He tried to pull his hand away then, but she held on. "Niklas.
I promise to be good. I promise not to ask any more questions or
ever to speak of the village again. Just please don't tell Mamma
and Pappa that Iris told me." She squeezed his hand and looked
into his face, so tight and worried. "Please."

Niklas sighed. "As long as you keep your promise, I won't tell
them. But I'm going to have to talk to Iris. She needs to know
how wrong she was to tell you."

"No." Milla's voice was louder and sharper than it should have
been, and Niklas jerked his head back. "Don't talk to Iris, Niklas.
Let me do it. It will be better."

Niklas looked at her through lowered eyebrows, and Milla saw
an expression there that she hadn't ever seen on his face before.
Suspicion.

"I feel guilty, Niklas. That's all. She's still so new here and
eager to please, and I made her tell me. And she was so upset
about it. She'd be terribly embarrassed if you knew. She thinks so
highly of you."

The shadow that had fallen over him lightened, but Milla
knew she would have to be more careful now. Something had
changed between her and Niklas, because something had changed
in her. She had become a liar.

✦ ✦ ✦

The next morning dawned bright and even hotter, and by the time Jakob and Niklas left for the fields, Milla was already sweating under her dress. She'd lain awake a long time the night before, worrying over Iris and the terrible mistake she'd almost made with Niklas. She had come too close to betraying Iris, much too close. She thought through all the things that might have happened if Niklas had told Jakob and Gitta. She thought about what her life would be like if they took Iris away. Then she felt terrible shame that she was worried more for herself than for Iris. Iris had trusted Milla. *Be my friend.* Milla hadn't been her friend last night.

But today that would change. Today, Milla told herself, Iris would feel better, and Milla would be a good girl, and she'd do her chores well, and she'd smile brightly at dinner, and soon the shadow of suspicion would entirely lift from Niklas and everything would be fine.

Doubt tickled her spine when Iris didn't appear at the kitchen door after breakfast. But maybe Trude had given Iris something to do that delayed her. Trude could be baking, and would want Iris's help for that. There were any number of reasons that Iris wasn't there. So Milla continued doing her chores, carefully, ever so carefully.

She poured the lines of salt especially straight that morning, with not a single break.

When every chore was done, and she had been told by Gitta that there wasn't a single other thing that needed doing, Milla walked to Stig and Trude's. She walked no faster or slower than she should have, and she thought that the very normalcy of her stride was proof that this was a fine day, a typical day.

She walked up to Stig and Trude's whitewashed door and she knocked in a way that wasn't too soft or too hard. It was a just-right knock, and then she waited for someone to open the door in a just-right way.

Instead there was no answer. So she knocked again, this time a little harder and louder than just-right. And again. And again. And then she called through the door. "Iris? Trude?"

Milla heard movement and then the door opened. Trude faced her, and Milla knew then what she hadn't allowed herself to know since Iris hadn't come after breakfast. What she'd felt in her gut even last night as she tried to convince herself to sleep. What she hadn't wanted to believe the moment Iris had tapped her forehead and said the demon was in there.

Nothing would ever be just-right again.

7

TRUDE REACHED ACROSS THE THRESHOLD AND PULLED Iris inside. The kitchen was oppressively hot, the windows shut tight.

Iris wasn't there; Milla could feel the emptiness of the house. There were two cups on the table and a pool of spilled tea that hadn't been wiped up. Trude herself looked unwell. Her gray hair, always neatly braided around her head, trailed down her back, undone. Her apron was dirty. Stranger than all of this was the expression on Trude's face, which was usually so plump and pleasant. It was terror. "Where is Iris?" Milla said.

"It's happening, Milla. Here. Where we thought we were safe."

"Where is Iris?" Milla felt that if Trude didn't answer her question this time that she might reach out and shake the old woman by the shoulders.

"She's run off! Stig's gone after her. And if your mother and father find out they'll take her and they'll put her in The Place. And then they'll send us away, too. Because we brought the demon here when we brought Iris here."

"What do you mean she's run off? She's run away?"

"She was so strange last night. So peculiar. And she didn't look well. And Stig and I, we looked at each other, and I think we both knew then, but we didn't want to know. So we all went to bed, and this morning I went in to wake Iris and she took one look at me and she screamed. She said I was a monster and what was I trying to do to her, and then she ran out in her nightdress. Stig went after her, but she ran so fast he said it wasn't even human. It was like something else was in her body making it go. Then he lost sight of her." Trude sobbed into her apron.

Milla had to think. She had to think what to do. She should comfort Trude, she knew, but instead she took a step away from her, wanting only to get away from her wet weeping.

"After that," Trude said, "Stig came back for his rope. He said that if he finds her and she's not herself, he'll tie her up and take her to The Place. Then he'll tell your mother and father that Iris got homesick and went back to the village. He said that was the only way your mother and father would let us stay here."

Milla had to get to Iris before Stig did. She couldn't let him take Iris to The Place. She turned away from Trude, desperate to leave.

"Oh, please, Milla. Don't tell your mother."

Milla held the door handle, her back to Trude. "That's what you care about." She turned around and looked at the woman whom she'd always thought of as a sweet old grandmother. "You don't care about Iris. You only care that Mamma and Pappa don't make you leave."

Trude's face changed, and Milla thought of the ugly old woman in the story of the snake tree, and how she transformed into a witch when angered. "Don't you judge me," Trude said. "Don't you dare judge me. You've never had a worry in your life. You don't know what that village is like. You don't know what it is to be afraid of your own child. You're a foolish little girl."

Milla's chin dropped a fraction lower with each word, each word that hurt even more for being true. She turned her back on Trude and left the door wide open.

Milla ran into the woods, thinking of all the places she and Iris had been together—the clearing that was so like where the witch in the story had buried her treasure. The spring where they'd sat the day before. But Iris wasn't anywhere Milla thought she'd be, and the longer she looked the more frantic she became, and the less certain she was that she would ever find Iris before Stig did.

She needed Niklas. He would calm her, and he would know what to do. She hoped he was alone and not with their father, because she couldn't possibly pretend in front of Pappa that something wasn't terribly wrong. In just over an hour Mamma would ring the bell for dinner, and she had to find Niklas before then.

Milla ran to the edge of the forest. There was a slight rise above a fallow field where she knew Niklas had gone that morning to chop a fallen tree into kindling. She heard his axe first, and then she saw him. He'd paused his work to wipe his brow. His light brown hair was dark with sweat. She waited to call to him until she was closer for fear that Pappa might be nearby and hear her. When she couldn't wait any longer she called to him while running. "Niklas!"

She could tell his first impulse was to smile at her—because that was always Niklas's first impulse when he looked at her. That made her heart break just a little. Then he took in her desperation and ran toward her, swatting aside tall, fluff-topped grass. "What is it?" he called to her. "What's happened?"

"Iris," she said. "She's run off." When they reached each other, she told him everything—how Iris hadn't seemed well yesterday, and what she'd just learned from Trude. "We have to find her before Stig does or they'll take her to The Place. We can't let them take her, Niklas. You love her, don't you? She begged me not to let them take her there, and I promised I wouldn't. Please, Niklas."

All the while she pleaded with him, Niklas moaned and ran his hands through his sweat-damp hair. "Oh, Milla," he said, pressing the heels of both hands to his eyes. "You should have told me last night that Iris wasn't well. And what will we do if we find her? What if she's as Trude says? If she's like the other girls, and the demon's really gotten into her?"

Milla didn't believe it. It couldn't be. "Well, then at least we'll know. But I have to see her, Niklas. I have to talk to her. I can't just let them take her." Then she said something that she knew would get him to come with her. "And neither can you. You said it yourself. You're the reason she's here. You owe it to her." Milla was almost sorry when she saw how her words landed on him. But not sorry enough to say that she was.

"All right, Milla. Let's go. But if we haven't found her by the time the dinner bell rings, and you and I aren't back soon after, Mamma and Pappa will know something's wrong anyway. And then neither of us will be able to protect her."

So *this* was how it felt when it happened. Just last night Milla had wondered if she'd ever heard another voice in her head—a voice that wasn't her own. Now she knew she hadn't ever heard one before, because she was hearing one now.

It wasn't the voice of a demon, though. It was Iris, and she was talking to Milla right inside her head. It wasn't wishful-thinking talking, the way Milla used to imagine that Niklas was with her and what they'd talk about if he were. This wasn't Milla making up the sound of Iris's voice in her head. This was Iris herself, telling Milla things that she didn't know.

Don't tell Niklas. He won't understand. Lie to him. Lose him. Then I'll tell you where I am.

"Have you looked everywhere you went together, Milla?" Niklas looked so concerned as they ran through the woods, choosing paths that Milla hadn't yet searched. She wanted to believe he cared for Iris, that he would help Iris once they found her. That he would keep her secret.

We can't trust him, Milla. He's not my friend. Only you are my friend, Milla. Be my friend.

Milla was sick with uncertainty.

He lied to you, Milla. He kept things from you. Everyone loves him more than they love you. Everyone except for me. Be my friend, Milla.

Milla ran along behind Niklas. Sweat dripped under her arms, and she felt hot and cold at the same time. She slowed. "Niklas," she said. "I have to stop."

He turned around.

"I have to pee," Milla said.

"Now?"

"I'm sorry. It's just that I'm so frightened."

Niklas shook his head. "Well go on, be quick."

"Walk ahead of me," she said. "I'll catch up with you."

Run left. Run fast.

Milla waited, heart beating painfully, as Niklas walked on. When the path took a gentle turn and she could no longer see him, she ran left, and she ran fast.

Keep running.

Branches snagged Milla's sleeves and skirt. Leaves slapped her face and twigs scratched her cheeks. She ran on, wondering if she was still going in the right direction.

You are.

She came to a clearing, and on the far side of it she saw Iris crouched beneath a tree. Her white nightdress spread limply around her. Her red hair streamed over her shoulders like the still-brilliant center of a wilted flower. When Iris lifted her eyes to look at Milla, a flame burned inside them.

Part of Milla wanted to run away, but the greater part of her pushed forward.

"Don't be afraid," Iris said. "It's me. I'm not anyone else."

"Oh, Iris," Milla said. "I thought I'd lost you."

Iris hugged her arms around herself as if chilled, despite the full heat of midday. "I know. I thought I'd lost me, too. But it's me. You can see that, can't you?"

What Milla saw seemed to be Iris, but so much brighter. Her syrup eyes flashed. Her wheat-brown skin seemed lit from within. It occurred to Milla that perhaps Iris had been growing duller ever since she'd arrived. And maybe this Iris sitting in front of her was the same girl who'd arrived on that spring day—only fresh and unharmed, her veil lifted.

Milla should have heard Niklas approaching, but even if she had, there wouldn't have been anywhere for her and Iris to hide. By the time the sounds of crackling branches and leaves under-foot were too loud to ignore, he was there, at the edge of the clearing, taking them in with wide, confused eyes.

He walked toward them, wordless.

"She's herself, Niklas," Milla said. She turned to Iris. "Talk to him, Iris. Show him."

Iris shook her head. Milla saw sadness in her eyes, and then something else. Something unrecognizable.

"Oh, Milla," Iris said. Then she laughed and laughed. And cried. And laughed some more. And laughed and cried at the same time, her lips hitching up over her teeth in a grimace. And Milla wanted to embrace her and run from her. Both.

Iris ran from Milla before Milla could decide which she would do. Iris ran so fast—too fast—and Trude's words came back to Milla. *It was like something else was in her body making it go.*

Milla felt Niklas's hand close around her forearm. "No, Niklas." She tried to pull away from him. "We have to go after her."

She heard a bell ringing. And ringing. Mamma's dinner bell.

Niklas yanked Milla back the way they'd come. She alternated between struggling and giving in. When she struggled she despaired that there was anything she could do if she caught up to Iris. And when she gave in she loathed herself for her cowardice. And all the way home, Niklas prayed.

Lord, protect us from demons.
Lord, protect us from demons.
Lord, protect us from demons.

8

JAKOB HAD ALREADY SAT DOWN TO EAT HIS DINNER
when Milla and Niklas arrived home. At the sight of their sweat-
streaked faces, Mamma's hand froze midair, halfway between her
pot of stew and Pappa's plate.

"It's Iris, Pappa," Niklas said. "She's changed. Like the other
girls."

Gitta dropped her spoon. She shook her head at Niklas and
then stared at Milla, her eyes rounding so they showed white all
around.

"I know about the girls, Mamma," Milla said.

"No," Gitta said, more breath than sound.

Jakob shoved away from the table. "Where is Iris?"

"She's run off," Milla said. "You'll never catch her. Please,
Pappa, just leave her be. Let her go."

Jakob ignored her. "Where's Stig?"

"Gone after her," Niklas said. "He's planning to take her to The Place."

Gitta twisted her apron so tightly between her hands that her knuckles whitened.

"I never should have let you convince me to bring her here, Niklas," Jakob said.

"I know," Niklas said. "I'll go with you to find her."

"No. You stay here. Don't let Milla out of your sight."

"I'm standing right here, Pappa!" Milla moved in front of him, grasping his sleeves like she hadn't done since she was a small child hoping to be picked up. "Why won't you listen to me? Iris is no harm to anyone. Please leave her be."

Jakob removed her hands from his shirt and pushed them aside. "Gitta, get this child out of my sight or so help me she'll never leave this house again."

Gitta moaned. Niklas pulled Milla away and wrapped his arms around her, half embracing her and half restraining her. "You must stop this now, Milla. Iris isn't Iris anymore."

When Milla heard Iris screaming, she tore through the front door before Gitta, Trude, and Niklas could stop her. Jakob and Stig carried Iris like a long bundle—Stig's hands hooked under her armpits, and Pappa's arms wrapped around her calves, fighting to keep a firm hold of her. She was bound with rope in two places—waist and feet—and she twisted her hands and her torso bucked.

"Let me GO leeeeeet me GO let me go let me go LET ME GO leeeeeet meeeeee goooooooo let me GO let me go let me go LET ME GO let me go let me go let me go." Over and over Iris said it, sometimes wailing it low and long, sometimes barking it sharp and insistent, sometimes crying it high and plaintive.

Niklas's arms were around Milla again, and she turned to him. "Niklas, you mustn't let them do this. It's not right. You know Iris. She wouldn't hurt anyone. And I promised her. I promised her, Niklas."

Iris stopped screaming. "Milla?"

She sounded so much like herself.

"Milla? Help me."

Trude buried her face in her apron. "Lord protect us from demons Lord protect us from demons Lord protect us from demons."

Iris wept now, her long hair forming red stripes across her forehead and cheeks, covering her eyes.

Milla fought against Niklas, but his arms were tight around her shoulders and waist. "Iris, I'm so sorry," she said. "Oh, Iris."

"Gitta," Jakob said. "Take Milla inside. Niklas, ready the wagon."

"Milla?" Iris said. "Be my friend, Milla."

"Lord protect us from demons," Gitta said as she pulled Milla away from Niklas. "Lord protect us from demons Lord protect us from demons."

Milla grasped her mother by the shoulders. "Mamma! Don't let them do this."

"Help me, Trude," Gitta said, taking one of Milla's arms in two of her own. Trude did the same on Milla's other side.

"Come, Stig," Jakob said.

Iris let out a howl and she bucked so hard that Jakob nearly dropped her.

Milla felt Gitta's and Trude's hands digging into her arms like claws as they dragged her into the house and closed and locked the door behind them.

They couldn't lock out the screaming.

Milla refused her mother's supper and sobbed herself to sleep that night. Niklas had gone with Jakob and Stig to take Iris to The Place.

Milla would never forgive Niklas for that. It was just as Iris had said. He was a liar. He wasn't Iris's friend, and he couldn't possibly love her. He'd betrayed both of them.

The only person who understood her, who'd never lied to her, was Iris. And Iris was being taken away from her, brought to somewhere horrible that Milla couldn't imagine. So horrible that Iris had said she'd rather die than go there.

When Milla rose the next morning, the sun was bright and cheery, and the green leaves danced on the tree outside her window, and it was all terrible to Milla's eyes. Each green leaf was an accusation. Milla could wake up in her soft bed and drink hot tea at her parents' table. Iris was bound and dragged off in her nightdress and called a demon. All because . . . why? She'd called Trude a monster? Trude *was* a monster, Milla thought. A monster in the skin of a grandmother.

The memory of the fire that burned in Iris's eyes, and her laughing that became crying that became laughing, flashed across Milla's mind. She shoved the thoughts away.

She would have stayed in her room, avoiding her mother forever, but her bladder was full and painful. She didn't bother combing her hair. There were no men in the house to try to please. Milla never wished to please another.

She walked through the kitchen in nothing but her nightdress and bare feet, hair streaming. She felt Gitta's eyes, but she didn't speak to her mother, nor did Gitta speak to her. After she'd relieved herself in the outhouse, Milla came back into the kitchen, where Mamma had poured her tea and set out bread, butter, and preserves.

Milla ate silently, hungry and disgusted with herself for being hungry. When she'd finished, Mamma reached out her hand and placed it over Milla's. Milla felt a tremor in her chest and willed herself not to cry. Not to seek comfort from anyone who would send Iris away.

Milla looked up at Mamma. Pretty Mamma, with her golden hair shot with silver, perfectly braided around her head. She saw the fine lines at the corners of Mamma's eyes and crossing her forehead. She looked into Mamma's cornflower-blue eyes and saw the same fear there that she always had. Milla looked away.

"I know you don't understand," Gitta said.

"I don't understand because no one will explain anything to me. All I know is that Pappa and Niklas dragged Iris away like they didn't even know her. Like she was a monster. Would you do that to me, Mamma?"

Gitta didn't take her hand away from Milla's, but Milla could see her recoil, the muscles in her face shrinking. "You mustn't talk like that, Milla."

Milla pulled her hand away. "I mustn't talk like that. I mustn't act like that. I mustn't think like that. Is there anything I may do, other than wash, and cook, and clean? I'm not you, Mamma. I'm not pretty. I'm not good."

"You're just fine, Milla. Don't carry on so. You'll forget about this soon enough." Gitta stood up and cleared the table, not meeting Milla's eyes now. "You don't know how lucky you are."

"Niklas says the same."

"Niklas is a good boy. You should listen to him. He knows we're safe here."

"But you don't know that, Mamma. Do you? That's why you're always so afraid when you look at me, isn't it?"

Gitta busied her hands while Milla spoke, then glanced at Milla as if she'd been too distracted to hear her questions. "Look at you, your hair all undone. What will Pappa think when he gets home?"

"I don't care."

"Nonsense," Gitta said. "A woman's hair is her glory, that's what my father always said. Let me brush it for you. Would you like that?"

Milla felt the tremor in her chest, the one that threatened to fill her eyes and make them spill over. She couldn't speak.

"I'll just get my comb," Gitta said.

Milla sat at the table, willing herself to move, to resist her mother's attention. But she couldn't move, and the thought of her mother's hands in her hair, of that little bit of comfort, kept her in her chair, tracing the wood grains on the table with one short fingernail. It was weak to want such comfort, but she couldn't help herself. It had been so long.

Gitta returned with her comb and stood behind Milla's chair, pulling it through Milla's dense, nearly black coils of hair. Milla closed her eyes, lulled by the light pressure of Mamma's fingertips holding her head in place while the comb gently tugged on the roots of her hair, then traveled down, sometimes pausing on a tangle. Mamma worked each tangle, ever so gently. Milla struggled against the desire to rest her head back on her mother's stomach.

Then Gitta stopped. "What is . . ."

Milla felt Gitta's fingertips searching her scalp just above her left ear. Then a sharp—a very sharp—pinch. "Ouch, Mamma!" Milla clapped her hand to the spot where it felt that Mamma had pulled her hair out by the roots.

Gitta sucked in her breath. "Lord protect us from demons Lord protect us from demons Lord protect us from demons."

Milla turned around in her chair. Gitta held something that squirmed between her two fingers. A tiny, emerald green snake, the length of her pinky, with a brilliant dot of crimson blood on its tail end. Milla said, "That was in my hair?"

Gitta shook her head. "No. No. Lord protect us from demons Lord protect us from demons Lord protect us from demons." Gitta dropped the snake to the floor and crushed it beneath her heel. "It was growing *from* your head. It was . . . Lord protect us from demons Lord protect us from demons Lord protect us from demons." Gitta backed away from the snake, still shaking her head.

"Mamma?" Milla said. She looked at the bloody pulp on the floor that was once a tiny, brilliant green snake growing from her head. Her own head. That wasn't possible. "Mamma?" Milla began to cry. She didn't want to be taken over by a demon. She didn't want to laugh and cry and laugh and cry like Iris. She didn't.

Gitta grasped Milla by both shoulders. "Listen to me, Milla. You must not speak a word of this. You must not. Not to Pappa. Not even to Niklas." Milla felt her mother's nails carving crescents into her skin. "You must behave. Be a good girl. A very good girl. It's the only way to keep you safe. To keep you here. Do you understand me?"

"Yes, Mamma. I understand."

✦ ✦ ✦

Milla awakened the next morning just as night was paling into dawn. She touched the spot on her head, just above her left ear, where Mamma had ripped out the snake. She remembered the way the tail end of the snake had dripped blood. Was it hers or the snake's? Or did their blood flow together—was it one and the same?

She expected to find a sore spot there. A break in the skin. A tender place. Instead, she sensed movement that wasn't her own, and something smooth and cool and dry wrapped itself around her finger.

The snake had grown back.

9

THE FOLLOWING AFTERNOON, WAGON WHEELS ANNOUNCED the men's return from The Place. Gitta went out to meet them, but Milla didn't follow. She had nothing to say to any of them, least of all Niklas. The traitor.

She lay on her bed, staring through the window at the tree that grew so large and wide its branches brushed the house. Its green leaves were the exact shade of emerald green of the snake that grew from her head. She stroked it with her finger, felt the gentle hiss of its exhalation on the outer whorl of her ear.

She'd been terrified when she first discovered it had grown back. Even now, her heart beat faster than it should, and she felt a tension in her belly, a sense that she should be doing something but she didn't know what. She wouldn't tell her mother about the snake. Couldn't. Her mother would only pinch it off again. And the fear in her eyes would grow.

But that wasn't the real reason she wouldn't tell Mamma. The real reason was that something was happening to Milla. She was growing accustomed to the feel of that small snake wrapped around her finger. It belonged there.

The sound of Gitta sobbing roused Milla, and she sat up in bed. She felt the snake tuck itself close to her scalp, hidden in her hair. Then she ran downstairs and out into the hot, bright afternoon.

She squinted at first, unsure of the meaning of what she was seeing. Mamma knelt in the dirt in front of Pappa, sobbing into her apron. "No, no, no, no, no. Not my boy."

Stig shook his head, turned, and headed down the path that led to his cottage, where Trude waited for him.

Milla felt a stab of pain in her chest and side, and her bladder threatened to release. Niklas wasn't there. "Pappa, where's Niklas?"

Jakob pulled Gitta to standing, gripping her by the shoulders. "Calm down," he said. "Calm down, do you hear me?"

Now Gitta sobbed into Jakob's big chest, clawed his shirt. "You left him there. You left my boy."

"Pappa?" Milla said. "You left Niklas?"

"He wouldn't come, do you hear me, Gitta? He wouldn't leave Iris. He insisted upon staying and looking after her."

"Noooooooooo." Mamma's crying had become a long wail.

Jakob freed his shirt from her grip and took both of her hands in one of his. "Milla, take her. There's nothing more I can do with her and I have work to do. These horses need water and feed."

Gitta's knees buckled and Milla rushed forward to catch her before she fell. "Milla. My boy. He's left my boy." Milla wrapped her arms around Gitta's back, and the feel of her mother's flesh under her hands was startling and unfamiliar. Sweat and tears mingled on Gitta's face where she pressed into Milla's neck and shoulder, and Milla felt the snake squirm on her scalp, as if it were discomfited by the invasion.

Pappa was already leading the horses away, straightening his back as if he'd been unburdened of a heavy load.

Milla led Gitta inside. "Come, Mamma. Come."

For an hour or more, Gitta could only weep, her words barely comprehensible between sobs. When she was spent and lay on her bed silently staring at the ceiling, Milla went down to the kitchen to make tea.

Milla tried to conjure more pity for Gitta than she felt. It wasn't that she was jealous of her mother's anguish over Niklas. Milla felt it, too. There was a gaping, awful emptiness, a worse loneliness than she'd ever felt, at the thought that Niklas wouldn't be home for supper, wouldn't be there at the breakfast table tomorrow morning. That he wouldn't be there to smile at her and call her silly Milla.

While she heated the kettle she thought about Niklas and what he'd done. She couldn't make sense of it. He'd thought Iris was demon-possessed, had even helped their father and Stig take her to The Place. But then he'd stayed with her like he loved her.

For the first time since she'd learned that Niklas hadn't come home, she allowed herself to imagine him inside The Place. A place so wretched that Iris spoke of it like a waking nightmare. A place so dreadful that Iris would sooner die than be sent there. Milla gripped the table edge. The room tilted around her. She scrambled to the door and vomited her empty stomach, hot and acid, into the dirt just outside. Her sweet, smiling brother. What had he done?

Milla wiped her mouth and face. Drank some water. *Think, Milla. You say you're not a child. Stop behaving like one.* She reached into her hair and let the snake curl around her finger. Already the snake seemed longer than it had that morning. Her heartbeat slowed. The room straightened.

She brought the tea to Gitta, and got her to sit up in bed to sip it. Gitta's face was puffed and reddened, and her blue eyes were watery gray. "Why did we have to bring that wicked child here?"

"Mamma," Milla said. "Iris isn't wicked."

"You don't know what they're like, Milla. The girls who turn. You only saw Iris at the start. But if she'd stayed, she would have gotten worse. Soon she'd have been howling through the night and swearing you were a monster with the eyes of a devil."

Something wasn't right with what Gitta was saying, and at first Milla couldn't puzzle out what it was. Then she realized. Just like Milla, Gitta was only ever here, on the farm. How could Gitta know what the demon-possessed girls were like? Yet Gitta didn't talk about them as if she'd been told stories about them. She talked about them as if she knew.

"You've seen them," Milla said.

Gitta began to weep again, and Milla took the tea from her, afraid she'd spill it. "It's all my fault. My poor boy. In that horrible place with those demon-possessed girls. My child. My poor boy." She brought her knees up to her chest and rocked and keened.

Milla's heart was only half warm toward her mother, but some deeper urge in her wouldn't allow her to stand by while Gitta suffered. "Mamma. How can any of this be your fault? What have you ever done but the right thing? What's happening in the village has nothing to do with you. And Niklas stayed with Iris because he's a good boy, like you raised him to be." It was true. He was a better, kinder person than Milla would ever be. She thought of her anger toward him, her accusations, and she was ashamed.

"It's because of what we did to Hulda."

"Hulda?" Milla said. "Who is Hulda?" Milla had never heard of anyone by that name.

"The demon. We thought we could get away from her by coming here. But there's no getting away. And now she's taken my boy from me. My own sweet boy." Gitta gripped her knees so tightly that the bones in her hands made sharp lines, and her veins wove over and around them like yarn. Her mouth opened and closed, and she stared ahead of her as if she were seeing something happen right in front of her, something she couldn't stop.

"Mamma, the demon hasn't taken Niklas."

"She will," Gitta said. "She ruins everything. She always did. That's why I hated her so much." Gitta looked at Milla now as if she were confiding something that Milla should understand. "I didn't always hate her. When we were little I loved her. But she grew up wrong, Milla. She grew up all wrong."

Her mother's anguish almost made Milla want to embrace her. But she didn't. There were too many secrets sending up little shoots through the floorboards and into the room, wrapping around them, ready to bear fruit. The snake growing above Milla's ear was restless, nudging her, its tiny hiss like a whisper, urging her to ask the question again. "Who is Hulda, Mamma?"

Gitta opened her eyes, and the moment she did so she no longer looked like a child. She looked like a confused old woman who couldn't understand how she'd arrived at this place. "She was my sister," Gitta said, as if perplexed—surprised—that such a thing could be true. "She turned into a demon and she cursed the whole village. All because Jakob burned her snake."

Milla's snake hissed so loudly in her ear that Milla thought her mother must have heard. The whole world must have heard. She fell back a step and her knees went soft beneath her. "Mamma?"

But Gitta didn't reach out for Milla, to keep her daughter from falling. Instead she shrank away. Then her eyes turned cold and small. "And now you're a demon, too."

PART
2

10

MILLA RAN INTO THE FOREST. SHE RAN TO GET AWAY FROM her mother, she ran to get away from her father, she ran to get away from what she was becoming.

At first she didn't know what she was running toward. And then she did. The spring.

It was the snake, she thought. The snake had made her a demon. So she would drown it. Even if it meant drowning herself.

She pulled off her boots and stockings and felt the coolness of the damp dirt and pebbles under her feet. She took off the apron that she hadn't stopped to hang on its hook in the kitchen. She wouldn't wear it anymore. She let it fall.

She took off her dress and dropped it to the dirt, too. She stood there for a moment in her shift, feeling the warm breeze through the rough weave of the linen, aware that she couldn't remember ever being so undressed outside. Her skin prickled, but not with chill; the day was still hot.

Then she pulled her shift over her head and she was naked. She felt the snake rising from her head, and she knew it was tasting the air with its tongue. She opened her mouth and explored the air with her own. She felt the tickling mist of the spring, but that wasn't taste. She closed her eyes, and there it was. Water mixed with moss mixed with rock. The specific flavor of the spring, forming itself on the tip of her tongue.

She had the strongest impulse to continue running. Through the forest, and on. On to somewhere else. Or nowhere else. The only destination would be the running itself, the moving, the never stopping. The never being trapped in one place.

But her fear came back to her. Her terror of the monstrosity she saw reflected in her mother's eyes. And so she pushed herself toward the water. She put a foot in, and another. She felt the cold run up her calves. She went deeper. The cold traveled up to her crotch and stomach, where it chilled the deepest parts of her. Then she went farther in than she had ever gone before, to the part of the spring that dropped away and became bottomless. She would sink there, to drown out the evil that she was becoming. To kill the demon.

Down she went. She hadn't sucked in a lungful of air, because the intent hadn't been to prolong, but to quicken. She pulled her knees to her chest, felt her hair swirl about her in the water, felt the cold in her heart like a stab. She tried to relax into the water, to let herself sink. She kept her eyes closed, willed herself to be heavy, heavy, heavy like the heaviest stone.

Her snake—and it was, she realized, *her* snake—pulled away from her as if trying to lift them both up to the surface, to save them.

She felt its panic. Its desire to live. Its will. She ignored it. She told herself no. That was the demon talking. Whether the demon was Milla herself, or the snake, or a creature that was once named Hulda—her mother's own sister . . . none of that mattered. She would not be a monster. Still her snake pulled. She put her hand there, not to smother it but to calm it. To say: I know, I know this is painful, but it's for the best.

Then, a voice.

I'm so cold.

Iris.

I'm so cold.

Iris. It was Iris.

Let me out.

Iris's voice was in her head again.

Milla opened her eyes and the pain there was piercing and immediate. The water was dark and heavy around her, but her body was light and wanted to be lighter and she uncurled herself and rose. She stroked forward until her feet touched rock, and then shallower still until she reached the edge.

She shivered and sucked in air and for a moment or more she allowed herself to bask on the rock where she and Iris had sat, to soak up the heat of the sun above her and the earth beneath her.

Then the voice again. Iris's voice.

I'm so cold.

I'm so cold.

Let me out.

Be my friend.

Milla's hand went to her head, searching. She found the snake, and relief brought tears to her eyes when she felt it curl around her finger. It was bigger than it had been even that morning. And stronger. Louder.

"I'm sorry," she said to it.

To Iris, she said, "I'm coming."

When she was warm and nearly dry, Milla pulled on her shift, dress, stockings, and boots. She left her apron where it lay. She knew what she had to do now, the promise she had to keep. She would go to the village, and she would free Iris from The Place.

First, though, she had to find it.

When Milla arrived at Trude and Stig's cottage, Trude was kneeling in her garden tending to her leeks and carrots. Wolf lay in the late afternoon shade nearby. He lifted his head and regarded Milla solemnly, then rested his head down and went back to sleep.

"Trude," Milla said, and the old woman reacted with a start.

"Oh, it's you, Milla," she said, a hand pressed to her heart. Her eyes seemed hesitant to light on Milla's face for very long, either because she didn't like what she saw there, or because she was protecting what her own might reveal. Milla wondered if she was ashamed. "How is your mother?"

"I left her weeping," Milla said.

Trude nodded. "It's a terrible thing to imagine Niklas there. That sweet boy."

"What about Iris?" Milla said. "Isn't it a terrible thing to imagine her there, too?"

Trude let out a lung full of air and her whole body seemed to deflate along with it. "Of course it is, child. She's my granddaughter. My daughter's only child. But she's lost to us."

"How do you know?"

"Hanna's not our only child, you know. We had another daughter. Leah." Trude stood and wiped her hands on her apron.

"What happened to her?" Milla said. Though she already knew.

"One morning Stig and I woke to Leah screaming like she was being murdered in her bed. We ran in to her and found Hanna crying in a corner and Leah howling at her, calling her a demon. At first we weren't sure which of them had been afflicted, but then we saw it was Leah. She wasn't right, Milla. She wasn't our girl anymore. She had this . . . this light in her eyes. There was something else in there with her, something wrong. Something mean."

Something else in there with her. Milla grew cold and then hot again, and her skin ached. Her body wanted her to leave, but she forced herself to stay.

Trude didn't sound like the woman Milla had known her entire life. She sounded like some other woman who had seen horrors, not the pleasant, chatty old lady who sat by the fire and told stories about princesses. "Hanna was just twelve when it happened. Our Leah was fourteen. The prettiest, sweetest girl she was. Never put a step wrong. That morning she wasn't her-self anymore. She screamed at us. Laughed and screeched and called us monsters."

It occurred to Milla that she hadn't really known Trude at all. She didn't know any of them. She only knew a version of Stig and Trude, and of her mother and father, that they'd constructed once they came here. A version that had been cleansed of the terrors that befell the village, a version that erased all the losses. But such things couldn't be erased. They were still inside Trude and Stig, and her mother and father, and they'd passed it all on to Niklas and Milla whether they'd wanted to or not.

Now Trude looked hollowed out and shrunken. "When the

midwife came to take Leah away to The Place, I cried like your mother is crying now. But your mother is lucky. Her son will come back to her. My daughter never will. Nor my granddaughter."

Trude had called Milla a foolish little girl. Milla refused to be foolish again. She would know everything, no matter how frightening it was, or how much it hurt. "Mamma told me about Hulda and the curse. I must know. Did Niklas know the demon is Mamma's sister?" Milla wasn't sure why this was so important to her, but it was. She thought she might be able to forgive all the other things that Niklas had kept from her, but she wasn't sure she could forgive that. The truth about Hulda—about the demon—felt so tied up with her own.

Trude paled, shook her head at Milla. "Lord protect us from demons Lord protect us from demons Lord protect us from demons."

"He didn't know?" Milla said.

"No, child, no. Your mother and father would never. They don't speak of that. Speak of evil and you call it to you. That's what demons want."

Something inside Milla released at that moment, another tight little knot of resentment toward Niklas. She could cry for missing him so. She had to find him, to talk to him, to see him. "Have you ever been to The Place? Can you tell me how to get there?"

"You're talking foolishness again, Milla. You're not listening. Why would you want to go where it's not safe?"

Milla could have said, *because I hear Iris's voice in my head, telling me how cold she is and begging me to let her out.* But that wouldn't get her what she wanted. That would get her tied up and dragged off, too. "Because Iris is there. And Niklas. And I can't bear to be separated from either of them."

"Oh, child. I know you love them." Trude seemed as if about to relent, but then she said, "You'll never find it. Even if you made it all the way to the village, someone would have to show you where The Place is."

"What about Hanna? Would she show me?" The expression on Trude's face told Milla something she couldn't have imagined. "Hanna doesn't know about Iris, does she?" Milla said.

Trude moaned. "Stig couldn't bear to tell her."

Milla latched onto hope. Hanna would help her—Iris's own mother would certainly want to show Milla how to find The Place, and then they would rescue her together. "Trude, tell me how to find Hanna and Tomas, and then I'll tell them what's happened to Iris. And I'll ask them to show me how to get to The Place." Milla sensed Trude hesitate, and she took one of the old woman's hands in her own. It was knobby and thin, as light and fragile-seeming as a bird. "I'm sorry for all that's happened to you. And I'm sorry that I didn't understand. Please let me try to help Iris."

"Your mother and father would never forgive me for telling you," Trude said. "This is their farm. They brought us here, and they could send us away just as easily."

Milla closed her eyes, willed herself not to show anger. She reminded herself that she didn't know what it was like to be Trude. To have seen and lived through what she had. "Then don't tell them," Milla said. "They don't need to know. I'll leave right now. They won't miss me until supper, which is still an hour away. And they may not even miss me then. Mamma's too upset to care what happens to me. Pappa will think I'm off sulking."

Trude nodded. "Come." She led Milla inside and wrapped a hunk of cheese, bread, and two apples, then placed the bundle in a rough-woven bag and handed it to Milla. She pulled one of her own shawls from a hook and wrapped it around Milla's shoulders. For just a moment, Milla let herself remember when she was a child and Trude told her stories by the fire. Milla would sit on a low stool next to Trude and put her head in Trude's lap. Trude would rest a hand on Milla's head in the exact spot where a snake now grew. Her snake.

"You won't make it to the village before dark," Trude said. "Not on foot. Good that it's summer so you won't catch your death sleeping outside. You need only follow the road with the fresh wagon wheel tracks. It will take you straight to the village. My Hanna lives in the center of town. Tomas is the blacksmith, so you'll see the smithy and then their cottage. You'll know my Hanna. Our Iris looks just like her." Trude's eyes were damp.

"Thank you, Trude."

"Tell my Hanna that I'm sorry. Tell her I thought we could keep Iris safe."

Milla thought Trude might embrace her, but she didn't. Milla touched the spot over her left ear where her snake nestled itself, and decided perhaps it was better that way. She wasn't a creature to be embraced anymore—if she ever was.

II

MILLA'S FEET FOLLOWED A ROAD WORN SMOOTH BY
her father's wagon wheels, and it was all unfamiliar. With each
step, her fear came back to her, washing over her like a stream,
lapping. She held two thoughts in her head at once. There were
the dark things that her mother and Trude had seen. And then
there was her belief that the same hadn't happened to Iris. After
all, Iris hadn't howled at Milla or called her a monster. Maybe
she was just . . . sick. Again the image of Iris's too-bright eyes
flickered across Milla's mind and she willfully shoved it away. Her
heart thumped in her chest, and the thought that she was doing
something terribly stupid threatened to overwhelm her.

No, she said to herself. Iris was Iris. She always would be. And
Milla would always be Milla, and she would always be a friend to
Iris. Milla's mind was her own, she told herself. The voice in her
head was Iris's, and Iris was no demon. How Iris spoke to her that

way, Milla didn't know. But Milla knew so little about anything that she was willing to believe that a great deal was possible. She was also ready to doubt a great deal of what she'd been told. The rules she'd grown up with made the world seem like such a small place. And so explicable. But she had proof growing from her own head that the world was much different from anything she'd been led to believe. She touched her snake, which was now the length of her hand. It settled her, and Milla felt her heart slowing to match its coolness, its calm.

The day had been very hot, but by the time the last light of evening turned to darkness, Milla was glad to have Trude's shawl. The moon rose big and bright, and Milla walked long into the night, wanting to arrive at Hanna and Tomas's as early the next day as she could.

As if it knew they were safe and alone, her snake rose up from her head, freed from its camouflage of dark ringlets. It gently bounced and undulated and tasted the air as Milla walked along, and Milla felt its hunger and excitement. Milla felt both in her own bones—and then in her belly. It would be good to eat, she thought. She stepped off the road and sat at the mossy base of a large tree, two roots on either side of her like armrests.

Crickets chirped around her and mosquitoes buzzed around her face. When one landed on her cheek, her snake snapped it up. She tasted its sweetness on her own tongue. She bit into one of the apples Trude had given her, then stuffed her mouth with cheese and bread, savoring fruitiness and saltiness and tanginess mixing together in her mouth. She couldn't remember when she'd enjoyed food this way, and then it came to her. It was back when she and Niklas were children, when they'd gone berry picking together and had eaten half of all they'd picked, the juice running purple and red down their chins. That was most certainly the last time. Since those days, meals had been about service and duty. She ate the food that she and Mamma made without thinking how she felt about it. There was no point, because there was no choice. It was what she was told to prepare, and then to eat. So she did. What was to taste?

What would her father have said to that? *A question that shouldn't be asked doesn't deserve an answer.*

After she'd eaten, she wrapped the shawl more thoroughly around her and curled up between the roots that hugged her on either side. She lay her head on the moss and closed her eyes. She felt her snake sway in the air over her, occasionally snapping up the beetles and other creatures that nudged their way into her hair or trekked across her shoulder.

She wiggled her fingers between fallen leaves and dug them into the cool, damp moss and soil, felt both accumulate under her fingernails. She imagined the dark crescents that would form there. She dug her fingers deeper. Her snake curled around her ear and rested its head on her cheek. She felt its tongue like a whisper. Like the stroke of one who loved her, but she had no memory to match with it. This was something new and restful and soothing. She felt her limbs and muscles relax into the earth. She slept.

Milla shifted, sleeping but not sleeping. She knew morning was coming, and she wasn't ready to wake. Morning should wait just a little longer, she thought, and yet some discomfort roused her. She felt as if one of her limbs were caught beneath her, but that made no sense because her arms were folded in front of her. Finally Milla gave in to wakefulness and sat up. The air was still cool and wet with dew. The bit of sky she saw through the trees overhead was a deep lavender.

Milla's first realization was that her snake was now fully grown—long enough that she could see the snake's lovely leaf-greenness where it rested its head on her shoulder. Her second realization was that another snake grew from a parallel spot just over her right ear—the side of her head that had been pressed to the ground. It was this new snake that had felt restless and stuck beneath her. Just as her first snake had done, this tiny new snake curled itself around Milla's finger when she placed her hand there—as if to say to her *hello, I'm with you, and I will never leave*.

Milla needed the comfort, because when she recalled what she was about to do, her gut clenched and she thought she might be sick. She felt a nip on her left shoulder, two sharp little teeth belonging to her fully grown snake, and then it hissed at her. Not a sweet, calming hiss. It was a hiss of anger—her anger. *All right,* she said to herself. *All right. I remember. I'm angry.* Her anger made her brave, forced her to her feet.

As she continued her walk to the village, Milla felt herself growing ever angrier. And the angrier she felt, the more her green snake lifted from her head, eager and urging her forward.

Her gut no longer clenched. It coiled and writhed. She should have been thinking of poor Iris, she thought. Or worrying for her brother. But instead she could only think of the wrongs she'd suffered. Of the lifetime she'd spent feeling never-enough and never-right.

Never-enough and never-right for her father, who mostly looked past her. On the rare occasions when she forced herself in front of him by speaking words, or spilling something, he looked at her as if flummoxed. Or worse: annoyed that such a problem should have intruded on his otherwise controllable life. Milla's value to him was like that of a tool he used on the farm. He didn't think of the axe's usefulness while he chopped wood. He only thought of the axe's failure if it dulled.

She had never been the pretty, compliant child her mother wanted, either. Oh, she'd tried. So hard. But always with Milla there would be an errant strand of hair that wouldn't bend to her mother's will. A hem that would drag. An off-kilter observation of Milla's that would cause Gitta to get that look in her eye—that look of fear. Now Milla knew why: because she was terrified that Milla would become like her sister. All her life Milla had been forced to suffer for a sin her own mother had committed: the sin of betraying Hulda. Was Milla any less strange than Hulda had been? Perhaps Milla was just better at hiding her strangeness, at pretending to be clean and free of voices. Well, she could hide and pretend no more. Her green snake hissed in agreement. Her new snake kissed her ear with its tongue. She wondered if it was as brilliant green as the other.

Then she thought of Niklas. A lifetime of resentment heated her from the inside out. She felt feverish with it. She *was* jealous that all their lives he was their mother's sunshine while Milla was their mother's dark cloud. She *was* bitter that for years he'd sat by and let Milla be the least loved in the family. He'd rested in the sure knowledge that he pleased their father and mother, that his mere presence on this earth was enough. And without a word of contradiction on his part, he'd allowed her to be less, even encouraged it. Because in contrast with her not-enoughness and not-rightness, he was always-enough and always-right. Silly Milla.

Silly Milla was dead. She died when her mother crushed her first tiny green snake under her heel. No one would do that to her again, or to her snakes. Milla touched each, and promised them aloud, "No one. Never again."

12

MILLA HAD NO IDEA WHAT TO EXPECT FROM THE VILLAGE;
all she had were fantasies. She knew there would be many more
people than she'd ever seen before. She imagined a hubbub, the
fuss and activity of a beehive. Everyone working and moving and
talking. She supposed that as she got closer, she'd first notice the
noise: the sound of all those people. But Milla walked and walked,
and there was no such sound. There were only the trees, which
were still and stolid on this already hot morning. Her boots were
loud under her feet.

Then the trees changed. No longer broad and reaching, they
seemed to give up, to give in. They drooped as if too tired, too
discouraged to continue standing much longer. Milla passed
through an orchard, and the trees were wizened, the apples
gnarled and blighted. The air buzzed with insects and the trees
crawled with them. The joints of branches were shrouded in web-

bing. Downy moth nests wrapped around leaves. Ants marched purposefully up every tree from neatly constructed anthills. Huge, threatening wasp nests hung high in branches. Milla had never been afraid of the creatures that occupied her world, but now she was. Everything was out of balance and trees that should be able to repel the assault of such tiny things were overrun with their number and losing the battle.

Black flies landed on Milla's hands and cheeks and stung, and landed again and stung again. Her snakes madly snapped back at the flies but there were too many. Milla reached for one of the small, twisted apples on a low branch, and as she pulled, it collapsed in her hand. It was the shape of an apple, but inside, it was soft and rippling with worms. Milla dropped the awful thing and wiped her hand on her skirt. She thought of the crisp apple she'd eaten just last night—hard in her hand and juicy when her teeth sank into it. It bore no resemblance to this. Ants swarmed the apple, worms and all, the moment it touched the dirt, and in seconds the pale apple flesh was black with them. Milla backed away, horrified. Then she walked on, waving her hands around her head, helpless to drive away the flies.

Still there was no sound other than the buzzing of the insects. So it was a surprise to Milla when the road widened, and there it was: the village.

And it was so . . . sad.

The village was laid out along a main street, just as Trude had described it. The houses crouched alongside it the same way the trees had—as if it was all they could do to stand up. They were tidy enough. But the green of the trees and kitchen gardens and sod roofs was less green than it should be. As if the whole place needed a good dusting.

The dreariness of the place seeped into her bones and made her feel hopeless. The fearful look she so often saw on her mother's face was everywhere here, and in every face. The town reeked of fear, like a rot. She'd so often dreamed of coming here, and part of her wanted to greedily take in all these new faces. They were all ages and sizes and complexions. All hair lengths and colors. Some round faced and some narrow, some thick browed and others thin lipped. But really, they were all the same. Each one regarded her not with curiosity but with suspicion.

Milla's snakes clung close to her scalp, hidden well beneath her hair. There was nothing outwardly strange about her, and yet each man, woman, and child stared hard at her as she walked toward them, then turned their heads to stare at her longer as she walked by them. She felt their eyes still needling her once she was past. She paused once to look behind, and she found that everyone she'd passed had stopped walking and was looking at her, eyebrows lowered, lips drawn tight. Milla told herself not to look back again. She supposed she shouldn't be surprised by their unfriendliness. It was a cursed village, after all. A village doomed to watch its sisters, daughters, friends, and cousins taken by a demon. A demon who was her aunt. Milla felt a cramp in her bowels.

These people couldn't possibly know who she was, she told herself. They'd never seen her before. But what if some family resemblance gave her away? She looked nothing like Jakob or Gitta, or even Niklas. Maybe, she thought, she looked just like Hulda. Right down to the snakes on her head. A slick of sweat formed along her hairline and ran down her sides under her shift. Oh, the many things she hadn't thought through before she set out on this journey. It was too late to think of them now.

Her heartbeat fluttered unevenly in her chest when she came to the smithy and saw a large, brown-skinned man, his shoulder-length black hair streaked with gray, holding a horseshoe with tongs. He must be Tomas, Milla thought. She raised a hand as if to wave, but then let it fall again. He watched her pass, and continued watching her as she knocked on the door of the very next house, where Trude had told Milla she would find Hanna. It was a modest place, at once clean and dismal, with a meager vegetable garden clinging to one side.

The door was opened by a woman who looked both like and unlike Iris. Like her in slim, graceful build and rust-red hair. Unlike her in that she seemed drained of the life that glowed from Iris like a flame. Where Iris's eyes were like candles, Hanna's were ash. Those eyes went round now and she grasped Milla by one shoulder and pulled her inside.

Light shone harshly through the closed windows, and inside the house, like out, was tidy but dreary. The air in the room was hot and stale. Milla felt breathless, and the more air she tried to pull into her lungs the less there seemed to be.

"Milla," Hanna said. "You're Milla, aren't you?"

"I am," Milla said.

"What's happened? Why are you here?" Hanna hadn't let go of Milla's shoulder once they were inside, and Milla felt nails digging into her flesh.

"It's Iris. Your father and mine have taken her to The Place."

Hanna pulled her hand away now and put both hands to her own mouth. "No," she said. "No, no. We kept her safe for so long." Then Hanna's eyes lost focus and her knees buckled, and Milla feared she might fall. She wrapped an arm around Hanna and led her to a wooden chair.

"I'm so sorry," Milla said. Milla had been distraught when Iris had been taken; she could do nothing but weep. Hanna was Iris's mother—how would she ever bear it? How had Trude borne it when her oldest was taken?

Hanna grabbed Milla by the wrist. "She was supposed to be safe with you. The way you've always been safe. Mamma and Pappa promised." Hanna squeezed her eyes shut and shook her head as if trying to banish a thought. "Now she's lost to us, just like Leah."

Hanna squeezed Milla's wrist so tightly it hurt, but Milla didn't pull away. Instead she put her other hand over Hanna's and held it gently. "I don't believe Iris is lost to us. She doesn't belong in The Place."

Hanna opened her eyes and Milla saw a bit of hope rise in them. "What do you mean? Wasn't she showing the signs?"

Milla hesitated, and Hanna's eyes turned hopeless again.

"She was . . . different," Milla said. "But still herself. And that's the important thing. She was *still herself.* Not lost. She was still Iris. And she shouldn't be locked away someplace awful. That's not where she belongs."

Hanna pulled her hand away from Milla and shook her head. "Oh, Milla. You don't understand. Gitta and Jakob have kept you so far from it, you don't know what it's like when the girls are taken. There's no making them better. The sooner you put them away and cease to think of them, the less your heart will ache from the loss."

The door opened, and a shaft of light scissored the room. Tomas. He closed the door behind him. Milla saw none of Iris in his face, but it wasn't a bad face. There was warmth there, and a desire to understand. Tomas's eyes searched Milla's now, but before Milla could speak, Hanna did. "Our girl has been taken." She said it blunt like that, as if there was no point in stepping up to it slowly or trying to make it any less awful than it was.

"When?" Tomas said.

Milla had to think for a moment. "Three days ago."

"Signs?" he said.

"Tomas," Hanna said. "You know the signs. Don't make me listen to them. Don't make me hear what our child has become." She put her face in her hands.

Tomas walked to Hanna where she sat and pulled her to her feet. Then he wrapped his arms around her and she sobbed into his chest. It was a moment so tender that Milla turned away from it. She had never seen anything like it—a man reaching out to a woman. A gesture meant to comfort, not to subdue. Her mother would occasionally touch her father, but only to placate a mood, to beg for calm. Not like this. And she couldn't remember her father ever reaching out to anyone—not even Niklas—with affection.

She listened to Tomas murmuring to Hanna. When there was silence, Milla turned toward them again.

"I came not only to tell you about Iris, but to ask you if you'd show me to The Place. And help me get her out."

Tomas looked at Milla, one large palm cradling his wife's head. "You don't know what you're asking. No one comes out of The Place. *No one.* And you wouldn't want them to. Our girl isn't our girl anymore. She belongs to the demon now." Hanna let out a whimper.

"But that's not true," Milla said. "She's still Iris. She talked to me. I know she's still herself."

"She talked to you? What did she say?"

Milla could tell that she'd surprised Tomas, sensed that he might be persuadable, so she kept talking in a rush. "She asked me not to let them take her there. She was frightened. She told me she was still herself. Does that sound like the talk of a demon?"

Hanna jerked her head away from Tomas. "It sounds exactly like the talk of a demon. The demon lies."

"Iris was Iris. And she never lies. I know it."

"Don't you think I want to believe you?" Hanna said. "Don't you think I want my girl back? I want my sister back, too. And my friends. All taken by the demon. All pretty and sweet one day, and the next screaming nastiness at me. Telling me they hate me. I won't see my child like that, do you hear me? Now you must leave. Get out of my sight."

"Hanna," Tomas said. "What if it's true what Milla says?"

"Tomas, ask yourself this. Why is it Milla standing here? Why is our child cursed and not this one, whose own aunt brought the curse upon us all? Why do you trust her? What if it's the demon talking through her?"

Hanna gripped Tomas's shirt in her hands while she spoke, looking him in the eyes, pleading with him. Then she looked at Milla, and Milla saw something in Hanna's face that she did not like. Not at all. Milla's snakes squirmed on her head. She felt their fear, imagined what would happen to her and to them if the suspicion she'd seen in the villagers' faces turned to accusation. She looked at Tomas. "I'll go," she said.

"Best," Tomas said.

The sun was high overhead outside, and Milla looked left and right. Then she felt a hand on her shoulder and she flinched before turning around.

It was Hanna, her face tear strewn. She pointed to her left. "Follow the road out of town. You'll pass through farmland and woods and then you'll come to a cottage. That's where the midwife lives. You'll have to talk your way past her. Or sneak around, through the forest. But I don't recommend that. Those woods are deep and once you're just feet from the road you won't know which way you've come from. Better to stick to the road and start thinking of your excuses. The Place isn't far from the cottage. There's no mistaking it."

Milla nodded the whole while Hanna talked, barely breathing. Now she didn't smile so much as open her face to Hanna. "Thank you," she said.

Hanna nodded. "You won't find Iris there. Not the Iris you know."

"But what if I do?" Milla said.

Hanna sucked air in, then out. "You think we're heartless, sending our girls to The Place. And maybe it's so. But if we are, then it's because our hearts have been taken from us. Look around this village and you'll know exactly who's lost a sister or a child or a dear friend to the curse. We all look the same, feel the same. Like we'll never be whole and happy again. When Tomas asked me to marry him I said no at first. I told him I wouldn't, because I couldn't bear to have a daughter taken from me. But. Well. I love him, and I relented. And then we had Iris, and there wasn't a day after that I woke up anything but terrified."

Milla thought of Gitta, always watching her, waiting for her to change.

"So I told Tomas, no more. I couldn't bear to have more children, not if the next might also be girl. When your father asked my father to work for him, and he and Mamma went to live there, I felt abandoned. My own mother and father leaving me for somewhere better. But they told me it was for Iris's good. That someday they'd bring her there to live with them, where the crops were always healthy and the trees still grew tall. And then Iris would be safe."

The words were out of Milla before she could stop them. "Iris would be safer here at home than in The Place, wouldn't she? How can you leave her there?"

Hanna's face closed up. Hardened. "I was like you once," she said. "I had ideas about how things should be. I hoped. I visited my sister there and told her I loved her and missed her. And each time I saw her there she was less and less my Leah. Then one day she only screamed when she saw me. She said I wasn't her sister, I was a demon come to drag her to hell with the other demons. I tried to touch her, and she hissed at me like a snake. After that, I never went back. It's too hard, Milla. Too hard. You'll see. Now go on with you. And don't come back here. You're not welcome."

Hanna turned away from Milla and walked into Tomas's arms. He looked at Milla over his wife's head, two stones where his seeking eyes had once been.

13

MILLA WALKED DELIBERATELY PAST THE VILLAGERS, keeping her eyes on the ground, hoping that if she didn't look at them, they might not look at her, either. When she'd passed the church, and the cemetery, and the market square that she'd so often dreamed of visiting with her brother, the homes grew sparser. Milla felt that she might soon be safe.

Farmland rolled on either side of her, the wheat stunted and shriveled, nothing like her father's fields. Why had Hulda cursed the village so, but allowed Jakob and Gitta their healthy fields only a day's walk away? An answer came to Milla. The torture was in the waiting. That was how Hulda cursed Gitta and Jakob. Their punishment was to wake each morning wondering if that was the day the aphids would come and suck the life out of their wheat, the day the demon would come and swap their daughter for their greatest fear—a demon just like Hulda herself.

Fields gave way to forest. The temperature dropped with the shade of the trees, and Milla's snakes peeked out of her hair. Milla was used to woods that felt alive—tree life, insect life, birds and animals all pecking and crawling, flying and scurrying. The drip of damp and soft rustle of leaves. But these woods were dying. There were no birds to drive back the onslaught of fat caterpillars and ants, grasshoppers and beetles that feasted upon the papery leaves and ate the trees from inside out. Milla felt queasy moving among the diseased roots and branches.

Milla felt a kiss of snake tongue on her left ear, and another on her right. She touched the snake over her right ear. It was so much bigger in just a day; it circled her wrist, not just her finger. She caught a flash of brilliant red, so beautiful. She was amazed by it, how it was part of her and yet not. How it moved of its own volition, and yet she felt what it felt. Its alarm was her own, its thirst was her own as well. Thirst. She was terribly thirsty. But if there had been water here, she wouldn't want to drink it. Even the air smelled wrong.

The sun was halfway to the horizon, the light just turning golden, before the forest turned green again. She caught the homey scent of wood smoke and soon she arrived at the midwife's cottage. It hugged close to the side of the road. Next to it was a barn and paddock with a single horse standing outside looking back at Milla with mild curiosity.

A dark-haired woman peered out from one of the cottage's two front windows. If Milla had wanted to slip by undetected, she'd failed. She could try to keep walking, but if the midwife didn't want her to pass, she'd only come after her. The woman nodded at Milla, then moved away from the window. Within a moment she'd opened the door.

Milla could see that the woman was older than Gitta, but beyond that she couldn't tell how old she was. She stood tall and straight-backed. A slender, perfect streak of white sliced across her dark hair, which was thick and unbraided, and swept over her right shoulder. Milla hadn't thought what to expect of the midwife, but upon seeing her in the flesh she realized she'd assumed her to be ugly and craggy, with a face to match what was surely the blackness of her heart. She wasn't expecting a woman so striking, so interesting to look at. The midwife seemed strong and capable, alert and intelligent. She smiled. Her lips were full and her teeth were straight and white. "What are you doing so far from the village, and so late in the afternoon?"

Milla had prepared herself for questions, and she forced herself to breathe evenly, not to betray her lies with shaking, and not to tell more lies than she absolutely had to. Not because lying to this woman troubled her, but because she was afraid she wouldn't be very good at it. "I'm looking for my brother," Milla said.

True.

The midwife raised her eyebrows. They were full and arching. "And who might that be?"

"Niklas."

True.

"Ah, Niklas. He came with Iris and didn't want to leave her, is that right?"

"Yes," Milla said. Also true.

"Come inside." The midwife stepped back and to one side, inviting.

Milla's snakes hissed softly, so softly. A warning that only Milla could hear. "I . . . I shouldn't. I need to get to Niklas. Before . . . before it's too late."

The midwife's eyebrows shot up again. "Oh my. That sounds serious. Well. All the more reason to come inside." She smiled again, closed-lipped now but not unkindly. Milla tried to remember Iris's warnings. Iris was terrified of this woman, and Milla knew there were good reasons for that. And yet Milla felt herself drawn to the midwife. Admiring her, even. She seemed like the kind of woman Milla might want to grow into being—so sure, so certain. She didn't seem like a woman who ever tried to puzzle out what would please someone else. She simply knew what was right. And not the way Gitta knew the right way to serve Jakob's dinner or to feed the chickens. Milla sensed a deeper sort of knowing in this woman, and underneath that, something else. A lack of concern. Of trepidation. There was only solidity where Milla so often trembled and shook. This was not a woman who said sorry. Or felt regret. What must that be like, Milla wondered.

As the distance closed between her and the midwife's door, Milla looked down at her feet and wondered at the strangeness of knowing that she shouldn't be doing this—even feeling that she didn't want to do this—while her feet continued to carry her forward. Soon she would be in the midwife's cottage and the door would close behind her. She felt like the stupid girl in a story that Iris might have told her.

Still Milla's feet carried her forward. As she moved past the midwife and stepped inside the cottage, the warmth of the woman's hearth met Milla's face and perspiration chilled her temples. The chill traveled to her snakes and down her spine. Then the midwife closed the door and Milla saw that she wasn't alone.

There was a girl in a chair by the fireplace. She seemed to be hugging herself so closely that her hands disappeared behind her, which Milla thought odd. Then Milla saw that the sleeves of the girl's dress were twice again as long as they should be and had been used to bind her arms to her torso. The girl's hair was parted down the middle and pulled smoothly behind her. It shone blackly as if wet. Milla couldn't tell how old she was. She seemed tiny, the shelf of her collar bones forming a straight line that was visible through the drab gray wool of her strange dress. Her eyes were a deep brown. She looked at Milla and blinked once, twice. She pressed her lips together, just enough that Milla could detect the effort. Milla recognized that expression. It was the same one Gitta turned to Milla every day. Fear of what might happen, combined with willing oneself to remain silent. The girl looked past Milla to the midwife.

"Milla, this is Asta."

So the midwife knew Milla's name. But of course she did. Milla had said her brother was Niklas. Which meant that the midwife also knew the demon was her aunt.

"Hello, Asta," Milla said. The girl said nothing in response, though she looked at Milla again and blinked. Once. Twice. Milla looked at Asta a beat longer, a question in her own eyes. Still the girl said nothing.

Milla looked around the room. It was about the size of her mother and father's cottage. It had all the same features. A kitchen, a table and chairs. But it all felt too close. And there was no scent—not of apples or bread or stewed meat. Panic tightened her belly and Milla wanted to shove past the midwife and run. "And your name?" Milla said to the midwife.

The midwife raised one dark eyebrow. "Ragna."

"Thank you for inviting me in, but I can't stay," Milla said. "I need to take a message to my brother. To tell him that our mother is ill."

"Is she dying?" Ragna said.

Milla felt herself pale. It would be a terrible thing to say her mother was dying, like bringing a curse down upon her. But Milla reasoned that the midwife wouldn't let her see Niklas if the news weren't very bad. The contents of Milla's stomach rose up, stinging the back of her throat. She swallowed. "Yes."

"There's nothing to be done then," Ragna said. "You'll only upset him if you tell him. He'll want to see her and even if I allowed it, which I won't, by the time he got home she'd be dead. No. You may stay here the night, but you go back home first thing tomorrow. And I hope your mother is still alive when you get there. It was foolish of her to send you here. I'm surprised Gitta would do that." Ragna's voice was drained of emotion. Unyielding. Challenging.

Where Milla had felt only panic a moment before, anger bloomed. She felt the quick flicks of her snakes' tongues against her scalp. Ragna was so sure she knew what was right and that Milla would do as she was told. And if Milla didn't . . . then? Milla looked at Asta, so quiet and so still on the outside. Yet Milla saw how her stillness cost her. The restrained terror in her eyes.

"Sit," Ragna said. "Are you hungry?"

"Not a bit," Milla said.

"Well, sit anyway."

"It will be dark soon. I should go," Milla said.

"You'll stay here," Ragna said. "I told you."

Milla's anger unfurled some more. It didn't make her stupid, though; it made her sharp. "Why doesn't Asta speak? And why is she bound like that? Is she ill? Is she your daughter?"

Milla could see that her last question caused a flicker of unease to pass across Ragna's face. "She's my daughter, in a way. All the girls are my daughters."

"She's from The Place?"

"I'm helping her," Ragna said. "The girls say bad things sometimes. Cruel things. Asta says especially bad things. She upset her mother and father very much when they visited her yesterday. So we're having a talk. And when she's ready to be a good girl I'll take her back."

"Back home?"

Ragna's eyebrows formed two soft crescents over her eyes, rough imitations of kindness. "Oh, aren't you a sweet child. I know it's hard to understand. But these girls are stricken. Cursed by the demon. They can never go home. The best I can do for them is to keep them safe and calm." She smiled. "See how safe and calm Asta is. She's feeling better already."

Asta blinked. Once. Twice.

Milla imagined Iris in that chair, and she thought she might be sick.

Ragna crossed her arms over her chest and cocked her head. "You look like her, Milla. Has anyone ever told you that?"

"I don't look like anyone in my family," Milla said. Her snakes coiled tighter around her head and she felt an ache in the bones of her face, tears about to form and spill.

"So much like her," Ragna said. "Hulda was never pretty like Gitta. There was always something strange about her. And then we found out why. It's a miracle you haven't been taken. Isn't it?"

Ragna's eyes were on Milla, enjoying her agony. Milla couldn't bear to look back at Ragna, so instead she looked at Asta. And that was how she saw the silent word that formed on Asta's lips. *Go.*

By the time Ragna had finished feasting on Milla's pain and had turned her attention back to Asta, the girl's expression had once again stilled to barely controlled terror.

A thought entered Milla's head then. It was her own but also not. *The secret to lying well is to give them what they want.* Lying to Ragna, Milla realized, was no different from lying to Niklas, or to her mother or father. What Ragna wanted was sweetness and obedience to her wishes. So Milla would give that to her. Or at least the appearance of it. Milla allowed her bottom lip to tremble, but ever so slightly, as if she were trying not to. "I've made a terrible mistake," she said. "You're right. Mamma was foolish to send me here, but she loves Niklas so. I should go home to her. If I leave now I can stay the night with Tomas and Hanna and I'll be that much closer to home in the morning. Maybe they'll even lend me a horse so I can get home faster. Would that be all right? I feel that I'm intruding here . . . while you're so busy helping Asta." Milla made her eyes as round and innocent as a hare's.

She thrilled a bit. It was a very different thing to lie simply to please someone than to do what she was doing now—to lie to get something she wanted. Or it felt different, anyway. This felt like a game that she could win.

Ragna looked at Milla as if measuring her, and Milla tensed inside while exerting every bit of will she possessed in order to relax herself to soft compliance on the outside.

"Stay to the road and walk straight back," Ragna said. "It will be dark in a few hours and these woods are thick. You'll be lost before you've taken a step."

"Oh, I would never step into the woods," Milla said. "Mamma and Pappa wouldn't allow it. And anyway, I'd be frightened." Milla moved toward the door, not too fast, she told herself.

"As you should be," Ragna said. "Fear will keep you safe."

Milla reached to open the door while smiling at Ragna in a way that was at once sad and grateful and apologetic. "Thank you, Ragna." Once the door was open, Milla turned back to look at Asta. "Good-bye, Asta." She wanted to say to Asta, *I won't forget you.* She wanted to rush past Ragna and pick up that slight, frightened girl and save her. But in that moment Milla had no idea how she would keep herself safe, much less Asta. And Ragna loomed over Milla, strength of purpose and conviction rising off her like a threat—a reminder of the fate that would await Milla if she didn't do as she was told. Milla made her smile a lie but kept her eyes honest for Asta. Then she blinked at Asta once. Twice. Asta did the same.

Milla didn't breathe while her legs took her back to the road and pointed her toward town. She didn't breathe while Ragna followed her out to the road and stared after her. Milla's snakes stayed close to her scalp as if they, too, could feel Ragna's eyes. Milla took in her first breath only once she'd passed Ragna's barn. She kept walking without looking back until her snakes began to move in her hair and she felt them peek out and lick the air. Only then did Milla look behind her to see that Ragna had disappeared.

14

THE WOODS WERE SHOWING THE FIRST SIGNS OF INFES-
tation when Milla left the road. It was revolting to pick her way
through the caterpillars and webbed leaves. She'd traveled well
past Ragna's cottage before doubling back again. She was certain
Ragna hadn't followed her, so the trick now was to conceal herself
should Ragna be keeping watch on the road. Milla wasn't afraid
of the woods. She never had been and she wasn't now. She felt
certain that no matter how thick the forest, she'd find her way
straight. Her greater fear was that Ragna might take it upon
herself to go to The Place tonight—and that she'd be waiting for
Milla when she got there. But Milla had to hope she wouldn't
be, not with Asta there to look after. Milla shuddered to think
of what that might mean. Maybe, somehow, she and Iris—and
Niklas, too, if Milla could convince him—could save that poor
girl. But first, Iris. Iris was the one she'd made a promise to.

As the woods grew healthier and thicker and wetter, the air was sweeter to breathe but the traveling was harder. So as not to find herself moving farther and farther from the road, she clambered over rocks and branches rather than around them. When she drifted left, her snakes rose up and leaned her right, closer to the road.

A breeze rustled through the leaves, sending a chill through her dress. Then the rustling became whispering.

Let me out.

I'm so cold.

Let me out.

Iris. Wasn't it? But not only Iris. Not one girl. Many girls. And women. All whispering together.

Let me out.

Milla turned abruptly right, heading for the road. She had to be well past the midwife's cottage by now. And those voices told her she was close.

The woods were so thick that darkness seemed already to have fallen, but as she drew closer to the road and the trees thinned, Milla saw that the sun hadn't yet dipped below the horizon. When she emerged from the woods, the whispering grew louder, as if showing her the way. Her snakes were on high alert, tasting the air over her head. She felt their excitement and her pace quickened. The road made a soft turn and she reached a wide meadow, blue-green in the twilight and dotted with yellow flowers. It might have been beautiful.

The Place rose up in front of her, a curved wall of stone so covered with moss that it looked like a flat, green hill.

The whispering that had sounded pleading before had become howls. The wind carried them to Milla's ears in screeches and shrieks.

LET ME OUT.

Milla's snakes retracted into her hair and she felt them tremble. Her bravery dissolved. The Place was so big, and she felt so small and alone. The only thought that calmed her terror was that Niklas was within those walls. He would help her, she told herself. He must. Maybe she could even tell Niklas what was happening to her, make him understand that though Iris had changed—and though Milla was changing, too—that they were still themselves. If she could get him to believe that, then he would have to help her free Iris. He would know that Iris didn't belong there. And then they could all leave here and find someplace where the curse couldn't reach them.

Darker thoughts crept in, pestering her and giving her no peace. Did she really think that she and Iris weren't cursed by the demon? Did she think that once away from The Place, Iris would get no worse, or for that matter that Milla herself wouldn't become a demon like Hulda, snake by snake? Then Milla wondered: If she continued to transform, would she merely look like a monster—which would be horrible enough— or would she actually become one, as well? Would her brother be safe with her? Would anyone?

She was a coward. She looked down at her feet, once again willing them to stop carrying her forward, into something that terrified her. *Stop, Milla. Turn around. Leave. Go somewhere safe, to a village where no one knows you. Cut the snakes from your head and pray they never grow back. Keep cutting them off if they do. You can't help Iris or Asta. You can't even help yourself.*

Her snakes rose up in protest, and Milla felt the sting of tears in the corners of her eyes. All she wanted in the world was for her brother to call her silly Milla and to tell her that everything would be all right.

Silly Milla is dead.

Was that her voice, or Iris's, or the demon's? Milla didn't know anymore. Were they all the same?

The howling grew ever louder. So many voices, each singing her own song of misery but using the same words.

Let me out.

I'm so cold.

Let me out.

The sun was fully down when Milla stepped through the open, arched entrance of The Place. She could see that it had once been a ring fort. Trude had told her stories about them, safe places where farmers took shelter from marauders. The stone wall was thicker than a grown man's arm span. Milla felt swallowed by it, made even tinier and less significant. Inside was a broad dirt yard with a large bell hanging atop a stone pillar. Beyond it was a wide well, also stone. Around it the dirt was muddy and puddled with spilled water. Clinging to the outer wall of the fort there was a stable with an attached corral where five horses stood dozing, and a chicken coop, and a small barn—all made of ash-gray wood. She might have heard the clucks of chickens or bleats of sheep if it hadn't been for the howling.

Let me out.

I'm so cold.

Let me out.

The Place was a building at the center of the ring fort—two stories high and made of stone. The second story had windows that overlooked the yard, too small to bring in much light or air. The wooden doors of the entrance also seemed too small for such a large structure. Milla walked to the doors and rapped twice. She waited.

The door opened slowly and a fair-haired boy appeared in

the opening. Milla thought of him as a boy, because he was as long-limbed and awkward as a colt, but the beginnings of a beard sprouted from his chin. His eyes opened wide.

"I'm here for my brother," she said. "Niklas. I . . . I have a message for him. From home."

The boy peered past her into the night.

"I'm alone," Milla said. "It's just me."

"I'm not supposed to let anyone in," the boy said. "It's not allowed. Midwife said so."

"What's your name?" Milla said, attempting to smile brightly. *What does he want,* she reminded herself. *Give him some of that.*

"Petter," he said.

"And do you know my brother, Niklas? He would have arrived just three days ago. Sandy hair. And tall?"

"I know him," Petter said.

"I could wait right here, and you could go get him for me, and then he and I could talk?" It was all Milla could do not to scream. To say, *You oaf, I haven't time for your wide eyes and your surprise—I need to talk to my brother.* Instead she kept smiling.

Petter nodded. "All right. But you can't come in."

"Oh my goodness," Milla said. "I wouldn't. I'd be frightened to." She arranged her face while imagining this boy was someone she very much wanted to make happy. She stood off to the side of herself and marveled at her cunning. Here she was, a girl who'd grown up with just one boy, her brother, and she was unmoved by talking to another boy, a boy she didn't know. His good opinion of her felt so . . . unimportant. Which was a surprise to her after all the stories Trude had told about magical first meetings between boys and girls. She'd assumed when it did finally happen to her that the expected response would churn up inside her. She'd feel some measure of what Trude had described as the most potent kind of joy. Milla looked at this tall, gangly boy. His face was nice enough, she supposed. But it certainly wasn't magic.

He nodded again, closed the door and left Milla alone. She tried to calm her desperation to see Niklas. She'd have to be careful not to make a fuss when he came. She shouldn't draw attention to herself in a place where any sign of oddness, of excitement, might get her locked up along with Iris.

The air was cooler here than at home. She thought about Trude's shawl and then realized she'd left it in Hanna's kitchen. Well, she thought. Just as well that Hanna should have her mother's shawl. Milla wrapped her arms around herself.

Her back was to the doors when she heard them open, and she stayed where she was, fearing what she'd feel, or do, if Niklas hadn't come. If he told Petter to send her away.

"Milla?"

A box inside her that she'd kept tightly closed since she'd set out from home opened in that moment. So much climbed out of that box—fear, relief, sadness, joy, regret, love, guilt—that it was all she could do not to sob. Instead she turned around and threw herself into her brother's arms.

"Oh, Milla," Niklas said. He wrapped his arms around her and she felt his size and strength and she wanted to stay there. But after a moment he gently held her away from him and said, "What are you doing here? And all alone? Where are Mamma and Pappa?"

"At home. They don't know I'm here. They wouldn't have let me come, and I had to. I had to see you. And Iris."

"Oh, Milla," he said again. In just three days he had become a different boy. There were angles in his face she hadn't seen before. Purple half-moons under his eyes where before there'd only been cream dotted with freckles. She waited for him to admonish her, to ask her why she must worry their parents so. Why she couldn't behave. Instead he brought her to him again, and she pressed her cheek to his chest and felt a tremor there like he might be crying. After a moment he pulled away and looked up at the dark sky, taking in a deep breath. He wiped both eyes with the back of one hand. "All right. We need to figure out what to do with you. You can't stay here. It's not safe. I'll tell Petter that I'm taking you to the midwife. You can stay the night with her, then go home tomorrow."

The snakes on Milla's head hissed so loudly that she thought Niklas must have heard them. *"No,"* she said. "No. Please, Niklas, don't make me leave until I've seen Iris. I've come all this way."

Niklas breathed out heavily. "I suppose you can sleep on my cot tonight. But, Milla, are you sure you want to see her? She's not as you remember her. And it will only upset you to see her here."

"How terrible is it here, Niklas?" She looked up to the small windows in the second story, where the howling spilled out in waves of agony and begging. "Why do they complain so of being cold? What does the midwife do to them?"

Niklas looked at her without blinking. She could see in his eyes that he was making a decision, and she knew him well enough that he didn't need to speak the words once he had. He was going to take her inside.

Niklas led her past Petter, who sat on a stool leaning against the wall of the fort's open central courtyard. From the way he startled, she thought he must have been dozing.

"My sister is staying here tonight, Petter. It's too late to send her home."

Petter looked at Milla with narrowed eyes. "You're sure she's all right?"

All right, Milla assumed, meant that she wasn't possessed by a demon. She almost laughed. Her snakes squirmed.

"She's my sister," Niklas said. "I'd know if she weren't."

Petter shrugged and closed his eyes. Not bothering to open them again, he said, "You can explain to the others. And the midwife."

"I'll have her out before the midwife comes in the morning." Niklas looked at her as if to say, *and no argument from you.*

Milla thought to herself that he needn't worry that she'd want to stay here. It was the dreariest place she'd ever seen. Worse even than the blighted village. Bad things happened here.

"The only time the girls are allowed out of their cells is when they're brought here to the courtyard," Niklas said. "That's because the ground is covered in stone. The midwife says the demon comes from below, from deep in the earth, and so the girls mustn't touch earth or else the demon will get an even tighter hold on them. Make them stronger and impossible to control."

"What's that?" Milla said. She pointed to a stone slab in the center of the courtyard, five empty buckets lined up next to it.

"When the midwife thinks a girl is being troublesome, she has the boys tie the girl up and lay her there. Then we're to douse the girl with water. The midwife says demons are made of hellfire and hate the cold. Water subdues them."

"I saw a girl named Asta at the midwife's cottage."

"You met Ragna? You didn't tell me. So she knows you're here?"

"Not . . . really."

Niklas frowned. "That's not good, Milla. You don't want to make an enemy of her."

"If she douses the troublesome girls here, what was she doing with Asta at her cottage? She said Asta told her mother and father terrible things."

"I don't know. I tried to find out, but the other boys wouldn't tell me. They're all so miserable, Milla. Most of them don't want to be here, but they're forced to be. And the few that do want to be here are the ones you want to stay away from. The midwife chooses what boys come here to be guards and there's no saying no. It's the deal every villager makes in order to be kept safe from the girls. And the oldest boy isn't allowed to leave until there's a younger boy to come in to replace him."

"That's horrible."

"It is. But, Milla, it's so much worse for the girls." His eyes traveled to the stone slab.

"Have you seen it happen?"

"Once," Niklas said. "It's awful. I haven't had to help tie up any of the girls yet. But it takes four boys just to tie up one girl and carry her down here. The girls buck and scream so. And it's no wonder. The water is icy and once the dousing is over they're wearing nothing but their soaking wet shifts. Then Ragna sends them back to their cells to shiver."

Milla thought of that happening to Iris. No. She couldn't let it. And she didn't believe Niklas would either. "No wonder they howl so."

"I feel sorry for them," Niklas said. "It's not their faults. It's the demon who deserves to be punished. Not them." In that moment he looked to Milla like the sweet Niklas she played with in the woods when they were children—the boy who didn't want to believe in any of the dreadful things that Milla could make up in her head. As dear as he was, and as much as she knew he loved her, he'd surely never want to know that his sister had snakes growing from her head—and that most of the time she rather liked the company. She despaired that she could ever tell him.

"Come," he said. "I'll show you the rest. Then I'll take you to Iris."

Niklas led her back through the stone tunnel that led from the courtyard to the corridor that circled the entire first story of The Place. The first room they came to was a large, dank chamber lined with ten straw-padded cots and lit by hanging oil lamps. Small windows high in the walls opened out onto the courtyard they'd just left. Four boys sat or lay across the cots, not talking, only staring, as if too spent to do anything else. Niklas said to them, "This is my sister."

All four looked up at once, like dogs catching a scent. One of them, round-faced and dark-haired, said, "Are you mad, Niklas? You think we're allowed visitors here?"

Petter walked in then. "I told him he'll have to explain to Ragna. I'm not getting blamed for this."

Milla could tell that Niklas didn't like this Petter. Neither did she. "And what's Ragna going to do to Niklas if she finds out I'm here? Make him leave? Good!"

Milla saw two of the boys exchange looks between them as if to say, *she has a point.*

Niklas, for his part, looked at Milla in horror—as if he could see the snakes on her head.

Petter, who for all his gangly dimness clearly did not like being bested by a girl, narrowed his eyes at her. "I think this one's showing the signs. She's got a demon light in her eyes."

Milla sensed the other boys shifting behind her.

Niklas stepped in front of her. "Milla is overtired from her journey. But she's as meek as a mouse, I promise you."

Bile rose in Milla's throat at being dismissed so. She wanted to let the snakes rise from her head and attack Petter with her nails. Let him see the signs of her claw marks then. Let him release his bowels with fright at the sight of her green and crimson snakes, jaws wide and ready.

Then Milla wondered if maybe Petter really had seen the demon light in her eyes.

"Come, Milla," Niklas said, pushing her out of the room. When they'd walked five paces he turned on her. "You must be more careful or I can't keep you safe here. These boys would sooner lock you up right now than worry that you'll turn demon-possessed by morning."

"I'm not as meek as a mouse, Niklas. And I was defending you. You should be thanking me."

Niklas searched the ceiling, as if for strength. "Milla, if you have any love for me at all, then you will stop defending me."

She smiled at him. "You didn't say that when the forest witches were after you. Then you made sure I didn't leave your side until we were all the way home."

"You are a strange girl, Milla."

She wrapped her arms around him and put her head on his chest. "But you love me."

He sighed. "I do. Though you'll be the death of me." He let her rest against his chest for a moment longer, then he pushed her gently away. "Are you hungry?"

Milla thought back to when she'd eaten last. Had it really been a full day since she'd had Trude's apple, bread, and cheese? "Starving," she said. "And so thirsty."

Niklas took her to the kitchen, a large room with a massive, cold hearth at the opposite end, and a long wooden table and benches in the center of the room. Against one wall there were shelves with baskets of apples, cabbages, and potatoes, also a bowl of eggs and some cloth-wrapped cheese. He poured water into a cup and she drank it so greedily that it ran down her chin.

"A village woman cooks dinner for us once a week. The rest of the time we fend for ourselves." Niklas handed her an apple, then tore off two large hunks of brown bread. He handed her one and tucked the other and a second apple into the pocket of her dress. "Give those to Iris."

Milla devoured the food without tasting it.

"I'll take you to Iris now. But, Milla, you must prepare yourself. I can see the hope in your eyes, and I'm sad for you."

"There you go again talking to me like you're so much older and wiser." Her snakes twitched. "You don't know what I've seen. Or what I know." She saw Niklas withdraw from her, and she calmed herself. This wasn't the way to get what she wanted. She breathed, settled herself. "Niklas, if there's something I don't understand, then help me understand it. Right now I can't think of a single reason that you and I shouldn't take Iris out of here tonight."

"You don't know what you're asking, Milla."

Her impatience flared again. She wanted to shake him. Why should she have to pretend to be settled in her heart and mind when he was the one in the wrong? "You're just like Tomas and Hanna. They said the same thing to me. But I *do* know what I'm asking. You can't let them do this to Iris. She's our friend. We love her." Milla gripped Niklas's rough linen shirt in her hand.

He closed his own hand over hers. "You don't know what you're asking because you haven't seen the girls, Milla. Come. I'll show you."

15

NIKLAS LED MILLA TO A WOODEN LADDER THAT WENT up to an opening in the stone ceiling. He climbed up first, and she followed. As she climbed she was struck by how quiet it had become. No howling or crying. She wondered if the girls were sleeping. When she'd climbed all the way to the second story, the moment her face was just above floor level she was hit with the overpowering scent of sour milk. It was so strong she could taste it in her mouth. She let out an involuntary grunt of disgust.

Niklas reached out a hand to help her all the way up. "Another of Ragna's ideas. The girls get cups of milk every four daylight hours. It's supposed to calm them. From what I can tell it just makes them angrier. None of them drink it and half of them throw it back at us. I've only been here three days, and I don't think I'll ever want to drink milk again."

Milla didn't think she'd ever wish to, either. They paused

before continuing on. Milla realized that as badly as she'd wanted to see Iris, there was now a tremor of hesitation in her. A fear of how Iris might have changed. "Is it always so quiet at night? Do they sleep?"

"I've never heard it quiet like this since I've been here. It's . . . strange." Niklas looked worried. She supposed that if howling seemed normal to you, then the absence of howling might be a cause for concern. "Come. Iris's cell is toward the middle." He held her eyes. "I think it would be better if you didn't look in the cells, Milla. Keep your eyes forward, on me."

Milla nodded while knowing it was a promise she couldn't possibly keep.

The stone hall circled the courtyard, just as the one beneath it did, and was lit by oil lamps that hung from iron hooks sunk into the walls. Milla felt the damp chill of the place in her flesh, and she thought of those poor girls, soaked to the skin and then left to huddle alone in their cells.

A whispering rose along the hallway. Milla could tell by the way he faltered for just a moment that Niklas had heard it, too. It sounded like wind through leafy branches, only sharper, crisper. Then she thought, *No, that's not what it sounds like at all. It sounds like hissing.*

Then the hissing became words.

She's here.

She's here.

She's here.

Niklas held one hand behind him, quickly squeezing one of hers. "Remember what I said. Don't look. And . . . don't listen, either. They'll say things to you. It's the demon talking. Remember that."

Milla noticed he hadn't prayed the way they'd been taught to do whenever anyone mentioned the demon. Nor was there salt around doors and windows. Come to think of it, there was none in Ragna's cottage, either. She wondered if everyone who spent any time here realized it was pointless. The demon was already here, and would do as she wished.

Milla could see the iron bars of cells, one after the other, curving along the outer wall of the corridor, and as they passed the first, hands shot out at her through the bars, fingertips grazing her arm and nearly catching hold of her sleeve. Niklas threw an arm around Milla and jerked her backward until they both leaned against the corridor's inner wall, beyond the reach of the girl.

Though she was not a girl at all. She had a woman's shape beneath the rough burlap she wore—more sack than dress. There were lines cobwebbing the corners of her eyes, and her cheeks were hollow, her lips thin. She stood pressed up against the bars, a smile across her face from ear to ear exposing her teeth, yellow with age. She laughed and hissed—laughing on the intake of breath, hissing on the exhale—and gripped and shook the iron bars. "She's here! She's here! She's here!"

More hands and arms emerged from the iron bars along the corridor and the whisper-hissing grew louder and constant.

"I'm taking you out of here," Niklas said. "It's not safe."

She turned to him, calmed her face and willed herself to be convincing. "I'm fine, Niklas. They're all locked up. They can't get out. And I've come this far to see Iris. Please don't make me leave until I do."

Niklas took her hand, less with affection and more, she felt, out of a desire to keep her close. Then he turned and led her on. Milla made no pretense of not looking at each woman and girl that they passed, their faces lit up by the oil lamps. She saw that there seemed to be two kinds of prisoners here. Those who smiled and whispered and held the bars as if waiting for something to be brought to them. Their faces were bright with expectation, from the oldest to the youngest. One of these women, old enough to be her mother, had hair and eyebrows that looked as if they might once have been the same rust-red as Iris's. She wondered if it was Leah, Iris's aunt. These women frightened Milla—their smiles were so wide as to be grimaces. They seemed to have teeth too numerous, too large. They were frenzied.

But there was another kind of prisoner here, too—girls who didn't whisper or grip the bars. In their faces Milla saw what Asta would become, whenever Ragna was finished with her. These girls huddled in the dim of their cells, only staring, the fight gone out of them.

Niklas stopped in front of one of these cells. Inside, on a low cot covered with dirty hay, sat a girl, her knees pulled up to her forehead, her arms wrapped around them.

It was Iris.

Niklas stepped up to the bars. "Iris. It's me. Niklas."

Iris lifted her head from her arms, and Milla was overcome with relief and anguish—both. Relief because here was Iris. Anguish because here was Iris. *Here.* And in this way. She wore the same rough, dirty burlap sack that all the other girls and women wore. Milla rushed to the door of the cell and thrust her arms through the bars. Iris leapt up and reached for Milla before Niklas could pull Milla away.

"Oh my dear. My dearest. I'm so sorry they've done this to you." Milla held Iris through the bars, felt the bones and muscles under the skin of Iris's back. Iris seemed at once thinner and stronger than she'd been just a few days before. Milla wanted to push her face through the bars and press her cheek, wet with tears, to Iris's. But the bars were too close together. She looked at Niklas. "Let me inside. Let me sit with her."

"Oh, Milla," he said. "Don't you know how I'd love to let you? But it's not safe."

"Niklas, please," Iris said, in a voice that was all her own. "I'm me. You know me. I would never hurt Milla. She's like my own sister."

"Iris," he said. "You know that won't keep her safe from the demon."

What he meant, Milla knew, was that Iris's love for Milla wouldn't keep Milla safe from *Iris*. "Niklas, what is the worst that could happen if you let me inside? What is the worst these girls ever do? Say bad things? Look at her, Niklas. She's just as she ever was." What Milla thought, but didn't say, was that Milla herself bore far more proof of possession than any of these girls. If Ragna knew there were snakes growing from her head, they'd build a new prison, just for her.

Niklas raised an eyebrow at her. "Milla."

"I know Iris. All you have to do is let me in and lock the door behind me. And if anything happens I'll call to you. Anyway, I'm hardly going to sleep in a room with all those boys looking for their proof that I'm demon-possessed. I'm safer here than there. Then you can come get me in the morning and let me out before Ragna arrives."

"Petter's on guard duty tonight," Niklas said, "so he'd be the first to hear you if you called. Not that I imagine I'll be able to sleep a wink knowing you're in here."

"You could stay with us, Niklas." Iris smiled at him, and

something in the brightness of her smile gave Milla pause, but then she told herself that she was being silly. It was just Iris's usual smile. Wasn't it?

"Yes, Niklas," Milla said. "Do that." She looked to Niklas hopefully, realizing with shame that she'd welcome his company. As the damp chill of the stone walls settled into her and the whispering circled and circled the corridor like a creature prowling, Milla felt suddenly afraid to be here alone.

Niklas thought for a moment. "No. It will make the other boys suspicious, and that will be no good for you. Besides, I can only lock the door from the outside. And . . ." He looked at Iris. "Leaving it unlocked wouldn't be a good idea." He pulled Milla away from the iron bars. "Milla," he said quietly. "You must listen to me now. And believe me. Trust that I love Iris, too, and I wouldn't lie to you. Do you trust me?"

Milla nodded. She did. Didn't she?

"Then trust me when I say that Iris isn't always like this. I know she seems like herself now. But I've seen her act just like the others. She hisses and laughs and throws her milk back at me like she doesn't even know me. She says terrible things. Things Iris would never have said to me before."

Milla wanted to protest, to say it was no wonder—after all, look what they'd done to Iris. Shouldn't she be angry? But something in Niklas's face told her that he'd seen things she hadn't. That arguing with him now would be unkind. That he was frightened for her, and trying his hardest to do right by her.

"Promise me that you'll scream your loudest if you need me," he said. "I don't trust some of those other boys. I see how they act with the girls. So far I've kept them away from Iris. And I'll keep them away from you. I'll stay awake in there with them, and I'll keep an ear out for Petter, too. You call me if you need me, do you hear?"

Again, Milla nodded, then put her arms around him and squeezed tight.

"All right then," Niklas said. He walked toward the door to Iris's cell and unclamped the wooden bar that held the iron-barred door closed. "Iris, you'll take care of Milla tonight, will you? Don't let anything happen to her?" He lifted off the bar and pulled the door open.

Milla squeezed Niklas's hand one last time and then she walked inside Iris's cell.

"Milla is my friend," Iris said. She put a gentle arm around Milla's shoulder and smiled at Niklas, so brightly.

16

ONCE NIKLAS HAD LEFT THEM, MILLA FELT SHY AND uncertain. She pulled away from Iris and circled the cell, touching the cold, rough stone of the walls, looking up toward the small window—more an opening than a window, too high and tiny to offer much light during the day, but big enough to let in the night chill. The moon shone weakly through it now. The only other light came from the oil lamp that hung from the wall outside. Milla looked around the floor, at the bucket in the corner where she supposed Iris must relieve herself—the stench rising from it revealed as much—and then, finally, at the cot with its layer of old straw. Clearly Iris wasn't the first girl who had lain upon it. And if she wasn't the first, then what had happened to the others?

"The girl who was here before me died," Iris said.

"How did you know I was wondering that?"

Iris shrugged. "I know you, Milla. I read the question in your eyes. It's natural enough to wonder. I did, too. It's the first thing I thought when they put me in here. I could smell her in the straw. I could smell her in the bucket."

"How did she die?"

"Fever."

Milla imagined a girl curled up on that straw, sweating and shaking, all alone. Ragna did that—she was responsible for that poor girl's death.

"I found out this morning what the girl's name was. Her name was Beata. My dearest Beata. She glowed, Milla. Like a flame. And they put her out."

Milla heard a whisper. Iris went to the door of the cell and crouched down, pressing her face to the bars. "It's Milla," she whispered back. "Niklas's sister. She's come to save us. I told you she would."

Whispers hissed up and down the corridor then.

shesheresheresheshereshereshereshereshereshereshereshere

Iris stood and turned toward Milla. Milla groaned and put her hands to her face. How would she save them all? The most she could hope to do would be to convince Niklas to let Iris out. But even that seemed remote. She saw the fear in his eyes when he looked at Iris. He didn't trust her.

Iris stood there, thin and dirty, barely dressed, and still she looked so strong, so alive with certainty. Iris walked toward Milla and put her arms around her. "Milla, dearest. I knew you'd come. I knew you'd hear me. And you did."

Milla had never felt so uncomfortable to be embraced by Iris. She pulled away. "How can I possibly save all of them? I'm not even sure I can save *us*."

Iris looked at her oddly, as if she weren't listening to Milla's words at all. "Why do you hide them from me?"

"Hide what?" But Milla knew what Iris meant. What chilled her gut now was not that Iris knew. It was *how* Iris knew.

"Your snakes." Iris reached out both of her hands as if to cradle Milla's head, and then turned them palms up, the way you would to reassure a dog. Milla felt her snakes emerge from their hair nest and watched as they rested their heads on Iris's hands and tasted the salt of her skin with their tongues. Milla's crimson snake was now as fully grown as her green, both of them as slender as her little finger, elegant and beautiful, and long enough to rest their heads on her shoulders. "You're so lucky," Iris said.

"Lucky," Milla said. "How can this be lucky?"

"The demon gave you snakes but left you this." She tapped Milla's forehead with a finger. "You're still you. You're not taken."

"You're not taken, either," Milla said.

"No? Then why do I hear her voice in my head?" Iris gripped her skull in her hands, squeezing as if she would crush it if she could. Her face crumpled like a dry leaf. "She's always in here. I want her out, but she won't leave."

And there she was. There was Iris, Milla thought. Her Iris. This time, Milla was the one to embrace Iris, and neither of them pulled away.

They sat on the old straw of the cot while Iris ate the bread from Niklas and told Milla about The Place. And about how Stig and Jakob had left her with the midwife. By then, Iris said, she'd so exhausted herself with crying and begging and terror of what was to come that she no longer tried to escape. When she was led to her cell she walked meekly by the other girls and women, who stared at her, blinking. Once. Twice. She sat on the dirty cot and obediently changed out of her nightdress and into the burlap she now wore.

"You say the girls blinked at you," Milla said, thinking of Asta.

"When we're not alone but can see each other, that's our way of talking."

"What does the blinking mean?"

"Anything. Everything. *I see you. See me.* There's a lot you can say with your eyes when you can't use your mouth. And there isn't time for anything more than that, because the only time we're out of our cells is when one of us is taken out for punishment or on visiting days. And most girls never get visitors. At night, when Ragna's gone and there's only a boy on guard, we talk to each other in whispers, from cell to cell to cell. The woman next to me is Agnetha, and she's the youngest of four sisters, all taken. Agnetha will give me a message for her sisters and then I pass the message to Rebekka in the next cell. And then she passes it on. It's how we spend our days, whispering to each other. They like my stories. Sometimes we get loud. We howl." Iris wrapped her arms around herself and looked around at the grimness of her cell as if seeing it again for the first time. "It's so cold here, Milla. And lonely. So lonely. It's only been three days and already I feel that I can't survive another. The last woman to be doused was my mother's sister, Leah. I heard her screaming, then crying. It hasn't happened to me yet, but it will. Agnetha says there's no rhyme or reason to when they come for you. You could be sleeping in your cell and next you know they're dragging you away."

"Oh, Iris," Milla said. "I can't bear to think of them doing that to you. I won't let them." Then Milla remembered the blinking. "I was in Ragna's cottage and saw a girl there, named Asta."

Iris nodded. "I heard about her. From the whispers. She made Ragna angry."

"How?"

"Her mother and father came to see her on visiting day. It's only the newer girls who get visitors. Their families still miss them. The older ones, their families have given up. Can't bear to see them here, I suppose." Iris's face changed, became all planes and edges, and she seemed to go somewhere else in her head. "Or maybe those mothers and fathers didn't love their daughters much in the first place."

"Asta," Milla said, wanting to bring Iris back to her, frightened of the sudden distance she felt between them. "What did she do that angered Ragna?"

Iris spoke urgently, as if she thought she'd be stopped even though she and Milla were alone and there was no one to interrupt them. "The thing you need to understand, Milla, is that not all the girls here are the same. Some of the girls aren't taken by the demon at all. They swear they can't hear her voice in their heads."

"Then why are they here?"

"They just misbehaved. Some only once, some more than once. But they say it wasn't because the demon was making them do it. They just got . . . angry."

"That's all?"

"The villagers are so frightened their daughters will turn on them that some of them, if their daughters make the tiniest misstep, they'll send for Ragna. And the thing is, Ragna never examines a girl and says she's *not* possessed. Once Ragna is sent for, the girl is doomed. That's what happened to Asta. She slapped another girl and that girl told her mother and father, and they insisted on sending for Ragna."

"Asta's mother and father should have taken her away before Ragna could get her. She doesn't belong here."

Iris cocked her head at Milla. "And I do? And these other girls who hear the demon's voice in their heads? Do they deserve to be here?"

Milla felt hot with shame. "No! No, that's not what I meant."

Iris smiled at her. "It's not? Then what did you mean?"

"I meant . . . I meant . . ." But what had Milla meant, really? She'd meant what she said. She could make an exception in her head for Iris. She knew Iris and loved her and didn't want her to be here. But those other girls, the ones who smiled too wide and hissed . . . she could understand why their mothers and fathers were frightened of them. She was frightened of them, too. She knew she was wrong to make such a distinction. To make allowances for the known while shutting herself off to the unknown. Did Milla think she herself deserved to be here? What made her better or different? She had snakes growing from her head, and hadn't she heard Iris's voice in her head? Why did anyone deserve this? There was no good reason. No one did. "I'm sorry."

Iris patted her hand, but looked away.

"Please finish telling me. Why is Ragna keeping Asta at her cottage?"

Iris turned back to her. "It's only the girls who insist they're not possessed who are taken there. And when they come back they don't insist anymore. They give up. When Asta's mother and father visited her, she told them that she didn't belong here, that she'd just been angry with that girl she slapped. And I suppose she must have seemed quite herself to them, and maybe that got them to thinking. They must have gone to Ragna."

"And then Ragna took Asta," Milla said.

Iris nodded.

"What's she doing to her?"

"Ragna has a way of getting in your head. Of making you give up. It's like she's a demon herself. Kari, one of the girls who came back from Ragna's, said that after being forced to listen to Ragna for days on end, she wished she *were* demon-possessed. She said she would prefer it to having Ragna's voice in her head, telling her things about herself that weren't true. She said Ragna talks and talks until you start to wonder if you really aren't who you think you are—if you know yourself at all. She said Ragna's voice was worse than any demon."

"Ragna. Hulda," Milla said. "They're the same, aren't they? Putting their voices where our own should be."

"But now you've come, Milla. And you'll get us all out."

"How can we get everyone out, Iris? Niklas wouldn't agree to it. And even if he wanted to, the other boys would stop him."

"It must be tonight," Iris said. She stared past Milla, as if watching her plan unfold. "You'll call to Niklas, tell him that you want out. When he comes to let you out, we'll lock him in the cell here and then we'll let the other girls out. And then we'll all escape."

"We can't lock Niklas in here, Iris. He helped me. And he wants to help you. No, the only way is to tell him that we need to get you out. And then he'll help us."

"You said yourself that he won't let the other girls out, and I won't leave without them. Milla, how could you expect me to after everything you know now? And can you imagine what Ragna would do to them if I got away? How much worse it would be for the rest? Anyway, if Niklas let only you and me out, we'd still have to get past the other boys. And that Petter.

He's a nasty one. We need the other girls to help us if we're to get out."

"But locking up Niklas, in here?" Milla looked around her and couldn't imagine it. She'd never forgive herself.

"I've survived it for three days. It would be a few hours for him. Ragna or the other boys will let him out by daybreak, if not sooner."

"How can you be so sure he won't help us, Iris? Why can't we explain to him?"

"Have you shown him your snakes, Milla?"

"No."

"And why not?" Iris's voice was mocking.

"Because he wouldn't understand. He'd be frightened. But maybe he'd come to understand. Someday."

"Someday, of course." Now Iris was soothing, stroking Milla's arm. Something inside Milla recoiled from Iris. The feeling she'd had when she first walked into the cell had returned to her. The fear that maybe Iris wasn't entirely Iris anymore. "But someday isn't right now," Iris said. "And right now, Milla, I promise you. I will not leave here without the other girls. And if I don't leave here, I'll die. Just like Beata."

17

"WHEN SHOULD I CALL TO HIM?" MILLA HOVERED AT THE iron-barred door to the cell, peering into the dim passageway. Now that she had decided, she wanted to get it over with. To get past the horrible disappointment she'd see on Niklas's face when he realized what she was doing.

"Not yet. Wait a bit longer. Petter is supposed to stay awake all night, but he won't. Let him get good and sleepy. Then you'll call to Niklas."

"And Petter won't awaken at the same time?"

"He won't come up here. He's a brave bully during the day, but when night falls he stays well away." She smiled. "We tell him the demon is coming for him."

Iris's smile chilled Milla. "Does the demon really talk to you?"

Iris looked troubled for a moment, then her face cleared and recomposed. "I told you she did."

Milla wanted—and didn't want—to know more. She worried that asking more about the voice, how it felt in Iris's head, what it sounded like, might somehow make it worse. Might even conjure the demon. "After we leave here, how will we get her out of your head? And how do we stop her from turning me into a demon, too?"

Iris looked at the wall, wouldn't answer. Milla couldn't tell if she was hurt, or angry. Milla sat down next to her. "I'm sorry. I didn't mean to make you sad. We'll figure that out later. There must be a way." Iris smiled back at her vaguely, patted her hand. Milla looked down at Iris's slender brown fingers, the delicate weave of blue-green veins just under the surface, and she thought of something else. "How will you and I lock Niklas in here? He's twice as big as either of us."

"I'm stronger than I look," Iris said. Milla believed her. There was a hardness to Iris now that was new. And Niklas might be far bigger than she, but he was also far softer. Iris tugged on a lock of Milla's hair, and Milla's crimson snake peeked out. "Let me play with your hair," Iris said. "It will calm me."

Milla sat on the floor, her back to Iris, and Iris sat behind her, running gentle fingers through Milla's hair, softly tugging on the ends. Despite herself, Milla's eyes drooped closed and she allowed herself to be soothed for a moment, as if she and Iris were back home, and not in this cell. If it weren't for the chill and the smell, and the snakes rising from her head, preening for Iris, she might have believed it.

"Tell me a story," Milla said.

"Oh . . . a story. All right. Let me think."

Iris continued to comb Milla's hair with her fingers, and Milla's snakes rested their heads on her shoulders as if they wanted to listen as well.

"There was a young man," Iris began. "A beautiful young man whom everyone loved. He was as sweet and gentle of disposition as he was handsome of face. Oh, and he was also a prince, which meant he was rich, and of course all the girls in the village wished to marry him. But the prince was sad. There was only one girl the prince could love, and she was dead. She was his childhood sweetheart and they had loved each other long before either of them thought anything of beauty, or gold, or marrying well. For this reason, the prince knew that she was the only one who would ever truly love him for himself. The prince carried on despairing and making everyone around him miserable as well, until finally the prince's father told him to go out for a walk and not to come back until he was in a better mood."

"No one likes a moody prince," Milla said.

"Indeed. So the prince walked and the sky was blue, and still he despaired. He said aloud, if only I could see my beloved one more time, maybe I could be happy again. And just as he said that, who should appear but a small, wizened woman who looked very much like the witch in all the stories that the prince had ever been told. And the witch said to him, I can take you to the smoothest, glassiest pond where you can see the face of your beloved in the water. You can even talk to her. But you mustn't try to get her back or you'll die, too. Will you promise not to try? The prince was so overjoyed that he agreed. When they arrived at the pond, the prince saw that the pond was so glassy that when he leaned over it, he saw his own face as if looking into a mirror. But then he wasn't looking at his own face anymore. He was looking at his beloved's face, just as he remembered her, so fair and full of love. His beloved said to him, my dearest, how I've missed you. And he said the same back to her. He told her how lonely he'd been for her and how he didn't think he'd ever be happy again. But, he said, perhaps now that he'd been able to see her one last time, maybe he could find a way. His beloved wept, and her tears bubbled the surface of the pond. My darling, he said to her, why do you weep so? And she said, because I have never stopped loving you, but you have stopped loving me, and now you are going off to love another. So the prince promised her that he would never love another, not as long as he lived. His beloved stopped crying and once again her beautiful face shone up at him smooth and unperturbed. And then she said, now come to me, my darling."

Milla tensed, and Iris laughed a little. Then Milla laughed a little, too. "Poor, silly prince," she said.

Iris continued. "This gave the prince pause, because of course the witch had told him that he mustn't try to get his beloved back, or else he'd die, too. And he told this to his beloved, and she said, but, my darling! You're not getting *me* back, I'm getting *you* back. Because you'll be coming to me and living with me forever and we'll never be parted again. So you see, she said, you'll still be keeping your promise to the witch. And this caused the prince to pause just a bit again, because *had* he told his beloved that he'd made a promise to the witch? He wasn't sure that he had. But in any case, if his beloved told him it would be all right, then he believed her. And so he dived in. As soon as the prince broke the surface of the water, he realized his mistake. His beloved wasn't there, and he wondered if she ever had been. Instead of his beloved, there were water snakes. Hundreds and hundreds of water snakes. And even as they ate him, the prince wondered if he might ever see his beloved again."

As she neared the end of the story, Iris had stopped combing

Milla's hair with her fingers and she rested her hands on Milla's shoulders instead. Now Iris's fingers gripped Milla there, and Milla felt Iris shaking. She turned and found Iris weeping, tears streaking her face, her mouth in a pained, tight line.

Then Iris began to laugh.

Then she began to cry again.

Laugh.

Cry.

Laugh.

Cry.

Milla rose to her feet and backed away from Iris, not entirely meaning to. But perhaps meaning to, a bit.

Iris's face went still, and she wiped her nose with one long swipe of her forearm. "Do you know what the moral to the story is, Milla?"

"What is it, Iris?" Though she was afraid to ask.

"The people you love are dead and want to kill you." Iris sobbed with an anguish so deep that Milla would have gathered Iris in her arms if she hadn't been so frightened. Then Iris stood up abruptly, stopped crying, and looked around her in expectation. A smile hitched up the corners of her mouth—ghastly, all wrong. Up went the left, then the right, then the left. "She's here."

"Who's here?"

"The demon," Iris said.

"Hulda?" Milla said.

"Oh no. No, no, no, no. No, it's you. You're the demon, Milla. You've always been the demon." Iris's face was lit up from the inside, her eyes bright and wide. And that hitching, twitching smile.

Cold sweat slicked Milla's forehead, her skin burned and prickled. "No. I'm not. I'm me."

"Even with those snakes on your head? Come out to play . . . *snakes*."

Iris pulled back her lips and hissed between clamped teeth. Milla fell backward away from Iris and cowered in a corner of the cell. Iris went to the bars of the cell and shook and howled. "Come get her, Niklas! Come get your sister!"

The shaking of the bars grew deafening as every girl and woman shook the bars of their cells, too, and hissed and howled, "Come get her, Niklasssssss. Come get your sssssissssster! Come get her before the demon comes for her. She'ssss coming, Niklas. The demon is coming."

Milla had thought her worst fear was to be a demon herself. But now she knew what her worst fear was. It was this. Locked in this cell with Iris, the demon who was eating Iris up from the inside coming to make a meal of Milla, too. She'd lost all her bluster, all of her belief in herself and in Iris, and it was all she could do to keep from emptying her bladder in her dress.

"Are you afraid, Niklasssss?" Iris shouted. "Afraid of me? Is that why you never touch me, Niklasssssss? Because you're afraid? Is that why you put me in this cell, Niklasssssss? Because you're afraid? You've always been afraid, Niklassssssss. That's what Milla told me. I know eeeeeeverything about you, Niklasssssss. How you used to cry when she told you stories. Because you're such a big baaaaaaby, Niklasssssss."

Milla's terror turned to shame. Things that Milla had confided in Iris were coming out of her as poison. Nasty and cutting and bitter. Milla hadn't intended to hurt Niklas by telling his secrets, had she? Milla had only been lonely, had only wanted a friend— someone to love her. To *see* her. But now Iris was using Milla's words to hurt Niklas, and Milla knew it was her fault. All her fault. She had betrayed Niklas, and Iris had betrayed her.

"Stop it! Stop it, Iris!" Milla jumped up from her crouch and tried to drag Iris away from the door. "Don't say those things!" Iris shrugged Milla off, her back to Milla. Milla grabbed back on, pulling at Iris's dress, her arm. "Please, Iris. Please. Come back to me. I know you're in there."

Iris stilled for a moment. Milla allowed herself to hope. Then Iris turned around to her, and Milla's shame and hope dissolved and fear and abandonment rushed into their place.

The face that looked back at Milla wasn't Iris. Her eyes were the same amber, her skin the same wheat-brown. But something else moved under the surface of her skin, altered its shape. And the voice that passed between her lips wasn't Iris's at all. It belonged to someone else. Someone older and filled with a hate that had been festering for years upon years.

The face that was Iris and not-Iris was so close that Milla could see the bones bulging and reforming themselves as if something had climbed into Iris and was wearing her body as its own. This thing—Iris and not-Iris—smiled at Milla. "Iris is mine now."

18

MILLA HEARD NIKLAS'S BOOTS POUNDING ON THE
stone floor as he ran down the corridor.

When he came to the door Iris backed away from it.

"Let her out, Niklas," Iris said.

"No, Niklas," Milla said. "I'll stay in here. Don't open the door."

Niklas's face was tight with worry, his eyes blinking fast.
"Milla, are you all right?"

"I am," Milla said. "I'm fine. But if you open that door, Iris is
planning to lock you in here and release all the other girls."

"Why would you tell him that?" For a moment Iris looked like
Milla's dear friend whose feelings had been hurt. Her face was
her own face, not the demon's. Then the moment passed, and
Iris's face turned hard and strange and horrible again. Iris walked
toward Milla and pinned her against the wall of the cell, one
hand around Milla's throat, leaning in so close to Milla that their

foreheads touched. Iris squeezed, and Milla's snakes rose from her head and snapped at Iris's face, but didn't break skin. Milla tried to push Iris away, leaning into Iris with all her strength, but Iris was like stone. Immoveable.

Iris was calm in a way that was more dreadful than her laughing and crying had been. "I'll kill her, Niklas." Her voice was a chorus, Iris mixed with not-Iris.

Milla heard the clank of metal and then the crack of wood hitting stone and the door crashing against the wall as Niklas opened it. And the moment he did, Iris released Milla, and she turned on Niklas and shoved him so hard that his head knocked against the stone wall behind him and he sank to the floor.

"Niklas!" Milla screamed, and she ran to him as Iris dashed through the door.

The girls and women raised such a din of hissing and clanging metal that it was as if the noise were inside Milla's head and chest. She held Niklas by each shoulder. His eyes were closed and his skin was more gray than cream. "Niklas, please. Please be all right, Niklas." She felt tears in the corners of her eyes and panic rise in her belly. She could hear Iris opening the doors of the cells one by one, and the slaps of the girls' bare feet as they ran down the passageway, a quick and excited pitter patter. Niklas's eyes fluttered and then he opened them. "Niklas!" Milla let out a moan of relief.

"Milla," he said, and touched his hand gingerly to the back of his head. It came away with a slick of shiny red on the fingertips.

The clanging had stopped and now Milla could hear the girls' whoops and shouts and hisses as they taunted the boys.

"We're coming to get you, Petter." They shouted down to him. "We're coming to get all of you. Time for your dousing!"

Milla struggled to calm herself and think through how best to keep Niklas safe. If Iris—her Iris—could threaten to kill Milla, if she could do this to Niklas, then what might the rest of them do to him? To them he was just another boy, like the others who'd tortured them. She hoped for those other boys' sakes that they'd run off. Then again, she was hard pressed to feel sorry for them. "Can you get up? We need to leave, Niklas." Milla rose and held him by the hands to help him stand. He wavered on his feet at first, but then steadied himself. "Can you walk?"

He nodded, and she picked up one of his arms and brought it around her shoulder. She looked outside the cell and saw the corridor was empty, then she led Niklas out and toward the ladder. She looked down at the girls and women in burlap running below, hair streaming around them, laughing and hollering like children playing a game. One stopped and peered up at her. Faded red eyebrows, faded red eyelashes and hair. Leah. She smiled wide and sharp. Then she ran off.

"All right, Niklas," Milla said. "Can you climb down?"

Niklas nodded at her, but looked troubled. "I saw something. But I couldn't have seen it."

"What?" she asked, even though she knew already what Niklas meant. Her snakes had hidden themselves away again, under her hair. But Niklas had seen them rise up when Iris's hands were around her throat, had seen them try to fight off Iris.

"There were . . . snakes. Coming from . . . there." He pointed to her hair, like a small child pointing at something he didn't know the word for. "I saw them. But I couldn't have."

Milla couldn't lie to him now. She didn't have the will. She loosened her hair with her fingers, encouraging her snakes to show themselves. They rose up to greet her brother.

Niklas stared openmouthed. Then he took a step backward, just as she had done with Iris. Milla didn't think she had more heart left to break, but as it turned out, she did.

"I'm still me. I'm Milla." Her snakes hid themselves away again. "Please. Come with me."

As she climbed down the ladder, she looked up at him all the while, begging him with her eyes to follow.

When Milla reached the bottom, Niklas paused one moment longer, leaving her to wonder if he'd stay where he was rather than go with her, a girl with snakes on her head. But then he started down, and Milla scanned the passageway for signs of danger. The girls had all run out, it seemed, and there were no signs of the boys, either. Perhaps they'd had the sense to get away. Milla hoped it was that.

She stepped away from the ladder to make room for Niklas. At the bottom, he turned toward her and then he took one of her hands in his. "Let's go home," he said.

Milla knew they had no time to waste, but she threw her arms around him nonetheless. They held onto each other one moment longer than either of them needed to, and then they both turned toward the doors that led to the outer ring of the fort. Milla could hear the screams and laughter of the girls. She hoped they were so consumed by their escape—by the joy of breathing in clean night air after so long crouched in dank, airless stone—that they wouldn't notice or care that Milla and Niklas were making their own escape. She took Niklas's hand as they emerged into the moonlight.

To their left, most of the girls and women were gathered, hissing and laughing and undulating like one creature with many heads—Iris's coiling, rust-red hair a bright spot among them. After traveling all this way to save Iris, Milla felt sick with defeat and self-disgust. Was she really going to leave here without Iris? Milla's eyes lingered on Iris, willing her to look back, to show her the eyes of a friend and not a demon.

"Come, Milla," Niklas said.

Milla looked back at him. "Iris," she said.

"She's a demon girl now," he said.

Demon girl. Is that what the boys called them? Did that not make her still a girl? Or did the girl part of her no longer matter? Once again she looked at Iris, willing her friend to look back, to show Milla some part of herself that was still Iris. As if in response, Iris threw her arms up in the air and hissed. Then all the demon girls did the same, their arms rising up together, then weaving and interlacing.

Niklas grabbed Milla's hand and pulled.

The arched passage to the outside of the fort was directly in front of Milla and Niklas, and they both looked at it, measuring the distance between them and it. She and Niklas began to walk toward it slowly, purposefully, silently agreeing that a frantic sprint would only draw the girls' attention. Milla wanted to believe that the girls wouldn't hurt her—that they sensed in her someone as afflicted as they were, someone who would never wish to hurt them. But then she thought of Iris's hand tightening around her throat, of the blood darkening Niklas's hair, and of the howling and the frenzy, and she knew she couldn't be sure of what any of them might do. They weren't girls with thought and reason of their own anymore; they were all Hulda. Single-minded and furious.

Milla and Niklas walked. Each step caused her heart to tighten painfully, anticipating the moment that the girls would turn on them.

The hissing was terrible, but it was a different kind of eerie when the hissing stopped. As one body, the girls fell silent and stared at Milla and Niklas as they walked past.

Halfway between the door to The Place and the arch in the outer wall, Niklas halted. Milla looked at him, confused. Was he faint? Was he unwell?

Niklas looked to his right, and in an instant Milla knew what he was looking at. The bell.

She shook her head, horrified that he'd even think of it. "No, Niklas."

"Milla, I have to ring the bell. Then Ragna will know the girls are out. She'll warn the village."

"Warn them of what? Those girls won't go back to the village. That's the last place they'll go. Those are the people who sent them *here*. Besides, the boys have all run off. Surely they'll have warned Ragna."

Niklas gave her a skeptical look. "Milla, they *hate* her."

Milla was painfully aware of the stares of the girls, the passage of time, everything slipping away. She could feel them behind her, their interest ever more aroused. "Niklas. *Please*. Do not ring that bell." She looked at the horses in the paddock. "When we ride by Ragna's cottage we can warn her." She would say anything to get Niklas out of there, to get out of there herself, and she reasoned that the girls would still have plenty of time to scatter. Ragna couldn't go after all of them by herself, and by the time she'd gotten to the village, the girls would be safe somewhere else. Iris among them.

Niklas nodded and they walked to the horses. Then Milla saw them: five more girls, crouched on the far side of the paddock. Milla's lungs tightened and she grabbed Niklas's arm. The girls blinked at Milla. Once. Twice. Milla saw in their eyes and how they clung together that they were as frightened as she and Niklas were. Milla moved toward them, her hand cupped in front of her as if she were approaching a wary, possibly dangerous animal. "Come with us," she said to them. "We'll take you home. You're safe." Were they, though? How could she promise them that? They were so thin, like girls made of sticks. Like Asta, bound and mutely suffering in Ragna's cottage. Milla wondered how these girls could have the strength to move, but when they saw that Milla and Niklas meant to help them leave, they scrambled to their feet. Milla and Niklas handed the girls the reins to three of the horses and together they led the horses through the outer arch of the fort, the demon girls behind them still silent and watching.

The moon washed the meadow in shades of blue and darker blue. The strongest of the girls mounted one of the horses; the other four mounted horses two by two, their burlap dresses hitched up around their legs showing their livid bruises and scraped knees. The girls were all knobs and angles, but they looked fiercer now, the night air expanding their lungs and ruffling the ends of their matted hair. Milla and Niklas each mounted the two remaining horses. They would go to Ragna's, but not to warn her, as Niklas wished to do. Milla knew it was evil of her—and she could taste the nastiness of her loathing on her tongue—but she didn't care whether Ragna survived this night. The girls could have the midwife and do what they wanted with her. There was only one reason to visit Ragna tonight, and that was to save Asta.

19

LIGHT FLICKERED IN THE WINDOWS OF RAGNA'S COTTAGE, though Milla could tell by the angle of the moon that it was now well past midnight. Then the light shifted and Milla saw Ragna's tall, strong outline.

Milla and Niklas dismounted, but the girls stayed on their horses. "Asta is in there," Milla said to them. "Will you help us get her out?" She looked at the girls' shadowed faces, at the way memories of this place passed across each one, the pain still fresh.

As the girls all dismounted, Niklas whispered to Milla, "They're so small and worn out, Milla. I don't think they'll be much help."

"We're stronger than we look," one of the girls said. Her voice came out hoarse, unused. She was Milla's height but half her width. Still the girl shoved between Niklas and Milla, sending each of them stumbling to one side, and she slapped barefoot up to Ragna's door. "Open up, you witch! And give us Asta!"

A girl's voice called from inside the cottage. "Ellinor! Is that you?"

"It's me, Asta!" Ellinor looked over her shoulder at Milla and Niklas. "I'm getting Asta out of there if I have to burn this cottage down, and Ragna with it."

"There won't be any need for that," Milla said, walking toward the window where Ragna stood, staring back. "Will there, Ragna? Open up. We want Asta and then you can stay or leave as you please."

Milla saw Ragna's eyes widen, circled with white. Ragna retreated backward from the window, and then Milla saw why. Two of the girls were dragging something between them toward the window. An axe. Niklas started to run toward them, but Milla put herself in his way.

The girls lifted and swung, and Ragna's front window shattered inward.

"Milla, this is wrong," Niklas said.

"Ragna had her chance to open the door. They just want Asta. They won't hurt her if they don't have to."

Niklas tried to move past Milla, but she put herself in his way again. While Ellinor and the other four girls cleared the window of glass and climbed into the cottage, Milla grabbed Niklas by the shoulders. *"Go."*

"Home? Without you? No!"

"You don't belong here, Niklas." This hurt him. She could see it in his eyes.

"Milla! You don't know what you're saying." It struck Milla how strange that phrase was, and how often she heard it, or some variation. *You don't know what you're saying, Milla. You don't know what you're doing, Milla. You don't know what you're thinking, or feeling, or wanting, Milla.* Anyway, when people said that to her they didn't really mean that she didn't *know*. Of course she knew. They meant she was wrong. But she wasn't wrong.

Milla placed a hand on either side of her brother's face, which was hopeful even in this moment, and so different from her own.

She felt full of knowing. The knowing rose to her throat; she tasted it in her mouth. It tasted of grass and dirt and the undersides of damp rocks. This knowing had been growing inside her ever since her mother pinched the first snake from her head.

"Look at me, Niklas." She took her hands from his face and ran them through her hair, encouraging her snakes up and up. "What do you think Mamma would say when she saw me? What do you think Pappa would *do*?"

Niklas's open face collapsed. "No, Milla. No. Please. I can't leave you. I won't."

She wrapped her arms around him, pressing her cheek to his chest, feeling his heartbeat in her ear. She listened for two beats, three. She memorized the sound. Then she looked up at him, and she had to blink to see him clearly. "If I can ever come home again, I will."

Niklas's face changed, and he wasn't looking at her any longer, he was looking past her, over her. His mouth slid open.

Then she heard it: the sound of breath forced between many sets of teeth. The demon girls.

She turned around and her own mouth gaped. The moon had set, and she felt the chill of predawn. But that wasn't what raised the hair on Milla's arms. The demon girls surged toward Ragna's cottage—they flowed, they *snaked*. They were still minutes away and yet their hissing sizzled through the air like meat hitting a hot pan. "Iris is with them," Milla said. "I can't leave now. I have to try to talk to her one more time. But you must leave, Niklas. They'll hurt you. They're so angry. I can feel it in my bones like . . . like it's a part of me, too." And she did feel it in her bones. Like a hum. She looked up at Niklas again, took his shirt in her fists and shoved him backward toward the road. "Go." Her snakes reared back and snapped, hissing in chorus.

Niklas looked at her—all of her, girl and snakes—and then behind her at the surging, roiling, hissing mass. "You'll come home Milla. Someday. I know you will."

She blinked at him. Once. Twice. *I see you. See me.*

Niklas mounted his horse and looked back at her. She held up a hand to match the one he held up. She hated herself for wanting to catch his hand in her own, for wanting to say, *You're right, Niklas, I don't know what I'm saying. Tell me what to do, Niklas. Tell me this doesn't have to be so hard, Niklas. Tell me how to go home.* But she didn't do that. Instead, she watched as he turned away from her and kicked his horse forward toward the village. Milla's snakes wrapped their cool bodies around her neck, rested their heads on her shoulders, and hissed softly, reassuringly. She hated herself again for half hoping Niklas might still turn around. But he didn't, and she told herself that she didn't really want him to.

20

THE FRONT DOOR TO RAGNA'S COTTAGE OPENED, AND Ellinor emerged with her arm around Asta's waist. The other girls trailed behind. Milla didn't have to tell them the demon girls were coming. They all turned toward the sound of their hissing. "We have to leave. Now. Or they'll make us stay with them," Asta said.

Milla said, "Why?"

"Because the demon will tell them to," Ellinor said. "It's not their fault. They can't help themselves."

Asta's legs wobbled under her, and Ellinor urged her forward toward the horse she'd ridden there. The girls all mounted their horses, two by two, but Milla hesitated, stood staring down the road. She could see Iris. She could call to her if she wanted. What if Milla could talk to Iris, she thought. What if there was still hope for her? For them? She remembered back when she'd first met Iris. Iris had said that the two of them could leave, could go . . . anywhere. Maybe she could get Iris to go somewhere, anywhere, with her now. Now that she was free.

"You go," Milla said to them.

Ellinor's eyebrows came together. "You think you'll be able to talk to her. But you can't. You'll see. For a moment she'll seem like your friend, but then the demon will snatch her back."

"I have to try," Milla said. Asta reached out, and Milla took her hand for just a moment, felt the bones under her skin, and the sinew holding them together. "Good-bye. I hope . . . I hope you find home again."

Asta looked over Milla's head and her face filled with loathing.

"There's no home for them." It was Ragna. She stood in her open doorway, her arms crossed over her chest.

"You're not in our heads anymore," Ellinor said. Then she smiled. "They're coming, Ragna. They're coming for you."

The other girls laughed. Repeated what Ellinor had said in singsong voices. *They're cooooming for you, Ragna.* Even after the girls were off, Milla heard their laughter carried back on the dawn breeze, chiming like bells.

Ragna took a step backward. Whatever certainty had remained in her after the girls shattered her window, it fell away from her now. Milla said to her, "You should have opened up when we asked. You still had time to get away. Now your only hope is that your shutters hold."

Ragna slammed her door, and by the time she'd closed and locked the last shutter, Milla and her mare were surrounded on all sides by the demon girls. She remembered the first one she saw in The Place, and how she realized that the girl who stood in front of her was no child; she was a woman whose life had been taken from her. But since the girls had left The Place, even the oldest among them looked like a girl again. They might have lines on their faces, and even touches of silver in their hair, but their eyes were bright and they crackled with energy, like fires that had just caught, their flames licking high and thirsty.

Iris, though, was calm, as if something in her had been quenched. She stepped out of the mass of girls that circled Milla, and Milla could see in her eyes that the only light in there belonged to Iris. Her face was its familiar heart shape. "Iris?" Milla said to her, turning her friend's name into a question.

Iris took her hand. "It's me," she said. "For now."

Milla looked around her at the other girls, not hissing now, but staring and quiet, as if waiting for a signal—or an order. She kept her voice low. "Leave here with me," she said. "We can climb on this horse and go."

"Go where?" Iris said. "You with your snakes growing from your head, and me with the voice inside mine. Where would we go that people wouldn't run us off or lock us up?"

"We don't need people," Milla said. "We can take care of ourselves."

Iris cocked her head. "Chickens don't grow on trees. And nothing grows on trees in the winter."

"What else can we do?" Milla said.

"Come with us." Iris squeezed her hand. "To the mother."

Spark. There it was. The light that wasn't Iris, and yet inside her. Getting brighter by the second.

"The mother? You mean your mother? My mother?"

"Not them," Iris said, her lips thinning. "They don't want us. They never did. No. *Our* mother," Iris said. "*The* mother. We're going to her. She loves us, and she's going to take care of us. But first"—Iris looked over her shoulder at Ragna's cottage—"the mother is going to take care of *her*."

The anger that Milla had felt humming in her bones now vibrated so powerfully that her teeth chattered. It was all around her—under her as well. She felt it from her feet to the tips of her hair. A spot of heat bloomed in her belly so suddenly that Milla looked down, but there was nothing there, and the heat expanded through her torso like a live coal in a pot. Milla scanned the landscape around her to find a source of the humming, but there were only the demon girls, quiet, still, and waiting, and Ragna's cottage, shut up tight, and the clear dawn sky, all pink except for a few soot-black clouds.

Something about those clouds held Milla's attention. Her snakes stretched high, straining even higher, as if trying to get a closer look. The clouds were moving, spreading, changing shape faster than any clouds Milla had ever seen. It was as if the clouds were gathering together overhead—pulled to this spot from north, south, east, and west. Then it seemed to Milla that the humming was even louder and the quality of the sound was different, more jagged. It was no longer a humming; it was a buzzing.

Milla's eyes widened and she sucked in air and she realized those were no clouds at all. They were swarms upon swarms of wasps, pulling together, forming a funnel pointed directly at Ragna's chimney.

The girls were no longer silent; they were giddy. They giggled and clapped. They danced. Milla thought she might be sick. She grabbed Iris by the wrist. "What's happening?"

"It's the mother," she said. "She sent them to punish Ragna. Now she'll never hurt us again." Iris smiled.

The demon girls had lost interest in Milla, they were so over-joyed at the sight of the vicious cloud of wasps filling the air overhead, pouring now into Ragna's chimney.

Milla heard screaming inside, and she clapped her hands over her ears. The girls circled the house as if about to sing and play a child's game. They held hands and looked up expectantly. The sky was turning more golden than pink and the light shone down on their faces and Milla might almost have thought them beau-tiful if it weren't for what she imagined was happening inside Ragna's cottage—just the midwife and all those angry wasps.

Iris had left her side and joined the other girls, her joy as thorough as theirs. Milla put her hand on the mare that still stood patiently beside her. She didn't paw or stomp the ground. Her ears were up and alert and she looked back at Milla. Milla's father had trained her not to view animals as anything but what they were. Creatures to be worked, or eaten. Or worked and then eaten. They weren't people. They didn't have thoughts. But if Milla were looking for something or someone to tell her what to do, she saw it in her own mirror reflection in the mare's wet eyes. Milla looked like a lonely, terrified child who didn't belong here. She pulled herself into the saddle, and then she buried her head in her hands and wept. She didn't belong here, but she had no idea where else to go.

Milla felt the earth move beneath her, but it wasn't the earth, it was the mare, walking. Milla gathered the reins in her hands but she didn't attempt to direct her, because the mare had ideas of her own. She wasn't taking them back to the village; she was headed in the other direction, toward The Place. Milla had no desire to go back there, but nor did she want to go back to that sad, suspicious village. Milla's snakes circled her neck. All that mattered to Milla at that moment was that the mare had made a decision and Milla didn't have to. She was taking them away from the midwife's cottage, the demon girls, and the swarming wasps. If there was anything else that Milla might hope for—in this moment or the next or the one after that—she hadn't the strength to imagine it.

PART
3

PART

3

21

MILLA HAD EXPECTED THE MARE TO TURN TOWARD The Place once they came to the open meadow that led there. That would make sense—for her to return to the last place she'd been fed. But instead the mare kept walking. Milla let the reins go slack and the mare continue to lead the way.

The sun was high overhead and the day was hot when the road passed through another lushly green meadow and the horse veered off. At first Milla thought the mare planned to gorge on clover, but she continued on. Through the meadow they went until they came to a path wide enough for the horse, and with only the occasional branch hanging so low that Milla needed to duck. It seem to be an old cow path, grown over but still passable. The mare took her time, careful of her footing, and Milla fell into a thoughtless trance. Then the path widened into another hard-packed road.

"Well, aren't you smart," she said to the horse. Milla felt a pang for Niklas at that moment. He would have liked this horse. Iris would have, as well.

Except for stops at streams, where both the horse and Milla took long drinks, the horse walked on until afternoon became evening became night. Milla's eyelids were so very heavy, and her empty-hearted exhaustion, combined with the gentle rolling gait of the horse, lulled her dangerously close to sleep. More than once she jerked herself awake having nearly fallen off the horse.

The night air grew chill again, and for the first time since the horse had led them away from Ragna's cottage, Milla allowed herself to feel frightened for herself. Perhaps the horse had no more sense than she did, and they were simply wandering. Perhaps they'd both starve. Milla had no idea if another village lay down the road. She was hungry, and she was cold, and she was scared. And then she cried. Her snakes caressed her cheeks, licked her salt tears, and she felt comforted by them. Once she stopped crying, her panic was replaced with a hollowed out feeling, a desolation. A sense of aloneness so profound that she couldn't imagine it ever ending.

When she thought she couldn't possibly go any farther, whether this mare continued on or not, Milla noticed that the forest on either side of the road was thinning to scrub. Then scrub became meadow, which became pasture and then farmland. Farmland meant a farm. A farm meant a house, and a barn, and people. Milla sat up straighter in the saddle. If there was a farmhouse nearby, it was hidden in the dark—too late for a lamp to be burning. Milla struggled to make out a darker mass among the trees. Then the horse turned off onto a smaller road and Milla smelled the familiar scents of home—a place where people lived.

People who made fires, and baked bread, and chopped wood. People who milked cows and spread hay in barns. Then a barn and paddock rose to her left, and beyond it Milla made out a cottage, a bit larger than Jakob and Gitta's. The horse didn't take them to the cottage. Instead she stopped suddenly at the gate to the paddock, and Milla got the distinct sense that the mare felt they'd reached the end of the road.

Milla slid off the horse and unlatched the paddock gate. The mare followed her through the paddock and then into the barn, which softly vibrated with the rhythmic night noises of heavy, deep-breathing animals. The mare made straight for the manger, and while she ate, Milla sat down on the straw-strewn floor. She might have been sitting in manure for all she knew, and she couldn't begin to care. The night spun around her and her ears closed to sound, and then there was nothing.

"Pappa! Fulla is back! And there's a girl with her!" The voice was young, high-pitched, and excited. Then it was gone.

Milla sat up and looked around her. The mare stared at her, still in her saddle and bridle. Not knowing what else to do, Milla stood and took the mare's reins in her hand. The barn door was open, early morning light catching dust so it sparkled in the air. In walked a girl who looked to be about nine. Her hair was a mass of black curls that sprang from her head like living things, and she had bright, lamp-lit amber eyes. Milla thought instantly of Iris. Not because she looked like her, but because there was the same restlessness sparking inside her.

The girl held the hand of a man whose hair was a shorter, neater mass of black curls. He didn't spark the way his daughter did. "What's this now?" he said.

"I'm sorry," Milla said. "It was late, and I was tired. I thought it would be all right if I slept here."

At first she thought she read suspicion in his eyes, but then she realized it was simply puzzlement. "Why were you out in the middle of the night all alone? Where's your home?"

"I don't have one." Her first answer was her most honest. "I lived with my grandmother. But she died." Milla didn't know where the words were coming from, but she let them flow and decided to see where they led her. "So I left the village and decided to find somewhere I might work. You wouldn't need help around here, would you? I can cook and clean. Tend a garden and feed chickens. I work hard, and I'm never sick." Words, words, and more words, and she wasn't even sure what she was angling for. Did she really want to stay here and work on this family's farm? How would that be any different from the life she'd always led? But hunger and the craving for a bed were powerful things, and she thought she might tolerate more of the same for a while—till she got her bearings and formed a plan for what to do next.

The man cocked his head at her. "You're hungry, I expect. Liss, take her in to your mother." He nodded to the mare. "Fulla, you found your way home." He removed her bridle, stroking and patting her, then he unsaddled her.

Liss smiled at Milla so wide that her oval face went round. She grabbed Milla's hand. "Come. It's time for breakfast. Mamma will take care of you."

The girl's words caused Milla to bristle and lean away from her. Milla didn't want a Mamma to take care of her.

Liss's smile shrank. "What's wrong?"

Milla struggled to control herself, to make her face placid and pleasant. "Nothing," she said, closing the space between them again. "It's just that I've never been away from home before."

"Oh," Liss said, her face serious and thoughtful. Then she brightened again. "But you'll like it here. You'll see." Her tone turned confiding. "And just so you know, Mamma needs help with my brother. Babies are terrible. Anyone who tells you otherwise is lying."

When they reached the log cottage, the front door was open to the morning breeze. The cottage's grass roof was brilliant green and sparkled with damp. Everything here was healthy and bright and untouched by the insects that marched in lines under the doors of the village and turned the surrounding fields and forest to dust. Maybe Milla had truly left it all behind. Maybe the worst was over now that the girls had been freed and the midwife was surely dead. Milla wanted to believe that, but then her snakes squirmed.

Milla's hope was a delicate creature, and it bruised at the lightest touch.

22

MILLA SAT AT KATRIN AND OTTO'S WOODEN TABLE breakfasting on bread with butter and jam, and slices of cheese and cold chicken. She tried not to look as wild as she felt. The moment Katrin had set the food before Milla, it was all she could do not to tear it apart and stuff it in her mouth by the handful.

Katrin's face had made an O of surprise when she first saw Milla at her door, but then she smiled and welcomed Milla to her table as if it were a typical sort of thing to have a girl awaken in your barn. First though, Katrin led Milla to the well in back and handed her a washcloth and a bar of soap. Milla saw Katrin's eyes travel to Milla's hands. Her nails were black with dirt. Milla flushed with embarrassment, and Katrin smiled wordlessly and touched her arm before leaving her alone.

Milla scrubbed her hands, face, and neck with soap and crisply cold well water, and the cloth came away brown. Her filth was something she hadn't thought about in days—not since she left home for The Place. It was disconcerting to be doing this routine thing in a place that looked like home, but wasn't home. Milla wondered if she should drop the cloth right there, fetch Fulla, and keep going. Then she thought that Fulla would be very unlikely to want to go with her. Nor could Milla blame her. The mare had done enough.

In any case, Milla knew that she wasn't going anywhere. At least not right now. She was starving. And so tired it was an effort to breathe. For the moment she needed food and shelter. That was all she could think about. All that made sense.

So she sat at the breakfast table like a good girl, and after she'd eaten enough that she could concentrate on something other than her hunger, she began to examine her surroundings. Liss was a chatty one. A little sly, but well-behaved. She made faces at her baby brother, Kai, who was just old enough to walk and babble nonsense. He sat in a high chair scooping up fistfuls of oatmeal despite Katrin's attempt to guide the food to his mouth with a spoon. This made Liss laugh. Katrin was gentle. Motherly. She smiled.

Milla took this in: Katrin smiled at Liss. A mother smiled at her daughter. She didn't look at her with fear.

Then Milla scanned the rest of the room. There were no streams of salt across the window frames or doorways or hearth. Katrin and Otto lived like people who didn't expect to lose their daughter to a demon. Who might not even know what a demon was.

Otto chucked Kai under his chin and the baby cackled and sprayed oatmeal. This caused Liss to laugh harder. Katrin wiped drool and milk from Kai's chin and handed her husband the spoon. "Here, you take it. And just so you know, the idea is to get the oatmeal *inside* the baby."

Otto took a big spoonful of the oatmeal, started for Kai's mouth, but then reversed the spoon and began to steer it toward his own. The baby's mouth and eyes opened with anticipation and Otto held the spoon just outside his mouth, held it, held it, and waggled his eyebrows at the baby. The baby screamed with laughter and reached for the spoon, and then Otto ate the oatmeal himself. Then he handed Kai the spoon and said, "All right. Now you."

Kai took the spoon in his hand and Otto looked at Katrin triumphantly. "See," he said.

Kai slapped the spoon down on the surface of the oatmeal, sloshing and spraying it over the sides of the bowl. Slap, slap, slap.

Katrin raised an eyebrow. "Yes," she said. "I see. Very smart."

"Kai, you rascal!" Otto scooped him up.

Liss looked at Milla. "I told you. Babies are terrible."

Milla smiled despite herself.

Katrin stood and wiped Kai's face and untied his bib. "You," she said to him, and kissed him on his round, sticky cheek. Then she kissed Otto's cheek as well. "Liss, take your brother out to play while we talk to Milla."

"But, Mamma," Liss said. "I want to talk to Milla, too. You'll let her stay, won't you?"

"Liss." Katrin looked at her daughter, and Milla sensed unspoken communication. An understanding. Trust between them that there were reasons for what mother was asking daughter.

Liss sighed and took Kai from her father.

The baby looked at Milla. Then he made a sound that caused Milla's hair to rise all the way from the nape of her neck down to the small of her back.

"Sssssss. Sssssss. Ssssssssssss." He hissed. Right to *her*. To Milla. Had the rest of them heard it? She looked around the room frantically, searching for proof that they'd all heard it, seen it, and would also stare at her and point and call her: *Demon. Snake girl.*

Liss laughed, oblivious to Milla's panic. "That's what he calls me, Milla, isn't it funny? Say my name, silly. It's not Sssssss. It's *Liss*. Say it, silly. *Liss*."

"Ssssssss. Sssssss. Sssss."

"You sound like a snake," Liss said. "Mamma, I wanted a baby brother, not a snake. Send this one back and ask for another."

"Liss," Katrin said.

"All right. All right, I'm going. Come, Snake."

"Snnnnnn. Snnnnnn. Snnnn."

"Oh heavens, Liss. You'll have him thinking that's his name. Off with you." Otto waved her toward the door.

Liss held Kai in front of her and looked over her shoulder at Milla on her way out. She smiled. "Come find us in the meadow. Kai likes to try to catch butterflies. But don't worry. He never can."

Katrin placed a mug of tea in front of Milla. "How did you happen to come by our Fulla? We were sad to sell her, but she's one more than we need, and she's getting old for pulling."

Milla couldn't think what to say, so she stalled. "She's a wonderful horse. Took me right here. And now I know why."

"Sweet old thing," Katrin said.

"The woman from the far village who bought her from me," Otto said. "I can't remember her name, but she said she was a midwife. Any relation?"

"No," Milla said. She felt her snakes tighten around her head, insulted by the suggestion. "How long ago was that?" Milla wondered what he'd thought of the village. If it was as sad and threatening a place then, Otto would have to say so. It was too glaring a thing not to mention.

"Oh, let me think. Had to have been a year ago," Otto said. "No one in the near village wanted our Fulla. At least not at the price I wanted. So I took her to the spring market in the far village. I hadn't been to the far village in years. It always felt . . . unfriendly to me." He shrugged. "Liss insisted on going with me, and I should have said no. Oh how she cried when I sold our Fulla."

"She gets attached to the animals," Katrin said. "A dangerous thing for a farm girl to do. Our horses aren't pets. But she doesn't have much company here," Katrin said. "She gets lonely. She looked forward to Kai coming, but then once he was born she realized that he wouldn't be much of a playmate for a few years yet. In the meantime, he's just more work for her."

"Yes," Milla said. It occurred to her that Otto and Katrin were so chatty that she could let them talk and maybe she'd never have to say anything at all.

Katrin looked at her with gentle eyes, her thick dark eyebrows knit together in the center. "You must miss your grandmother. And you've really no other kin?"

"No," Milla said. "They're all dead."

"It happens," Otto said. "I lost all of mine when I wasn't much older than you. But at least I had the farm." He looked at Katrin and raised his eyebrows. She nodded.

"Milla," Katrin said. "We really could use your help. We haven't much to offer. But you'd have your own bed, and we'd treat you as one of our own. We'd ask no more of you than we'd ask of Liss if she were your age."

"Oh," Milla said. "Oh. Yes. I'd be most grateful." Milla felt a combination of relief and dread in her belly. Now that she had been offered what she'd hoped for, was this really the right thing? How could she possibly know? Not for the first time, she wished there were a voice in her head to say, *yes, yes, Milla, exactly right, stay there.* But when she needed it most, there was no voice. There was just her own trembling, uncertain heart. She told herself that for today, this was the right thing. When it was no longer the right thing . . . then she would figure out what was.

Katrin smiled at her. "Good," she said. "Good."

Otto smiled, too. "It's settled then. To the fields with me. I'll see you at dinner." He kissed Katrin on the forehead and ran a hand over her tightly braided hair.

Once he was gone, Katrin led Milla up to a pleasant room with a peaked ceiling, a window looking out over the garden, and two narrow beds. "You'll share with Liss." She ran her eyes over Milla's dress. "You're slimmer than I am, but taller. I have a few dresses and night shifts I'll give you."

"Oh," Milla said. "But not if you need them."

Katrin smiled at her, touched her arm. Milla was learning that this was Katrin's way of saying, *I understand, and we don't need to speak of it.*

"And an apron, too."

An apron. Milla remembered the apron she'd left in the mud next to the spring back home. She felt overcome with weariness and the recurring, heart-numbing fear that she was making a terrible mistake. If she wore Katrin's clean apron, would that change her back into the sort of girl who did such things? Would her snakes shrink away to nothing, or possibly worse: rise up in protest? Her green snake nipped her scalp.

"You must be tired," Katrin said. "Rest. I'll wake you for dinner."

"I can help with dinner," Milla said. "I should help."

Again Katrin smiled, touched her arm. Then Katrin left and quietly closed the door behind her. Milla looked at the bed that was now hers. She lay down on it, and her aching body sank into its softness. What a weak-willed creature she was. Defiant one moment, and crying with relief the next. She reached her hands into her hair and gave each of her snakes a long stroke. "You must keep us safe," she said. "These people are kind, but they won't understand you. So. Please. Keep us safe."

Milla closed her eyes, and her snakes settled in, hidden away in her thick, black hair. She slept.

23

IN THE SLENDER MONTH BETWEEN SUMMER AND WINTER, there was more work than could be done by Otto and Katrin even with Milla's help. Two men from the near village helped Otto with the harvest, while Milla helped Katrin preserve jar upon jar of vegetables to hold them through the frozen months. Milla fell into the familiar rhythm of working alongside another woman, doing the things that must be done to keep a family fed and clothed and clean.

Once that fall, Milla visited the near village with Otto and Liss. She hadn't wanted to. Katrin was being kind in encouraging her to go, thinking she might enjoy the distraction, but Milla would have preferred to be left alone. That was when she felt most comfortable, most herself—when there was no one around to please. With Katrin and Otto she felt the need to be sweet and grateful—and in truth she was grateful—but the effort involved in showing it all the time made her feel trapped. Milla thought of all those people in the village—so many people to try to be well-behaved for—and sweat dampened her hairline. She felt cramped and breathless.

This village hugged the road, same as the other village had, but the people were more curious than suspicious. And the market was full of ripe, healthy apples and unblemished potatoes and fat livestock. There was a din of haggling and sociable chatter and shrieks of children chasing each other among the stalls. Otto bought her and Liss sweet buns studded with raisins.

Milla was only half in her body all that day. She felt the curious eyes on her, the strange girl whom Otto and Katrin had found in their barn. She'd taken care with her appearance, wearing an old dress of Katrin's made of moss-green wool. She combed her hair. She no longer worried that her snakes might show themselves; they knew better. But still she felt like an oddity. All around her there were people, their mouths perpetually wagging with words. Milla couldn't imagine having that much to say to anyone anymore. The only people she'd ever been able to talk to that way—never running out of things to say—were Niklas and Iris. And just the thought of how much she missed them turned the doughy bread in her mouth to sand.

Liss chatted and pointed and laughed, filling the too-wide space between her and Milla. Milla had a feeling that Liss did this on purpose, that she knew how Milla struggled with words. Beneath Liss's easy smiles, there was a bright intelligence—the snap that Milla had sensed in her that first morning in the barn. Milla wondered if she'd buzzed the same way when she was that age. She remembered how easily stories had come to her as a child, but it was as if her desire to make words had died at The Place. Now she just wanted to be quiet. Still, despite herself,

Milla felt herself warming more to Liss every day. She told herself not to get too attached, not to let her guard down. She imagined what Liss's face would look like if she ever saw Milla's snakes. Best not to get too close, Milla told herself. Not even to Liss. Especially not. If Liss ever looked at her the way Gitta had, Milla didn't think she could bear it.

Then there was Katrin. Milla sensed Katrin's desire to be motherly with her, and it was a struggle for her to be kind in the face of it. Why must a mother's love come with so many rules? Katrin was warmer and easier with Milla than Gitta had ever been, but still Milla felt the judgment in her eyes. The gentle nudge toward the wash basin. The reminders that she probably meant to be subtle, but weren't subtle at all. And always the observations about Milla's appearance. Katrin seemed to think it a nice thing to tell Milla that she would look pretty with her hair braided. But what Milla heard was that Katrin didn't approve of Milla's hair the way it was. Too wild, too unkempt. Once Katrin had offered to show Milla how to braid her hair around her head the way Katrin wore hers. When Katrin lifted her hand as if to touch a lock of Milla's hair, Milla flinched away from her. Katrin's face showed hurt and surprise.

"I'm sorry," Milla said. That old, familiar word. She was using it again, so often. "I'm just tender-headed. I wouldn't even let my grandmother touch my hair." Then Milla smiled in a way that she hoped said, *let's forget all about this.* Katrin smiled back in a way that said, *you're a strange girl and I certainly won't try to touch your hair again.*

The air had smelled like snow all day, and the clouds were so low and heavy that they seemed to settle on the treetops. Just before supper, the first snowflakes fell. By supper's end, the world out-side the cottage was frosted white.

Once dishes were cleared and washed, Milla and Katrin worked on a pile of mending, while Otto rubbed grease into his boots. Liss rolled a wooden ball across the floor to Kai, who was supposed to roll the ball back to her. Instead of rolling it, though, he cackled louder each time and carried the ball back to Liss, dropping it at her feet. Then he waddled away from her as fast as he could.

Liss put her hands on her hips. "Kai, that's not the way you play the game."

"Apparently it's the way Kai plays the game," Otto said, and winked at Liss.

Liss walked over to Kai and picked him up like a sack. "All right, you. Time for a story." She sat at her mother's feet with Kai in her lap.

Katrin set down her mending and ran her fingers through Liss's springy curls. "Such beautiful hair you have, Liss." She lifted up a curl and wrapped it around her finger.

"She's getting to be as lovely as her Mamma," Otto said.

Milla kept her hands moving—needle through fabric, needle through fabric—and her eyes on her work.

"Once there was a little snake," Liss said. She tickled Kai.

"Sssssssss. Sssss. Sssssss," Kai said.

"And that little snake thought himself very smart and very beauti-ful. And also very big. He went around quite puffed up, as a matter of fact. He slithered by an anthill and said, you're all so very little. I could eat every single one of you with just a lick of my tongue. And the ants all said, oh please, don't eat us. We're too small to be much of a meal. A big snake like you wants something big to fill his belly. And the snake agreed that the ants weren't at all a worthy dinner for him, so he moved on. Then he saw a ladybug, and as he passed her, he swished her with his tail. The ladybug called after him, saying, well that wasn't very nice. The snake looked back at her and said, you shouldn't say such things to me because I could eat you. I'm a very big snake. And she said, oh, you wouldn't want to eat me. I taste very bad. And the snake thought he'd heard that about ladybugs, so once again he moved on. He passed all kinds of creatures after that. Flitting moths, busy grasshoppers, fierce dragonflies. And to every single one he bragged about how big he was and how he could make a quick meal of them. And every single one talked him out of it, flattering the snake that they were much too unimportant and not tasty enough for such a pretty, smart, big snake as he. And the snake agreed with every one of them. By the end of the day, the snake was feeling so pretty and so smart and so big, that he slithered right up to a . . ." Liss stopped her story and tickled Kai. "What do you think he slithered up to, Kai? Do you remember?"

"Goose! Goose! Goose!" Kai clapped his hands.

"That's right! The snake slithered right up to a goose, and he very proudly said, you look like a plump, tasty meal for a snake as big as me! Well, that goose was so amused by this that she laughed and laughed. And the snake was quite offended at first, but something about the way that goose laughed and stomped her quite large goose feet, made the snake think that perhaps he wasn't *quite* as big as he thought he was. So the snake said to the goose, yes, ha ha ha, that is very funny. And you are a very big, very handsome goose, and I think I'll be going. Well, the goose looked at him with two black, beady goose eyes and said, oh no, I don't think so, little snake. I think I shall be making a meal of *you.* Well, now our smart little snake needed to be a fast little snake, and he slithered right between the goose's legs and down a tiny little hole that only a very tiny little snake could fit into. And when our snake was safe down that hole, he heard the goose above him go snap snap snap with her beak." And here Liss stopped to snap at Kai with her thumbs and index fingers like little jaws. Kai squirmed and giggled. "And our smart little snake thought that really, after all, it was a very fine thing to be quite tiny."

Otto and Katrin clapped. "Liss, you tell a very good story," Otto said.

"Silly snake," Katrin said. "I'm glad he learned his lesson. Best not try to be something you're not."

Milla resisted the temptation to reach into her hair, to remind herself of what she was. Instead, she kept her eyes on her sewing. Needle through fabric. Needle through fabric.

That night, when Milla and Liss climbed into their beds, Milla thought of Iris and her stories. "That was a good story," Milla said.

"Kai likes it. Mamma and Pappa, too. My favorite is one about two children, a brother and a sister, who get lost in the woods. But Mamma doesn't like that one."

"Oh? What happens to them?"

The room was dark, but Milla could hear Liss turn on her side. "They meet a witch. But they don't know she's a witch. And she offers them wishes."

"Wishes never go well, do they?"

Liss laughed. "No."

"So what happens to these poor doomed children?"

"The witch eats them, of course."

"Of course," Milla said. "They must have broken the rules. That always happens with wishes."

"Not in my story," Liss said.

"No?"

"No. In my story, they get eaten *because* they follow the rules."

"That's a twist," Milla said.

"All those stories about doing what witches tell you are silly. Why would you do what a witch tells you?"

"Hm," Milla said.

Silence fell between them, and Milla knew Liss's night noises well enough now to recognize the moment she'd drifted off.

It was only at such times that Milla's snakes emerged from her mass of hair and rested their heads on her shoulders. She looked forward to these moments. She closed her eyes and stroked their cool, smooth skin and thought, *I wish I knew your names.* It didn't occur to her to name them herself. She felt certain they had names already.

Then she heard two soft, smooth, distinct voices in her head. And two distinct words to go with those voices. The first voice said, *Sverd.* The second voice said, *Selv.*

Milla lifted her hands so they hovered just above each snake. "Sverd?" The green snake over her left ear raised its head and tasted her hand. She stroked him and said, "Well, hello."

Then she said, "Selv?" The red snake over her right ear did the same. Milla smiled—genuinely, widely. *It is right to know their names*, she thought. *Only a stranger is nameless.*

24

At first it was pleasant to be cocooned in that warm place. For much of the winter, Milla spent the few daylight hours sitting in one of the cottage windows, looking out at drift upon drift of snow. There were days when the sky was so blue and the sun on the snow so bright that it hurt to look at it. But mostly the sky was a pale gray, and snow became more snow, became even more snow. Only the sharp, dark spikes of the evergreens broke the sea of whiteness.

Then the cocoon grew too tight, and Milla felt suffocated. She envied Otto strapping on snowshoes and venturing into the woods to lay his rabbit traps. He'd come back with his beard frosted with ice, his cheeks bitten red, and Milla could smell the forest on him as he blew into the door. She was so desperate for air, for rough bark, for the sky over her head, that she asked him if she could go with him to check the traps. Katrin laughed at this. "Oh, Milla," she said. "You don't want to do that. You'll freeze to death." Milla nearly said that she'd take her chances, but she stopped the words before they could spill out. She sensed it would mark her as even stranger in Katrin's eyes. Then once again she grew resentful of the effort not to appear odd.

Finally, when even Liss grew blank and prickly and tired of telling the same stories, the snow turned to mud. Rivers of mud. Which meant oceans of laundry, but Milla never thought she'd be so happy to be scrubbing until her hands bled. Soon, she thought. Soon she could walk in the woods. She felt the need for it in her bones. In her snakes' bones.

Once the first wildflowers poked through the last of the melt, Milla had begun to notice a change in Katrin. She seemed heavier, slower. Tired all the time. Then Milla noticed how Katrin filled out her dress, and the round of her belly under her apron, and she knew: Katrin was expecting another baby. Milla said nothing, knowing this was news that you waited to be told.

One morning as Milla and Katrin were cleaning up from breakfast and Liss played with Kai, Katrin sat down in a chair at the kitchen table and said, "Milla, I don't think I've ever been so tired."

Sunshine poured through the windows and the trees were budding. The air was fresh and just barely cool. It wasn't a day to be tired. Katrin was pale with exhaustion, and Milla nearly touched her arm, but didn't. "Why don't you nap?" Milla said.

"No, no," Katrin said. "It's time to knead the bread for dinner. And you must tend to the goats while I do that. And the chickens. There's too much to do." Katrin rested her forehead in her hand for just a moment. "There's always too much to do."

"Liss and I can do it all. Not as well as you, but it will get done. You rest."

Katrin nodded and pushed herself up to standing. "You're a good girl, Milla. Thank you."

Milla scattered a handful of flour on the table, and fetched the bowl of risen dough. She plopped the dough onto the floured wood, and just as she was about to begin kneading, she saw that the surface of the risen dough was alive with weevils, spread out over and through it like seeds. She opened Katrin's crock of flour. It was crawling with tiny, pale brown worms.

Milla told herself that these things happened. Weevils got into flour. It was nothing more than that.

"Liss," Milla said. "Why don't you take Kai outside? He'll like picking some flowers for your mamma. I'll find you when I've finished here."

"I can help you," Liss said.

Milla covered the dough with her hands, wishing away it and the dread that was growing in her belly. "No. Go out, Liss." Her tone was sharper than she meant it to be, and Liss looked hurt.

After Liss had dressed Kai in boots, she turned back to Milla at the door, and said, "You'll come when you've finished?" Her face looked so hopeful and eager to be loved and attended to. Milla felt a mixture of tenderness and revulsion.

Milla conjured a smile that she hoped carried an apology as well. "Yes, of course."

Liss smiled back, her face opening up like one of the crocuses dotting the meadow.

Milla tossed out the infested dough and flour. She fetched another crock of flour and the sourdough starter. She ran her fingers carefully through the flour and saw nothing amiss. There, that was proof, wasn't it? Weevils had gotten into one crock of flour. It was nothing more than that.

She set to mixing more dough. She'd tell Katrin that the first batch hadn't risen. Such things happened, and no sense worrying her. That was the right thing to do, Milla thought—for Katrin's sake, because she was so tired. She practiced what she would say, the lie forming on her lips.

Once Milla had set the dough to rise, she fed the chickens and milked the goats. She told herself to ignore the busy anthills in mounds around the paddock, the trails of ants that marched row upon row, single file into the barn. *They're just ants,* Milla told herself. *This is what ants do.* They hadn't been there yesterday because this was the first truly dry day.

It was nothing more than that.

She also ignored Sverd and Selv, who'd grown unusually restless. She tried not to notice their whispers in her ears. She told herself that it wasn't they who whispered warnings to her. It was just the ghost of a memory of something terrible that had happened but was over now. In the past.

It was nothing more than that.

As the sun was nearing its peak, she remembered that one of Katrin's hens had gone broody the day before. The hen had pecked Katrin's hand when she'd tried to come close, so Milla knew to stay well away from her, but she wanted to look in the coop to see if the chicks had hatched. It would be a little surprise she could offer Liss, something to make her smile.

Milla reached the yard to find the chickens in a frenzy of pecking. Milla swatted something black from her arm. Then from her other arm. Sverd and Selv hissed.

Termites. They swarmed up from the ground, an oozing mass, thick and black like smoke. Milla swatted more from her skirt, kicked them from her boots. The chickens pecked and pecked at them. Then, as quickly as the termites had risen, they subsided again and the yard was back to normal, the chickens calm and incurious. Among them, Milla realized with a start, was Katrin's brooding hen. The hen shouldn't be in the yard with eggs still to hatch. Perhaps she'd given up on them. That would be a shame.

But nothing more than that.

Sverd and Selv hissed at her again, impatient.

Milla walked toward the coop telling herself that she'd find a clutch of unhatched eggs.

Instead, she found six eggs that had hatched, and six chicks lolling inside, all dead. Their pale yellow feathers crawled with ants; their eyes were gone, and in their place were more ants. Milla backed away, her hand to her mouth, willing herself not to scream.

The curse had followed her. It was here.

When she dropped her hand from her mouth, she sucked in her breath so hard the intake burned her lungs. The skin on her palms was a pale, shimmery, grassy green. Cool and scaled. She dropped her hands to her sides.

Milla walked into the kitchen, her mind turning and turning but unable to settle on a thought or action.

Katrin was placing a round of cheese and a plate of cold meat on the table. "There you are," she said. "Where are Liss and Kai?"

Milla tried to create order on her face, to arrange her mouth and eyes in a way that wasn't horrifying to behold. Katrin had asked her a question, but the effort required for Milla to compose her face and string words together was too much. She opened her mouth and nothing came out.

"Milla? Is something wrong?" Katrin's eyebrows knit together. "Where are Liss and Kai?"

"The meadow. Playing."

Katrin cocked her head at Milla. "Would you go fetch them for dinner? It's a cold meal today. There isn't time for anything else. Take Fulla. She could use the exercise."

"Of course," Milla said. She heard how flat her words were. She willed herself to walk calmly to the door, to keep moving her feet, and perhaps soon thoughts would form out of the sick panic that was rising inside her.

25

MILLA RODE FULLA TOWARD THE MEADOW WHILE WORDS screamed in her head. Her panic had turned to anger, and that had turned to speech.

Why, she demanded to know. Why was it not enough that she'd been forced to leave her home, that she had these snakes growing from her head? That the girls had all been freed and the midwife was dead? Everyone who had betrayed Hulda had been forced to pay in some way. And their children—and their children's children—they had paid as well.

Why was it not over?

Sverd and Selv whispered to her. *You know why.*

The delicate hope that Milla had just barely sustained since she arrived on the farm was now gone, choked and breathless. The curse had followed her, because the demon wasn't finished with her yet. Milla had become a half-thing. Herself inside, and yet something else on the outside. Demon-like and yet not a demon. And everywhere she went, she would bring the curse with her, causing anyone she touched to suffer as well. She should have drowned herself in that spring. She remembered how Sverd had kept her from killing herself then. She'd thought of Sverd and Selv as her snakes. But maybe they were really Hulda's. Maybe she should rip them from her head.

Sverd and Selv rose up from her head, whipped themselves downward, each staring into one of her eyes. *We are not Hulda's snakes,* they hissed, *we are yours.*

She reached out to them, stroked their leafy-green and crimson heads, wanting to believe them, wanting their comfort. "I'm sorry," she said. "Help me. I don't know what to do." She touched the palms of her hands, as scaled and beautiful as Sverd and Selv. And yet so wrong. She was fascinated by herself and disgusted at the same time. She wanted to look and also to look away.

Liss and Kai weren't in the meadow. The sun was high overhead and though it was still early spring and Milla wore a winter wool dress, her riding trousers underneath, and a coat of Katrin's, she could feel a hint of warmth on her shoulders. Maybe, she thought, they'd sought shade.

The orchard.

It was a voice in her head, and not her own. It was a voice so familiar and dear to her that despite everything that had happened, she was too grateful to be frightened. Milla looked around her, scanning the meadow and the forest beyond. She caught a flash of movement and color—the color of rust. The color of autumn leaves. The color of Iris's hair.

The orchard, Milla.

Then the flash of color was gone, and the voice was, too, and

Milla turned Fulla toward the orchard. She squeezed her legs tighter around Fulla's belly. "Faster, Fulla. I know you'll do just as you please, no matter what I do. So please go faster."

She could hear the buzzing over her own heartbeat and breath and it grew louder and louder the closer she and Fulla came to the apple orchard. She saw the orchard ahead of her—neat rows of slim trees separated by lanes of green.

The apple trees should have been white with blossoms, but instead they were white with the webbing of moth nests. Where there should have been fresh, new petals there were chewing caterpillars. The buzzing was now loud in Milla's ears, but there were no flies, and the deeper Milla walked into the orchard, the more intense the buzzing grew and yet there was no sign of where the buzzing came from. Then, amidst the slender tree trunks she saw a large, round mass of black and livid yellow, like a storm cloud that had settled to the ground.

In the center of that mass were Liss and Kai.

Milla slipped off Fulla and ran toward the black and yellow cloud, and the angry, eager buzzing was all she could hear. The cloud was made of wasps—so many wasps. It was as if every wasp that had funneled into Ragna's cottage had come here, now, and all were circling their prey. Milla stood just outside the cloud—so close she could feel the air shift around their vibrating wings. The wasps ignored her, their focus trained on the children caught inside. Liss sat on the ground, Kai pulled into her lap. She wrapped her arms around her own head and his.

"Liss!" Milla screamed over the buzzing. Liss didn't move.

Milla screamed again, a sound that started out as a word—*why*—and became a howl. She screamed at nothing, at everything. At Hulda. At Iris. *Why.* Why her? Why these children? Why must hurt breed more hurt, pain breed more pain? What sense did any of it make? She alternated between anger so bitter she could taste it in her mouth and despair so deep she wanted only to sink to the ground and sob. But she couldn't, because those children were in that cloud of wasps, and it was her fault. And she would not let them suffer for what someone else had done.

Sverd and Selv rose from her head and hissed at the cloud, and Milla saw a parting open in front of her, big enough to put an arm through. "Again," she said. "And louder." Another hiss, and the opening grew larger, as big as a window.

"Liss!" Milla called to her.

Liss looked up. "Milla!" She started to stand, and Kai squirmed in her arms.

"Don't move," Milla said. "Keep holding Kai close to you." Milla saw Liss take in Sverd and Selv, but she didn't scream, only grew open-eyed with wonder.

Then Milla spread her arms wide as if they too were snakes, and from deep in her belly, a place where there was nothing but gut and anger, she hissed. She hissed her anger and her demand that those wasps disperse and leave those children. Her hiss was louder than the buzzing, it was louder than the wind. In response, the cloud widened and widened, and grew, and thinned, and Milla felt the wasps pass her, withdrawing and withdrawing.

Then they were gone. Liss remained crouched over Kai, their faces and eyes hidden, just as Milla had told her to do. Sverd and Selv tucked themselves away in Milla's hair, and Milla went to Liss and touched her shoulder. She felt Liss's trembling, and she said, "They're gone, Liss." She wanted to say *you're safe*, but that would have been wrong. Because they weren't.

Kai struggled out from beneath Liss, and Liss stood. Red-faced, his dark curls matted to his forehead, Kai looked at the air around them. "Fly! Fly?" Then he tugged on Liss's hand. "Sssss! Sssss! Fly!"

Milla said, "Wasps, Kai. Very mean wasps."

Liss looked at Milla with round eyes. "You saved us. I knew you would."

"How did you know I would save you, Liss?"

"She told me."

Milla felt as if she'd pitched forward off an unexpected step. "She?"

Liss tapped her forehead. "The voice in my head."

"What did the voice say to you, Liss?"

"It said, *she's here.*" Then Liss smiled, her eyes alight.

26

MILLA'S EYES SEARCHED THE SPACES BETWEEN THE trees. The voice Liss heard in her head could have been Iris's. But Milla feared it wasn't. The blight, the cloud of wasps, the brightness in Liss's eyes . . . there were too many signs that the *she* who was here—who was nudging her way into sweet Liss—was not Iris.

It was Hulda.

"Come, Kai." Milla scooped him up and handed him to Liss. "Go straight home. Tell your mamma and pappa about the wasps, and the moth nests. Tell them I told you I've seen it before—that it's what killed . . . my grandmother. Tell them I was afraid that I'd caused it, and so I needed to leave. Tell them all of that."

Liss nodded. "I will, but I don't want you to leave." Liss's bright eyes were wet and shiny.

"I have to, Liss."

"What if they don't believe me? What if they think it's a story?"

"They won't. You're so smart and so strong. And your mamma and pappa love you." Milla's voice broke. "They'll believe you."

Kai struggled to get down. "Sssssss! Home!"

"All right, Kai, all right," Liss said.

For the first time, Milla took it upon herself to embrace Liss. She held Liss close and kissed the top of her head, her curls tickling Milla's nose. Then she released Liss and walked away from her fast, looking back just once and seeing that Liss was doing the same.

Fulla stood her ground stolidly. Imperturbably. Milla thought the mare would follow Liss and Kai back home. Fulla had become more dog than horse to the family. But she didn't. She stood there staring at Milla, waiting. "Really, Fulla?" Milla said to her. "You know we're not going back." She reached for Fulla's reins and tugged gently, expecting the horse to finally resist and turn around. But instead Fulla followed Milla out of the orchard and into the mossy evergreen forest. What she would do with Fulla, Milla had no idea. But the mare had a mind of her own, and whenever she wished to turn around and go back home again, she no doubt would.

Anyway, the mare calmed her. Sverd and Selv rose up and craned forward, as if they knew the way. As Milla had done before with dear old Fulla, she allowed her snakes to lead them, trusting that they could taste Iris in the air the way Fulla had tasted home.

The forest was so thick that the sky was just a sliver of blue above her head, and Milla felt a chill even under all her wool. Evening would fall soon, and she hoped Iris would show herself before then. The forest floor was soft with evergreen needles and Milla was tempted to curl up between two tree roots and rest her head.

Rustle. Flash.

Milla looked quickly to her right and there she was—Iris.

She wore a man's shirt over pants that she'd rolled up over leather boots that looked at least a few sizes too large for her feet. Her eyes were syrupy amber, no brighter than they should be. She smiled at Milla. "I'm happy to see you," Iris said.

Milla wanted to run to Iris, to embrace her, but this was the same girl who'd threatened to kill her, who'd hurt Niklas. Who'd hissed and writhed under a full moon, who'd held hands with the other demon girls, who'd tried to get Milla to join them. "You seem like yourself, Iris. But you seemed like yourself before. And you weren't. Or you weren't for long. I want to trust you, but how can I?"

"Because you love me. And I love you back."

Milla sighed. She wished it were so simple. But everyone she loved most had hurt her. Or she had hurt them. She thought of the moral to the story Iris had told her in her cell at The Place. *The people you love are dead and want to kill you.*

But Iris wasn't dead. Niklas wasn't, either. And sweet Liss hadn't ever hurt anyone. Liss deserved so much better than whatever fate Hulda had in store for her. "If you really do love me, will you take me to Hulda and help me end this?"

Iris led Milla and Fulla deeper into the woods. She dug into her trousers' deep pockets and handed Milla an apple, and she ate one herself while Milla asked her question after question. They gave the cores to Fulla. Often they paused while Fulla stopped to chew on the leaves of low-hanging branches and shrubs.

"How do you live?"

"You'll see," Iris said.

"Where did you get those clothes?"

"Hanging on a line." Iris smiled. "I'm awfully quiet when I want to be."

"Do you see the other girls?"

Iris's face closed and she seemed to recede. "Sometimes. They frighten me. Only the girls who hear Hulda's voice are left. The ones who were never possessed in the first place have run off. I stay away as much as I can, but sometimes Hulda calls to me, and I have to go."

"Why do you have to?" Milla struggled to understand, but she couldn't. Why couldn't Iris resist? Shut out that voice, and refuse to do what the demon said?

"Because she's the mother. And when she's in here"—Iris tapped her forehead—"I have no choice."

"What does she want from you and the other girls?"

"She wants us to hate everyone. She wants to punish our families and the people who hurt her. But each time she curses another girl, it doesn't ease her pain. It only stokes it. Makes it hotter. Nastier. So then she sent the insects after the village's harvest. And then that wasn't enough, either. When we all escaped from The Place, and she sent the wasps for Ragna, even that wasn't enough."

"What does she want from me?"

Iris looked at Milla with pity in her eyes, and Milla's heart went cold. The chill seeped outward, wrapping tightly around her rib cage, squeezing the air from her lungs. She looked down at her hands, the scales pale green and spreading to her wrists. "I suppose I already know, don't I? She's turning me into a demon like her. But why?"

"She hates your mother and father most of all. She's punishing them for what they did to her by turning you into a monster, too."

"If only Hulda knew how little Mamma and Pappa care for me she wouldn't have bothered. It's Niklas they love."

"Don't tell Hulda that. You saw what she did to Ragna. You don't want Niklas catching her attention. She'd kill him if she knew, and make Jakob and Gitta watch. That's why I keep you and Niklas in a special place in my head. A place she can't touch. She can fill the rest of my head with her pain, but not that place. That place is mine."

"Why didn't you come find me before now? I've missed you so. I've felt so lost."

"I haven't been right, Milla. I knew you were out there, and I wanted to find you. But I remember what I did to you at The Place. I remember my hand around your throat. I remember wanting to squeeze, and squeeze harder, and I didn't know if it was all a trick or if I really would hurt you then. Or if I might hurt you if I saw you again."

Milla reached out and held Iris's hand. She tried to imagine the pain of a head so torn in two. She thought she could. A bit. Sverd licked her cheek. But no, her snakes weren't like that. They didn't make her do things. Or think things. "And now? Your head is more your own? And that's why you came to find me?"

"No," Iris said. "My head isn't more my own. It's mine right *now*. Right at this moment. But I never know when she's going to take it."

"Now that I'm with you, maybe we can keep her out of your head for good. Maybe we can find a way."

Iris stopped walking and her face rippled, the outlines of not-Iris reforming the planes of her face. "No . . ." Iris said. "No . . .

I . . . I don't think so." She shook her head, hard, as if she were trying to shake something out of it. Then she smacked the side of her head, harder still. "No. No. No." *Smack.*

Milla let go of Fulla's reins and took Iris's hands firmly in her own. Iris struggled against her, but Milla wouldn't let go. "Iris, no, please, dearest. You mustn't hurt yourself. And you're here now. With me. Yes?"

Iris nodded. Her muscles were hard under Milla's hands, as if flexed with the effort to hold herself together. Slowly her face reassembled itself again, and she was wholly Iris.

Milla gathered Fulla's reins and they continued walking, quiet for a time. Then Milla said, "Why do you suppose I can hear your voice in my head?"

"I don't know," Iris said.

"I think I do. I think it's because I want to, so badly."

"But I don't want to hear Hulda's voice in my head, and yet I do."

"True," Milla said. "But that's different. You didn't invite her. The moment I met you I found the person who'd never let me be lonely again. The person who really saw me, all my strange parts, and loved me all the same. I invited your voice into my head and you never left. And I never wanted you to leave."

"That's a nice story," Iris said.

"Shall I tell you another?"

"Yes, please."

"There was once a girl who loved to lie in the grass and let it tickle her skin. She liked the feel of dirt under her fingers. She didn't like aprons or making dinner or washing dishes. She didn't like being told to behave. She didn't like feeling that no matter what she did her mother and father looked at her with disappointed eyes. She could never be pretty enough or sweet enough or pleasantly talkative enough. And she grew angrier and angrier and angrier that all anyone wanted her to be was an idea they held in their head that had nothing to do with her. And this anger became bitterness, and this bitterness turned her into a monster. And the monster that she became wanted to hurt everyone that had hurt her. So she did. She punished everyone until there was no one left to punish. No one at all."

"That's a sad story," Iris said.

"It is."

"It has a bad ending."

"It does," Milla said. "But I think maybe it hasn't ended yet."

Iris stopped walking and looked at Milla. "I'm afraid it will go on and on, Milla. The punishing. The anger. The sadness. I feel Hulda's sadness inside me, her resentment. It's growing stronger, and it's making me weaker. What if I leave you again, and what if I never come back? What if I'm gone for good?"

Milla took Iris's hand. "Iris, I promise you this. I will never abandon you. I don't care what you say to me. What you do. What Hulda makes you say or do. You're my sister as much as Niklas is my brother. My mother couldn't be a sister to Hulda, but we are not them. We get to choose. And I choose never to leave you." Milla's voice was shaking now, tears rimming her eyes and spilling over. "And I will get Hulda's voice out of your head. Because no matter how deep her pain, no matter what she's suffered, she doesn't get to take my sister from me."

Iris threw her arms around Milla and Milla held on tight. Milla swore to herself: No demon above or below would ever separate them again.

PART
4

27

Iris led Milla and Fulla up the ledge of a low rock slope and into a cave. "This is where I come when I can shake Hulda's voice from my head."

There was a battered basket of clothing. Another of apples, and yet another of potatoes and onions. Everything stolen. Iris gave Fulla an apple and then knelt in front of a circle of stones where she built a fire. The ceiling of the cave was black with soot. Milla looked around, imagining how many long nights Iris had spent here, alone and dreading when Hulda's voice would return.

After a supper of berries and hazelnuts, Milla and Iris slept cocooned in blankets that smelled of damp and smoke. Whenever Milla woke in the night, which she did often, she sensed that Iris was just as awake beside her. Sverd and Selv squirmed, restless. Fulla slept so deeply she snored.

As soon as the sky was light, they set off to find Hulda. Iris was quiet as they walked. Milla sensed Iris's fear, her worry that the closer she was to Hulda, the greater her risk of losing herself. The same fear twisted in Milla's belly. If Iris became that other version of herself, Milla would have to face Hulda alone.

They hadn't gone far when Milla felt Iris tense beside her. "What is it?" Milla said.

"Listen." Iris eyed the woods around them.

Fulla nosed the back of Milla's head when she stopped walking. At first she heard only the horse's breathing and the shushing of air through evergreen needles. But then she realized it wasn't shushing, it was hissing. Soft and low. Then there was a flash of movement through the trees and a woman leapt in front of them wearing only an apron and a man's trousers. Her hair and eyebrows were faded russet-red.

Leah.

She hissed at them, her breath a sizzle between her teeth. Sverd and Selv rose from Milla's head and hissed back.

Iris extended an arm in front of Milla. "Let us pass, Leah. Milla is here to see Hulda."

"She's here," Leah hissed. Then she leapt and slithered through the trees—over rocks and roots, weaving out and in among the tree trunks.

The words *she's here* were picked up and passed along in urgent whispers, and then more demon girls emerged from the woods like gathering fog. First there were only tree trunks, and then there were girls and women, some still wearing the rough burlap dresses they'd worn in The Place. Others wore odd combinations of rags and clothing, knotted and sewn together. All had bright, lamplit eyes. All hissed.

She's here.

She'ssss here.

She'ssssssssssss here.

Iris led Milla on, her eyes fixed forward. "Talk to me, Milla. Remind me who I am."

Milla reached for Iris's hand, held it tight. "You're Iris. And you're my sister. And I'm yours."

"Yes," Iris said. "That's right. Tell me again. Keeping telling me."

And so Milla did. Over and over. *You're Iris. And you're my sister. And I'm yours.* Each time Milla said it, Iris squeezed her hand more tightly, as if she were holding onto herself, as much as to Milla.

They came to a clearing with an evergreen tree larger than any Milla had ever seen. Its grooved trunk was as wide as a cottage, with a jagged opening in the front. The tree grew so high, and its thickly needled branches spread so widely, that it seemed endless, like the tree from which all other trees had sprouted—like something that had existed forever, and would exist forever.

Iris let go of Milla's hand and slapped her hands to her ears. Milla was losing her. Iris was being shoved aside, and something else was taking her place.

"You're Iris," Milla said. "You're my sister, and I'm yours."

Iris dropped her hands from her ears and smiled at Milla. "She'sssss here," she hissed. Then she ran into the woods to join the other demon girls.

Milla threw Fulla's reins over her saddle, then pushed her fat rump. "Go on, girl. This is too much even for you." Fulla let herself be driven off, and Milla knew that if any animal could find her way home, that one would.

As the girls moved around her through the trees, Milla was reminded of the cloud of wasps that had surrounded Liss and

Kai. Now she was the one surrounded, only there was no one outside the cloud to save her. If it hadn't been for Iris's hair, Milla wouldn't have been able to pick her out of the swarm of girls.

Then, from the jagged opening in the tree, Hulda emerged.

She was a woman made of snakes—constructed of snakes. Instead of hair she grew countless snakes, all of them lifting from her head, eyes forward, tongues out and tasting. The snakes shimmered black, blood-red, brilliant green and yellow. All were longer and thicker around than either Sverd or Selv, who hissed and whipped the air above Milla's head madly, frantically. Hulda's shoulders and arms were woven with snakes where a woman's muscles should be. Even her fingers were slender snakes. She had snakes for veins, snakes for ribs. She wore no clothing, so Milla could see the snakes that corded her chest and belly, her thighs and legs. When Hulda moved toward Milla, the snakes that made up her legs spread out, slithering across the ground and carrying her forward, so her motion was more like undulating than walking.

Hulda's face, like the rest of her body, was both beautiful and terrible. Her skin was the texture of snakeskin and brilliantly colored. Her forehead was grassy green, her cheeks blushed red-orange, her lips were the blood-brown of clay. They drew back over fangs that were long, sharp, and starkly white.

Milla's voice came out high and childlike. Querulous. "I'm here to give you what you want," she said. She'd wanted to sound strong and sure, but looking at Hulda made that impossible. Ridiculous.

Hulda opened her mouth and every snake that made up her body seemed to hiss as one. "What isssssssss that? What isssss it you think I want?"

"An apology," Milla said.

Hulda's snake legs swirled and whipped the ground, lifting leaves and dirt in violent gusts. "An apology? An apology? An apology?" Hulda rolled forward and wrapped her snake arms around Milla. She pulled Milla so close that Milla could look into her lidless eyes, her slender, black pupils encircled by amber that quivered yellow and green. Where Hulda should have had eyebrows, her scales arched upward, blackberry-purple. "Can there be an apology for thisssss?"

Milla struggled to speak and not whimper. "I know you've suffered."

"You don't know *what* I've suffered." Hulda's breath hissed hot and acid between her fangs. "How my own sssister betrayed me. Gitta, my love. My best love. How I wished she could love me back. How instead she despised me. How they buried me in the snow. How they left me there. Alone. How I shook and froze and cried out for my snakes to comfort me. And how then . . . I became this."

Hulda unwrapped her arms from Milla and she stretched them out and the snakes that made up her body moved and shifted and her snake arms whipped the air around her. Her face became a grimace, and the hisses that made up her voice vibrated with sadness. "Will an apology make me a girl again? Will it give me back my life?"

The demon girls hissed in response, a chorus of abandonment so profound that Milla felt it vibrating in her chest.

Then the air around Milla grew thick with bitterness. The scent of it kissed the tip of Milla's tongue and it tasted like bile. She despaired. "Hulda, I would give you back your life if I could. Instead I'm begging you. Please let the curse end with me, and then you can let these girls go. Let them have their lives back."

"Why do you care about these others?" Hulda hissed. "No one cares for you. Silly Milla. Loveless child."

Milla felt Hulda's hatred rising from her, burning Milla from the outside in. Milla was overcome by Hulda's desire to hurt her, to make her suffer, and it made her stupid; it opened up her mind to Hulda's words and they latched onto her like thorns. Milla's years of isolation, of being called *silly Milla* by the one she loved the most, heated her up inside. She felt on fire, would have doused herself with water if she could.

"You can't know that," Milla said.

"But I *do*. I know because the one you call *friend* told me. She'ssss telling me right now. She'ssss telling me you're the least loved. That your brother shines like the sun. Your brother makes everyone happy. And you . . . you are the one they wish had never been born."

Milla looked around her for Iris. Then she spotted her, russet-haired and hissing. Traitor. She said she'd keep Niklas and Milla in a safe place in her head, but she hadn't. Sverd and Selv writhed and nipped at her cheeks, sensing her resentment toward Iris rising, her feelings of betrayal making her stupid and incautious. *Stop*, they hissed. *Stop*. But Milla couldn't stop.

"Iris lies," Milla said. "None of that is true."

Hulda rolled and writhed to Iris, who cowered away from her now, whimpering. Hulda wrapped five snake fingers around Iris's neck and dragged her to Milla. She held Iris in front of Milla, the tips of Hulda's snake fingers all snapping and hissing around Iris's throat. Her eyes were round and panicked, the eyes of Milla's friend. More than friend: sister. And Milla had betrayed her in a heartbeat. Milla had thought herself so much better than her mother, but now, overwhelmed by shame and self-loathing, she knew she wasn't.

"Milla?" Iris said.

Milla lurched toward Iris, but Hulda jerked her out of Milla's reach. She squeezed Iris's throat, and the air around Milla was coal-hot. Milla felt it scorching her cheeks. Then there was no air, only burning. Milla felt that she was suffocating, surely turning to ash.

"Iris can't lie to me, Milla. She *belongsssss* to me."

Iris screamed, slapped her hands to her ears. "Get out get out get out get out get out get out get out."

Then Milla screamed as well. "Stop it!"

Hulda smiled, triumphant, and she dropped Iris to the ground. Iris sobbed and covered her head with her hands.

Milla wanted to pick up Iris from the ground, to tell her that it wasn't her fault. Milla had thought she'd understood Iris's pain. But she hadn't had any idea what Hulda was really like. Milla had really only thought of her own pain, her own resentments. She was worse even than her mother; Milla felt no less a bitter, hateful monster than Hulda was.

"Please, Hulda," Milla said while pulling up one sleeve and showing how the pale green scales had spread to the crook of her elbow. "I'm a monster already. You've gotten your revenge. Let this stop with me."

Hulda wailed from her belly, not a hiss but a howl. "I CAN-NOT."

Iris scrambled away from Hulda on hands and knees.

"But you can," Milla said, trying to make her voice sound calm and certain. "You're the demon. It's your curse."

Hulda's snakes rose from her head and froze in midair, staring.

"You think *I'm* the demon?" Hulda said. "I'm not the demon. The snakes brought the demon to me, and then she turned me into"— she looked down at her own slithering body—"*this*. A monster."

Milla tried to imagine a demon that wasn't Hulda—a demon more powerful and horrible than Hulda was. She couldn't. Milla's thoughts couldn't stretch that far. "But you cursed us. So you can lift the curse. Can't you?"

"The demon has all the power," Hulda said. "It was her voice in my mouth when I cursed the village."

"Then you must ask her to lift it," Milla said. "Go to her and tell her that it's enough. Or take me to her, and I will ask her myself."

Hulda whipped her snake arms and legs so wildly that Milla stumbled backward to avoid being flattened. Hulda's words came out in panicked hisses.

cannot . . .

frightened . . .

the demon . . .

terror . . .

terror . . .

terror . . .

The girls responded to Hulda's wild panic with their own, hissing and writhing.

terror . . .

terror . . .

terror . . .

Hulda rolled back and back, a swirl of snake hair, snake legs, snake hands, snake fingers, and back and back and back until she disappeared into the jagged, dark opening in the tree.

The hissing of the girls grew louder, and Milla saw that they were closer than they had been before, and closer all the time. Iris still crouched on the ground, her arms over her head. "Iris," Milla said. "We must leave. *Now.*"

Milla reached for one of Iris's hands to pull her to her feet. Iris snatched her hand from Milla while twisting up and hissing. Iris was gone again. "Terror," she hissed at Milla. "Terror. Terror."

Milla backed away from Iris, looking around her for a path through the writhing, hissing, encroaching swarm of Hulda's girls.

Then she ran.

28

EACH TIME MILLA TURNED HER HEAD TO SEE HOW close the demon girls were, they were too close, and so she kept running. The girls slipped and slid through trees and over rocks and branches as if they were no barrier at all. All the while they hissed. *Terror.*

Then, in an instant, the girls' hissing stopped. Milla turned around to find them gone, the woods quiet except for the scurrying of small animals and the calls of birds. She was alone. Strangely alone. Hadn't the girls been there just a moment ago? It was as if they'd vanished. Milla should have been grateful, but instead she felt unnerved. She wondered if they might be hiding, waiting for her to stop running so they could surround her.

Sverd and Selv tasted the air, alert to danger. "Which way should we go?" she said to them. There was no answer. She felt herself crying and that made her angry. She said aloud to herself,

"Stop it, Milla. Since when has your crying gotten you anywhere?"
She didn't want to be the stupid, frightened girl in a story. "Think,
don't cry," she told herself.

Then she knew: She would go to Niklas and warn him that
Hulda was coming for him. That was the only thing to do. It was
already late afternoon, and if she was going to find her way back to
familiar ground today, then it must be before nightfall. The forest
canopy was so thick here that sunlight only trickled through in slender beams. At night, the way ahead would be black and treacherous.

Milla had been walking for some time, when she heard a sound
like humming. Not a buzzing. Not the humming of wasps. The
humming of a person. A woman, Milla thought.

Her snakes strained forward, as curious as she was. If this were
a story, Milla thought, the girl wandering in the woods and hearing a song would find a witch at the end of it. But this wasn't a
story. And if a woman lived here and might give Milla food and
shelter for the night, well . . . it was worth at least a peek.

Milla walked toward the humming, and as she drew closer
she smelled wood smoke and something more pungent. Then
Milla saw light shining into a clearing ahead and she dropped
to a crouch. She moved from tree to tree peeking around each
to see what she could glimpse until she was nearly to the edge of
the clearing. From there, Milla saw a ragged little cottage at its
center—and the humming woman. Or rather: witch.

Because that was what she must be—a witch out of stories.
Her long white hair was in a tangle atop her head, her eyebrows
were as woolly as caterpillars, and her face was as creviced as a
walnut shell. She appeared so impossibly old, and her pallor so
gray, that had Milla seen her lying down she'd have thought her
dead. Her lips were as cracked as her cheeks, and were puckered

as if stitched into a knot. And the tip of her long, warty nose nearly met the tip of her long, warty chin.

Milla sucked in a breath.

The witch was puttering around a kettle hung over a fire, out of which curled a stench so vicious that Milla's eyes teared and she feared she'd sneeze. Hanging from two posts held together by horizontal pieces of wood were three bloody animal carcasses, scraped of most of their flesh and drawing flies. The cottage looked more like a loosely constructed pile of sticks than a house, and was topped with a high-pitched, thickly-grassed roof. Chickens pecked about the yard, the one thing about the place that made it look at all homey.

Sverd and Selv hissed in Milla's ears, then tucked themselves into her hair as if to say, *if you don't have the sense to avoid a witch, then we certainly do.*

Milla backed away over soft evergreen needles that she hoped muffled both her scent and her sound. Gradually the witch's humming grew softer and the clearing was just a spot of brightness behind her, and Milla allowed herself to breathe.

She stopped for a moment, looking forward, left, and right. Which way? She was more lost than ever and the only thing she knew for certain was that she should leave the witch as far as possible behind her. Finally deciding that straight ahead was the likeliest route back, Milla took a step forward and her foot sank into soft needles. Then she felt herself sink farther and farther, and then she was crashing down and down and grasping at branches, but the branches weren't holding and before she'd reached bottom she knew: She'd fallen into a trap.

Her fall was mostly broken by damp, rotting leaves, but she landed stomach-first on a bowl-shaped rock that knocked the wind out of her. She rolled off it and lay there for some moments feeling stupid.

Sverd and Selv tasted her cheeks and nudged her neck and shoulders. "Yes," she said to them. "I'm all right." She sat up and her hand brushed the rock, which wasn't a rock at all, she realized. It was a skull—a man's, judging by the size of it. She held it up and centipedes oozed from its eye sockets. She tossed it away. She stood and felt along the sides of the pit, looking for something she could hold onto. She scraped and clawed until her hands bled, but any root she grabbed pulled free. She dug her hands into the earth, finger deep, and tried to climb up while kicking footholds, but she could manage to lift herself no more than three feet from the bottom before the soft earth gave way and she lost her grip. It was hopeless—the top of the pit was a good five feet above her head.

Milla sat down on the floor of the pit. In the dim she looked around for what else might be down here with her—some sign of what this pit was used for, and how recently. The poor fellow whose skull she'd fallen on had clearly been down here a long time. The bone was smooth and picked clean. She searched about with her hands, brushing away leaves and evergreen needles, and she found more bones, some person-sized. Some deer-sized. Some tinier. This accounting of the dead things that occupied the pit with her kept Milla's brain from spinning into panic. If some-one had gone to the trouble of making this pit, she thought, and then covering it over, then that someone would surely come back and check what they'd caught. Surely Milla wouldn't be left here to starve, she told herself. Her very next thought was that perhaps whoever dug this pit intended it for unsuspecting wanderers like her and was content to leave them here to die—however long that took. Hence the skull Milla had landed upon. Milla thought of the humming woman. Wasn't that just the kind of thing a witch would do?

Sverd and Selv hissed to her. *Sleep.*

"How can I sleep?" Milla said. "I'm in a trap. With bones."

It's the only thing to do, they hissed back at her.

Milla gathered wet leaves together, cushioning a spot under her head. She lay down, looking up at the darkening trees. Sverd and Selv rested their heads on her shoulders, and she stroked them.

There was a soft crackling of life and movement around her. Bats fluttered above, dipping into the pit and circling her head. She looked at them through the darkness with wide, curious eyes, and they looked back at her with their own. Her panic subsided, and she felt strangely at peace here with these crawling and flapping things. She would sleep tonight, she told herself, and tomorrow someone would come for her. And then she would get out of this pit and go find Niklas.

Just as her lids grew heavy, Milla felt something shift beneath her—deep beneath her. Something dark and endless. Something that was waiting . . . waiting to be called. Milla hadn't said her prayers in such a long time, but in the seconds before sleep the words came back to her.

Lord, protect us from demons.
Lord, protect us from demons.
Lord, protect us from demons.

29

MILLA SENSED LIGHT THROUGH HER EYELIDS, AND morning damp in her hair. She opened her eyes and looked up to see two faces staring down at her from opposite sides of the ditch. One was long and familiar: Fulla, the dear. If not for the other face that looked down at her, Milla might have smiled. But the other face—cackling and hideous—belonged to the humming witch.

"That is one nasty curse you've got on you, girly." The witch slapped a knee. "I haven't seen a curse that nasty in . . . well, since the last time I cursed someone myself!" She slapped her knee again.

Milla looked up at the old woman. She knew her first request should be that the witch throw her a rope, but she was more curious about something else. "How do you know I have a curse on me?"

"I can see it," she said.

"Do you mean my snakes?" Milla said. "Anyone can see them."

"No, I don't mean your snakes," the witch said, rolling her eyes as if affronted. "I mean I can see your curse all around you. And the demon who did *that*? Well, there's not much I'm afraid of, but she's a doozy."

Milla sat up. "You know what demon did this?"

"I'm a witch, girly."

"I need to find her. Can you help me?"

The witch scratched her nose. There was a lot of nose to scratch. "I can. Are you sure you want me to? She's not one you sit down and have a chat with. Not without coming away more cursed than you already are."

"It's really not possible to be more cursed than I am," Milla said.

"You're wrong there, girly," the witch said. Then she walked away.

Milla waited, staring at the wall of the pit and the beetles that scuttled in and out. Then, in front of her eyes dropped a thick rope.

The witch's name was Hel. She led Milla to her yard and offered her a stump to perch on, then handed her a cup of something hot. Milla looked at it suspiciously. Her snakes tasted the air over the cup. "Smell it, girly," Hel said. "It's tea."

Fulla had refused to step any closer to the witch's cottage than the forest's edge. She'd simply stopped in her tracks, immovable as a mountain. Her mouth full of leaves, the horse hadn't look frightened, merely decided. Milla had patted her neck and said, "Smart, Fulla. Very smart."

Milla sniffed the cup. It seemed like tea. Smelled like tea.

Still, she didn't take a sip. She'd heard too many stories to sip the first cup of tea a witch had handed her. This witch seemed kind, though, if that was the right word for her. Strange, yes. But she didn't look at Milla as if she were a monster, and for that Milla was grateful.

Milla peered around the witch's yard. The animal carcasses still hung there, flies feasting. The witch tracked the direction of Milla's gaze. "My maggot farm," she said. "There's not a potion I know that isn't made better by maggots."

Milla nodded as if this made perfect sense. The steam from the tea wafted up, warming her face. She was so tired and chilled from the night spent in the ditch. She took a tiny sip from the cup. It really was tea.

Hel narrowed her eyes at Milla. "What do you know about demons?"

"Nothing, really," Milla said. "I only know that my aunt, Hulda, used one to curse me and my family and her whole village. And I'm trying to break the curse. My aunt says she can't do it, that only the demon can do it."

"Hm," Hel said. "I think your aunt is lying to you."

"How do you know that?"

"Because I know her demon. She's my demon as well."

"Does she have a name?"

"She does," Hel said. "She's the oldest of the demons, the original. You don't want to tangle with her, girly. Like I said, she's a doozy. Always hungry. Never satisfied."

"But *you* tangled with her," Milla said.

Hel smiled, lips puckered over teeth that crossed over each other like fingers, and were so yellow they were brown. "Keep drinking your tea."

Milla looked down at her cup. What was that floating in it?

Hel laughed and slapped her knee. "Taking tea from a witch, girly! Taking tea from a witch!" And she slapped and laughed until she coughed and spit into the dirt.

What Hel spit up was black. It squirmed. Milla blinked her eyes at it and watched as the black mass crawled across the yard and into the grass. She felt the world shift just slightly around her. She wasn't dizzy, or disoriented. But what she saw around her was different. Clearer. Colors were brighter and sounds were louder, and when she looked at Hel she saw something forming over the witch's face, like a mask. Every one of Hel's already exaggerated features became more so. Her nose was so long it curled under her chin. Her eyebrows weren't just woolly *like* caterpillars, they *were* caterpillars. The largest wart on her nose puffed and curled mushroom-like, then began to vibrate. It burst open and out oozed a nestful of tiny gray spiders that spread across her face.

"Do you see it yet?" Hel asked her.

"What is happening to you?" Milla said.

"Oh, it's not what's happening to *me*. It's what's happening to *you*. I gave you something to help you see. We don't just cast our curses, girly. We become our curses."

"Who did you curse? And why?" Milla hoped that it was worth it, and that whoever was on the receiving end of something so ugly deserved it.

"Years and years ago, I was pretty," Hel said. "Would you believe that? I was a pretty farm wife with a husband and no children. And then one day my husband died. He left me with the farm, but no sons to protect me, and no daughters to take me in. But I didn't think I needed sons or daughters, because I had a farm, and that was enough. I was wrong, though. Of course I was." Hel laughed, but it didn't sound like a laugh. It sounded like an axe striking wood. "My husband's brother arrived on my doorstep and told me the farm was his. I could live there, but he'd run it. Well, I was always mouthy, and I wasn't interested in having that man run my farm, so I went to the village elders to complain. My husband's brother didn't like that, and so he and his wife spread it around the village that I was a witch and that I'd poisoned my husband. The elders never liked me anyway, and they had no trouble believing I'd done such an evil thing. So they let my dead husband's brother take my farm. And then I cursed all of them. I cursed their harvests and their children's harvests and their children's children's harvests."

"And did it work?" Milla asked.

Hel leaned forward and smiled, and a shiny green beetle raced across her front teeth. "They all starved."

Black smoke curled from Hel's nostrils, so sharp and biting that it caused Milla's own nose to curl and her eyes to sting. Then the smoke filled the air around Milla and the scent took on meaning, and Milla felt that she knew the name of Hel's demon, and of Hulda's. The smoke had told her the name. "Vengeance," Milla said. "Your demon is Vengeance."

Hel laughed, and her face reconfigured itself into something a shade less hideous than it had been. "And a fine demon she is. She's done right by me all these years."

"You don't . . . you don't feel . . . sorry . . . for all those people who starved?"

"Did they feel sorry for calling me a witch and taking what was mine? They got what they deserved. They wanted a witch, and I gave them one."

Milla wanted to believe that Hel was weakened by her curse.

But she didn't seem weak. Twisted, yes. But not weak. Milla wondered if the strength Hulda drew from Vengeance was as unbending as Hel's, then why would she ever let it go? "You said you saw my curse on me. Can you show me?"

"You've drunk the tea. You only need look at your reflection." Hel went to the well and drew a bucketful of water, then placed it in Milla's lap. "Look. You'll see."

Milla stared into the water and saw only her own unkempt hair and serious face staring back at her. Sverd and Selv rested their pretty green and red heads on her shoulders. Then something formed around Milla. A cloud. A dark cloud, shot with flashes of yellow. No, not a cloud at all. A swarm.

A swarm of wasps. Thick and hungry. Tireless. Buzzing. And they were all over Milla. In her hair, her eyes, her mouth. Laying their eggs in Sverd and Selv, their larvae growing plump and eating her snakes alive.

Milla cried out, dropping the bucket to the ground, sloshing water over her boots.

"*That* is Vengeance," Hel said. "I told you not to tangle with her."

30

"THERE MUST BE A SPELL FOR LIFTING CURSES," MILLA
said. "You must know one?"

"There isn't," Hel said. "Else it wouldn't be a curse. Curses are
powerful magic, and only the one who casts a curse can lift it."

Milla thought about the curse hanging over her like a swarm
of wasps—the same curse that also hung over Iris and now Liss.
Milla had made the mistake of thinking she could escape it, and
instead she'd brought it to Katrin and Otto's door.

"Maybe Hulda doesn't realize she can lift the curse," Milla said.

"Hm," Hel said. "Doubtful. More likely she's a liar."

Milla knew Hulda was a monster, and yet she struggled to
believe she was a liar. She'd seen the torture Hulda inflicted on
the girls and everyone who loved them. But the part of Milla that
felt rejected and abandoned by Gitta was drawn to the part of
Hulda that felt the same way. Milla remembered the anguish in

Hulda's voice when she said, *Will an apology make me a girl again? Will it give me back my life?* The demon Vengeance had kept Hulda alive but at the cost of almost everything else. At the cost of any impulse other than the desire to punish.

Milla shook her head. "I don't believe she's lying. I think she's in pain, and the pain is all she can think about or feel." Milla thought for a moment. "Hel, I'm not the only one Hulda has cursed. She's cursed many girls, including my friend. Hulda gets inside their heads. She makes them feel what she feels and do things they wouldn't do ordinarily. She's not inside my head, not yet. But I'm afraid she might do that to me."

"And you want to stop her from doing that? You want some sort of potion for that? Don't think there is one."

"No. Not a potion for that. I wonder, is there some kind of spell that could put me inside Hulda's head?"

Hel crossed her arms over her chest and squinted at Milla. "You want to possess Hulda? You'd need your own demon for that."

"No. Not possess her. Just get inside her for a bit. Find out what she wants and if there might be a way to appease her. To end all this."

Hel scratched her chin thoughtfully. "Could be there's something could get you in there. Could be. But I'm going to need more maggots. Lots more."

Milla's stomach rolled and rose up to her mouth.

Hel took the cup from Milla and hummed happily while she worked. Milla forced herself not to look, not wanting to know. She heard Hel mashing something in the cup. Her stomach lurched and cramped, readying itself to refuse.

"Oh yes," Hel said. "That's nice. That's very nice." She brought the cup to Milla. Too late, Milla realized she should have held her nose. The steam that rose from the cup was as brilliant yellow as dandelions but the scent reminded her of dead mouse. The liquid itself was a sickly brown. And chunky. Milla thought she'd lose what was in her stomach before she even brought the cup to her lips.

"Now you drink all of that down," Hel said.

Milla looked up, her eyes stinging, fat tears rolling down her face. "All of it? There's so much."

"All of it. Hold the cup with two hands. You don't want to drop it when . . . well. You might want to drop it, but don't."

Milla pressed her lips to the cup and at first all she could think of was the unexpected thickness of Hel's potion. Or not thickness, sliminess. It was like drinking a slug. She took one sip and recoiled, sticking her tongue out like Kai spitting oatmeal.

"Drink it while it's fresh! You're wasting time, you silly girl."

"I'm not silly," Milla said. "I'm *disgusted*."

"You're not even a girl. You're a baby. A silly baby who wants to boo hoo about how hard her life is so someone else will fix it."

Milla narrowed her eyes at Hel, then she put the cup to her mouth and drank down every slimy, chunky sip and morsel. When she'd drunk it all, she continued to look at Hel while she ran her finger around the inside of the cup and licked it.

Hel laughed and slapped her knee. "That's my girly. My little demon girly. Now close your eyes and think of Hulda, not a thing else. The potion can't do all the work—you have to help it along."

Milla did as she was told, but other thoughts kept flooding in. Iris's confusion. Niklas's disappointment. Gitta's revulsion. Milla's own shame. The shame was dark and hard to see through and it made everything else ugly and untrustworthy. Milla's shame made her angry. She felt it consuming her, like fire. And this was how she found her way back to Hulda. The anger was where they both lived. The anger had transformed Hulda into a monster and it was transforming Milla even now. The anger burned up the air between them. The space. Then there was no air or space between them; there was nothing between them at all, because they were one and the same. They were Hulda.

Hulda remembered a time when she could be alone and not lonely. She remembered how she'd lay in the meadow, the grasses swaying and stroking her nose. She remembered having skin and hair and all the sensations of girlness. She remembered the salty taste of sweat that dotted her upper lip on a warm day. The delicious tickle of gooseflesh that bloomed in the night breeze. The vibration of her own laughter in her ears. She remembered all of this.

And then she remembered how it was taken from her. How aloneness became loneliness. And how loneliness became pain and then pain became terror and then terror became hate.

And hate became monstrosity.

Hulda didn't know why these memories were coming back to her now. Oh, but yes she did. She knew why. It was the girl's fault. Milla. The girl she'd cursed to be like her. The girl who wanted to apologize to Hulda for things that weren't her fault.

She remembered the cold. So cold. She remembered the midwife burying her. She remembered the snow in her face. How it froze the blood in her veins. The breath in her chest.

Hulda wrapped her snake arms around herself, listened to all the life that buzzed and crackled and squirmed in her tree. She was safe here. They couldn't hurt her anymore. She could talk to her snakes. She could talk to her demon girls. They would never leave her.

They couldn't.

Hulda writhed. They *would* leave her if they could. But they couldn't. They couldn't because she wouldn't let them.

So alone.

But. But. But. Hulda gestured with her snake hands, making her argument to the air around her. Their mothers and fathers didn't love those girls. Not the way Hulda did. Their mothers and fathers didn't *deserve* them. Hulda did, because Hulda understood them. And Hulda loved their ugliness. Their anger. These girls were lucky. Hulda had saved them. Now none of them would ever have to see the disappointment in a mother's eyes. Or a sister's.

Hulda was the mother now, and the sister. She was the one they loved, and who loved them back. She would never betray them.

Hulda remembered the mother, still. But those were sad memories. She remembered wanting something from her, something she could never have. It was like being hungry always. There was never enough for Hulda, because the sister got it all.

The sister. Gitta.

Why these memories now, Hulda asked herself. Told herself: *You don't need these memories. They only hurt you. Call to your demon girls. Make them come and tell you stories.*

But she didn't want the demon girls. They only loved her because she forced them to. Hulda knew that. She was a monster; she wasn't stupid.

Hulda wanted the sister. It had always been the sister she wanted.

Gitta.

31

MILLA DROPPED THE CUP. "SHE'S SO . . . SO LONELY."
Milla shivered in her dress, though the day was warm.

Hel rolled her eyes. "Boo hoo."

"Haven't you any feeling at all? She's *sad*. And I don't think she has any idea how to lift the curse."

"Don't be a weak boo hoo baby," Hel said. Sverd and Selv hissed at her. She laughed.

"How can I call up Vengeance?" Milla said.

Hel cackled. "Calling her up is the easy part. But what are you thinking you'd say to her when you did? Girly, she's not called Vengeance because she lifts curses. She punishes. That's what she does. That's why she's a *demon*. I'm just an old witch, not even the meanest, and even I wouldn't lift a curse. You hurt someone, they hurt you back. You hurt a witch you get hurt back worse. You go against a *demon* and you wish you were dead.

That's the way the world works and it makes good sense to me."

Milla looked at Hel, at the nightmarish mask her curse had made of her face. That was the price of so much hurt and hatred, and it did not make any sense at all to Milla. "You said it's easy to find her. So tell me how."

"You know, girly, you should be more respectful. Don't forget I'm a witch. You've got one curse on you already. You don't want another."

Milla's cheeks grew hot, half with anger and half with embarrassment. Half wanting to strike Hel, and half wanting to apologize for being rude.

Hel drew her white eyebrows together and lowered them over her small black eyes. She pinched her lips together so tightly her mouth seemed to disappear, sucked into her face. Black smoke poured from her nostrils and the stench of Vengeance rose around her.

Still, Milla refused to quake or step back. Instead she took a step forward, and Sverd and Selv rose up and hissed at Hel.

Hel laughed. "Good, girly. Never be nice, that's my advice to you. I spent years trying to be nice, though it wasn't in my nature. Then my dead husband's brother showed up on my doorstep and stole my farm. After that I didn't wish I'd been better at being nice. I resented every bit of time I'd wasted trying to be nice at all. Girls who run from what frightens them don't get what they want. Now let's call us a demon. It's a blood sacrifice we'll be needing. Demons like blood sacrifices."

Milla felt needles of suspicion at the nape of her neck and Sverd and Selv wrapped themselves around her throat, hissing. "What kind of blood sacrifice?"

"Something you can kill yourself. Maybe one of your pretty snakes?"

Milla backed away from Hel, and the witch closed the distance.

"I bet they'd make a powerful potion," Hel said.

Milla took another step backward.

Hel stomped her foot. "Girly! You're not going to find a demon by being a well-behaved child who runs away from scary things and hides behind your mother's legs."

"I don't do that," Milla said, feeling spite rising inside her.

Hel sighed. "I've lost patience." She walked over to a placid chicken pecking at the maggots that fell to the ground beneath the reeking hides. She grasped it by the neck in one hand, and pulled a knife from the pocket of her trousers with the other. She raked the knife across the chicken's neck, spraying blood across the earth between her and Milla.

Black smoke curled and rose from the blood, grew thick and alive and fierce with intent.

Hel smiled. "Girly, meet Vengeance."

Smoke poured into Milla's mouth, her ears, her eyes—choking her, deafening her, blinding her. She fell to her knees, unable to breathe. Sverd and Selv trembled and vibrated and she cried out—she thought she could hear their cries, too. It felt as if they were being ripped from her head.

Then it was over, and she could breathe, and she gasped and felt for her snakes. They moved against her hands and she was so grateful she thought she might cry.

When she opened her eyes, her tears dried. Her mouth did, too. The hissed refrain of Hulda's girls came back to her. *Terror . . . terror . . . terror . . .*

Vengeance filled Hel's yard. Black antennae branched from her head like horns, and what at first seemed like two black plate-sized eyes on either side of her head were made up of countless smaller eyes, all reflecting Milla back at herself. The demon's flattened nose was bright yellow, and two jaggedly sharp black mandibles wrapped round her chin, resting under her wide, black, ridged mouth. Her broad upper body was shiny-black and armored, her waist slender and flexible, and her lower body was all stinger, black slashed with yellow. Two sets of translucent, finely veined wings stretched out on either side of her from her shoulders, and her arms and legs were bright yellow and viciously serrated.

"Who calls me, and why?" Vengeance said.

Milla didn't know what she'd expected Vengeance's voice to sound like, but it wasn't this. Her voice was full, round, and motherly. If Milla had closed her eyes, she might have been deceived by it, but she kept her eyes open to remind herself what Vengeance was. A demon. The original demon.

No fear, she thought to herself. *Girls who run from what frightens them don't get what they want.*

"I called you. I want you to lift a curse," Milla said.

Hel muttered under her breath, "*Want,* she says. Like she's giving orders. Spoiled boo hoo baby."

"I see your curse," Vengeance said, "and I'm admiring of it, but it's not my curse."

"Hulda told me it was. That your words were in her mouth when she cursed all of us."

Vengeance hummed and Milla felt the vibration in her feet. "I am her demon. I cannot do what she doesn't ask me to do. Her curse is her own."

"Is there a way . . . a way to *make* her lift the curse?" Milla said. "Could you do that?"

"Nooooo," Vengeance said. "But you could."

"How?"

"You have three choices. The first is to ask for her forgiveness. And then she must grant it."

"I tried that. No. She's too"—Milla hesitated for a moment, then said—"vengeful."

"Hmmm," Vengeance hummed, shifting her wings. "Her demon suits her well." Vengeance took two steps forward. Milla felt each of the demon's eyes examining her. "That was a terrible thing her own family did to her. I remember how she cried out to me in the cold and dark because no one else would come to her. What kind of a mother and father would do that to a child?" The demon sawed the air with her mandibles, and Milla was all too aware of their sharpness and the wide mouth behind them. Then Vengeance grazed Milla's cheeks with her antennae, holding her still, and Milla was no longer in Hel's yard.

Milla was buried in snow, bound and shivering. Snow filled her mouth, her nose, and when she tried to breathe she breathed in snow. The cold was in her heart and in her lungs. The cold was in her bones. She tried to cry out, but she couldn't, so the scream was all in her own head and it wasn't a scream for Niklas or Iris, it was a scream for vengeance. She was dying, she was alone, and her only wish was for something to take this hurt away.

Milla cried out, and Vengeance released her.

"Settle yourself, girly." Hel patted Milla's shoulder, and it was almost soothing. "Don't be a boo hoo baby." Almost.

"What is my second choice?" Milla said.

"Kill Hulda," Vengeance said.

"No," Milla said. "Never."

"Hmmmm. I thought you might say that. Your third choice

is the best, really. Simplest. Most . . . effective."

"What is it?" Milla said.

"Ask me to be your demon and let me kill her." Vengeance stood up on her serrated back legs and brought forward her long yellow and black abdomen. "Look at my children," she said, exposing her belly lined with translucent eggs, each containing a quivering larva. "There are so many. Vengeance is endless. I go on and on, and you may use me, all of me. My strength is the only strength you will ever need."

Milla felt Vengeance's strength and knew she was right. With Vengeance, she could destroy Hulda and save Niklas and Iris and Liss. With Vengeance she would never have to fear the revulsion she saw in Gitta's eyes—or anyone else's. She would never need to be pleasing again. She could live inside her anger and feast on it.

Milla might have said yes to that. But then she remembered lonely Hulda in her tree. That was where Vengeance would take her. And Milla wouldn't go.

"No," she said. "You're evil. And you're no choice at all."

"Oh, girly," Hel said. "You've done it now."

Vengeance spread and flapped her translucent wings and the wind that kicked up under them was furnace-hot. It knocked Milla back on her heels and singed her eyelashes. The air filled with buzzing, the sound familiar and horrible, the sound of swarming. The sky blackened as if the sun had gone out, a blanket thrown over them all, but the blanket was made of wasps. Milla thought she and Hel were surely dead, but the wasps closed around Vengeance, encircling her, lifting her from the ground and carrying her up and up.

Milla and Hel stood openmouthed, watching her go.

All was now silent in the surrounding forest. Not even a leaf shook. Hel's yard was strewn with feathers, the remains of her chickens. Sverd and Selv peeked from Milla's hair, while Milla struggled to think of something to say. "I'm . . . sorry . . . about your chickens."

Hel's long white caterpillar eyebrows were sizzled black at the ends. "Girly, I don't want your sorries. I'm no boo hoo baby. What did I tell you? Never be nice. We messed with a demon." She shrugged. "This is what we get."

32

F ULLA STOOD CHEWING AND WAITING, UNMOVED BY the appearance of a wasp-shaped demon. Milla rested her forehead on Fulla's and stayed there, wishing she could absorb some of the mare's calm. "All right, girl. Help me think this through. I can't kill Hulda. I wouldn't know how to, anyway." The very idea of it was ridiculous. Milla remembered her games with Niklas when they were little. Waving their imaginary swords through the air, hunting trolls. She had no sword and Hulda was no troll. "And I won't ask Vengeance to kill Hulda." That would be just as bad. No, it would be worse, because it would be cowardly. And then where would it end? With more vengeance. That's what the demon wanted. "So the only thing left is forgiveness. But I've already tried asking for that, and it made Hulda even angrier."

Milla wanted to scream, but instead she tried slowing her breath to match the mare's. How wondrous it would be to be an animal, Milla thought. How easy. Any kind of animal would be fine. No matter how short the life span. She'd live, sleep, and eat. Death would come quickly. As it was, Milla imagined her life if the curse continued to run its course. It rolled out in front of her, interminably. Her body fully covered in green scales, only snakes where she once had hair. She'd be a monster, forever alone. Punished for the sin of another.

Milla lifted her head from Fulla's, a thought blooming, tickling, making her ears itch. *The sin of another.*

It wasn't Milla's apology that Hulda wanted—needed. It was Gitta's.

It had always been Gitta.

Bless this horse's sense of direction, Milla thought to herself more than once. She said it aloud to Fulla more than twice.

It took the better part of a day for them to find their way back to Iris's cave, skirting as far around Hulda and the demon girls' territory as they could without losing their way. When they arrived, Iris was huddled in the dark, her face pressed to her knees.

Milla ran to Iris and crouched in front of her. Iris blinked as if to be sure that Milla was really there. "I came back to myself," Iris said. "I'm me. Your sister. You can see, can't you? I'm me."

Milla wrapped her arms around Iris. "Yes, dearest. I can see. You *are* my sister. And I'm yours."

Iris pulled away. She squeezed her eyes shut and buried her face. "I don't know why you still trust me. You shouldn't trust me."

"None of this is your fault. I trust *you.* I trust *my* Iris, *my* friend, *my* sister."

Iris let out a muffled sob.

"Come with me," Milla said. "I'm going home to get Mamma."

Iris lifted her head. "Gitta? Why?"

"I'd thought I needed to protect Niklas from Hulda, but now I know that it's not him she wants, or me. It's Mamma. Hulda loved Mamma more than anyone else, and Mamma betrayed her. And it's Mamma who has to make this right. So I'm going to ask Mamma to go to Hulda with me. Maybe if Mamma apologizes, Hulda will lift the curse."

"But you saw how Hulda is. She'll never lift the curse."

"I have to believe otherwise," Milla said. "I don't want to end up like Hulda. Even the thought is unbearable. And I must get her out of your head. And Liss's. And all the other girls. And . . . well. I want Hulda to have some peace."

"She doesn't give me any peace, Milla."

Milla sighed. "I know. But there's some part of her that isn't awful. I think there's a way to convince her to let us go." She picked up a coil of Iris's russet hair and held it in her hand. "At least I have to try. Will you come with me to talk to Mamma?"

"It's not safe. What if I lose myself? They'll tie me up and drag me away again."

"They wouldn't. I won't let them. Niklas won't let them."

"Neither of you could stop them before. And what if they drag you away, too? What if they see your snakes?"

"My snakes know how to hide."

Iris reached for Milla's hands and turned them over, showing her scales. "What about these?" Milla felt Iris's agitation growing, threatening to ignite. "Anyway, Gitta isn't safe with me," Iris said.

"What do you mean?"

"I hate her. We all do."

"But Mamma didn't do anything to you. Hulda did. And I

don't think Mamma really knew what she was doing to Hulda. She was frightened. And selfish. But how could she know what the midwife would do to Hulda? She couldn't possibly."

"I still hate her," Iris said.

Heat rose off Iris in waves. The cave felt airless. This was Vengeance, Milla knew. She could smell her, feel her. Sense her larva hatching in Iris, eating her from the inside out. "Well, I love you," Milla said, hoping to soothe the parts of Iris that didn't belong to Hulda or Vengeance.

Iris dropped her face to her knees again, and Milla stroked her hair, crinkly with hay and leaves.

"I'll come back for you, Iris."

Iris nodded into her knees but didn't speak.

It was midmorning a day and a half later when Milla arrived home—or the place she'd once called home. The farm looked faded, like a dress forgotten in the sun. The air buzzed with black flies that harassed Fulla and Milla both. Anthills leaned against fence posts, undisturbed, no one noticing or caring to sweep them away. The cottage itself seemed to sag in the center, as if exhausted with the effort of going on. All was quiet, and still, and sad, just like the village had been.

Milla led Fulla to the barn, unsaddled her, and gave her a big bucket of oats. The poor beast hadn't had a proper brushing in days. "I'll make it up to you," Milla said. Fulla was nose down in the bucket, unconcerned.

There was no sign of her father or Niklas when Milla walked back to the cottage. She didn't expect there would be—they'd be out in the fields, working, at this time of the day. But there was also no sound floating over from Stig and Trude's cottage. No scraping of chairs or stirring of pots or flapping of laundry. Milla walked inside and the kitchen was cold and empty, no bread rising or dinner preparations underway, even though her father and Niklas would be back in a few hours for their midday meal.

Milla found Gitta lying in bed, eyes open and staring, her blond hair loose about her shoulders. "Mamma? Mamma!" Panic rolled over Milla. Her mother looked ill. Or worse. Milla remembered the lie she'd told the midwife, that Gitta was dying. Had she made it so?

Gitta stirred, then raised her head from the pillow to look at Milla, her eyes struggling to focus.

"Milla?" She sat up.

"Mamma, what's wrong? Aren't you well?"

"I'm not dying, if that's what you think. I only wish I were." Gitta put her face in her hands. Milla felt a flash of disgust for her mother, like lightning. Gitta was so terribly selfish. Milla thought of what Hel would say about her. *Spoiled boo hoo baby.*

"Why do you wish you were dead, Mamma?"

Gitta's eyes trailed over Milla. "Look at you. You haven't had a bath in days, have you?"

Milla wanted to scream. A bath? Milla hadn't been home in months, and her mother could only remark on how dirty she was. "That's what you have to say to me, Mamma? That I need a bath?"

"Oh, Milla. Why must you be like that?"

Milla should have gone to her mother by now, embraced her. Isn't that what any other daughter would have done? She imagined what Liss would do if she hadn't seen Katrin in so long. She imagined what Katrin would do. Katrin would have held onto Liss and never wanted to let go. But Gitta went on lying there in bed, feeling sorry for herself. No wonder Hulda hated her.

"Do you want to know where I've been? Do you care? Or is it enough that you have Niklas home now?" Milla could see her mother's pain, how she suffered, but she didn't stop talking, remembering what Hel had said to her: *Never be nice.*

Gitta cringed, shrinking backward and inward.

And there, in her cringing and shrinking, was the face that Milla had grown up looking back at. The face that looked at Milla with fear. With dread instead of love. "Are you afraid of me?" Milla said. "Of these?" Sverd and Selv rose from her head, not hissing, only placid and staring. Milla's anger felt clean and right. It didn't belong to Vengeance or to Hulda, it was her own, and she could control it—and use it.

Gitta cried out and covered her face with her hands. "Don't make me look at you. Don't make me look at what I've done to my own child."

A space opened up in Milla at that moment. A space that allowed in a crack of pity, and of curiosity. She moved closer to Gitta. "What do you mean? What have you done to me?"

Gitta wept. "It's all my fault."

Milla remembered her mother's weeping when Niklas went to The Place with Iris. How was this any different? Gitta was more sad for herself than she was for Milla. "You mean you're disgusted by me."

Gitta dropped her hands to her lap and looked at Milla with anger. "You're so . . . *mean.* You always have been. Why are you so mean?"

"Mean? What have I ever done but what you've told me to?"

"Always begrudgingly, though. Always treating me like I'm simple-minded, such a bother to you. You and Niklas with your little jokes and secrets. Making me feel stupid. Niklas isn't the same with me now. I don't think he loves me anymore. He's so angry. And I can't make him understand that all I've done is to try to keep you safe."

"Safe? You mean from the curse you brought down on me? The curse that made me this way?" She turned her hands over and then rolled up one sleeve so that Gitta could see the scales, shimmering green.

Gitta reached out a tentative hand, and Milla didn't pull back, though she wanted to. Gitta stroked Milla's scales, and Milla trembled from her wrist to her shoulder. Her mother's hands were gentle, and Milla felt sudden relief that she could still feel the touch of fingers. She was overcome with longing to be a baby again, to start all over and be the kind of girl her mother could have loved. "Mamma," Milla said, "I'm a monster." And she sank to her knees and wept.

"Oh no, child. No, no, no." Milla felt her mother's arms around her, caught her mother's familiar scent of milky tea and parsley. Milla wanted to stay there, to put her head in Gitta's lap and pretend to be a girl again. A girl like she never was, with a mother like she never had.

Milla stood up, resisting all that temptation to soften. "But I am a monster. Or I will be. Even if you don't want me to be. And if you really want to help me, if you're truly sorry for what you've done, then you need to apologize."

Gitta reached up to grab Milla's hand. "But of course I'm sorry. I told you so."

"No, Mamma. I'm not the one you need to apologize to. It's Hulda. You must come with me to see her and tell her so."

Gitta scrambled backward on the floor and looked around as if for somewhere to hide. She shook her head wildly. "Oh no. No, no, no. I can't. I won't. You don't know what she's like. I didn't tell you that part, Milla. She's not like you. She really is a monster." Gitta wept and carried on so that it was all Milla could do not to roll her eyes.

"Don't be a boo hoo baby," Milla said.

Gitta looked at her strangely. "What?"

"A boo hoo baby, Mamma. That's what you're being. You lie up here crying because you haven't gotten your way. Hulda made messes for you, and then I made messes for you, and you can't wish your messes away. I'm here, Mamma. A big mess. And I'm taking you to your other big mess. And you will apologize, and you will make this right."

Gitta wiped her nose with the back of her hand and looked up at Milla with wet, pleading eyes. "Now?"

"Right now," Milla said. "Get dressed and I'll saddle the horses. We're leaving before Pappa and Niklas can try to convince us otherwise."

As she walked to the barn, Milla imagined Hel off to one side cackling, slapping her knee.

33

MILLA WAS SADDLING FULLA WHEN SHE HEARD HIS
voice. "Milla! You're back!" Niklas ran to her and embraced her.

She held onto him for just a moment and then pulled away,
fearing she'd break down if she didn't. "Not for long, though."

Niklas searched her face. "What do you mean? Why not?"

"Nothing has changed, Niklas. I'm still cursed and so is Iris."

"Milla, please don't go." Niklas looked so sad, so alone, and
for a moment Milla felt a shameful sort of pleasure. For so many
years she had been the one pining for him, pulling on his sleeve,
wishing he'd stay. "It's awful here without you. Every day I wake
up hoping you'll come home. Every night I go to sleep disappointed. Mamma clings to me so that I can't leave her alone for
long. Pappa pretends nothing's changed. He won't even speak
your name."

"He hardly ever spoke my name before, Niklas." Milla knew

it was unkind to be so cold in the face of his suffering, but she couldn't ease it right now. She had barely enough strength to cope with her own.

"Niklas," Mamma said, standing in the door to the barn.

Niklas looked Gitta up and down and confusion passed over his face. "You're wearing riding trousers." Then he turned to Milla and saw that she was saddling a second horse. "What's happening?"

"Mamma is going with me to Hulda, Niklas. She's going to apologize to her."

"What! No! Neither of you is going to Hulda. She'll kill both of you!"

Niklas was a full head taller than Gitta, and she reached up to place a gentling hand on his shoulder. "If she'd wanted to kill me she could have done so long before now. She wants me to suffer, not die."

"I'm going with you," Niklas said.

"*No,*" Gitta said. "There's no telling what Hulda would do to you, Niklas. And I can't bear to lose you again. That would truly kill me."

Milla bit her tongue and tasted blood. It wouldn't help to say what she was thinking—that, as ever, Niklas was everything to Gitta. That Milla could sink into the earth and it would mean less worry for her mother, not more.

"Milla, talk sense to her," Niklas said.

"I did talk sense to her, and that's why she's going with me. And she's right, Niklas. You should stay here. If you come along you'll only give Hulda something to use against us. She wants to hurt Mamma, and she'll know that the best way to do that is through you." She held his hand for a moment. "And I couldn't bear to lose you, either. You must let us go."

Gitta embraced him. "Stay safe, my sweet boy."

Niklas looked at Milla over his mother's head. "Come home to me. Both of you."

Milla nodded. She would make sure Mamma did, but could make no such promise for herself.

They rode for hours, until it was so dark Milla couldn't see more than a few feet in front of them. By then, she and Gitta were long past the village. They'd passed Ragna's empty cottage, falling in on itself, and then the wide, flower-dotted meadow that led to The Place.

"You know what that is, don't you," Milla said.

Gitta nodded, staring at the hulking fort off in the distance. "Niklas won't speak of it. Whenever I try to talk to him he tells me I don't want to know."

Milla cocked her head at Gitta. "*Do* you want to know?"

Gitta looked back at Milla. "No."

Mostly, the ride had been quiet. Gitta hadn't voiced a word of complaint since they'd left the farm. Gitta hadn't even delayed, though she'd had the chance. Milla thought her mother might make the excuse of stopping to speak to Hanna and Tomas, but she didn't. And she paid no attention to the stares of the villagers. Milla had grown so used to being an oddity that she'd forgotten what a strange thing it was to see a woman her mother's age in riding trousers, astride a horse. But Gitta seemed not to notice their gapes; she simply rode, her eyes forward.

After they'd eaten supper and rolled out blankets for sleeping, Milla said, "You don't seem afraid."

"I am."

"But you don't *seem* so," Milla said.

"I've had a lot of practice, not seeming afraid."

"Hm," Milla said. "I don't know if you were very good at it."

Gitta pulled a blanket around her and turned on her side to look at Milla. "What do you mean?"

"I mean, you've always seemed frightened. For the longest time I thought you were angry with me. There was this particular expression on your face when you looked at me, and it was so different from the way you looked at Niklas. I can't remember when it was that I first realized you were afraid. But once I did, it was all I could see."

"Well," Gitta said, "but did I seem terrified? Did I seem like I could barely get out of bed each morning because I lay awake every night wondering what might have happened in the night? Did I scream all the time, or look like I wanted to?"

"No."

"Then I'd say I was doing just fine at pretending. Because there wasn't a minute of any day since you were born that I didn't feel that I might die of dread."

Milla felt overcome by grief. The waste of all that time, neither of them having any idea how the other was tortured by the unsaid. "Why didn't you tell me? If you'd told me, then at least I'd have understood why you looked at me that way. I'd have understood why you couldn't love me."

Gitta shifted to her back and looked up into the branches overhead. "You're my daughter. Of course I love you."

"You can't even look at me when you say that."

"Oh, Milla. Why must you make everything so *hard*? Life is hard enough without your daughter making it more so."

"That's not the first time you've said that to me, you know."

"Well," Gitta said. "This must not be the first time you've needed to hear it then."

Milla closed her eyes, fighting back tears. Willing them not to come. "Goodnight, Mamma." She turned on her side, her back to Gitta. Sverd and Selv tried to soothe her, but Milla was ashamed to admit even to herself that it wasn't their comfort she craved.

When they arrived at the cave, Milla knew before they entered that Iris wouldn't be there. Even from the outside Milla sensed its blankness. Wherever Iris was, there was energy. Spark. But the cave was cold and empty. Gitta stood in one place, her eyes circling it. "This is where she's been living? That poor child."

"You said she was wicked, Mamma. You let them take her away."

Gitta turned on Milla. "You know, you resent me so much for how I've looked at you, and for what I did to Hulda. But you're looking at me right now like I'm a monster. Like I have no feeling. Like I should be the one with snakes growing from my head."

Milla sucked in air, stung.

Gitta's eyes widened. "I didn't mean you! That's not what I meant!" She buried her face in her hands. "Everything I say to you is wrong. You want something from me that I can't give you. But I've tried, Milla. I've tried."

"Mamma, listen to yourself. You act like everything's been *done* to you. I'm just me, Mamma. I've always been me. And all I've ever wanted is for you to love me. Even a bit."

"I told you I loved you."

"They're just words when you say them to me, Mamma."

Gitta reached for Milla, held her by the wrists. "I haven't

known a moment's peace since Hulda went . . . wrong. And everything I've done, I've done because I wanted to make things right. I was brought up to please. To please my mother and father, and then to please your father. Because that's what women do. That's how we live, how we survive. But Hulda couldn't be pleasing—she never could. I loved her when we were little, but when we got older I grew impatient with her. I wanted her not to be so . . . strange. And it made me angry that she was. I was afraid that Jakob wouldn't want to marry a girl with such a strange sister."

"Strange . . . like me?" Milla said.

Gitta's eyebrows knit together. She paused. "A bit, yes. And, Milla, just think. If you were like her, and you know how she turned out, then don't you think I was right to be frightened? And so every day I taught you how *not* to be like her. I taught you how to please. That's how I hoped to make your life easier."

"But you didn't," Milla said. "You made it harder."

"I know it, Milla. I know it. And I'm sorry for it."

Milla closed her eyes, felt her stony heart tremble and shake. She wanted to say something terrible to her mother. Wanted to make Gitta hurt, wanted her to feel the rejection that was as much a part of Milla as the snakes that grew from her head. But then she thought of Hulda and of what Milla asked her mother to do—to apologize to Hulda for all the pain. And if Milla held out any hope that Hulda could forgive Gitta, then Milla had to forgive her, too.

Milla looked into her mother's pale blue eyes, round and wet. "Thank you, Mamma." And as she said the words, she knew she meant them.

34

THEY SPENT THE NIGHT IN IRIS'S CAVE, HUDDLED CLOSE for warmth. As Milla lay awake, she wondered what the future might hold for her and Gitta if Hulda lifted the curse. Milla forgave Gitta for the past, but would Milla's heart ever fully open to her? Could she bear to risk the terrible heartbreak of not being loved well enough? Milla fell asleep not knowing.

The next morning they were both quiet and neither could eat. "We should leave the horses here," Milla said. "I'm not worried about Fulla, but your horse might get spooked."

Her mother nodded, then did something strange. Gitta had neatly rebraided her own hair that morning, and now she reached out to tuck a curl behind Milla's ear. When Sverd grazed her hand, Gitta didn't gasp or lurch backward. "Oh," Gitta said. "Oh." Her face remained gentle, and her hand as well. Milla's heart opened to her mother just a tiny bit more.

Milla and Gitta hadn't walked far when the hissing started. Then the demon girls stepped from behind trees and crept over rocks and the hissing grew excited. Frantic.

She'sssssss here. The sssssssssister. The ssssssister is here.

When Gitta reached for Milla's hand and squeezed it, Milla's heart opened still more.

They walked farther, the hissing building and blending and overlapping.

She'sssssss here. The ssssssssssister. The ssssssister is here.

When Milla and Gitta arrived at the clearing where Hulda's tree stood wide and tall, they were encircled by the demon girls. Among them was Iris. Milla searched her heart-shaped face for some sign of her friend, but there was none. The face that looked back at her belonged to Hulda.

"Sister," Gitta said, her voice hesitant at first, then growing stronger. "Sister, I'm here. And I have something I would say to you, if you'd let me."

Silence fell over the girls, and each of them cocked her head as if listening to a single sound.

A blast of heat rose from the ground, and Milla felt terror and a sense of wrongness so sudden and acute that she thought she would lose the contents of her bladder and her stomach at once. She wanted to take her mother by the hand and run. She wanted to tell her that this was a terrible mistake. Milla and Gitta had both been wrong: It wasn't safe for Gitta here. Because in that heat, Milla felt all the hatred and resentment that Hulda had nursed for her sister since Hulda had been abandoned in the snow. It was a well so deep it would never run dry.

But there was no time to speak, because from the tree slithered Hulda's snake legs, followed by the rest of her. And then so fast, too fast, and Milla should have known, should have *known* this would happen, Hulda had undulated forward and grasped Gitta around the throat, tearing her from Milla's side.

"Mamma!" Milla screamed.

Gitta's toes scraped the ground, and she struggled to stay on her feet.

Hulda pulled Gitta to her, her face just inches away. Her purple lips pulled back into a grimace. "After all thissss lonely time, Gitta, you've finally come to visit. You were always so frightened of me. Even when I was nothing but a strange girl who talked to snakes, you thought I was a monster. So what makes you sssso brave now?"

"I wasn't always frightened of you, Hulda. I loved you."

"Never."

"I did, Hulda. When we were little we slept so close our hair would tangle together in the night. Mamma would have to unknot us in the morning. Do you remember?"

"I remember you called me monster," Hulda said. "How the mother and father let them take me. Bury me in the snow. How the girl died that day and turned into thissss."

"I died that day, too," Gitta said.

Hulda howled, and her howling spread to the girls until the air was full of their agony. Milla felt their pain in her own heart, in her brain and lungs and blood. A sleek black snake with intricate golden diamonds down its back lifted from Hulda's head, and arched downward to graze Gitta's cheek with a long fang. "I could kill you right now, Gitta. And I should. For daring to compare your pain to mine. For *daring*."

Milla stood helpless, watching Hulda tighten her grip around Gitta's throat, so tight her mother couldn't speak. Then Hulda dropped Gitta to the ground, and Gitta sank to her knees. Milla ran to her mother to help her to her feet, but then Milla felt herself lifted off her own.

Hulda dragged Milla backward toward her tree. Milla struggled to free herself, but it was like trying to bend iron. Iron that only coiled tighter the more she fought. "I could kill you, Gitta, but this is better. This way has always been better. I hurt you best by hurting what you love. Your child is mine now. She's a monster like me. And we're both monsters because of you."

Mine now.

Mine now.

You're mine now.

The voice was in Milla's head. Hulda's voice. Milla tried to resist. Tried to remember what her own voice sounded like. What her own heart felt and wanted. But where her heart had been there was only smoke. Hot and black and choking out all air, anything that wasn't hate. That wasn't vengeance.

Then there was another voice inside her, fighting through the smoke. A voice that Milla remembered but couldn't name.

The voice of a friend.

Come back, Milla.

Iris.

Iris was shaking Milla, then clawing at Hulda's iron-snake grip. Shaking and clawing, wild and frantic but herself, all herself. Milla was looking into the face of a friend, heart-shaped and russet-haired and syrup-eyed. "Iris," Milla said. And the friend smiled, but then the friend was flying through the air, hurled by Hulda. "Iris!" Milla screamed.

Hulda dropped Milla to the ground. Enraged, she rolled toward Iris, her black and diamond snake ahead of her, fangs spread and ready. Then a figure was between Iris and Hulda. A figure with long blond hair breaking free of its once-perfect braid.

"Mamma, no!" Milla cried out.

But Gitta had already thrown herself at Hulda, and the snake had already sunk its fangs into Gitta's exposed neck. Gitta's body jerked from the force, then went limp and sank to the earth at Hulda's feet.

Hulda screeched. "No, Gitta! No, sister! Not you!"

Milla ran to her mother, lifting her up, cradling her head in her lap. Touching her face as she never had. Stroking her hair as she'd always wanted to. Gitta's lips whitened and her skin chilled from pink-white to stony gray.

"Mamma," Milla said. She took one of Gitta's hands in hers. Milla remembered how she'd always loved the coolness of her mother's hands. But now Gitta's hands were cold. Too cold. Milla brought them to her cheek. "I'm sorry, Mamma. I'm so sorry."

Gitta looked up at Milla. "I love you, child. I always have."

Snake hands and snake arms wrapped around Gitta, taking her from Milla. "Wake up, Gitta. Wake up, Gitta. Wake up, Gitta." Hulda petted and petted her sister, hiss-whispering, "You are not to leave me, Gitta. Never to leave me. You stay. Sister. *My* sister. Most beloved. This was not my curse. Not my curse. You *stay*."

Gitta's lips moved, forming words. She looked up at her monstrous sister, eyes open and unflinching. "So much pain I caused you. Please forgive me." Then she closed her eyes, took one shallow breath, and no more.

For a long moment, Milla knelt by Gitta while Hulda held her, and the only sound in Milla's ears was Hulda's weeping.

Then her ears opened to the sounds of the forest. Wind shushing through needled branches. The call of birds.

So quiet otherwise.

Milla felt Iris beside her. Her friend, whom her mother had sacrificed her life for. Unafraid of Hulda, Iris kissed Gitta's forehead.

Milla set her mother's hand on her belly and she and Iris stood, backing away from the sisters, one cradling the other. Sverd and Selv settled their heads on Milla's shoulders.

Hulda's grief rose from her in waves, replacing the vengeance that had once radiated from her like heat. The girls gathered around Hulda and Gitta in a circle, each bringing their own sadness with them, like offerings. They laid hands on each other, on Gitta, on Hulda. And in the quiet of that clearing deep in the woods, where a monster had long lived while waiting for her vengeance, they wept together.

EPILOGUE

"TELL ME A STORY," LISS SAID, HER EYES BRIGHT WITH
mischief. "The one about the girl and the witch."

Milla smiled, reaching out for a plump, red apple hanging from
a low branch. She took a bite of the apple, warm from the sun, and
juice ran down her chin. She caught the drip with a finger, then
she wiped the stickiness on her skirt. The sound of a bell chimed in
the air. "That's Mamma," Liss said. "Time for dinner. Come with
us, Milla. Mamma and Pappa are always asking for you."

"Hm," Milla said. "Another time."

Liss sighed. "That means never."

"Doesn't." Milla tugged a chunk of Liss's hair. "It just means
not now."

Liss took Kai's hand and picked up her basket of apples.
"Mamma's making applesauce for the baby. I don't know why.
None of it ever seems to make it into his mouth."

Liss's memories of the day when the curse found her had mostly faded. Just once, Liss had turned to Milla, a shadow passing over her face, and said, "Tell me about the wasps."

"It was a blight," Milla told her. "And it's over now."

Milla watched Liss and Kai walk away from her. When they were just two smudges off in the distance, Sverd and Selv untucked themselves from their hiding places in her hair.

Hulda's curse had lifted when Gitta died. Hulda had withdrawn to her tree, alone, and the girls no longer heard her voice in their heads. Many of the younger girls had returned to their homes, met by families who were happy to know that curses could lift. There were some who didn't feel they could go home again, though. Those women and girls made new homes for themselves where no one knew what had happened to them, where no one pointed or whispered or wondered if they really were themselves again. Iris was one of those. She'd visited her mother and father, thinking she'd stay. But she told Milla that they kept looking at her, like she might change back at any moment. And anyway, it was stifling living at home. And she was a curious girl.

Milla's pale green scales had faded away, leaving fresh skin behind, but her snakes remained—perhaps because she wanted them to. Life would have been easier without them, she supposed. But they were a part of her now. She could tuck them away in her hair when she needed to, but that never felt right. Sverd and Selv were restless creatures; they kept her honest. She couldn't pretend to be what she wasn't—or at least not for long.

When Milla had returned to the farm to tell her father and Niklas that Gitta had sacrificed herself to lift the curse, her father blamed Milla. He said she wasn't welcome in his house, that she'd as much as killed her mother and was just like her aunt: strange. Niklas had protested and said it was Milla's home just as much as Jakob's. Their father grew so angry he turned a shade of purple as dark as a bruise. His anger didn't frighten Milla the way it used to, though. She hugged her brother good-bye and told him not to worry: She would make her way. She hadn't wanted to stay there anyway, not really. The only hardship in leaving the farm was how much she'd miss Niklas. She'd been crying nonstop for a good two miles when Niklas came riding up behind her and said he was coming with her. "My home is with you and Iris," he said. Then she cried harder.

When Niklas, Milla, and Iris rode up to Otto and Katrin's farm, Liss spotted them first. Her squeal of delight split the air. Otto's and Katrin's smiles were wide and genuine. They didn't believe that Milla had caused the strange blight that descended upon them one day and lifted the next, and hadn't understood why Milla thought she had to leave. They never would have blamed Milla for such a thing, Katrin said. Milla thought of Hel and Hulda and Gitta, of vengeance and curses, and she smiled. People blamed other people for all sorts of things.

Katrin thought it odd that Milla hadn't mentioned having a brother, but was too polite to ask why. Otto's and Katrin's delight in having help with the farm and the children was so great that Otto offered to give Milla, Niklas, and Iris a plot of land and to help them build their own log cottage. Such a shame, Katrin said, that they were all orphans. She wanted them to know that they were always welcome at their dinner table. Niklas, Milla, and Iris responded gratefully, then chose a plot too far from Otto and Katrin's cottage to allow for casual visits.

"Are you sure you wouldn't like to live closer?" Katrin said.

Niklas shone his sunshine smile on her. "No, thank you." And in Niklas's usual way, he made it all right.

Milla was happy. She and Iris and Niklas made a companionable home together. When they weren't working on the farm, they took long walks in the woods telling stories about witches and lost children and demons. Well, Milla and Iris told the stories. Niklas mostly listened and laughed and criticized the endings.

Some nights, long after Iris and Niklas were asleep, Milla stepped out into the moonlight, alone. Sverd and Selv stretched themselves and tasted the night air.

Milla walked deep into the woods, ferns brushing her legs. She settled herself in the soft, pillowy moss at the base of a tree. Then she tapped her fingers on a tree root.

Tap. Tap tap tap.

On the fourth tap, the snakes emerged from their hiding places to gather around her. Green and brilliant yellow. Beetle-black and blood-red. Some wrapped themselves around her ankles and wrists; all raised their heads to look at her.

"Now," Milla always said to them, "from where we left off last time. Tell me your names."

ABOUT THE AUTHOR

Peternelle van Arsdale is a book editor, essay and short story writer, and the author of *The Beast Is an Animal*. She lives in Brooklyn, New York, where she is at work on her third novel.

Visit her at PeternellevanArsdale.com

If you enjoyed
The Cold is in Her Bones,
why not try ...

The Beast is an animal
You'd better lock the Gate
Or when it's dark, It comes for you
Then it will be too late

A fairy tale with a difference:
shivery, dark, and deeply satisfying.

LISTENING HELPFULLY

LISTENING HELPFULLY

How to Develop Your Counselling Skills

JEANNE ELLIN

A Condor Book
Souvenir Press (E&A) Ltd

First published 1994 by Souvenir Press
(Educational & Academic) Ltd,
43 Great Russell Street, London WC1B 3PD

Reprinted 1998, 1999, 2000, 2003, 2007

ISBN-10: 0 285 63208 6
ISBN-13: 978 0 285 63208 0

Printed and bound in Great Britain by
Creative Print and Design Wales, Ebbw Vale

This book is for my daughters,
Serena, Verity and Kendra

Contents

Acknowledgements

I want to thank my daughters, Verity and Kendra, for their loving support, enthusiasm, encouragement and acceptance of a mother even more absent-minded and busy than usual. They have had to be more self-sufficient than ever and have cheerfully put up with many inconveniences. Kendra has brought me welcome and unasked-for cups of tea at my word processor, even coming down from bed when she heard me working late at night. Verity has believed in me and willingly helped in many tedious practical tasks, like word-counting.

Bessie has been a loving rock in many storms, with the rare grace of being able to make her gifts a natural expression of caring, never a burden of obligation. Evelyn has had a great hand—literally—in the writing of the early chapters of this book, typing and reading patiently about subjects completely new to her, and offering me a valuable viewpoint. When she had to go abroad, Bessie gallantly read the manuscript for errors and they both made helpful suggestions.

My colleagues in my support group are a vital part of my personal and professional life, offering support, stimulus, honesty and challenge.

My grateful thanks also to the following:

Mary and George, my first counselling teachers, who lived what they taught.

Louise, for sensitive and challenging supervision, and for holding which enabled me to hold my clients through the dark places.

All those who have generously contributed their experiences to this book, clients and colleagues alike.

The clients and students with and from whom I have learnt so much.

Gwen and Michelle for loving support and encouragement.

'The Man at Rochdale Bus Station' for everything.

Jeanne Ellin
April 1994

Introduction

My aim in this book is to offer you a starting point if you feel that your work could include an element of helpful listening—indeed you may already be in a job where such a role is required of you. You may feel a need to increase your skills and confidence in this area; or you may simply be following an interest, wondering if counselling might be work that you could do.

I have based the book on my experiences of running basic counselling skills workshops and training courses for a variety of people. Over the years, certain questions and concerns have emerged as common to most of those with whom I have worked, including many from the caring professions, voluntary workers and those contemplating full counselling training. As I wrote I imagined that I was talking to a small group representing the range of backgrounds and experiences of the people who have attended my training workshops. It could well include the following, perhaps in a situation similar to your own.

Maggie has a young family and is looking to widen her experience. She is mainly on the course from curiosity and wonders 'what this counselling thing is'. Her friends all say she is a good listener—perhaps she might become a counsellor later. Geoff has taken early retirement: he wants to learn more about himself and to help others. He feels that he still has a lot to give. He is also a voluntary worker and is aware how much people need someone who can listen to them; listening is therefore a skill he wants to develop. Jo is a practice nurse and wants to find out if counselling skills could be useful in her well person clinics and in her work with patients who have weight problems or who want to stop smoking. Chris is studying part-time to qualify as a practitioner of an alternative therapy and feels that counselling skills will help her take a better case history and reach a clearer understanding of her clients.

Here are some of the questions that I am asked most frequently:

- How does 'helpful listening' or counselling differ from social or friendly listening, offering advice and information or tea and sympathy?
- Can it be combined with other helping activities, such as giving advice?
- Can it be useful to alternative practitioners?
- Can you help someone whose experience is very different from your own?
- Can you help someone who is going through what happened to you?
- How do you help when someone is in great distress or experiencing very strong feelings?
- Is there a 'right thing' to say?
- How can you tell when someone needs more experienced help?
- How can you help them find that help?
- How do you take care of yourself?
- How do you find supervision and support?
- How do you choose further training?

By itself this book will not teach you how to counsel, any more than you could learn first aid solely from reading about it. But a book can provide a good introduction and can help you decide whether the subject is one you want to study more deeply. I hope to give you some idea of what counselling involves and some of the difficulties and dilemmas you may encounter. There are skills to practise and many questions to discuss and think about, which could form a useful preparation for counselling training and may help to improve your communication skills and your self-knowledge.

You may find it interesting to keep a journal while you are working through the book. It need not be seen by anyone else and can be particularly helpful if you have no colleagues who share your interests, with whom you can discuss various points. If you decide to do this, choose a notebook that looks and feels good. Use it to record your thoughts and feelings and to answer the questions raised in the following chapters. Have a discussion with yourself: write out more than one point of view. Have fun with it.

The book is divided into three parts: counselling, combining counselling with other skills and the clients' experience.

COUNSELLING

Getting ready

This part of the book covers preparing for counselling— both the external aspects (the setting and conditions) and the internal (the development of the skills and attitudes needed to counsel). There is a strong emphasis on self-understanding, self-development and self-acceptance. Yes, it may be uncomfortable or even painful for you at times. I do not apologise for that. Counselling is painfully honest and the pain is not all one way, nor is the gain in growth and development. What is the difference between me (the counsellor) and a client? Simply that for the moment we are focusing together on his problems, concerns and needs using my skills and resources. At the same time we are mobilising and enhancing his coping skills and increasing his problem-solving capacity.

First things first

Since Part One is planned to reflect the order in which things happen, the first chapter will look at beginnings in counselling, for both counsellor/listener and client. For example, we shall examine what boundaries there are and what hopes and fears we may bring to this work. The client will also bring his or her own hopes and fears to our first meeting, and will need to know the boundaries.

An example of a boundary might be how long your meetings will last. Another early task is to come to some joint understanding with your client about what you are doing together. For ourselves, as writer and reader, an early priority is to come to some understanding of what counselling (listening helpfully) actually is.

What do you think counselling is?
Throughout the book I shall be offering suggestions for work you can do to increase your skills and understanding of counselling, so your own thoughts and experiences and the conclusions you might come to from reading this book will contribute to your own unique understanding. The client, meanwhile, brings his (or her) unique feelings and experiences to counselling and then, with your helpful listening and his own thoughts and actions, comes to his own decisions and draws his own conclusions.

So this first part deals with the basic skills of listening helpfully and some of the preparations, both practical and personal, that you would need to make before you could listen effectively. This part also includes some information about supervision and support.

COMBINING COUNSELLING WITH OTHER SKILLS

Part Two looks at how different practitioners combine counselling with their other roles. They discuss the difficulties and dilemmas they have encountered and assess the usefulness of counselling skills in their jobs. The contributors range from managers and trainers to alternative practitioners, from a speech therapist and people involved in education to an individual who is a good listener and finds herself lending a helpful ear to friends. I have asked these people to say what they think counselling is as well as to describe how it fits or does not fit in with their work. I have also asked them to write about some of their ethical and other problems. I hope this will be valuable for those of you intending to combine counselling with your other roles. It could help you to plan ahead and discuss possible difficulties and dilemmas with colleagues and managers before introducing a counselling element to your work.

THE CLIENTS' EXPERIENCE OF COUNSELLING

Part Three is made up of the experience of counselling from the clients' points of view, mostly in their own words. The reports are theirs rather than mine, but I have added some of the discussion we had as we prepared for this book and I have also responded to questions they raised.

Because counselling involves understanding, exploring and accepting a variety of powerful feelings and experiences, I shall invite you to look closely at your own. This has two benefits: first, it is easier to be accepting of others if you are also tolerant and accepting towards yourself; second, it is easier to work out what is going on if you are at least familiar with one set of feelings and experiences—your own. It is then a simpler task to separate the client's feelings and reactions from your own, and to keep your feelings from getting in the client's way.

This is why, throughout the book, I suggest exercises that you might do, and raise questions for you to think about and discuss. Sometimes this may be painful and uncomfortable. If you feel distressed by any of the issues raised, please stop and consider whether you could benefit from some 'helpful listening' yourself. You could end up feeling much better and the experience would certainly make you a better counsellor.

Learning and practising these skills is a little like going to an aerobics class. If you had any doubts about your fitness or concerns about your health you would get some advice first. You would also listen to your body while doing

the exercises. I hope that, for you, learning about counselling will also be about being more comfortable with yourself
and that you will take the same care of your emotional
health as you do of your bodily fitness.

PART ONE
COUNSELLING

1 First Steps

From the beginning I hope to make this process of exploration a shared task, by encouraging you to contribute your thoughts and conclusions, as well as by offering some of my own experiences.

Let's see if we can begin to answer the following questions.

1 What is counselling?
2 What do you need to think about to get ready to do this work?
3 Do you have the ability to counsel?

What is counselling?
I would like you to pause briefly at this point and think of how you would describe counselling. You might find it helpful to write a brief note or two—not to show how 'right' or 'wrong' you are, but to offer you a marker by which to measure your developing understanding of counselling as you work through the book.

I could give you British Association for Counselling definitions or could quote from dictionaries, but I hope the following descriptions of counselling offered by ex-clients will give you a richer flavour of the experience. They come from a wide range of people, of different ages (11 years to 50+), life experiences and perspectives.

Counselling is . . .
'A journey . . .'
'Something that freed me.'

'Helping people who have problems to talk, just gently and kindly easing things out.'

'Just a kind of mirror, really.'

'A demonstration of the power of self-observation.'

'I talked a lot; you didn't tell me anything; things got clearer.'

'My strongest sense is of channels clearing and connecting and of something being received and transmitted.'

How counselling differs from other helping activities

Imagine that you are lost at night in a strange place. You are cold, wet and beginning to feel rather nervous. Perhaps there is no one near to ask for help, or maybe you feel anxious about asking those around you. You have heard that I have some maps and have helped other people, so you telephone me. If I said, 'Oh, how dreadful! that happened to me once, so I know just what you should do,' this would be sympathetic and well meant. It might even be helpful if your circumstances and mine were similar and we felt the same about them.

I might tell you to 'pull yourself together' and that someone of your age should be able to cope if you tried, but this would be unlikely to help you. If it felt that easy you would not have asked me what to do. It might just add to your difficulties by encouraging you to feel bad about yourself and your coping abilities.

Nor would you find it helpful if I told you that you should have started out earlier or from a different place and should be somewhere else—preferably Manchester, as I have an excellent map of that city! Preaching, lecturing or scolding have no place in counselling. Nor is it helpful to have rigid sets of beliefs to which you expect your clients to conform. It is important to accept people as they are, starting from where they are, not from where you feel they ought to be.

If I gave you factual information, such as bus or train times, and told you where your nearest bus stop was, this would be purely an information service, useful only if you knew where you were and where you wanted to go.

Now suppose that you tell me that it is wet and cold and dark where you are, that you don't feel it is safe to ask directions, and that the street signs are missing or obscured. If I accept that as being true for you where you are, even if the sun is shining on me and I am not afraid of strangers, then I gently encourage you to search for clues to where *you* are and to move towards a better-lighted area. Here you can see more clearly where you are and what your travel options are.

That would be counselling: my offering you attention, respect and acceptance of where you are, supporting you as you move at your own pace towards your own choice of destination.

Counselling philosophy

It may be useful to you if I explain how I see counselling and what my understanding of the work is, so that you can make a clearer evaluation of how my understanding of theory is put into practice. You might then also find it easier to establish your own viewpoint, and see whether or not you agree with the counselling theory that I follow, and with the way I attempt to put it into practice.

It is important to find a way of working that fits who you are and what you believe about people and the way they grow and change, and even your understanding of what it means to be alive and human. I have a profound belief in people's ability to grow and change throughout their lives. I also believe that only they can choose whether, when and how they do so.

As a counsellor I am prepared to use any theory or technique to help, provided it satisfies the following criteria:

- I am competent to practise it.
- It is respectful of the individual, and of his wholeness and capacity to change and grow, in his own time and in his own way.

- It is acceptable to the client.
- He understands it.
- We both feel that it fits the stage he is at and the work we are doing together.

I feel that my task is to work with the client so that the conclusions he comes to are his own and new coping skills become his to practise in the future.

What do you need to think about to get ready to do this work?

You may become aware that a lot of work in this book—the exercises and questions to think about—seems to be more about you than about the client. This is because I believe that first of all counsellors need to listen to themselves. We need to understand our own reactions, thoughts and feelings before we can begin to listen to those of the client. This familiarity with our own 'baggage' helps us to recognise it and disentangle it from the client's.

We also need to be comfortable with strong feelings—our own as well as the client's. It is better to practise with our own feelings first, and perhaps with those of fellow students where this is possible. We then have the chance to remember how vulnerable we can feel in 'helping situations' when we are the client.

Starting out in counselling

You may be 'counselling' as a volunteer or as an extension of your work role. For example, many care workers find themselves involved in listening to clients' difficulties while performing their other duties. They often become aware of the clients' need to talk things out and feel uncertain about how to help them do this. Some of us simply start with a vague interest, a feeling of 'I'd like to do that'. Whatever your reasons, there are the same basics to consider before you begin.

Are you ready?
You will need to consider your own readiness and to discuss this with more experienced colleagues, and to begin to identify the skills and experiences you will have to acquire. I hope that working through this book will help you do this.

You will need to think about who you will be counselling. You might have special areas of experience and skill to offer, or the agency for which you work might have a particular field of expertise and offer its own training. You will need to think carefully about which training course to choose: distance and cost matter, but more important still is to choose a recognised course. The British Association for Counselling can help with information on approved training courses. You will need a source of clients, for although most courses can provide you with supervision or at least advise you on suitable individuals, all require you to have people whom you can counsel. This may be possible in your existing setting or you may need to explore the voluntary sector.

What does counselling involve?
Listening helpfully (counselling) involves offering another person your focused attention: concentrating together on areas of concern and difficulty. You may be helping him to think about what he is feeling and come to his own solutions; or to expand his view of what his choices are and how to live with them.

Fortunately, this does not require us, as listeners, to be wise and all-knowing or infallible. We offer our focused attention to help the client think about his feelings while keeping *our* feelings out of his way. We offer him space to explore new ways of looking at his situation and we respect his ability to make choices he can live with.

Setting the scene
You will need to look at the setting in which you will be listening—lights, seating, privacy, co-operation with colleagues.

Since listening helpfully is an intense activity that demands privacy and consent, you need a quiet, interruption-free space where both you and the client can be comfortable. Take whatever practical steps you feel necessary to ensure this.

The environment in which you will work is important and there are several practical points to consider. You are trying to create a warm atmosphere where two adults can work in partnership.

Telephones, interruptions and unspoken messages

Is there a telephone in the room, and can it be disarmed? Your client may be finding it hard enough to tell his story, and the disruption of the phone ringing at a critical moment may make a difficult task impossible. Another important point is that by answering the phone, you might be giving a silent message—'You are not important enough to have all my attention'. Our aim is to offer our concentrated attention, without distractions.

It is vital that people around you respect the counselling room. It is not permissible to 'just pop in to get . . .' Your client is vulnerable and exposed—the emotional equivalent of having her knickers round her knees. Interruptions show a great lack of care and respect.

Equal seating

Are both the chairs you will be using of equal height, comfort and status? Is one obviously more expensive or shabby? Is one more 'official' and important? When people are feeling vulnerable and at a disadvantage, they are sensitive to anything which may give the impression that they are less important than you. It is hard enough to build an equal partnership without the furniture giving unhelpful messages.

Is there an obvious barrier, like a desk, between you? Again, your aim is to create a warm, accepting atmosphere, and a formal barrier like a desk can literally get in the way of this. It puts a distance between you and underlines a difference in status and power that you will have to work hard to equalise.

A matter of timing
You will need to be able to check the time discreetly, so you should choose your own seat with this in mind. It can be very distracting to have to manoeuvre to see the time.

Seeing and being seen
When you think about lighting and seating, remember that you need to see and be seen clearly. You will be watching for fleeting changes of expression that can underline or contradict what is being said.

Windows and privacy
If the room in which you will be counselling has windows which can be peered through or overlooked, you will need to check the curtains. Remember that nets alone are useless for privacy in a lighted room, so you might consider blinds.

Personal space, permission to cry
Remember that each of us has a comfortable distance that we like to maintain: this varies with cultures but also with individuals. Be alert to signs of discomfort and have chairs that can be easily moved.

Since people may need to cry copiously, it is useful to have a box of tissues placed where clients can see them and help themselves. Do not offer the tissues, as the client may then feel you are trying to stop her crying.

Does your appearance matter?
This has nothing to do with vanity, but is simply a part of your increased self-awareness. This is where working with colleagues can give you so much valuable feedback. How do people see you? What assumptions do they make about you because of the way you dress? Are they picking up

clues that you do not know you are giving out? What do you think about people who dress in bright colours, who wear beads plaited into their hair or nose rings? Or people who dress very conservatively? Would you respond differently to a counsellor who dressed in a style very unlike your own? These questions are worth considering and perhaps looking at again after you have done the exercise in Chapter Two (p. 28) on appearances and your perceptions about other people. You may also want to compare your answers here with the results of the exercises on pp. 20–2, analysing what made you feel comfortable or uncomfortable in a helping relationship. Did the way the professional was dressed have any bearing on how you felt when you were with him, or how he thought about you? There is no rule about this, it is just more material for you to think about, consider and use in order to come to your own best decisions. If you are wearing something very eye-catching, it might be distracting for your client.

This is something that did not occur to me until it actually happened in practice. If you are leaning forward, trying to be encouraging and warm, it's fine if you are offering warm eye contact; it's rather more dubious if you are offering an increased view of your bosom! So think about this when choosing something to wear to work, especially if you are a woman. What happens when you lean forward? Do you have the sort of wrap-around skirt that will suddenly come adrift? There is nothing more distracting for you or the client than for you to be wearing clothes that you must constantly be aware of or which you have to fiddle with.

Dress to be comfortable

I think it is important for you to wear clothes in which you feel comfortable, that reflect who you are, and that you feel will be acceptable to your client. This is a very individual thing, so to illustrate what I mean, let me give you an example.

Some years ago I was invited to teach on a workshop with a colleague. It was several years since I had last stood up in front of a group of people and I felt very nervous and uncertain with some of the material, but even more anxious about how to present myself. The colleague with whom I would be working had a lot more current experience, and she dressed quite conservatively in neat little grey suits. So the night before the course was due to start, I raked out a little grey skirt I had from goodness knows when and a very plain blouse, and I went the next day and felt totally self-conscious, miserable and uncomfortable, simply because I didn't feel like myself. I was therefore less able to forget myself and get on with the job of being there and facilitating. The following day I wore a smart pair of purple trousers and my very favourite jumper at the time, which was purple with a beautiful yellow swirling pattern, and in that I felt completely at home. I went in to work, forgot all about myself and my appearance and could give all my attention to the workshop and the people on it. But as I say, it is a very personal thing.

What does appearance tell you about people?
While your client is taking in your appearance and perhaps making deductions about the kind of person you are, you might find yourself doing the same thing about him or her. It is worth being aware of the assumptions you might make about someone (see the exercise on p. 27).

There is also another point: sometimes people's clothes do not actually reflect their free choice, but rather their circumstances. There was a time when all my clothes came from jumble sales; if a garment fitted me and was free of holes I bought it and wore it regardless of style and colour. Now I never forget the possibility that what people wear may be a reflection of their financial or other circumstances rather than their taste. For instance, depression can affect how people care for themselves, the way they present themselves, the way they choose their clothes. More serious mental conditions, such as Alzheimer's and other confusional states, can also result in very odd choices and combinations of clothes and strange grooming habits, or the lack of them. So although all this information is important, it is wise not to jump to any conclusions until you have more information on which to base them. Is this somebody simply with a bizarre dress sense, someone very eccentric, someone who is currently depressed, someone who has very little access to or choice of clothes, or is this an expression of some kind of mental or emotional problem?

Discuss your plans beforehand

If you work with colleagues, it is helpful to talk to them about what you hope to do before you begin:

- Will there need to be any changes in work routine?
- Can you have uninterrupted use of a quiet room?
- Do they share and support your aims in doing this work?
- Can they offer support and continuity of approach in your absence? (For example, in a small team working in a residential setting, one staff member 'counselling' can have a big impact on the rest of the community.)
- How will your regular absence for an hour affect the work load of the other staff?
- Will other residents feel left out?
- Will your exclusive use of a quiet room inconvenience them?
- Do your colleagues share your understanding of counselling and its aims?

The time you spend doing this preparation will pay dividends in the support and confidence you and your client gain. If the client is seeing you in an atmosphere where your 'listening' is valued and supported, positive results are more likely. You will also find yourself more relaxed.

If you are working as a volunteer, counselling may already be an acknowledged part of the work. However, if your 'listening' is taking place in a home setting (yours or the client's), you will need to ensure the understanding and co-operation of the other people around before you begin.

Boundaries

You will need to have a clear understanding of the guidelines or boundaries within which you are working.

Contracts

As you and your client are in a partnership working together, you both need to be clear about what you are doing and why you are doing it, and how you will know when it is finished:

- What do you both understand to be the point of these meetings?
- Who will you discuss the work with?
- What records will you keep and who else will be able to see them?
- Under what circumstances, if any, would you break confidentiality?

You, as the listener, need to be sure in your own mind about these questions. If you have a line manager or supervisor, discuss this with her. If you are a member of a professional body or service with a code of ethics, check them to see if there are any possible contradictions or confusions that might arise. These are better dealt with before they happen. The British Association for Counselling has two codes of practice, one for counsellors and one for those using counselling skills. You may well find them valuable.

Safe to speak

Having worked on achieving the right physical setting in which to work—comfortable and private—you then need to think about providing a safe emotional atmosphere. Before you can encourage someone to tell you his story, you need to look at how you can help him feel safe enough to begin.

Fear

Most of our pain and uncertainty, in situations where we feel vulnerable, can be boiled down to fear: fear of being labelled, of being judged, of being rubbished; fear of being found out, of being unacceptable, of being misunderstood, of taking up too much of someone's time; fear of being seen as too demanding, too boring, too emotional, too wimpish; fear that the other person may not be honest or trustworthy, or may harm us.

Below are two written exercises that I hope will help to clarify some of the concerns that a client brings to a new counselling relationship. The results should help you to think about how you can most usefully deal with them.

EXERCISE: AN UNCOMFORTABLE PROFESSIONAL ENCOUNTER

I would like you to remember a recent encounter with a 'professional' that left you feeling uncomfortable or even distressed. If you have no recent event, choose one that you remember vividly. An example of a 'professional' might be your bank manager, child's teacher, or a member of one of the helping professions. Briefly describe what happened, then list your feelings in as much detail as you can. How did you feel before, during and after the meeting? Were you aware of being disturbed by any particular thing that was said or done? Were you uncomfortable because of the surroundings (for example, a telephone ringing, people coming in and out) or was your discomfort more subtle? Did you sense an attitude that made you uncomfortable? Concentrate on how you felt and how you thought the other person felt about you. However well-intentioned the helper, if the person being helped feels bad, the encounter has not been as successful as it could have been. Feelings are just as real as facts, and of equal value. If you feel put down, the fact that I only meant to help you does not make your feeling less true.

When you have completed this exercise, please ask one or two friends or colleagues to do it. Then compare notes and see if you can find any feelings in common. What were you/they most afraid of? Boiled down, most lists would say things like:

I felt stupid.

I felt powerless.

I felt like a silly child.

I was afraid that he'd think I was a bad person.

I was afraid he'd think I was irresponsible.

I was afraid that he'd think it was my fault.

We all know how that can feel, even if we are not being expected to talk about painful personal matters.

EXERCISE: A COMFORTABLE PROFESSIONAL ENCOUNTER

Now repeat the exercise, this time focusing on an encounter that went well and left you as the client feeling good. It is proverbially more blessed to give than to receive and this can be especially true in 'helping situations'. The person on the receiving end has the problem, and to some degree the embarrassment, of asking for help and exposing his or her need, and perhaps the burden of feeling under an obligation or grateful. The helper has more power and prestige and is not at a disadvantage.

Again, concentrate on how you felt when you began and how you felt at the end. What effect did what was said and done, and how it was done, have on how you felt? Try and condense this to a couple of sentences that describe how you felt and how you think the helper seemed to feel about you. Compare notes with your colleagues and make a list. You may have something like this:

I felt very nervous, afraid of wasting his time, but he let me take my time.

He listened carefully, seemed to understand how I felt.

I didn't feel stupid to have come.

Attitudes and assumptions that are helpful to develop:

That people are capable of change.

That people will work harder for their own goals.

That people can come to their own understanding of the
  'meaning of their life'.
A successful helping relationship helps a person to feel
heard but not judged. From the beginning, the client is
treated with respect as an equal adult. He is given an honest
warmth that is not possessive, and he is free to expand and
grow in his own way. I find it helpful to think of myself, as
counsellor, being responsible *to* my client for the quality
and sincerity of my work, not responsible *for* him.

How far do you think the attitudes and assumptions listed
above were present or absent in the encounters you have
written about? How did their presence or absence affect the
outcome? How far did physical factors, like noise, or
barriers, like desks, affect you?

There may be other aspects you might wish to consider
and you may find it helpful to record these observations in
your work book. If you have found it helpful to do the
exercises and reflect on them, the following thoughts may
also be useful:

As you go about your everyday business, begin to notice the
  quality of your encounters with others. How often do you
  unconsciously or consciously apply the attitudes and
  assumptions we have discussed?
How can you extend the range of situations in which you
  practise them?
Are there any that you feel need special attention?
What happens when you try applying them in new situations or, more consciously, in old ones?

There are no right or wrong answers here. If you are
becoming more aware of what you do and how you do it,
then you have succeeded! You will then know what you
need to work on developing.

What are your responsibilities?
There may be situations where these are contradicted by
your other roles and responsibilities to your client. If there
is any possibility of confusion, get it clear in your own
mind, then explain it equally clearly to your client.

What do you expect?
Perhaps at this stage we can mention a rather more delicate point: what does the counsellor expect of the client?
Whatever your expectations are, you need to be honest with
yourself about them. Do you expect that all your clients will
get 'better', and do you define that in a particular way?
Does it meet criteria of your own? What is 'better'? Do you
expect that your clients will let you down or are are you
able to let go of all expectations and simply offer your
clients the space to work in the way and for the length of
time that they wish for their goals?

You need to be able to accept that these goals might
change—the client might change his mind, he might not be
able to finish the work, he might decide to finish it with
somebody else, he might not feel able to do it at all. That is
his choice and if it leaves you with feelings, then those are
your feelings and you need to deal with them. It is quite a
complicated issue, but if you have expectations that in order
to be a good client somebody must progress in a particular
way and make noticeable progress, it becomes an unseen
burden on your client and on you.

It is very difficult to give up all expectations. Perhaps a
more manageable one is that people will do what they are
ready to do in the way that seems 'better' to them, within
their own time-scale, and that you may or may not have the
privilege of being a part of it. The expectation I hold is that
all of us have the capacity to grow and change, and make
our own choices about when this might be.

And yes, I'd like it to be with me: I'd like to be involved
with it because I'm a nosy sort of soul, because I find it
interesting, fascinating, good to be part of. But that's my

affair, not theirs, and I work very hard to hold the expectation that they will do what they are ready to do when they
are ready to do it, whether or not they do it with me. It's a
tough one, I know.

Perhaps this is something to talk about, discuss in a
group, or to use as the basis for some listening work
between yourself and a colleague. There are some interesting issues there to explore: why we want to be counsellors,
what we are in it for, what we expect to get out of it, what
we can put in, what being a client is about.

Change is painful
Think what a painful thing it is to change even something as
small as your diet. It takes a lot of effort, a lot of motivation
and can be a continuing struggle—you must really want to
and you must have a good reason, one that makes sense to
you. Then you need support, and even so your success
depends on how you make the change. You can do it
gradually, so that it fits in with your life and becomes a part
of it, which is the easiest way in the long run. Or you can
make an immense effort that doesn't last and you slip back
because you have failed. In the same way, actually to make
changes in your life, in the way you think and feel and react
to events, is very, very difficult.

Counselling costs
For the people coming for counselling the process is expensive in terms of time, energy, commitment, the disruption in
their lives, the changes it might make in relationships or in
other areas and possibly in money. The time they spend in
counselling is not available to them to earn their living or be
with their family or enjoy themselves in other ways.

I think that the degree of change someone makes is a very
individual choice, dependent on how ready they are. If they
have no supportive partner or loving family around them,
no satisfying job, or if they have other worries, whether
financial, emotional or marital, they might not have the

First Steps 25

resources to make all the changes that they want or need at
the time when you are seeing them. Or they may persevere,
and I am often awestruck at the courage of people who have
made changes in the midst of immense difficulties with
what seem like minimal resources; they work through and
they come out at the other end with a life that feels so much
better to them than it has ever felt before. That is a very
worthwhile thing and they have put tremendous hard work
into it, but I do not think you can ever say that people
should be doing more than they are.

People do what they are ready to do, given the resources
they have, and we have to think in terms of that. Very often
you will wonder why people do not change particular
attitudes that seem not to be working for them or that are
making others around them uncomfortable, but if you yourself have been in that situation you will know that it is
rather like a weighing scale. You have the pain of how you
are at the moment, the difficulties it is causing you and the
people around you, and the limitations it is putting on your
life. First of all you have to recognise that these drawbacks
exist and are changeable; secondly, they have to be heavier,
so that the discomfort they cause you is greater than the
discomfort of actually changing them. And if you want to
add something in the balance, perhaps consider how you
feel life would be without these hindrances: if I were only
able to think about how I felt more easily, I would have
better relationships and I would feel a lot happier. If that
seems a desirable goal, then it is an added weight in the
scale and makes the pain of change worthwhile for you, but
it is a very individual weighing-up process. Will what I gain
be worth the difficulty and pain I must go through to
achieve it? Is it going to hurt less than it hurts to be as I am
now? These are big questions and you cannot answer them
for someone else. What you *can* do is help them explore the
options and come to their own right answer for this particular time.

The right helper

The only factor to bear in mind is that you might not be the right helper, not simply in terms of skills but due to a possible mismatch in terms of personality, or your technique—there could be a whole range of reasons why you are not the best person to help at this moment. It might be that no one could help this particular person at this stage in his life. He may not be ready for change and may lack the resources, or the time may be wrong for him. It could be, however, that you are simply the wrong helper for him, and don't feel bad about this—you can't be the right helper for everybody, any more than one key can fit every lock. We are all very individual and you can be far more effective if you accept that there will be people for whom you are not the best possible counsellor.

You may be wondering about the answer to the third question—'Do you have the ability to counsel?' Perhaps we should change that to 'What do you need to do to develop your ability to counsel?' As you work through this book, I hope that you will find your own answers to this key question.

2 Are You Ready?

Having worked on preparing the room and your colleagues for counselling, the next area to consider is yourself. In some ways this is a similar task. You have looked at the resources of the room and considered how they will meet your needs as a counsellor. Now you need to look at the furnishings of your mind—your attitudes, assumptions and the information you already have, as well as any gaps you might become aware of. The attitudes and understanding of colleagues are also important. A good starting point is to explore your habits in the way you think about people. Again this is not about being 'good' or 'bad' in how you think about others, but about becoming more aware of your own attitudes and assumptions and then deciding for yourself how useful or helpful they will be to you as a counsellor.

Sorting the attic
Imagine that you have a day to spend in clearing and sorting out the contents of an attic. You are curious and interested in what you might find, ready to trust your own judgement about what to keep, to cherish or renovate, and what to discard. In this same spirit of openness and curiosity, you might like to work on the following exercises.

EXERCISE: EXPLORING ATTITUDES AND ASSUMPTIONS
If you are in a training group, you may choose to do this exercise with someone you have not yet got to know. Write a description of all you notice about this person and what your guesses are based on. If you are not in a group, try speculating about strangers you see travelling to work or

while shopping. You will not be able to check whether you have guessed right but should still get most of the benefit of the exercise. Working very quickly and intuitively, guess your subject's favourite food, television programme, music, holiday destination and so on. Then decide what you think is his or her secret ambition.

This exercise is not about being right about someone else, though you might be surprised at your accuracy, but about trying to notice what 'clues' you used in making your guesses and what they told you about yourself.

EXERCISE: HOW IMPORTANT IS APPEARANCE TO YOU?

What aspects carry the most weight with you? For example, which would matter most to you, dirty fingernails or uncombed hair?

Would you see people differently if they were unshaven and wore a designer suit, or if they had stubble and wore dirty overalls?

Do you feel more at ease with people who look as if they read the same daily paper as you?

What do these people look like?

Could you draw a picture of a floating voter? a car salesman? a justice of the peace? If you were to guess about them, using the questions posed in the first exercise, what would that tell you about yourself?

Choose the first two strangers you meet in the next week, one who you feel would be a good friend and one with whom you feel that you would have nothing in common. Decide what their views are on important issues and also answer the questions posed in the first exercise as if they applied to them.

You should by now have quite a lot of information to sort and here is one way to do it. Make two columns, one for positive and one for negative. Write down all the things you have noticed about the people you chose: appearance, clothes, voice, accent, build, clothes sense, posture and so on. Then look at the number of positive entries for each person and compare them with the things you guessed about them. How often did you guess good things, things that you like or approve of about people with certain characteristics? How often did you guess things that you don't approve of, or dislike or are uncomfortable with, about people with certain characteristics? How much do you have in common with each?

As before there are no right or wrong answers here, just a chance for you to become more aware of the attitudes and assumptions in your 'attic', so that you can decide which will be useful in counselling work and which, if any, you no longer find useful.

Making the links
So now you may have become aware of something we all do to a greater or lesser extent—sort and label each other as a short cut to finding out those we will like or dislike. Because this habit can get in the way of counselling, we need to recognise it so that we can prevent it from coming between us and our clients.

If you look again at the exercises in the first chapter (see pp. 20–2), how many of the discomforts you felt in the unsuccessful helping situation could have been due, in some part, to your feeling of being labelled, or even to your labelling the other person or yourself? Someone who .... (fill in this blank for yourself) couldn't possibly like, sympathise with, understand someone like me?

You might like to pause here and compare the results of the exercises in Chapter One with those you have just completed. Are there any links you can make between the two? If there are links, might they be worth thinking about in your approach to your clients?

Basic counselling theory
One basic counselling theory, the Egan three-stage model, begins with the client telling his story, and moves through

exploration and the gaining of new insights to the planning and carrying out of a course of action. I feel it is useful to start a stage earlier and look at how we can make it safe for the client to decide to tell his story, and for us to be able to hear him.

Atmosphere

Atmosphere is a subtle thing; certainly the physical surroundings matter, but so does the emotional climate, and that is the area we are going to concentrate on now. Remember the exercise in which you looked at helping interviews that left you feeling good (p. 21)? What attitudes did you feel the helper held towards you? In general most people would say, and research backs this up, that they felt accepted rather than judged, respected and valued for themselves; really listened to; and that the helper was a genuine person, sincerely interested in them.

Core conditions

These qualities of *respect* (non-judgemental acceptance), *genuineness* and *empathy* are described by Carl Rogers as the core conditions for a helping relationship, and are the foundation on which good helping relationships can be built. Let us look at these deceptively simple qualities in more detail.

Respect, acceptance, trust and being non-judgemental

It often takes a great deal of courage to admit that you need help and then decide to risk exposing your pain and confusion to a stranger, not to mention the difficulties of working through that confusion in counselling. I do not find it hard to respect the courage and vulnerability of my clients.

It can be confusing to think of not judging someone. Does this mean that we are to have no values and standards of our own? I do not think that this is what it means. I find it more helpful to think about finding a way to value and respect the person sitting opposite me, while not sharing all or any of his beliefs or values—even at times feeling pain or revulsion at some of his actions. I have thought, said and done 'bad things', but I do not think that I am an irredeemably bad person. I want to be seen as the whole person I am, struggling, often in pain and confusion, with the consequences of actions I now regret.

I feel that most of us could say the same. We are often more aware of our faults than our strengths and individual value. Which is the more important self-knowledge, or do you think that we need to be equally aware of both?

EXERCISE: HOW WELL DO YOU KNOW YOUR STRENGTHS?
This exercise could give you a lot to think about.

Which good things other people say about you do you find it easiest to believe?

Are there any good things that other people say or believe about you that you 'throw away' or find hard to accept?

Are they things you admire in other people?

Are they qualities that you have been trying to develop?

Did you notice them in your answers to the attic questions?

Did you get any pleasant surprises?

Is the whole area of looking at good things in or about yourself too embarrassing?

Does it make you feel silly or self-indulgent to try to look at your strengths or good points?

You might like to try describing some of the unexpected good things about yourself that you became aware of while doing the exercise, or perhaps some of the good qualities for which other people praise you.

Make a brief list of your weak points—the areas you would most like to improve. Choose only those that cause you or others most inconvenience. Do not make too long a list—you are not that bad! There is value in being aware of and owning our weak points. When you own and befriend your 'fault' and take responsibility for it, it can be transformed into a source of sensitivity and strength.

Imagine that a large, savage dog has been hanging around your house. You accuse your neighbours of being responsible for it; they insist that it is yours. Well, it does hang around outside your house the most, it did scare away several dubious characters and you do slip it the odd bone, don't you? Perhaps it is yours. Now it has started threatening the postman and some of your friends, and you decide to take charge of it. Take it to the vet, get it a collar with your name on and a strong lead. Together you go to obedience classes, and soon you have a watchdog to be proud of.

Acknowledge your weakness and make it work for you; it can be a source of strength, a resource for you, whether it makes you aware of your own humanness or is a source of increased sensitivity to the varied ways in which people respond to painful or stressful situations.

There is nothing wrong with being as aware of your strengths as you are of your weaknesses. This may be an area of self-development that you need to work on. Many of us are good at blaming and nagging ourselves but are unable to take in or believe good things about ourselves. If you feel that this is an area you need to work on, keep the work you have done on this exercise safe and add to it any thoughts and comments that occur to you later about the way you respond to praise and criticism, and how you praise and criticise others. I think we need to feel safe enough to look at the best and worst in ourselves before we can begin the sifting and sorting process which is part of the growth that continues all through our lives, in or out of counselling.

Liking

Do we have to like our clients? Are there different types or degrees of liking?

I feel that respect is the key here. With respect comes acceptance and the possibility of learning to like the person we have come to know. On the other hand, dislike and disrespect make counselling impossible. Sometimes we need to see the client separately from his actions, or try to understand the meaning they had for him.

Genuineness and congruence

The counsellor has to be honest with herself and be genuine with her client. You have to feel what you say as well as mean it. If you do not, you will be transmitting two conflicting messages: as if a simultaneous broadcast on Radio 3 and BBC 1 had gone wrong and the Proms were being broadcast with *EastEnders*—two popular programmes but, combined, a confusing and irritating experience. Clients are sensitive to how we listen and what our body language is saying. Just as we need to listen to the unspoken messages they are offering us, we also need to listen to ourselves so that we can 'broadcast' a clear signal: 'I am genuinely interested', 'I mean what I say', 'What I say reflects what I feel'.

In case you think the courage has to be all on the client's side, I find it takes great courage to be honest, open and vulnerable. So I attempt to offer (and, yes, it is a struggle sometimes) my clients a respect for their unique human selves. When this has been most difficult, I have often found that something in the client's own life or attitude has mirrored something about myself or my life that needs my attention. This may mean that I have some personal work to do, in supervision or with my own counsellor. Very rarely, it might mean that I cannot work with this person and will have to help him or her find another counsellor. And then I would probably work around that issue with my supervisor or counsellor. I cannot afford to miss any chance to grow.

Empathy

Empathy is difficult both to describe and to practise. It differs from sympathy, although it is often confused with it. Empathy is seeing the experience through the other person's eyes; feeling what he feels—from his point of view. As a young colleague once said to me after a rather vigorous group discussion, 'If I were twenty years older, wearing those colours and sitting in that chair—I could feel like that about it!'

Here are two true stories that I think give some idea of the difference between sympathy and empathy.

After a stillbirth

A newly bereaved mother was being comforted by a kind and concerned health worker. The worker was genuinely concerned and trying to find a way to understand and show that understanding. 'No one close to me has died . . . except my dog died two years ago . . . I was very fond of it.' A gallant but very misguided attempt at sympathy: definitely not as comforting as it was intended to be. Trying to understand someone else's experience and feelings by translating them into the nearest equivalent of your own is unlikely to work, because no one else's experience is identical to our own. Even the same experience is thought about, felt, responded to, differently by each person.

This is not to lessen the very great value of the work done by support groups and survivors' organisations, where the starting point is a shared experience which it is accepted that each person will have responded to individually.

A dog's death

This story is about a listening experience I had with a woman whose dog had died (no, not all empathy involves dogs!). I am not a dog lover, in fact at one time in my life I was so scared of dogs that I would cross the road to avoid one. Currently I can meet and respond to individual dogs, rather than to my 'fear picture' of a dog. I tell you this so that you can see how my listening to the bereaved dog lover enlarged my perceptions; for a little while I was able to see dogs through her eyes.

She had had her dog for 15 years, through many changes and difficulties. Her mother had died, her husband had left her, her children had grown, but Sandy was always there, loving, uncritical, glad to see her—a living link with the happier memories, someone there for her at the end of a long, hard day. Sandy even provided the incentive to go out regularly, so for her, losing him was losing much more than I, as a non-doggy person, could have imagined. Sandy even gave a final, loving, gift. His death helped my client to mourn the other losses in her life, which she had put off grieving for. This may seem like a small example, yet I think it gives a sense of how a counsellor can gain from the experience of empathy: it is not a one-way process.

Is your client ready for counselling?

This is an important point that is sometimes overlooked. The client's state of mind, beliefs about counselling, her understanding of it and her perceptions of your role are all-important. Has she been 'sent'—in other words, has the decision been made by someone else? Has she been strongly 'advised'? Is counselling seen as part of a disciplinary function, or as some compulsory improvement programme? If your client comes in the hope that you, 'O wise and wonderful person', will give him the magic, painless answer to the pain and confusion of his life, you are in for a difficult time. Perhaps he simply wants you to make 'them' or 'her' behave differently towards him, or just to wave your magic wand like a fairy godmother and transform his life. Unfortunately, such transformations are short-lived and the return to reality is likely to be distressing, with anger and blame flying about freely!

No one wants to feel that they have to change because someone else says so, and if overpersuaded or even forced into counselling, it is unlikely that anything helpful or positive will result. Remember, counselling is another of those activities best and most effectively undertaken by consenting adults in private. (Counselling children is a specialised skill and they need to be aware of and consent to the work as far as they are able.) The issue of working with involuntary clients is a complicated one. I shall cover it in Chapter Eight (p. 96).

Meet your first client

Your first client is about to arrive—how do you feel? You are feeling uncomfortable, anxious?

Good! This shows that you are noticing your own feelings and responses and are aware of how important the work is.

Concerned about your competence and ability?

Good again, because it means you are willing to review your own performance and monitor your own competence.

Worried about what the client will expect of you?

Good again, because you are ready to focus on what the client will bring and you realise that you don't know what that is. Your mind is open, you are willing to be told how it is, by the expert on his own feelings and experience—the client.

I find it helpful regularly to put myself in new situations and feel the uncertainty, vulnerability and discomfort of not knowing what to expect, and experience the fear of making a fool of myself. This makes me less likely to offer well-meant reassurances like, 'Don't worry, you won't shock me . . .' or, 'I've heard it all before', or, 'That's nothing, you should hear what happened to my cousin's friend'.

Hearing this sort of comment, a client can feel like just another bit of your day and a not very interesting one at that. It may well be a difficulty you have often encountered or one whose solution is obvious.

If it felt like that to your client, he would not be taking the risky step of asking for help. If it was just a question of offering a standard commonsense right answer, very few people would need counselling and we counsellors would not need training and supervision.

Another point about treating the problem as common is that it leaves out the individual element, the feelings and reactions of the person who has come to you. Divorce is very common but that does not take away the pain and sadness that the individuals involved might feel. It would be wrong to assume that sadness is the only reaction—for some people there is relief or even joy. There might be 1,000,000+ unemployed people depending on how you count them, but each one has his or her own unique feelings and reactions to the experience, as well as maybe having some in common.

Talking to a stranger, however good and competent, is making yourself vulnerable. This takes a lot of courage and so does admitting that you need help. For many people there has to be a lot of pain and confusion in their lives before they take this step. The pain of seeking help, the pain involved in looking at difficult areas in their lives and the pain of changing all have to be outweighed by the agony of continuing as they are. They may have tried to work things out alone or with varying amounts of help and support from friends and family, or they may feel that the problem is too bad to share with anyone close to them.

So the client will be feeling some distress and confusion, to which will be added apprehension and anxiety about counselling. Most people fear the unknown and many of us feel uncomfortable with officials. If you have an official or statutory role, this may increase the client's apprehension.

It will help both of you if you can relax and concentrate on welcoming your client. Greet him by name and confirm who you are—people often fail to grasp details like the name of a helper when under stress. Offer a place for coats and umbrellas, but don't insist on taking a coat or jacket. Some people feel safer with an added layer of protection around them! In time your gentle warmth will help him thaw out as far as feels safe. Take the time to explain the boundaries of your role. This is where your earlier work will begin to pay off. You will be clear in your mind about the conditions in which you can work and what you can offer, so your attention can be focused on what your client has to say about the following questions:

- What does he want or expect from these sessions?
- Does it match what you feel you can offer?
- How often and for how long will you meet?
- Is there a fee?
- What notes will you keep and who will have access to them?
- Who will you discuss the work with—your supervisor? Others?
- In what circumstances will you break confidentiality?
- What was your training and what sort of help can you offer?
- What are the arrangements for changing or cancelling an appointment? Is there a fee for missed appointments?
- Are you available between appointments? Can you be contacted at home, in the evenings or at weekends?

If you are too shy or reluctant to seem 'hard' in case you come over as uncaring, you risk causing problems later. For example, if you say, wanting to be kind and supportive, 'You can phone me any time,' and they do, you may find yourself feeling more and more resentful. This will get in the way of your being helpful and, even if you don't boil over, your resentment will leak out and your client will feel it. She may then decide that you are not sincere or reliable. I find that it is simpler in the end to be honest and offer only what I really want to give wholeheartedly, then it is a free gift without a bill of gratitude for the client to pay later. Do not be trapped by some image of a good helper. Think about what you need, too. This is a professional requirement for counsellors and written into their code of ethics.

Can you counsel your family?
No, you are too close and may become part of the problem—if not already! However, you can use listening skills and the core conditions to improve your communications and relationships. Your own personal growth as a counsellor can have positive spin-offs for your family, too.

Can you counsel friends?

The situation of listening to friends is complex and we shall explore it more fully later in Chapter Nine (p. 113). Many of the above conditions still apply. You might like to write down those you feel would not apply, and why.

3   Starting to Listen

Now you have seated and greeted your client and laid down the boundaries, it is time to begin listening. This is a simple-sounding task—many of us like to think we are good listeners. Just sitting and listening sounds like one of those dream jobs like mattress tester or taster in a brewery.

'You don't give advice, you don't tell people what to do, you don't share your experience with them. What do you do, then?'

The short answer is, 'Mostly just listen' (the long answer is book length.)

'And you get paid for that?'

There are many situations in which we listen to each other, with varying degrees of usefulness. You might like to list a few, including social and family situations. Here is my list:

Listening with half an ear
Mechanical auto-pilot
Listening to prove a theory
Scanning or surveying, screening or diagnosing
Me too: sharing or matching experiences, bonding
Gossiping
Sympathetic (expressing warmth and concern)
Compare and contrast (exploring differences)
Information/evidence gathering (useful, shows interest; can be misunderstood)
Focused attention (structure that is for the client to use, leaves counsellor open to surprise)

All these types have their uses and/or pleasures. How many different kinds of listening are you aware of doing? Do you listen differently with different people or subjects? You might like to jot down some brief thoughts about these questions.

Helpful listening is different because its purpose is to focus on the needs and feelings of one person, the client. There may be elements in common with some of the others, for example information gathering, but the whole point is that attention is centred on the client.

Counselling is hard work but at its best it is like invisible mending: the better your work the less visible it is. If your client feels that 'what happened was I talked a lot and things got clearer but you (the counsellor) didn't tell me anything', then you can feel pleased that the client owns the changes. You may smile wryly to yourself, aware of how much skill and effort went into helping him to get things clear, and the struggle you had to stay out of the way of the process.

How is counselling listening different?

The kind of listening that is used in counselling is different in several ways. It is deliberate, it is focused, it is inclusive rather than selective. It involves listening to feelings as well as facts, listening to unspoken thoughts expressed in body language as well as silences and pauses.

Listening in the counselling sense is done with the head, heart and gut. And of course the eyes and ears.

Hearing more than the words

The ears are fine-tuned, picking up changes in speech patterns, rhythms, pauses and differences in tone and volume. You are listening to the voice as well as the words. The human voice is a sensitive instrument and can carry many delicate shades of meaning. For example, just a simple greeting—'Hello, how are you?'—can be understood to have different meanings by the way it is said. I could be uninterested but polite, or any shade of meaning up to warm, concerned, glad to see you. Just the words on the page would give you no clue to this; you would need other information before you could decide.

Take a few minutes to write down a list of the sort of information you would need. Concentrate on what you would learn if you heard my voice but could not see me, perhaps during a phone conversation.

You may have listed things like tone of voice, the emphasis or stress put on certain words, the rhythm of speech and, perhaps less easy to explain, a sense of emotion felt by the speaker and how you felt on hearing the voice. This latter sense is a very important one to notice and develop.

Now you have a list of the sort of information that you can get from a voice, quite apart from the simple meaning of the words it utters. This is the kind of data you will be gathering and assessing while you are listening to your client.

Tuning in

As a listener you need to tune in to the client's choice of words and be aware of how he uses them. Are some feelings described more fully than others? What words or images does he use to describe his feelings and experiences? Does this language differ from the way he talks about facts? How does he talk about feelings—easily or painfully? Are some feelings easier for him to talk about than others? Does he tend to underplay painful feelings, or speak about them at great length? Someone who is feeling very depressed might simply describe himself as 'a bit down', but this might be part of a lifetime's habit of minimising his feelings.

Does he carefully detail everything that he talks about or is he vague? Does he wander and ramble from the point? Does he find some things harder to talk about than others or is he not really comfortable with talking much?

You might like to think of people you know well and consider whether they all use words in the same way. Think about how they express feelings in words.

You might also like to extend your awareness to characters on TV or to casual, everyday conversations, and record your observations in your notebook. How was the feeling expressed through the choice of words, the tone of voice or in other ways?

Concentration, attention, silence and memory

These are all listening skills, and they do become easier as you continue to work with them. If you find any or all of them difficult, do not be discouraged! Identifying and acknowledging that you have a difficulty is the first important step to overcoming it. It is an encouraging sign of your self-awareness as a listener. The ability to be honest with yourself about your level of skill and competence is a very valuable asset for any counsellor. These listening skills will all develop with practice, so do not rush yourself. They will come; be patient and encouraging with yourself.

Memory

I think memory is particularly important as I feel that taking notes during a session is unhelpful. It can make the client feel nervous or self-conscious and it makes it difficult to give all your attention to what is being said now if you are trying to write down what was said two minutes ago. Another disadvantage of writing is that it occupies your eyes and robs you of potentially valuable information. It also makes eye contact difficult and might interfere with the development of a comfortable silence.

Silence

Silence can feel difficult or uncomfortable at first, but it can be very healing and powerful. A working silence is where the client is thinking deeply or reliving old feelings, or pondering new insights he is not yet ready to share. Please respect this working silence.

If the silence is uncomfortable for your client you might try to encourage him to speak. How would you know if he was uncomfortable? Think of someone you know well: how does she convey discomfort or distress without speaking? She communicates her distress by using her unique body language. Is this different from the signals you use to convey distress? Yet again we come back to the fact that each of us has a different feeling language, both spoken and unspoken. As counsellors we need quickly to pick up our client's language so that we can respond to him sensitively. If the silence is uncomfortable for you, you need to put up with it and afterwards think about why you felt that way. You might want to talk about it with a colleague or take the problem to your supervisor.

Attention
This is a difficult skill, particularly as you have to pay attention to several different things at once:

1　What your client is saying.
2　The facts.
3　The words used.
4　Body language (more detail in Chapter Four).
5　Voice tone, rhythm, volume, pitch.
6　The feelings spoken and unspoken.
7　Any relevant information you already have.
8　Any relevant theory.
9　How relaxed or tense your client is.
10　The environment noise comfort/discomfort.
11　The time.
12　Your own feelings of comfort/discomfort.
13　Monitoring your own performance, concentration, etc.
14　Any distress of your own that the client's words may reactivate.
15　Concern for the client.
16　Concern for the client's safety or for the safety of yourself or others.
17　Awareness of the need for supervision.
18　Awareness of the need for action.

As you can see, there is a lot to do while you are just sitting there! But please don't be put off. It does become easier with practice to keep most of the balls in the air most of the time.

Can you develop these skills?

You may be wondering whether you can develop these skills and my belief is that you can, just as we can all dance or respond to music in some way and can develop our understanding and appreciation of it, which in turn increases our enjoyment. So, too, we can all develop our listening skills. We may not want to be on *Come Dancing*, but be happy to enjoy ourselves at a party or disco with confidence in our improved ability. You may want to become a professional counsellor and this book may be just a small step on your way, or you may want to bring in counselling skills to enrich the work you love. The amount of time and energy you put in to developing these skills will depend on how important they are to you.

Where do you start listening from?

The best starting point is the client's. Sometimes people need a little encouragement and you might prompt them with something like: 'What feels the most difficult thing about your situation?' or 'What made you decide that you needed to talk to someone?' Sometimes you might just say that you are ready to listen to whatever they need to talk about in whatever order it comes. Then your hard work begins.

I suggest that you listen with as few interruptions as you can manage until you feel that there is a natural pause or that you cannot hold any more detail in your head. Then offer a tentative summary of what has been said and ask if you have 'got it right'. Never be afraid of getting it wrong so long as you are open to being corrected by the expert (the client). If you have got it right, good; if the client corrects you or explains further, also good. Then listen again and keep checking that you are in tune with the speaker. If he finds it hard to speak, and even if he doesn't and you want

to let him know that he has your attention, you can offer
encouragement without interrupting his flow by making
encouraging murmurs or nodding, giving eye contact, looking and being interested.

Can you think of other ways of letting your client know
that you are still listening and interested, without speaking?

Concentrated attention

You may find it hard to picture this process in action and
might like to practise. Working with a friend, ask her to talk
for five minutes about something that interests her but
which has no very strong feelings attached to it. If you were
on a basic first aid course, just beginning to cover heart
massage and the kiss of life, you would not rush up to
someone who had collapsed in the street and whip out your
penknife and offer to practise open heart surgery! However,
you might well practise finding and counting the pulse of as
many friends and relatives as you could. Would you let
someone practise bandaging your newly broken arm? No,
but you might let them try the technique on your unin-
jured one. Feelings are powerful and potentially explosive
material, to be handled with care, and you will both feel
more relaxed if you know that you are practising on non-
sensitive material. You won't risk hurting your friend by
being clumsy or feeling inadequate to deal with the revelation of a twenty-year-old secret before you have developed
the skills and strength to hold it.

While your friend is speaking, your job is to try to retain
the main points of her story, so that you can check it with
her afterwards, and also to notice what you yourself are
thinking and feeling. An advanced form of this exercise is
also to notice how she is sitting and how often she shifts
position. When you feel ready you can add noticing her
choice of words and begin to monitor how she describes her
feelings. Then you might begin noticing your own physical
comfort and monitoring your level of concentration.

This work will obviously take place over a period of

time, during which you will add new elements to notice as you feel confident and comfortable to do so. You might do this with a number of willing victims, and you might also choose to practise with television programmes, focusing on one individual and, if you have the use of a video recorder, checking your accuracy. Take the time to practise these skills; a confident, relaxed counsellor makes for a more relaxed, secure client.

Recording your observations

You will develop your own note-taking style, or you may be expected to follow a workplace or organisational style. These are some of the points I find important to note:

It is good to get into the habit of writing your notes as soon as possible after your client has left, remembering to record feelings as well as facts. Has the interview had a theme? Was your client responding differently? Was there any significant change, new information, new problems raised? Is there something you need to follow up, prepare before your next meeting? Have you any concerns, anything you need to take to supervision?

One way to write up your results is in columns—one for the content (the facts and the details of what was said), two for your feelings and thoughts and what you noticed about yourself, such as posture and so on, and a fourth for what you observed about your client:

Facts	Own feelings	Own thoughts	Observations of client
what is being said	how you feel, body language	notice own thoughts	voice tone, words used, feelings? Body language

Please be patient with yourself as you develop these skills. Counselling is hard work, although hopefully most of the effort is invisible to our clients.

When working on the listening exercise you may have become aware of how you encouraged your practice client to continue. Did you find yourself nodding, smiling, making mmmm noises, leaning forward and giving good eye contact? These are all useful ways of encouraging someone to continue talking, without interrupting the flow of her story. Notice which techniques you use and then try out some of those that you don't use as frequently. Eye contact is a delicate art: it can be very encouraging and can convey real warmth and interest, but it can also feel intrusive, even menacing.

People vary, both personally and culturally, in the amount of eye contact with which they feel comfortable. In what circumstances do you use eye contact? How do you feel about a relative stranger looking deep into your eyes without an ophthalmoscope? Have you ever felt threatened by lack of eye contact? What about the sexual and intimate aspects of eye contact? You might like to consider these points, perhaps writing about them in your notebook or discussing them with others.

It can be a useful exercise to try listening with varying degrees of eye contact, but if you decide to do this, please work with someone who understands what you are attempting to do. Make sure that she is not going to talk about anything about which she feels sensitive. I have done this exercise with groups, all of whom knew it was a training exercise and that they were going to talk about unimportant things. Even in these circumstances feelings ran high. It would be interesting to note which caused more discomfort to you or your client—too much or too little eye contact. Even more interesting would be to discuss the reasons why, and the sort of feelings that came up, both for listener and speaker.

Helping someone to talk

Encouraging someone to talk is also a skill, and the attitudes we have discussed really are effective. There is no better encouragement to talk than feeling that someone really wants to listen. If what you have to say is painful, you need to feel safe and that takes time. As a counsellor you must feel that you want to hear whatever the client needs to tell you, and must feel confident in your ability to 'take it'.

Time

You need to feel that you have the time to listen. So another awareness that you will need to develop is that of time.

Interruptions

As counsellor you should feel secure from interruption. Remember that your client may be sitting there feeling emotionally naked: you can't relax and accept that situation unless you are confident of your privacy.

Noises from outside can be disregarded if you know that no one is going to barge in. I work from home and am aware of my two daughters when they are in the house. I know that they will not interrupt my work because they under-stand what counselling is. When they were smaller (I am a single parent) we had a simple yardstick to decide whether an interruption was essential—severe bleeding that would not stop (they were competent to deal with scrapes and minor nose-bleeds) or burglars breaking in!

I am very fortunate to have sensible, competent daughters who feel they are contributing to earning our living by accepting the occasional disadvantages of my working from home. I mention this to illustrate my point about the need for interruption-free privacy. I could not concentrate if I was anxious about being interrupted or if I felt that I would not be made aware of a real emergency. This way I can deal with my awareness of my daughters, notice the distant sounds of them in the house and carry on working.

Are there arrangements or agreements you would have to make to help you work?

What if it never happened to you?

You might feel hesitant about listening to someone who has had experiences that you have not, but you could not possibly have had personal experience of all the problems you will hear. This need not get in the way of your being helpful. On the contrary, believing that you know how someone else feels because it happened to you can make it difficult for you to hear and understand how it was for him. To acknowledge that you do not know how he felt about his experience (whether or not you have had a similar one) enables you to learn from the expert on his experience, the client himself. Be honest about not knowing and be open to finding out. You are aiming to be an expert listener, not an expert in all painful life experiences.

This does not mean that you should not learn all you can or that theory is useless. But I believe that theories should be examined to see how they are of use to a particular person and how they might help in understanding what is happening as the client tries to make sense of his experiences. An example of useful theory is the considerable amount of information available about the processes of grief and loss. If your client is exploring an area that is unfamiliar to you, take the opportunity to learn more about the subject, both the theory and its relevance to the real experience of your client.

Is an issue beyond your current skill?

You need to monitor the limits of your ability. If an experience is beyond your skill to work with, you need to discuss this sensitively with your client. To give an example, if your client has been sexually abused in childhood and wants to work to heal the damage, this is a situation in which you should very carefully consider referral to a more experienced practitioner. You and your client will need to decide together how you can support her in finding more experienced or skilled help. You can also offer to be there to listen supportively, at least until she feels the new helping relationship is established. The decision about whether or not you should refer on and whether or not your client needs more skilled help is one in which your supervisor can be of immense help to you. It is a difficult situation and of course you will avoid it happening if you can, possibly by making clear from the outset what you feel able to offer and ensuring that clients and colleagues understand exactly what you feel you can do.

4   Watch the Body Speak!

A lot of feeling is expressed through our bodies and a great deal is held in. As a counsellor it is very important that you learn to 'read' this body language, but you need to learn a new language for each person you work with. Yes, there are some general rules—for example, muscle tension usually indicates strong, often uncomfortable feelings being held in—but like dreams and symbols, everyone has a personal body language. Counsellors therefore need to spend time making an individual emotions/body language 'dictionary' for each client, with a section for the sort of words the individual uses to describe or talk about his or her feelings.

EXERCISE: BODY LANGUAGE DESCRIPTION
How well do you know your own body language? How aware are you of the way you describe your feelings? Timing yourself, take five minutes, just for fun, and see how many common phrases or sayings you can write down relating to feelings and the body. These can include bodily symptoms—for example, calling someone a pain in the neck. If you prefer you can make a picture or diagram to illustrate this topic.

EXERCISE: BODY LANGUAGE AND YOU
This needs help from a friend. Lie down on a large piece of paper (wall lining paper will be fine), and get someone to draw round you. Now fill in the outline in any way you choose—wild streaks of colour, collage cut-out words, drawn or painted patterns. Have fun, because this work will represent how you feel about your body—good, I hope!

Do not take too long to think about what you are going to do, just do it.

You might want to think about the result, however. What does it show you about how you feel about yourself? Are there any surprises, shocks? Did your actual shape surprise you? Do you want to use this in your listening practice, or write about it in your journal?

If the whole body seems too much to tackle, you could do the following exercise (or you might want to do it as well, for its own sake).

Draw round your bare foot and decorate the drawing (as in the whole body exercise). You might also write a thank you letter or letter of complaint to or from your foot.

I hope the exercises were fun and have given you some food for thought. They are equally useful as tools to help clients express thoughts and feelings about their bodies. I hope, too, that the exercises have made the links between body and feelings clearer for you.

The client's point of view
You might find it helpful to note whether or not clients tend to discount or minimise their feelings. An example might be:

'Well, yes, I am a bit concerned about the court order and the eviction and the bailiff's visit, and it was rather worrying to be told that I've got to have my leg amputated. But at least it's only one leg! I know lots of people have worse troubles than mine.'

This person consistently underplays her feelings and tries to keep cheerful. She may well be severely depressed and unable to let it show or ask for help. So when she says she is rather worried, her meaning will be different from that of the following person:

'I've had a dreadful day. I missed the bus and had to wait twenty minutes for the next in a leaky bus shelter in the pouring rain, and this really unpleasant-looking man was waiting, too. I just felt so anxious! Then this red Cortina drove right through this big muddy puddle and soaked me, and . . .'

Yet both of these people have felt real distress. Perhaps they have different distress thresholds.

The worst thing that has ever happened to you is just that—the worst thing YOU have yet experienced—whether it is standing in a check-out queue on Christmas Eve and discovering that you have lost your purse and car keys and don't know anyone you could ask for help, or being told that you are about to be made homeless or that you or someone you love is suffering from a deadly disease.

The point I am trying to make is that there is no value in comparing your client's distress with your own or anyone else's: this would amount to judging their feelings by some scale or rule book. The only rule to go by is, how did this feel to the individual? If his feelings are accepted, he can move on to place them in a wider perspective later, when he has made sense of the experience in his own way. People have the right to feel what they feel without denying or diminishing someone else's painful experience or having their own discounted as less than the other person's.

Learning body language
Just as we express emotions differently from each other in words, so we express emotions differently with our bodies. What does that particular smile mean in this client's language—nervousness, anxiety to please, fear, hostility, shy pleasure? I don't know, so I watch, listen and, when in doubt, ask the expert, the client. It is more useful to describe what you can see without sticking a definite label on it. Ask:

'I noticed you moved your shoulders in a sort of shrugging motion just then. I was wondering what it meant?' Or, 'When you were talking about how sad you were feeling, your mouth was moving as if you were smiling and I wondered what you were feeling.' Or, 'When you were talking so calmly just then, I noticed your hands repeatedly closing tightly and opening again. You have told me about some things that happened to you, that to me sound very painful. I wonder how you feel about them?'

Be sensitive
It is unhelpful and just plain rude to tell someone else how or what she feels. Yes, you may be right, but that might only make things worse. Imagine feeling that your counsellor sees you as such a pathetic person that you can't even be trusted to know what you feel!

I think that is disabling, and one of the important tasks of counselling is to help the client feel stronger and more competent—more able, not less.

Nor does this labelling of her feelings with you as the expert seem very respectful of her. Many people coming for counselling are feeling bad about themselves, finding it hard to work their way through their troubles. The very last thing they need is what feels like proof that they can't trust themselves or their own judgement. Counsellors who need to demonstrate how right and clever and insightful they are have a problem and are adding to their clients' problems.

Trust your client
So often the focus is only on building the client's trust in the counsellor. Yes, this is important—how desperate or damaged would *you* have to be to show the worst, most painful parts of yourself and your life to a comparative stranger? But equally important is the counsellor's trust in the client. I don't work well if I feel physically unsafe or if I feel that the client is not ready, willing and able to work with me. Sometimes I need to remind myself of my basic beliefs in people's capacity to change and grow when they choose to. Sometimes I have to struggle to see the person behind the labels, to listen to who they are now and trust myself and them and that spark of eternal light within us both.

Touching

It can seem the most natural and comforting of gestures to reach out and touch someone's hand, to hold a distressed person comfortingly in your arms. It can also feel invasive, intrusive, uncomfortable, false, unnatural.

The difference lies in our 'touching history', the experiences we have had of touching and being touched; the sense we have made of that history, and what we have been taught, often without words, about touch. This not only varies from culture to culture but from family to family.

What were you taught about touching when you were a child? Did you belong to a family of natural 'touchers' who hugged frequently and spontaneously? Was a kiss a natural greeting and goodbye? Is it natural now for you to use touch to communicate warmth, friendly interest and concern?

Or did you grow up in a more reserved family, one which seldom displayed their affection for each other in physical ways, which hated to be 'fussed over' physically? Do you find that it is still more natural for you to express your closeness and concern and interest in words or through your thoughtful actions, rather than through touch?

Neither family style is wrong. As always, what matters is that the way you are works for you and those close to you. However, problems can arise when a family of non-touchers—let's call them the Catts—marries into a family of enthusiastic touchers—we will call them the Doggs. The couple themselves may not have too many problems initially. After all, both sides agree on the rightness of close physical contact between partners. (The Catts would reserve this for what they would consider private and appropriate moments.) The problem is first felt by the various in-laws. Each side is filled with good intentions, trying in their own 'right' and 'natural' ways to get to know their new relatives.

The poor Doggs feel rejected by the 'cold', reserved Catts—'There is no getting close to them, they are so standoffish.' The unfortunate Catts feel overwhelmed and threatened by the 'over-enthusiastic' physical friendliness of the Doggs—'Smarmy Doggs, they are all over you like a rash.'

As you can see, there is a basic misunderstanding here, each side assuming that their 'natural' way to behave is the norm. They might never be completely comfortable together, but if they could accept the other view as equally 'natural', they would get on better.

What do you think would happen in a counselling situation if a distressed Catt was offered comfort, a touch or pat or hug, by a Dogg counsellor? What would happen if the roles were reversed—a distressed Dogg expecting a warm physical gesture of comfort from a Catt counsellor?

This is just another part of your client's individual body language that you have to learn: how he uses touch, what meaning it has for him. Then, if there is a big mismatch, you have something to think through, to work on in your journal and to use in listening practice or group discussion.

The dilemma for Dogg counsellors is how to find a way to express warmth in less physical ways, and for the Catt counsellor to consider expanding her range appropriately, too. Remember congruence—it will not work if you do not really want to do it. It is fine for Catts to stay Catts and Doggs to stay Doggs, but perhaps Catts and Doggs with a wider perspective than before and a somewhat enlarged range of responses.

The wrong sort of touch
There is another important thing to say about 'touching histories'. Some clients' histories will include experiences of being physically hurt, beaten or sexually abused. This will have had a profound effect on how they experience touch and the meaning it has for them.

You may not be told this initially. Look for body signals that would indicate it. A stiffening or jerking back as a response to the counsellor leaning forward, for example, could be a clue. An unnatural stillness, almost a frozen stillness, as a response to a touch on the hand could be another indicator. These could be seen as a sort of basic response to a perceived threat—to either run away (jerk back) or freeze into the background in the hope of being overlooked. This latter response is also often adopted by abused children who feel powerless to avoid or escape, so withdraw into themselves, shut down, or freeze, until 'it' is over.

So use touch sparingly, sensitively. Always signal your intention and move slowly, even when offering a gentle touch on the hand or elbow. Use touch in a way that fits your natural style, and primarily in a way that is comfortable for your client.

Sex and counselling
No sex, please, we are counsellors! It is always unethical and, I think, abusive for counsellors to have a sexual relationship with a client.

Can you think why there is this restriction?

Could there be exceptions to this rule?

Could you imagine this issue ever being a problem for you?

What could you do, what *would* you do? Would you seek help?

Is this only a problem for male therapists/counsellors?

Why the restriction?
There is a special warmth, trust and closeness that can and should develop between counsellor and client. This can feel very like a sort of love, and perhaps it is. But it is a kind of love, a special intimacy, that remains focused on the needs of the client.

What kind of sexual relationship would it be that ignored the needs of one person to fulfil the needs of the other? Yes, an abusive one! The sad thing about a sexual relationship between counsellor and client is that the focus moves from the needs of the client to the needs of the counsellor. Even though the client may seem to want the relationship to become sexual, it is not helpful or healthy for him. Issues of power and dependence arise. Why does the counsellor need this relationship to be sexual? Does she want or need to be looked up to or depended on, or to feel in control?

It is not unusual for clients to feel strongly attracted to their counsellor, to feel dependent, willing to please, even to act as if they want a sexual relationship. I feel very strongly that this vulnerability on the clients' part means that we as counsellors have a heavy responsibility to protect them.

This is particularly true of clients who have been abused. They are especially vulnerable, and sometimes, in their attempt to heal old wounds, may act in what can be seen as a 'seductive' way. This is because the only way they know to attract or please or placate someone who is important to them is by being sexual; and because, even if they are unaware of it, they are looking for an experience of being cared for which does not include being exploited.

To have a sexual relationship with a client who has been abused in the past is to repeat and reinforce that damaging experience. It can feel like incest and involves a similar breach of trust.

The current BAC guidelines state that it is unethical to have a sexual relationship with a client, but the guidance on relationships with ex-clients is more flexible. My own feeling is that a sexual relationship with a client is never possible, even years later.

This does not mean that counsellors have no sexual feelings. The difference between an ethical counsellor and an abusive counsellor is what he or she does about those feelings. This is the sort of situation in which good supportive supervision is vital.

What to do

If you are strongly attracted to your client, work on it in supervision; there may be useful information to be mined on the relationship. Look also at your own life, and remember the maxim about not going shopping when you are hungry!

Look at your closest relationships, look at yourself. Why is this situation arising? Is this a frequent problem for you? A one-off, a response to old, unfinished business of your own? Does the client remind you of someone? What unmet need of yours is pulling at you? Get it sorted, urgently.

Whose problem?

This is a problem for both male and female counsellors. Female counsellors may find the issue arising with clients who have had sexually abusive experiences with women in their childhoods. Clients of the same sex can also invoke this response in their counsellors, or can behave towards them in ways that indicate a need to experience a non-abusive intimate relationship in which, this time, their trust is not betrayed.

And both sexes are vulnerable when their resources are low, when their own relationships are going through difficulties, when they feel lonely or depleted. We need to take care of ourselves.

Do you think it couldn't happen to you? Why? Aren't you human, too? If you believe that it couldn't or shouldn't happen to you, then you will be less able to deal with it sensibly. Feelings are not the same as actions; if you allow yourself to look honestly at your feelings you can take appropriate action, but if you deny your feelings they may act without guidance or control.

If you are wondering whether I have ever had sexual feelings towards a client, yes I have. And very shocked I was, too! I had thought that female counsellors were immune. I read with new eyes all the excuses and self-justifications of counsellors who had broken this taboo. It was too close to home for comfort (read *Sex in the Forbidden Zone* by Peter Rudder, Unwin, 1990). It was very disconcerting to find how easy it would be to fall into that trap. Thank heaven for a good supervisor and supportive colleagues. No, I never said or did anything to express these feelings, but I certainly had them. Oddly enough, once I had talked about them in supervision and to my support group they became much more manageable. When I looked at what lay behind them and worked on them both personally and with what my client's behaviours were telling me about his history and his needs from the counselling relationship, I was able to act appropriately for myself and for my client. It was a surprising, painful and very valuable experience.

Appropriate warmth
You do not have to be cold and distant with your client: think about appropriate warmth, trust and respect. One of the greatest gifts you can give an abused client is the experience of warmth and non-possessive 'love', enabling him to prove for himself that he can trust himself and others, that there can be closeness without abuse.

'Love' in counselling
Counselling is a warm and intimate relationship, perhaps the first that your client has experienced. Strong, positive feelings are natural, and your client may interpret them as 'being in love'. This is not unusual. You need not panic or withdraw, or become more distant (but it is always a good idea to talk over the situation in supervision, and to look at the relationship and your reactions and responses). If you have been working within your boundaries, you can focus on how to deal with this in the way that is most helpful for your client. Your boundaries should include a clear understanding of the difference between a counselling relationship and a friendship or romantic relationship.

You might like to pause here and clarify for yourself what these differences are, the chief one being the question of whose needs are to be met in the counselling relationship. All other relationships are two-way and are meant to be so, but although a counselling relationship moves towards equality of power and is mutual in trust and respect, it is built around only one person's needs and concerns—the client's.

Can you define 'love'?
Are there different kinds of 'love'? I believe that there are many sorts of 'love' apart from the obvious romantic love and nurturing or parental love. There is the 'love' that means infatuation or need or, simply, sexual desire (to call this on its own 'love' is a prudery similar to the Victorian passion for covering piano legs). There is the sort of 'love' which is really gratitude out of proportion; there is a feeling, often called love, that is warmth, familiarity, habit, affection; and there is a feeling of respect and admiration that acknowledges the fine qualities in the other person, and rejoices in them. In this last sense I often feel love for my clients. It is a feeling that confers no obligation on the person loved, but gives me the happiness of rejoicing with them, and wishing always for their good.

And there is another sort of 'love': the yearning for good qualities which you feel you do not possess. Clients often see in us the reflection of their own potential. They cannot believe that these good characteristics could belong to them, so, like their self-respect and confidence, they 'give' them to their counsellor. The counsellor's job is to keep them safe until the client can own them and take them back.

What would you do if a client said she had fallen in love with you?
Would it make a difference to you if she was the same sex? Or the opposite sex, but straight while you were gay/lesbian? Or the opposite sex and both of you straight?
Imagine how you would handle such situations. Use your journal and perhaps talk it through in a group of colleagues, or you might find that you have material for your one-to-one listening practice.

Your client is in love with you

Be sensitive, be clear. Remember your boundaries. You can acknowledge her feelings without leaving her in any doubt that your relationship will not become romantic or sexual. You can show that you value the gift she has offered you, her trust and vulnerability, without abusing it or putting her down. You can look together at all the good things you have achieved in the relationship, all the work you have done together. It is not surprising if such an intimate and worthwhile relationship should raise strong feelings. You can celebrate your client's capacity to have loving feelings, to be comfortable in an intimate relationship, perhaps for the first time. This can be a major gain for her.

5 Coping with Emotions

You may be wondering what will happen during the counselling process and whether you will be able to cope. You
may run through all sorts of disastrous scenes in your head.
It is natural to be concerned about the unknown, and to feel
anxious about being with and witnessing someone in pain.
If you feel worried about hearing sad and painful things,
that is human and acceptable. What matters is how you deal
with your own feelings, in order to keep them out of your
client's way. When you have done this you can begin to
help your client.

Be kind to yourself, take time to prepare yourself and to
develop coping skills. Learn more about emotions, become
more comfortable with the varying ways people express
them. Be patient and encouraging to yourself.

Facts or feelings
Many of us feel we could not cope with other people freely
expressing their pain. This may apply to all painful feelings
or to particular ones. We might feel able to hear the facts of
the story, but unable to cope with visible emotion. For some
people this is reversed: they can cope with the feelings but
find it hard to cope with the detail.

Which would you find hardest?
Why?
Is there anything you need to do to develop your ability
to listen and be with clients who are telling a painful part of
their story; or who are expressing grief and rage?

You can use these questions to ponder on in private, or you
might find it more helpful to explore them in your journal.

Developing the ability to cope
The first step is to know which aspect you find more difficult. Then you need to work on why, and you might need some help with this. It can be rather like trying to see the middle of the back of your neck—a friend with a mirror can be a real help. This can make excellent material for counselling listening practice.

When you understand why you find a particular emotion difficult, you can begin to work. Begin to work for yourself, on yourself; begin to find ways to let go of and heal your own old pain. You can find ways to understand and accept your history without being dominated by it. You may need to learn new ways of thinking about feelings—your own and other people's.

Some ways of thinking about the expression of feelings are more helpful to a counsellor than others.

Which ways do you think are likely to be the most helpful?

Doesn't it depend on what use and purpose you think counselling has?

Since I think that counselling is about the safe expression of feelings and their acceptance as being of equal value with facts, I believe that the ability to express and acknowledge them is of great benefit to both client and counsellor in their work together.

Avoid the cheery approach
Sometimes our instincts lead us to try and cheer someone up, or help him see things in perspective, or urge him to look for the silver lining. It happens every day among well-meaning family and friends, and even some members of the helping professions try to help in this way, but it is a trap for the unwary counsellor, leading her to act on her need to be protected from someone else's pain. It may be intended to help, but it can make the unhappy person feel misunderstood, isolated and perhaps at fault for feeling and reacting as he does. As a result his pain and fear are pushed

down, with perhaps other painful feelings added to them. There might be a superficial improvement, but months of work later with someone like me. So however helpful this 'jollying' approach may be in other circumstances, it is not helpful in counselling.

Do not 'kiss it better'

It may also be natural to want to comfort and ease someone else's pain, but it is better not to act on those feelings when you are counselling. Does this sound harsh or unkind? Counselling listening is different. Your job is not to 'make it better', but first to hear and acknowledge the pain, then to support your client in finding his own way of making it better.

Feelings are as true as facts

Feelings have their own standard of truth and may not always match the facts, or someone else's assessment of the situation. Four different people can have the same experience and feel quite differently about it. This does not mean that one of them is wrong, two are right and one half-right in what they feel. They are all 'right', since what each one feels is real and true for him or her at that time.

Knowing that people don't support how you feel, or that they think that you are unreasonable in feeling as you do, is not helpful. Let's look at one example.

A mother is knocked over while wheeling her toddler out in his buggy. She is badly injured and in a coma for many months, and meanwhile her frightened little boy has to be cared for by relatives he hardly knows. None of this is her fault, she is not to blame. However, the effects on her son are profound and lasting. As an adult he has difficulty in trusting and making relationships, although he knows that it was not his mother's fault and understands the circumstances.

Why is this not enough to mend matters? The facts are true and acknowledged, but his feelings, his experience and the sense he made of it at the time are also true and need to be recognised. He felt abandoned and betrayed, hurt, afraid and uncomforted. This was no one's fault but nonetheless real. He may need to cry and express the pain, fear, rage and despair that he felt, and have it acknowledged before he can let it go and begin to heal. The facts do not change or cancel out the feelings, or the truth of what the experience was for him.

This example may be nearer psychotherapy than counselling, but I have included it as it shows dramatically the contradictions of facts and feelings. The experience of having your pain acknowledged as real, of being allowed to feel as bad as you need to, to cry till you are ready to stop, is powerful and healing.

What if they don't stop crying?
A common fear of both new clients and new counsellors is that the person crying will not be able to stop. Well, it has not happened to me yet. What has happened is that people find a natural ending and recover in their own way, and feel better for having been able to let go. It is all about their timing, though I would never force anyone to 'let go', any more than I would try to make them stop. I trust that if people feel safe they will do what they need to do. And I trust myself to respond honestly and appropriately.

Strong feelings
This might be a good place to pause and think about strong feelings, to look at and explore your reactions and responses in the same spirit in which you did the attic exercise in Chapter Two. Again, this is not about being right or wrong in how you react, but about looking with understanding and warm acceptance at yourself, and choosing to keep reactions that suit you and possibly to change those that do not. I believe we all have a wonderful lifelong potential to change and grow happier and healthier.

Families and feelings

One way to think about the way feelings are expressed is as a form of nourishment, like food and just as essential for life. You might have come from a family which was vegan or a family which thrived on burgers and chips, or anything in between. Whatever your family eating patterns were, as an adult you will decide for yourself how you eat. If your family never ate cabbage you might never eat it now, or you might have tried it and liked it! You might eat the same diet as you did then or a completely different one, or betwixt and between. If you were taught that a certain food was good for you, for example, that sugar gives you energy and is good for shock, you might find it natural to use it in that way and give it to your children. Or you might decide as an adult to study diet and learn about healthy eating, choosing a very different diet from the one with which you grew up.

It is the same with what we were taught about the expression of feelings as we were growing up. You can choose to deal with feelings as your family did, if that works for you, or you can learn new ways that suit you better. Change takes thought and may be affected by new information.

Anger

This is a powerful emotion and one which many people are anxious about expressing. Fear of anger can come from very early experiences. If the people around us as we were growing up expressed their anger in a violent, uncontrolled way, it would be surprising if this had no lasting effect on us, but each of us tends to react to the experience in very different ways. One person might grow up to express his anger in a similarly violent, uncontrolled way and find this quite natural and unremarkable. Another might suppress feelings or expressions of anger and avoid people who gave vent to their rage. This person might also be very skilled at pleasing and placating others, avoiding arguments and confrontations. A third might have worked very hard to find a way to use her anger, to express it safely and effectively, and to teach her children to do the same. She might have tried to learn the difference between aggression and assertion.

EXERCISE: ANGER

Describe your anger. Is it quick to come to the boil and quick to cool down, or does it simmer slowly, then erupt like a volcano? Or is it more like a corrosive poison stored in a metal barrel, slowly eating its way through and leaking out of what was meant to be safe storage?

Write a short description of your anger and how you let it out (or don't).

You may prefer to draw instead. Working quickly without worrying about artistic ability, draw your anger. What shape, colour is it? Does it have a texture? If it were an animal, which would it be? Is it behind bars or running riot? Walking to heel or on a leash? If your anger were a climate or weather, or a landscape or environment or habitat, what would it look like?

You may prefer to answer these questions by writing about them. After doing this you could talk it through with, if you like, a counselling partner. Choose someone with whom you feel comfortable, someone for whom you feel trust and respect and a sense that they can safely look at this with you.

Sadness

Let us look at sadness next, the sadness that comes to us all through life. Try adapting the exercises suggested for anger, and in addition, answer the following questions:

What makes you sad?

How do you express sadness?

Does hurt or loss or disappointment cause you most sadness?

Do you feel and express sadness in the same way in every situation?

You may like to write about this in your journal or talk it through with a colleague.

Fear

For some people being afraid has to be covered with anger or with a sense of false confidence. For others being afraid means being compliant, trying to please, fitting in.

How do you react when you are afraid?

Do you react differently in different circumstances or to different fears?

What are you most afraid of?

What situations arouse fear in you?

You may also like to work on any of the other questions from the anger or sadness sections that you feel would be useful here, or you might like to do the drawing exercise described under anger.

The opportunity to learn

If, while doing any of these exercises, you feel you are touching on powerful, distressing old feelings, if you begin to feel uncomfortable physically or emotionally, do not be alarmed! This is not a sign that you are doing anything wrong or that there is anything wrong with you. It is a sign that you have uncovered an old wound, and that now might be a really good time to begin to heal it. It is in fact a healthy response, part of our wonderful healing capacity.

You could see this as a positive outcome of doing these exercises, and a very important one. If potential counsellors do not feel positive about being a client and being counselled, I think this says something quite sad about their attitude to their future clients. If you think only wimps and hopeless cases, forlorn and friendless folk, the lost souls and the inadequate need counselling, that must surely lead to an attitude towards your future clients that is disrespectful, negative, judgemental and unhelpful.

If, on the other hand, your view of counselling is that it is a helpful, useful experience from which most of us could benefit, then this positive attitude will be picked up by your clients, even if it is unspoken.

6 Emotional Needs

Listening to your client's story unfold, you will become aware of her emotional needs and how she attempts to get them met. This subject is sensitive and rich in complicated feelings and actions. We tie ourselves up in some strange knots just trying to feel lovable and worthwhile.

Basic needs

The need to feel loved, loving and of value is as basic as the need for food and water, and just as essential for our survival. Babies and children who do not have these needs met fail to grow well physically, mentally or emotionally. Adults who are starved of this emotional feeding act in ways that reflect their desperation but do not always have the desired results.

They might develop coping strategies that are self-defeating. For example, desperate, clingy neediness does not usually result in the warm, loving, sustaining relationships the 'clinger' is trying to make. As a counsellor I think you will find it helpful to have an understanding of people's emotional needs and how they attempt to satisfy them, in ways that do not always seem to make sense if we look at them logically. Feelings have a different set of rules that do make sense, although not obviously. I find it helpful to think of emotional needs as similar to the need for food and to think of love and attention as emotional food.

Emotional food

We are all born with a need for love and affection: a need to be known and valued as unique individuals, to feel loved without strings or conditions. This need is as real and as vital to our survival and growth as food or water or the air we breathe. Because we originally get these needs met through skin contact, a theory was developed in transactional analysis which described this need as 'strokes'.

Strokes

A 'stroke' is a unit of emotional nourishment. We all give and receive a variety of 'strokes', and the aim is to achieve a healthy balance of strokes given and received. These strokes can be given in words, or without words, in ways to make us feel good or bad and with or without strings or conditions attached. A smile of greeting, for example, is a positive, nonverbal and unconditional stroke. A 'telling off' is verbal, negative and conditional—that is, it is given in response to some action and is spoken in a way that is intended to make you feel uncomfortable. For further information on transactional analysis I would recommend that you read *T.A. Today* by Ian Stewart and Vann Joines (see Book List).

I have found this theory of strokes a useful way to think about emotional needs and how we get them met, and also to talk about the topic with clients. Let's look at the subject in more detail.

Just as people who are starving will eat scraps in their desperation, so people who are emotionally hungry will take whatever they can get. Anything is better than the pain of starvation, and unkind or hurtful attention is better than being ignored. Being ignored hurts, being sent to Coventry hurts. The whining toddler who whinges and cries till he gets shouted at or smacked is hungry, and emotional scraps are better than being starved of his parents' notice. Like food, we also tend to like best what we know in the emotional food we give and accept.

Getting our needs met

A very important point for counsellors is how we get our own emotional needs met. You might like to spend some time thinking about this. It could be a fruitful topic to explore in your journal or, perhaps, to discuss with colleagues.

Which of your needs do you expect to be met by counselling?

Should you expect to get any of your needs met by doing this work?

Emotional healthy eating

It is not healthy to use your clients as a source of emotional nourishment. It is comparable to advertising yourself as a restaurant and then sitting down at the table with the hungry customer. You then choose the food you like and eat the choicest bits and, having taken the lion's share, present the bill and expect a generous tip (gratitude)! If your client is vulnerable and unsure of what should happen—and many clients are—this abuse may go unchallenged. That will not make it right.

You just have to make sure that you are getting your needs met outside the counselling relationship. I have already mentioned the old saying that we should not go shopping for food when we are hungry. This is because our judgement can be affected by our need, even if we are not aware of it. This also applies to emotional 'food': do not counsel when you are emotionally hungry, it might seriously affect your judgement.

Some needs that can be met through counselling might include the need to do a worthwhile job and the need for adequate pay. The need to be a helper can be more doubtful.

I do think that it is healthy to feel satisfaction in doing a worthwhile job. To take pride in your skill and competence is not harmful to the client unless there is a weight of expectation on him to 'get better', to prove how good a counsellor you are, or an expectation of a particular outcome that meets the counsellor's own values and beliefs rather than the client's. Nor should the client be under pressure to recover to a time-scale of the counsellor's rather than his own.

There are dangers for both client and counsellor if this is the only or major source of emotional nourishment for the counsellor. If being a good helper is playing a large part in your feeling of being a decent, worthwhile human being, this needs urgent action from you. If your work is your only source of emotional feeding, you risk passing on your problem to your clients who *must* get better to prove how good their counsellor is. The counsellor needs this proof to reassure herself and to feel 'well fed', or satisfied with herself and the outcome.

EXERCISE: SOURCES OF SELF-FEEDING AND SOURCES OF FOOD
FROM OTHERS
You might find it useful to list the ways in which you are emotionally nourished—for example, by your partner, friends, lovers, children and your colleagues.

List also what nourishes you professionally, personally and environmentally.

Do you give yourself time in environments and settings that are healing for you?

Does it feel wrong to take care of and treat yourself?

List three things you could do easily, regularly and afford-ably to redress the balance. You already do three or more things regularly? Well done! Here is part of my list:

Soak in hot bath with six drops of grapefruit essential oil.
Read a bad book (mental chewing gum).
Read a book that inspires me.
Tea/breakfast in bed, a cup of tea when I come in tired.
Foot bath, foot massage.
Go out and take a look at the hills.
Give myself a hand massage.
Attend my support group.
Get lively, vigorous feedback on a course.
See someone's face light up with understanding when I've explained some tricky point.

Devise a new workshop topic.
See people blossom on a workshop.
Laugh with my friends.
A gossip and a giggle.
A night out.
Sing with my daughters.
Get/give a massage.
Window-shopping/clothes shopping
Writing poetry.
Playing Scrabble.
Occasional meals out or live entertainment.
Spiritual nourishment: silent retreat, Quaker meetings.

How long is your list? Would you like to add to it? Remember that it is all right to ask for what you need—you are improving communication and giving those who love you a gift. Yes, of course there is a risk they might say no, but you will know that you are both honestly communicating something that could improve the relationship or help you both to move on.

Valuing ourselves
Many of us find it hard to value ourselves enough to take care of our own needs. This can be because of things we learned about love and caring when we were growing up. There might also be cultural and gender influences. We might have learnt that girls look after other people's emotional needs and get their satisfaction that way, or that boys do not have emotional needs or do not express them.

What did you learn?

How useful do you find it now in helping you to get the emotional feeding you need?

If you really loved me . . .
Many of us grew up with the mistaken idea that we should never ask for what we need, that it would be selfish or demanding to do so. Some of us have the belief that

someone who really loves us will *know* without being told what we want, when we want it and how it should be offered! Some of us believe that if we love someone we should always know what they need and always meet that need in order to feel loved and valuable ourselves.

Do you share any of these beliefs?

Have they worked for you?

Many of us find that they do not work but don't know what else to do. Some of us have not managed to make them work yet but feel that if we only tried harder, if 'they' cared more, really loved us, it would work. Some of us feel very angry that what we have been taught is not working as we feel it should! Many people feel sad or resentful about this.

I have found that these beliefs do not work for me and that it is unhealthy for me to try to live by them any more. I think they come from an idea of the world as a marketplace, where even love and respect have to be bargained for. I find it more useful and effective to think of love and respect as feelings that cannot be exchanged or bartered, only freely given. If they are not a free gift they become a burden, a debt. I think it is possible to confuse a wish for certainty and security with the need to give and receive love.

Imagine that you had a plentiful supply of food which you regularly prepared, cooked and served to the people you loved. Imagine also that you never served yourself any. You might sit with an empty plate waiting for someone to notice and serve you some. If you were lucky they might, but they might not give you what you wanted. They might give you too little or the wrong thing, something to which you were allergic. Whatever happened, you would never tell them or ask for what you wanted or serve yourself. You would behave like this because of your belief that if they really loved you they would know exactly what you wanted and would give it to you without your having to ask.

Or you might be acting on your belief that you should get enough to eat from the cooking smells and the scraps! Or you might be waiting for them to feed you because of your belief that if you were a good enough cook they would feed you without your having to ask or serve yourself. Perhaps you would eat the scraps and leftovers later in the kitchen. (Do you believe that is all you deserve?) None of those behaviours would be a healthy or effective means of getting adequately fed, would they? Yet many people do just that when it comes to getting their emotional food.

I find it helpful to remember to love my neighbour as well as, not instead of or better than, myself.

If what you feel and believe, based on your own life experiences and values, is very different from this, I would not disagree with you or think my way was better than yours. If your beliefs are working for you and those close to you, then we are both lucky: we have found ways that work for us. Still, I can only speak and write from my own experience. Please take from it what is of value to you and leave the rest.

7   Developing a Fresh Point of View

During the course of your work together your client may well develop new insights into his situation. It is very important that these develop at his pace and are his insights, not yours. At times this can feel very slow and frustrating work for the listener. No, you cannot take short cuts and just tell him what is so obvious to you! It will not speed up the process, it will not help.

Telling him will break his trust in you and, more importantly, in himself. It will disable him, not help him to find his own strength. What message would you be giving him by telling him? You would be showing him that you did not believe him capable of finding his own answers, that you did not respect his individuality and integrity.

Good advice can be bad for your client
There is another good reason for not giving answers or advice: they may not be right! Or they may be good advice, useful insights and still wrong for him. Even worse if they are right and work! Worse? Yes, worse, because you have just proved to him that you are right and wise and powerful and that he needs you or someone like you to hold his hand through life. What a terrible disability for you both.

The goal of counselling is a client who feels more able, more competent, less dependent. I hope that my client will feel more confidence in his own judgement, and more self-reliant. I hope that he will feel better about himself and have more coping skills for the future. This aim means that

I accept that people flail around and fumble their way through, and may choose not to change.

My job

Clients take risks, make mistakes and learn from them. My job is to hold for them that confidence in themselves that they do not yet have. My job is to believe in their potential strength while helping them to be honest with themselves about their current abilities and resources.

What I help clients to do

To look clearly at their actions and the consequences.

To accept their current weaknesses and confusion as real and painful and changeable.

To share my understanding and acceptance of our human-ness.

We need to be accepted for all that we are

We can be strong, resourceful and fearful, weak, confused and selfish all at once. We do not have to be one and not the other. We can be full and complex and many-coloured. How often do we feel surprised at someone who shows a contradictory side? We seem to have a need for people to stay in neat, labelled boxes. He is a war hero so he is always brave. She is disabled so she is always patient and uncomplaining. He is fat and middle-aged so he can't write romantic poetry. She is plump and always the life and soul of the party.

People need to be seen in their full richness. As a counsellor I find that strong, competent people may need a safe place where they can feel weak and confused and wimpish while still being respected. Weak, fearful people need to be acknowledged for their strength (living with fear and vulnerability takes strength), actual and potential. Sometimes people cannot see their own good qualities. So they give them to me, and all they see are reflections of their inside selves. I keep these safe for them, knowing what is mine and what is theirs. When they are ready they take them back. I do not give them back, they are not mine to give. If this sounds complicated, I am sorry. It reflects an important and delicate part of the counselling relationship. It is easier to experience than describe.

Standing in
Sometimes the counselling relationship is the first healthy, honest relationship people have experienced. They may have experienced exploitation and manipulation from those close to them. They may have grown up feeling that all love has to be 'paid for'. They may have been intimidated or criticised and grown up with little trust in themselves, and they may find it difficult to trust anyone else, either. When people are carrying this sort of pain, part of their healing is learning to trust, perhaps for the first time in their lives. You may find yourself 'standing in' for important people in their past.

They may feel the need to look up to you, to depend on you for a short time. In these circumstances I try never to lose sight of the fact that I am an adult working with another adult. I find it helps to acknowledge and accept their needy feelings and also to acknowledge them as competent adults, so I talk to them about my understanding of what is happening and respect the adult in them while accepting the fearful, childlike feelings. I share 'adult' information with them, discuss their feelings and accept them as real, and together we decide how best to deal with them. I attempt to build a partnership in which we both take care of the hurt child inside them. Gradually my part in this lessens as they grow healthier and better able to heal their old hurts. It is important not to lose sight of their own adult strength and abilities even when at times these are more potential than actual.

Feelings are real and when they are acknowledged they can begin to change. Denying them doesn't make them go away, they only get stronger and have to shout louder and become more and more disruptive until they are heard and dealt with.

Developing insights and new perspectives

I want to offer an example from my own experience. This has grown and changed over time. Clients have similar processes, but the best insights may come long after counselling is finished. I am also more comfortable revealing myself than asking my clients to do so in a book.

I was born into a partially practising Catholic family (Easter duties only!). I was sent as a day girl to a convent and made my first communion and confession at the age of seven. Being a solemn child, I took it all very seriously. In those far-off times meat was forbidden on Fridays—I think it was a venial or minor sin. Now that I had just got my soul clean, as I understood it, I wanted to keep it that way. Little prig! One Friday, not long after my first communion, there was chicken stew for dinner. It smelt delicious! My favourite meal . . . I reminded my mother that it was Friday and we were not supposed to eat meat. She had forgotten and was not pleased to be reminded.

'This is what there is. You can eat it or have bread and butter,' was her response. I felt confused. It was wrong! It was not fair! The others were going to eat it, and I felt angry but could not put these feelings into words. I ate bread and butter in a spirit of virtuous suffering.

Many years later, working on other issues in counselling, this memory popped up as part of my feelings of having only myself to rely on. I was able to express some of the anger and confusion of that little girl. To be told on God's authority that something was wrong and then be faced with doing it or feeling left out and different was hard. After all, it was my parents' choice that I went to the convent and was brought up a Catholic.

After expressing that pain I was able to see that from my mother's perspective things looked different. It must have been irritating to be reminded of what she regarded as a minor matter—only a small sin. The insight I gained at this time left me feeling that what I had acquired from that episode was a greater sensitivity as a parent. I have always

worked hard to be consistent about the standards and values
I hold and teach my children. Remembering that episode, I
have tried to respect their emerging beliefs. So, in the end,
there was a gain.

Then last year I attended a workshop with Dorothy Rowe
and found myself working on this memory again. We were
asked to look at a childhood memory and see how it had
ultimately enriched us, even though the experience had been
painful at the time. I suddenly realised what a special gift I
had been given. I do not know whether or not it was inten-
tional, and unfortunately my mother is dead so I cannot talk
to her about this.

Never, since the 'day of the chicken stew', have I doubted
that I am morally responsible for my own actions. It has
always seemed natural to think things through and make up
my own mind. This, I realised, is the lasting gift of that
experience and I am glad to have it. It had become so much
a part of me that I had thought nothing of it; now I know it
was nurtured by that and other early experiences. All that
smelly stuff makes good compost and you choose what you
grow with it.

If, during my first time of working on that memory, my
therapist had offered my mother's point of view or had said
how trivial the matter really was, or that it was not a sin
now, it would not have been helpful. There was truth in all
those things, but I was not ready to hear it. Once I had
dealt with my old anger and pain, once I had gained the
perspective to see the experience as helpful to me as a
parent, I was ready to see my mother's point of view. If I
had been offered the later insight earlier, I would have
felt less confidence in my own growth. I might have felt
stupid at not having seen it for myself. It would never have
been my insight, only my therapist's 'wisdom'. I might not
have believed it, might never have felt it as a strength of
mine.

Is there an incident from your past that you could now
see differently?

Can a painful experience be the beginning of a new strength or a new ability or insight?

If so, how did you become aware of these good things developing?

You might like to explore some of these questions with colleagues in listening practice.

How can you help your clients to develop insights?

Accept that they will work at their own pace and take in only what they are ready to own. Whatever the temptation, do not offer your insights. Use open questions and comparison to help them explore a situation. You might try looking at unexpected side-effects or gains from painful experiences. Please do this only after your client has fully expressed and explored his painful feelings.

Journal questions

Clients may use journal work, too, and you may wish to adapt some of the questions we have used in this book for work with those who enjoy writing. Some may find keeping a journal very helpful. They may or may not choose to share its contents with you, but just seeing and reading what they have written for themselves is useful. Please encourage them to get a special book and pen too (if they can afford it). If they can only afford a simple exercise book, encourage them to cover it with an attractive piece of wrapping paper or with a collage. This may be of pictures on a particular theme or may consist of words of encouragement and positive messages cut from newspapers and magazines.

The journal should be special because the person writing in it is special. Your client can use it to record dreams or thoughts or to keep her own record of counselling. Many of the writing and drawing exercises I have suggested in this book could be adapted for your client's individual needs.

Angry letters and party political broadcasts
Among other helpful writing techniques is the writing of
angry letters (not to be sent) and 'Party Political Statements'. This involves getting your client to choose to write
about a problem from two or more points of view, as if each
side were a political party wanting to persuade the elec-
torate to vote for them. This is not as complicated as it may
sound. Here is a simple example.

A working woman is approaching her thirtieth birthday.
She is under biological and family pressure to start her
family. She also has important ambitions as yet unfulfilled.
Further training or even a change or direction are possible
in the near future. If she does not take these opportunities
they may not be there for her in five or ten years' time; they
might not be open to a 'mother'.

She feels strongly that she would like children while she
is young enough to enjoy them, but she believes that good
mothering is a full-time job and she also feels she needs the
stimulus and challenge of a demanding career.

Do you feel tempted to offer your experience to suggest
strategies and advice? Do you have strong views on the
subject?

Does your own choice or your parents' choice in this area
seem to offer a clue to the right answer?

If you answered yes to any of these questions, beware of
the trap! We need a way for the client to explore this
for herself without getting confused by your feelings and
experiences. After all, if she needed true life stories—'How
I coped with being a superwoman. High-flying banker and
mother of ten shares her secrets', or 'How I gave it all up to
raise seven children on love, wholemeal bread and live
yoghurt'—she could go out and buy the magazines that are
full of them.

It can be very tempting to share our experiences and try
to help others avoid our mistakes. Resist the temptation.
That's what families and good friends are for! Your client
needs something else from you.

Taking the example of the young woman we have been thinking about, I encouraged her to name two parties, one to represent each conflicting point of view. They might be called the Real Mothering Party and the Career First Party. There was a marginal third party standing for Solo Career Excellence (without diversions for relationships or children), and she could have had representations from that, too. However, she felt that would split the vote unnecessarily and chose only to hear from the two main parties.

She wrote both manifestos and designed their 'broadcasts'. The work continued over some time as she talked through both arguments. This technique helped to separate her tangled thoughts and made it easier for her to hear herself think.

Then I suggested that, since it seemed neither party could win alone or get everything they wanted, they should form a coalition. More work followed in the form of writing, discussion and letters exchanged between the two sides. In the end a compromise acceptable to both was reached. This had to happen because otherwise each would have continued to sabotage the activities and efforts of the other.

You may not want to take things so far, but I hope the idea of helping your client to explore both sides of a problem like this is useful to you.

Alternatives to writing—two chairs

Some clients will not be at home with writing and you could try getting them to speak for the different points of view.

To help keep the two separate, suggest that the client uses two chairs, one to speak for each side. So she might be sitting in the 'Mother's' seat and ask a question of the 'Career Woman'. Before answering she would have to move and sit in the 'Career Woman's' chair. As long as the conversation continued, she would move from chair to chair according to the opinion she was voicing. This works well for some people, less well for others. Fit what you do to the client, not the client to the technique you want to use. It is equally important to use techniques in which you feel competent and which you are comfortable about using.

Drawing

Some clients may prefer to draw their feelings or situations or life maps. You do not have to be an art expert to do this, either as counsellor or client.

Basically, treat your clients' work with respect and interest. Encourage them to tell you what it means to them. Confine your comments to what you can see—colours, shapes, recurring themes: 'Your drawings seem to have a lot of red in them. What does this colour mean to you?' rather than 'You must be very angry, there is so much red in all your pictures.'

Try, 'I am interested in this blue shape here. Could you tell me something about it?' rather than, 'What is this grey blob? Were you trying to draw a cloud? It's a bit woolly, isn't it?'

If you are strongly interested in drawing, then I suggest you consider an art therapy course. This skill stands on its own and also combines well with other helping methods.

Dream work

This is another specialist area. If it appeals to you, look out for workshops on the subject.

As a general rule, if clients want to tell you about their dreams you can do no harm by listening helpfully. You can encourage them to record their dreams and help them to identify recurring themes. Please do not offer your interpretations or use standard dream dictionaries.

Dreams are very personal and individual and so are their meanings. You can help your client to explore what a particular symbol means to her. For example, what does she think of when she sees a black cat in her dream? It may be a happy memory or connected to a distressing experience, or may even relate to some everyday matter—for example, I need to take our black tom cat to the vet. It can be helpful in understanding the dream if she gives it a title.

Just remember not to tell the client what her dream means, instead, help her to find out for herself. Help her to come to her own understanding and find her own meaning.

Another helpful way to explore the dream is to suggest that your client describes it as if it were going to be in a television programme guide. She would give the dream a title and say whether it was a comedy or a soap or a tragedy, with a brief outline of the story.

These simple measures can be very useful to your client in understanding what meaning her dream has for her. They can do no harm and may well be helpful.

Other ways of working creatively
Some clients will respond well to using things that have memories to help them talk. Photographs are an obvious example. If a client wants to show you photos of important people or places in his life, accept gratefully. He is sharing important and special parts of his life with you. Look and listen and encourage him to tell you whatever he needs to tell you. Try not to put your meanings into the pictures, rather work to draw out the client's meanings and memories. Sometimes it can help to have photos of past and present to refer to. This can be especially helpful in bereavement.

Other ways to explore problems
We talked earlier about using questions sparingly, so you know I am not going to suggest a string of questions. However, it can be very helpful to use a question to help broaden your client's viewpoint, and in an atmosphere of respect and trust you might use a more challenging approach: 'I wonder if you ever find being so heavy has any good or useful things about it?'

I once got the reply, after some pause for thought, that it prevented the client 'falling pregnant'. This person had very little confidence in relationships, especially sexual ones, and felt unable to set boundaries. Being very heavy, she thought, protected her from situations in which she felt out of control. Obviously she had gained weight for what were 'good' reasons, even though she was not fully aware of them. Until she could have faith in other ways of taking care of herself, and could gain some confidence and assertiveness, it was unlikely that she would lose weight. All the logical, sensible, healthy reasons for losing weight would not count so long as the big hidden reason for staying heavy was left unexamined. Being breathless, being unable to take part in her daughter's school sports day, mattered, but so did feeling safe, protected from unwanted sexual advances to which she could not say no except by being seen as undesirable.

So long as what we do works for us we are unlikely to change. So long as we are unaware of what a particular problem or behaviour is doing for us or helping us to avoid, or what it is protecting us from, we cannot change it.

It is rather like a group of soldiers told to guard a building. The danger may have passed, their presence may be causing inconvenience, but they are dedicated, faithful and well trained. Until they are given the right passwords and formally relieved of command, they will fight fiercely to defend their post.

Often we behave in ways that are no longer useful to ourselves or helpful to others. We do this for long-forgotten reasons, but until we remember and acknowledge those faithful if misguided soldiers they will continue to 'guard' us.

Have you any old soldiers, still standing guard long after the battle is over?

If there is still something to protect, are they the most efficient and effective way of providing this protection?

If this way of thinking about this problem does not work for you, can you make up another way to describe it? Or can you draw your protective forces and the way they can be rewarded and released from duty? What would replace them?

If you do not have any protective forces which are no longer helpful, well done. How do the helpful ones look? What do they do for you?

8 Problems

There might be clients whose behaviour or reactions give the counsellor some challenges. There might be clients with whom you personally have problems, either because of a personality mismatch or because of the issues on which they need to work.

However, they remain people with problems rather than problem people, just as your having a problem working with them does not make you a problem counsellor, merely a counsellor with a problem. Pause here and think . . .

Which issues would you find it difficult to work with?

Are there any beliefs or life-styles that you would have a problem working with? For example, I knew a caring and competent counsellor who had a problem with a client's belief in spiritual healing. The counsellor felt this conflicted with deeply-held spiritual beliefs of his own.

How far would your own spiritual beliefs, or absence of them, affect your ability to work with clients whose beliefs were different from your own?

How much flexibility is there in your thinking?

Have you considered issues of sexuality and gender?

How would you respond to unfaithfulness within a relationship?

Would you respond differently if the relationship were lesbian or gay?

Could you work effectively with clients who were or had been involved in cruelty to vulnerable people like elders or children?

Would you be comfortable working with clients of a different race or culture?

Equally important, would they be comfortable with you?

Do you feel that more information or training in any of these issues would be helpful to you?

Is such special training available for you?

These questions may help you to clarify issues which may be a problem for you or in which your attitudes may be a problem for your client.

As I mentioned in Chapter Two, not everyone is able to benefit from counselling. While there might be people with whom you would choose not to work, there are also some situations and conditions with which you would be unwise to work.

Severe current mental health problems

Some people with current and severe mental health problems might benefit from treatment which could include counselling. This would be a very specialised task, needing great skill, experience and clinical judgement. It might also require a great deal of available support, both for the practitioner and for the client. Many people might think this was most conveniently provided within a residential (preferably not institutionalised) setting, where support, supervision and medical back-up were readily available.

However, although counselling might not be an appropriate form of help for some people with serious mental health problems, there is scope for good listening. Support and encouragement from a genuinely respectful listener can always be helpful. Again, it is the core conditions (see pp. 30–4) that are important here. Counselling may not be the most useful way to help, but a more low-key befriending relationship could be offered. Do be clear in your own mind what you are offering and how it differs from ordinary friendship. Be clear with your manager and/or supervisor and colleagues and clear with your client.

You might like to pause here and write down how you see befriending as differing from ordinary friendship. Also consider how they both differ from counselling.

Friendship and befriending and how they differ
Both generate warm feelings and offer support in times of
need. In a befriending relationship the balance of need and
support is heavily, if not exclusively, towards the befriender
meeting the needs of the client. The relationship is begun
because of the client's needs, not necessarily because of
mutual interests or liking. Would it be appropriate for a
befriender to lean on a client for support?

How counselling and befriending differ
Counselling usually entails a mutually agreed aim which
involves the client in changing either behaviour or perspective and/or in developing different approaches to the problems of living. This amount of work may not always
be possible for an individual at a particular time and he
may benefit instead from a warm, supportive befriending
relationship which accepts him (as does counselling) but in
which there is no expectation of efforts that the client may
currently be unable to make.

Personal boundaries for working on mental health issues
In general I do not work with anyone who is not securely in
touch with reality—that is, someone who is suffering from
delusions or confusion about what is real and what is
fantasy.
     Are you clear about what you will be expected to do in
this area? Are there professional or organisational guidelines laid down for you, concerning who you can see and
the issues you can work with? What procedures does your
workplace have for referral? How familiar are you with
them?
     If there are none, then I think this is a priority task
for you to work on with your manager and colleagues.
The British Association for Counselling ethical guidelines
might be a useful starting point for you. If you have chosen
a supervisor with experience in your main, non-counselling

task, she might be able to offer useful advice on adapting existing codes of practice to your work situation.

Violence

This is an important factor to consider. You need to be safe, and you deserve safety and security in your working conditions.

Do you know what the safety procedures and security guidelines are in your place of work?

If you are working for yourself, please take the time to think about your own safety.

How would you respond to the threat of violence, or to a violent incident?

How would you respond to an actual threat, an implied threat, to threatening body language, to a growing vague sense of unease?

If your client had a history of violence, would you be aware of it?

Would you set different boundaries with a client with a history of violence?

Would you refuse to work with someone with such a history?

I am not offering you answers, only asking you to think about the possibilities. You may use the opportunity to discuss issues with colleagues and take whatever action you feel is needed. Remember, you may not always know or be told about a person's previous history, or a client with no previous history may suddenly react violently. You cannot always know in advance. Trust your instincts—that is what they are for: your protection.

Safety measures

You might want to consider these measures:

1 Always have colleagues within call.
2 Have a bell buzzer or personal alarm to hand.
3 Sit nearer to the door than your client.

The following questions could be considered in a group discussion or as material for your journal.

What would make you feel secure/insecure in a counselling setting?

Do you feel able to discuss this with your line manager and colleagues?

Are you reluctant to raise this topic in case others think you can't cope?

Working with clients who seem too talkative

I am not talking here about the nervous new client who pours his whole life into your lap in the first half-hour you have together. I am thinking of someone with whom you are having difficulty working beyond the first session. The first questions I would ask myself are:

Why does he feel the need to do this?
Is he simply lonely and has he lost the fine edge of his communication skills through lack of use?
Is his level of social and communication skills a problem for him in general?
Is there a basic misunderstanding? Does he feel that he has to talk because he is being counselled?

There might be any number of reasons. The place to find the answers is within and between you and your client.

Finding the answers
I would expect to find the answers by:

1 Observation and reflection.
2 Discussion with my client.
3 Offering honest but sensitive feedback about how I react to his talkativeness, not blaming the client or making him wrong and me right, but owning my feelings, my difficulty.
4 Trying to find out how he sees the issue and if it is ever a problem for him outside counselling. If it is a problem,

considering how important it is to him to solve it. Is he aware of it as a difficulty for me in listening to him?

5 Discussing the difficulty with colleagues (bearing in mind confidentiality).

6 Taking the difficulty to my supervisor.

Protective camouflage

Is he trying to protect himself? Is this protection his general response to other people or does he react like this only in certain situations or in response to certain topics? Some people react in this way to 'authority' figures, people they see as more powerful than themselves. It can be an attempt to please or to avoid having to look or have you look at painful parts of their story. Here are some of the things we might consider:

1 Is the difficulty recent? When did it start?

2 Could it be related to stress or anxiety? Would it be helpful to explore further the underlying cause of the stress or anxiety. Do you need to work on stress management or relaxation or on reducing the anxiety? This is a situation in which you may consider referral to someone with skills in behaviour therapy.

3 Is he still recovering from a bereavement? If this is so you may need to work first on his bereavement.

4 Is he taking prescribed medication?

5 Is he taking recreational drugs, mood altering substances?

6 Do you sometimes feel as if you are drowning in a flood of words he is pouring over you?

7 Does he seem to have difficulty in sticking to one topic and flit from subject to subject without pausing to finish a story or explain an idea?

8 Do you find that, however hard you concentrate, what he says seems to be utterly divorced from sense or reality? Even though it sounds impressive and interesting, when you try to grasp the meaning of it, is there only froth and no beer?

Referral

If the answers to any of the last four questions are yes, you may need to seek your client's permission to discuss matters with his GP. There may be cause for concern; he might be suffering from potentially serious mental health problems. There are disorders in thinking and reasoning which could make it difficult for individuals to benefit from counselling and which need to be discussed with their doctor. Some of these can be heralded by the behaviours I have described in questions 6, 7 and 8.

You may want to consider referral to a specialist counselling service for drug or substance or alcohol related issues if the answers to questions 4 or 5 are yes. Remember to offer the suggestion of referral sensitively.

Suggesting medical help also needs to be presented in a positive and tactful way. Your own attitude to mental health problems and confidence in the doctor concerned will contribute substantially to a positive outcome from the referral.

Safety barriers and unhelpful behaviours

We usually behave in ways that have helped us. Sometimes the behaviours were the only option we felt we had to keep ourselves safe. They may no longer be working so well, but we might have forgotten that we did not always react this way, or we may be afraid to change. People have a range of protective behaviours that may in fact be making their lives more difficult for them in the present. Remember that they once had a very good reason for behaving in this way, and until they can feel safe they will not want to change.

I do not find it helpful to think of these protective behaviours as 'resistance'. I try to find out how they have been helpful to the client in the past. Usually when someone feels accepted she can begin to look at and change such behaviour, but unless she owns the problem as hers, neither she nor you can do anything about it. You may have to be clear and direct with your client about this. Counselling cannot solve or change the behaviour or attitudes of anyone except the client, and then only if she wants to change.

Unwilling clients

Clients who have been urged or advised to come by their nearest and dearest often bring a lot of anger and resentment or bewilderment with them. The work does not begin until they find a good reason of their own to do it. This is especially so with clients who have no choice about seeing you. Without their co-operation nothing useful will happen. They may feel angry and resentful, hostile, suspicious.

What can you do? Acknowledge their feelings, do not try to 'reason them away'. Accept that they may have good reasons for feeling as they do. Accepting their feelings does not mean that you have to take on the role of whipping boy for the whole system, for all their past unhappy encounters with authority. You can set limits to the amount of negative feeling you feel willing to absorb. Would you accept verbal abuse or swearing? Would this vary according to circumstances or individuals? You might need to acknowledge the boundaries and conditions of your working together.

Do you have to make a report on the work you are doing, and to whom?

What are the consequences for your client if your report is unfavourable?

What are the possible benefits for your client of working with you? Do not be vague about these; you need practical, concrete examples, gains you can both recognise.

Is there a practical, easily achievable task you can do together? Start small, and choose goals that really matter to your client, working towards a deeper understanding of the joint problem. Once you both accept that there is a problem, you can begin to discuss how it affects you both and how you might work on it.

Is your client depressed?
Watch for the following significant indications:

- Is her speech slow, heavy and dragging?
- Does it lack expression?
- Does she look sad?
- Or is she determinedly smiling, but with a smile that does not seem quite to fit?
- Does she have little energy or enthusiasm?
- Is her sleep disturbed?
- Does she sleep all day?
- Does she wake in the early hours of the morning?

Any of the above could be symptoms of depression. If you feel in any doubt, discuss your concerns with your client and suggest that she consults her doctor. See Chapter Nine, p. 114, for more on depression.

Problems of self-esteem
You have screened out the most serious causes, those which would need extra help, support or skills. Is the problem simply a habit in someone who believes no one is or could be interested in him? If this is the case you might agree to focus on building your client's confidence and self-esteem. However, he might prefer to continue to work on his chosen area. People always work harder for their own goals. Even if you do not change the focus of your work together you could see an improvement. The respect and attention you are offering, and the equal partnership you are building by consulting him, will contribute to this. The warmth of your interest in him, your concern for his feelings and ability to look beyond an annoying presentation will help. Just by the way you raise the subject you may already have begun the improvement.

Put simply, if the client thinks you are a good enough person, your good opinion and respect for him will be a starting point for him to think well of himself. In a way you lend him your respect for him so that he can use it as a pattern to make some for himself. It is also important that

your self-respect is solid and based on an acceptance of
yourself as a decent, fallible human being. Showing him
that you can accept yourself as less than perfect helps him
to build a realistic self-respect and esteem that fits who he
is. Do not forget to encourage him to cut generously to
allow for growth!

Loneliness or poor communication skills?

Your client is simply lonely and reacting to the novelty of
being listened to. Is this her major or only problem? Does
she need counselling or just a sympathetic ear? Would she
like your help in working on ways to reduce her loneliness?
Think and talk together about what she needs and how it
could best be provided.

A difficulty in presentation

You both agree there is a problem. One way to deal with
this is to get your client to list her concerns in her own order
of importance. Then she can choose which one to concentrate on. Help her to stick to her chosen topic. Honest
communication between you can be the starting point for
her to improve her communication skills. This situation also
offers her the opportunity to practise organising, planning,
prioritising and focusing. This should increase her sense of
confidence in her coping skills.

The Rime of the Ancient Mariner

Some clients simply repeat the same story, often in the same
words, again and again. Do not blame yourself if you feel
bored and irritated in this situation—you are only human!
Use your feelings, be honest, be sensitive and respectful.
Remember, you may be missing something important! In
these circumstances I have said something like:

'This is the third time you have told me about this. It is
obviously important to you. Is there something I have
missed, something that you want me to understand that I
don't seem to?'

What I try to do is be honest (congruent) about my feelings, even if only to myself, admitting to myself that I feel bored or irritated. Then I look further to understand what is happening. I feel it is important to do this in a way that does not put the client in the wrong. She may have the habit of repeating every little detail because she never feels listened-to. This behaviour may be a reflection of her life and relationships outside counselling. Unfortunately, the very act of repeating and repeating to make sure the message gets through can itself cause her listeners to switch off, so she helps to make what she fears come true.

People do not listen, so she tries harder to tell her story, with even less effect. It is rather like the way of communicating with foreigners that some English people used to have—if they don't understand, shout louder! Don't change your approach and try to learn new ways to communicate!

As you can see, these strategies are not effective in solving problems, only in perpetuating them. Of course they are useful in proving the worst about the world—'No one ever listens to me.'

How to help

If this is happening in a client's life, it helps her to know so that she can, if she chooses, work on the problem in a more effective way. Rather than working on the rambling, repetitious presentation, work on the feelings. Work on how it feels not to be interesting enough to be listened to, how it feels not to be important enough to be heard. Can you see how it helps if the counsellor is honest with herself and accepts her own feelings? How it deepens the work and gets nearer to the source of the client's pain? The counsellor is demonstrating that it is possible to be a healthy, effective human being who is sometimes wrong. You are not perfect, but you can own your mistakes and learn from them and still respect yourself. (You can be bored, you can fail to pick up what the client is trying to tell you. You do not have to

tell her that you were bored but you have to tell yourself.)
You are showing her this about yourself and showing her
that she too is acceptable, less than perfect as she is. She too
can own her mistakes, learn from them and keep or even
increase her self-respect.

Being human

Did you find the idea of telling your client that you might be
mistaken or have missed something important alarming or
uncomfortable? If you did, it might be an idea to stop and
think why.

Do you feel that a counsellor should know and always do
the right thing?

Are you afraid of losing the client's respect?

How do you feel about mistakes in general?

As always, throughout this book, your answers are the
'right' ones for you, even if they show you some attitude or
belief that you feel you would like to change. If thinking,
writing or talking about these questions confirms that you
are already comfortable with learning from your mistakes,
good! If the result of your doing this exercise is that you
have found some personal work to do because you are not
yet comfortable with being fallible, that is good, too.

How I learnt this

On the first residential weekend that began my counselling
course I was feeling very inadequate. I was sure every other
student was better qualified, more experienced and had
more clients than I had. I lay awake most of the first night
planning an early retreat. The course director had stressed
how many people had wanted to come on the course. She
urged anyone who was unsure to withdraw early, so that
someone from the reserve list could benefit instead. I was
sure she was speaking to me.

Our first lecturer the next morning gave me a gift that I
still treasure. He was a man of wide and deep experience in
counselling, well respected and very able. I was prepared to

be awed and instructed by this 'guru'. He started by saying how hard he had found it to sleep the night before, how nervous addressing a large group always made him feel. I was astounded. He was nervous and he admitted it! So it was possible to be experienced, competent, effective and fearful. You did not have to be perfect. Maybe I could be a counsellor one day after all. It did not look an easy option, just a more possible one than having to be perfect.

But what courage it takes to be honest and vulnerable, to be openly yourself. George showed me how to be human and fallible and competent, brave and fearful together. I realised it was not 'either or'—I could be both.

Later on the course I tried out both options on the same afternoon. I discovered that not everyone was comfortable with the combination. Some people still preferred things, especially other people, in black and white. Me? I was beginning to get a taste of the joys and pains of being more colourfully myself.

You might like to hear about that afternoon. The tutors were presenting a piece of theory and there was that heavy silence that comes when people haven't quite 'got it'. This happened to be a subject I had just spent eighteen months studying. We were always encouraged to contribute freely on the course, to build a learning community, so I suggested a particular angle that might make things clearer and was promptly and warmly invited to the rostrum. I made my presentation and it was well received. Later the same day, in my small growth group, for other reasons I was feeling vulnerable and uncertain and showed it. I was challenged, as one group member felt that I could not be confident and competent earlier and vulnerable now! One or other had to be a false reaction, a kind of front. Both were and are honest parts of me, real feelings but different because they were responding to different events, both inside and outside me.

I am still working on owning more and more of myself, and one day I shall stretch to all the colours in the rainbow, even if I choose not to use them all. We all have the potential to be great and terrible. I want to own all I can be so that I can choose how I respond rather than just react.

A good counsellor is . . .
A good counsellor looks honestly at himself. He is always prepared to work on himself and learn from his mistakes. I hope you find it as encouraging as I do that he actually does make mistakes to learn from! You really could not always be right. Think how inhumanly daunting it would be for those around you if you were. Imagine how disempowering it would be for your clients and what a terrible burden for you to carry!

Clients who say very little
The points I would consider in this situation are:

How long have we been working together? Has he just not had enough time to feel ready to confide in me?

Do we need to work more on building trust and confidence between us?

Am I just not a good match for him? Does he need to see someone of his own race, religion, age or gender?

Do we simply not work on a personal level? Am I wrong for him?

Would he be better with a form of help which did not rely so heavily on speech?

Would he prefer to draw or paint or work with sand or clay?

Would he be better with a more 'body work' approach?

Is there a problem between us that needs to be sorted out?

If this reluctance is new, perhaps he is trying to tell me something that is very important to him. He may be struggling to find a way to talk about a long-held secret. He may be afraid that I will judge him or those close to him, afraid that I may be shocked or revolted. He may be afraid that I shall blame him. He may feel a great deal of shame and fear. If you feel that this might be the case, proceed very gently and at your client's pace.

For the answers to all these questions, consult the expert, your client—not with a string of questions but gently and honestly in a way that you judge best fits your client and the relationship you have built up. For example, with a nervous, tense client I would carefully raise the question on our third meeting. I would handle things quite differently with someone who had been coming for some months and whose behaviour seemed to have changed. With someone who had a robust sense of humour I would tackle the problem differently from the way I would work with someone with a poor opinion of himself.

EXERCISE: HANDLING A CLIENT WHO WON'T TALK
You might like to imagine how you would handle the situation I have outlined above. A client has become reluctant to talk. Write out your planned approach with two very different clients in this situation. Consider how their temperaments and personalities and yours would affect the way you would approach this problem. How would your personal style and personality affect what you would feel able to do? It could be interesting to compare notes with a colleague.

The 'take care of me' clients
Some clients hide or deny their vulnerability. Others seem almost to flaunt it or wave it like a flag of desperation. The latter can be very demanding and draining, and in thinking how best to help them you must not lose sight of the need to take care of yourself. Remember your boundaries and the importance of only giving what you freely choose and want to give.

There is a need for a delicate balance between being warm and supportive and being disabling. If I ask you what help you require to reach your goals, I am assuming that you have the capacity to make plans and choices. If I negotiate with you the amount of help I can offer and help you find alternative sources for what I do not provide, then we are partners. If I assume that you are helpless and powerless, I might help to make that come true for you. Yes, you might need a lot of help and support, but you are still in charge, still responsible for yourself. This, I think, is a more respectful attitude and in the end more helpful and healthy for us both.

If I assume that my client is less than myself, I run the risk of developing a very unhealthy view of myself and of creating a mutually damaging relationship. I run the risk of becoming a victim of burn-out. I risk creating an unrealistic expectation of total help and support that will lead to disappointment, dependency and disability.

Rescuers, victims and persecutors

There is a piece of transactional analysis theory called Karpman's Triangle that I think illustrates this very vividly. It describes a 'game' played between two people, in which they both end up feeling bad in familiar ways. The prize is to have your opinion about yourself and other people confirmed.

You can begin to play in any position of the three— Victim, Rescuer or Persecutor. We all tend to have a favourite starting and finishing position. Those of us in the helping professions often start in the helper or Rescuer position. The client starts in the Victim position and for a while all goes well. The helper rescues, the Victim suffers. By 'rescuing', I mean that the helper tries to meet the client/Victim's needs. They both share a picture of the client as helpless, powerless to change; both believe that it is the Rescuer/counsellor's job to fix things, come up with the answers and make things better.

Often the client hopes that the solution will be effortless, painless and involve the Rescuer/counsellor getting other people in the Victim/client's life to change. Since this is unlikely to happen, and since the Victim/client will probably multiply his demands as the Rescuer/counsellor increases her efforts, a crisis is inevitable: something has to change, something has to give. Either the Rescuer/counsellor loses patience and moves into Persecutor, or the Victim/client does so, or the Rescuer/counsellor collapses into Victim, offering the client the choice of Rescuer/client or Persecutor/client.

In the switch from Rescuer/counsellor to Persecutor/ counsellor, the angry, needy counsellor blames the client for not getting better in spite of all her hard work. In the Victim/ counsellor option the counsellor blames herself for not being good enough, for not having made the client better. If the client wishes to take the Persecutor option he will agree and shower blame and anger on to the Victim/counsellor. Or he might prefer the Rescuer/client option and reassure the Victim/counsellor; he might enjoy the power and prestige that they both see in the role of Rescuer. Sometimes the players take all the options in turn, the counsellor moving from Rescuer to Persecutor to Victim, pursued by the client moving from Victim to Rescuer to Persecutor.

You might find it easier to picture this if you actually 'play it out'. You will need two players and three labelled chairs. Choose a role as either needy client or eager-to-help counsellor. Allow yourself as counsellor to help and offer lots of advice and suggestions, while your partner, playing the role of client, must find lots of reasons, good and not so good, for not acting on your advice. She may choose to explain how other people or events make it impossible for her to change, while telling you how much she is suffering. She may beg or plead or demand that you help her. Are you beginning to feel impatient with her whining, feeling that she would be the better for a kick in the pants? You are moving into the Persecutor role—change chairs! Perhaps she accepts this: it just goes to prove that she is as bad and useless as she has always feared! And for the Persecutor role you have proved that you just can't help some people!

Wait a minute: something else is happening. Your client has shoved you off the Persecutor chair and is saying that it is all your fault! You are a hopeless counsellor, you give useless advice, you have made her worse.

You, poor counsellor, go and sit in the Victim's chair. You feel guilty and miserable. It is all your fault, nothing you ever do is any good . . . You start to cry and your client moves into the empty Rescuer chair and begins to comfort you and offer good advice and tell you she is sure you do your best.

This game can go on for a long time. You ex-client may decide to go back to the Persecutor chair or try to go back to the Victim role, or you might return to Rescuer or Persecutor. I hope this gives you some idea of the complicated things that go on between helper and client if there is no commitment to build a respectful, equal relationship.

Too close to home

If the experience that a client is going through is similar to one that is still fresh and painful for you, it may not be helpful for you to counsel her. For example, the counsellor might be going through a difficult divorce which involved a dispute about the children, in which case he would be very unwise to counsel another parent going through a divorce. It would be extremely difficult to keep his concerns and feelings and reactions separate from those of the client.

Sometimes these 'matching issues' suddenly arise in an established counselling relationship. This is definitely a situation to monitor closely and to take to your supervisor. He can help you to assess how much overlap there is and how best to handle it. Extra awareness on your part may be all that is needed, or you may decide that the problem is one that you need to work on in therapy for yourself. However, you may decide that referral is in the best interests of you both.

This can be particularly so if you uncover an old booby trap, a piece of your past that you had forgotten. Working on your client's problem may have caused it to surface, and it may feel as if it has blown up out of nowhere in response to a painful and strangely upsetting part of your client's story. I say 'strangely upsetting' because in this situation the strength of your reaction surprises you. It does not seem to be in character. This problem is always a possibility for any of us working in counselling: what matters is how we handle it—how quickly we notice what is going on inside us and how effectively we act on what we have discovered.

What is going on between you?

As a general rule, if you cannot find a specific cause for a problem in counselling it would be a good idea to look with your client at the amount of safety and trust you both have in the relationship. You might examine together how the relationship is working. This can seem a daunting prospect, almost inviting the client to tell you where you are failing her. Yes, it is daunting, and inviting the truth is seldom comfortable. However, in my experience, if something is not right between you, you need to know.

You may, quite unintentionally, have said or done (or not done) something that distressed your client. This hurt or disappointment then got in the way of your communicating with each other. A healthy counselling relationship must include the client being able to say when she feels hurt or let down or misunderstood by her counsellor. She may have completely misread you, but you need to know and so does she. This kind of misreading of signals may be causing her problems in her life generally, and your honesty may be her best chance of dealing with them. She may have read your reactions as if they were those of someone in her childhood, or you may be doing something without being aware of it.

Old faces in new places

Sometimes we encounter this puzzling difficulty in communicating with people: something just does not seem to add up. The response we give or get does not match the obvious facts and feelings and intentions of those in the situation. You may make a comment and receive a response that is very intense, so intense that it seems out of all proportion. Or you may find yourself feeling very strongly

about an ordinary event or simple conversation. When this
happens, one possibility to consider is that one or both of
you are reacting as you did long ago, in other situations
with people from your past.

Or you may have got it wrong. You may have been
clumsy or insensitive or inattentive (this does not apply to
your client: he has a lot on his mind and has reason to be
any or all of these). You are human and you can make
mistakes, in spite of your best efforts, and you can take
responsibility for them.

Can you make mistakes and still be good enough?

What would you regard as being good enough?

As a counsellor and a woman I do not claim to be perfect.
I do promise to be responsible for what I do and answerable
to my clients for the quality, integrity and honesty of my
work.

9 Situations

In this chapter I want to discuss several potentially difficult counselling situations and dilemmas, all of which you are likely to have to face at some time. What impact does counselling have on your client's partner and family, and how does this affect the client? Are there risks in counselling colleagues, family and friends? What special skills are needed when counselling people suffering from depression, stress and anxiety? What risk factors should you be aware of? And how do you set about dealing with any feelings of discomfort or unease you may have after a counselling session?

Whose side are you on?
Clients are often inhibited by their belief that it is unfair to talk about a third party in his or her absence. Sensitive people feel uncomfortable discussing the impact on them of their family's or partner's behaviour, for they are aware that the other person has a point of view which is not being presented. They feel protective of their partner and concerned that I may judge or criticise the absent party. This anxiety can make it difficult for them to speak freely. There may also be pressure, direct or indirect, from the family or others closely concerned.

I find it helps to remember that we are concentrating on the truth of one person's perceptions and feelings. There may be other strands, other experiences that would enlarge the picture or reveal a completely different story, but we are looking at the client's experience, coloured by her feelings, her thoughts, her history. The time may come when that picture can be enlarged by an understanding of other people's difficulties, but in fact many clients have an all too detailed understanding of other points of view and too little experience of their own.

I do not find it helpful to blame or judge the absent parties. Keeping the focus on the client is more effective, and trying to understand someone else's actions and feelings in his absence is pointless. The question may need to change from, 'Why does he treat me like this?' to 'Why do I allow myself to be treated like this? What can I do about it? What am I willing to change or let go of in order to alter this situation?' This may involve abandoning an image of oneself as unworthy of respect or as someone who suffers bravely, or giving up a hope that 'if he loved me enough he would know what I want'. To take responsibility for yourself and your own feelings is the first step to taking back your own power.

Do not turn your client into a defence lawyer

There is another reason not to 'take sides', even when you feel strongly. Attacking her partner may result in your client working hard to defend him, rather than working hard for herself. You would also be demonstrating a critical, judgemental attitude and your client might fear that she could be next for sentencing. You do not have to pretend to accept the other person's behaviour, but nor do you have to condemn him.

Listening over many weeks to the story of a woman who had experienced mental, emotional and physical violence in her relationship, I often had to bite my tongue. My client knew and felt my concern for her, but what she needed from me was the space also to feel and express her love and concern for the confused and deeply unhappy person with whom she had lived. Of course I was sometimes crying inside or wanting to ask, 'Why do you feel you deserve this?' I did not have to ask her. When she was ready she asked and answered this for herself. I did not hide my concern, but found that what she needed more was my confidence in her strength, rather than a reinforcement of her vulnerability: 'Everyone sees me as helpless and weak. I don't need that.' She taught me a valuable lesson.

This is not a prescription for treating all clients with similar problems in the same way, it is just something for you to consider.

Partners or others close to the client
Often those close to the client feel uneasy about the counselling relationship or excluded by it. They, too, may fear that they will be judged, and feel anxious about what is being revealed. This is only natural. It can be very unsettling, imagining your most private relationship exposed to the critical gaze of a stranger, without having the opportunity to speak for yourself—a stranger, moreover, who is becoming more and more important to the person in your life. Partners wonder where they have gone wrong, worry about the effect of counselling on their relationship, feel left out and vulnerable, even resentful. The client seems to be receiving all the support and attention while the partner has to cope alone. Clients working intensely deep in painful feelings are not always able to be supportive, they may simply be too much in need of support themselves. Partners, however, need to feel supported, and family and friends can help. They may decide to seek counselling for themselves and often find it helpful to read about the subject or about their partner's problem.

The other end of this spectrum is taking responsibility for someone else while feeling powerless—for example, trying to focus on solving your partner's or child's problems while ignoring your own. Since you cannot change the other person and you are not even looking at yourself and your own difficulties and needs, things can only get worse.

'Tell him he is wrong'

Sometimes the problem is the opposite: the client wants you to agree that the other party is wrong. Her preferred solution is for the other person to change and she would like you to tell her how to get this point across. She would love to be able to quote you, imagining the impact of going home and saying, 'My counsellor says you are a nag and neurotic and uncaring, all I need is a loving, supportive relationship (so there!).'

As a counsellor you will help her to focus on what she can do, wants to do, needs to do, for herself. Help her to reclaim her power, which includes being responsible for deciding not to accept being nagged! Help her to look at her own behaviour and ways of improving communication, taking her share of building a loving, supportive relationship, perhaps even looking at why she expects to have things done to her or for her.

Horror story

I have even encountered the counsellor equivalent of this viewpoint on a counselling skills course. On one painful occasion—the first and last, I hope—I was facilitating, and one of the participants seemed to be having a problem with the course content.

When we sat down to talk together we found to our mutual dismay that we had totally different expectations of the outcome of counselling. He had a very well trained and logical mind. He liked things to be orderly and efficient. He was genuinely concerned for his clients and took a parental interest in them. Before he had gone much beyond the 'getting to know you' stage, he had what he described as a 'preferred scenario' worked out: he knew what the outcome of this particular counselling work should be, for his client. He was confident of what would be a good and moral outcome, especially in sexual matters.

He was on the course to learn more, effective and faster methods of getting his clients to his preferred best outcome.

As you can imagine, we decided he was on the wrong counselling course!

Does the idea of being able to speed up the counselling process attract you?

What is the single biggest difference between this man's view of counselling and the approach I have been describing?

How close is your view of counselling to either of these?

Yes, I do feel tempted on occasion, but I find the process works better and lasts longer when the decisions are the client's own and the pace acceptable to her.

There are now 'quick counselling' techniques that some people find effective, which enable more people to have some counselling help. Do seek out special training if the idea appeals to you, rather than trying to speed up the process without learning these techniques. There are many approaches to counselling, some of which offer a greater degree of structure and could be seen as more directive. Again, I would advise you to seek out training for yourself in these approaches.

I am writing about what works for me, fits my beliefs and personality and works for my clients. It is not the only way to counsel, but I admit to having serious reservations about any approach which assumes that the counsellor knows what is best for the client and works for that without the client's full, informed involvement. The biggest problem I had with the course participant's approach was the emphasis on *his* choice of outcome, *his* conviction that he knew what was best for others.

Counselling family, friends and colleagues—or not?

Now that you have worked through and thought about many of the difficulties and concerns involved in counselling, it seems a good time to return to this question that we raised in Chapter Two. You may want to discuss the issues or write about them in your journal. Remember that my answers are the result of my experience and reflect only my viewpoint.

I think it would be unwise to offer to counsel family members in any circumstances. I would have great difficulty in getting my feelings out of the way and I might be part of the problem! The difficulties with other family members who were not being counselled would also be even greater than if I were not involved. This does not mean I could not help. I could listen, I could offer the core conditions, I could be accepting of feelings, honest and open and real. All this could be supportive and comforting, and I could also help my relative find good counselling help.

I would be very reluctant to counsel a friend, for many of the same reasons, but it would still be possible to help, to be supportive, to listen rather than to counsel.

Colleagues? This is a greyer area. It would depend on circumstances, on our working relationship, on how close we were. I would be particularly uneasy if one of us were senior to or responsible for the other and would want the boundaries to be very clear to us both. The problem is that what you know as a counsellor you cannot unknow as a manager. Issues of ethics and discipline are all tangled up together here; I would want to get them as clear as possible before starting to counsel.

Counselling other professional colleagues, other counsellors with whom I do not work, offers a challenge and stimulus and is not a problem.

Depression
What do you understand by depression?
Do you see it only as a medical problem?
How far can counselling help?
How would you assess and handle the risk of suicide?
What are the workplace or professional and ethical guidelines
   you will be working under on the subject of suicide?

How I see depression
There are many views about depression. Some people regard it purely as a medical condition: a disorder in thinking and

reasoning resulting in an inner confusion, or the result of a chemical imbalance; others see it as being of two types: an understandable response to a distressing event (reactive depression), and a state that just drops out of a clear blue sky without rhyme or reason (endogenous).

My own understanding of it is nearer to the idea of a disorder in thinking and reasoning, with the additional possibility of a deeper meaning in some cases.

The Chinese characters for 'crisis' are the same as those used to write 'opportunity'. The depression can be seen as trying to draw the person's attention to something which needs to change, either in himself or in his life. It has an individual meaning and significance for each person.

I think it is very important for counsellors supporting clients who are depressed to be able to share information with the doctors involved. Do seek your client's permission to do this.

There is an excellent reason for having good communication between all those involved. Too heavy a dosage of antidepressants will make counselling extremely difficult; on the other hand, sometimes the support of antidepressants will lift the weight of the depression just enough to make it possible for the client to work on the underlying causes.

The risks of suicide
Another good reason is that you can be involved in helping to monitor the likelihood of suicide and you can rely on support and consultation in helping your client to feel secure. Do not hesitate to raise the question of suicidal thoughts with your client. No, you will not put the idea into his head if it is not already there. You may be offering him a chance to discuss something he was afraid to talk about, the chance to make positive choices for his life and the opportunity to tell someone just how desperate he feels. By asking, you are saying that you are willing to look at it if it is a problem.

Do not believe the myth that those who talk about it never do it. This is just not true. Often people have thought and planned and talked about killing themselves long before they actually did it. People who can tell you not only that they want to kill themselves, but just how they would do it, are serious! Another serious sign is the amount of time a person spends on thinking about killing himself. If he is dwelling on it frequently, daydreaming about it as if it were a dream holiday, you should worry. Take action within your code of ethics to ensure your client's safety.

In order to work effectively you need to have your client's consent to an open confidentiality between you and his general practitioner and perhaps other people whom you both feel are important in supporting him. Do not even try to carry this on your own. Make good use of your supervision and seek the support of your colleagues.

Be clear about your beliefs and boundaries around suicide. Have a clear contract with your client and a definite understanding with others involved about boundaries.

Do you have strong religious beliefs about suicide? Does your client or his family? What about the other professionals involved?

Do the ethical guidelines you will be working to on this issue fit or conflict with those of others involved? If in doubt, ask. It never hurts to have things clear, and it can cause harm not to.

Stress or distress
When thinking about stress I find it helpful to remember that it is not always a source of *di*stress. Some stress is helpful and stimulating, but the type and amount vary for each of us.

What stresses you and why?

What challenges and stimulates you? Why?

What causes you distress?

How far do you think the attitude we have to a particular source of stress affects whether we see it as distress (a threat) or a challenge?

How could you increase one and decrease the other?

Anxiety and anticipation

In the same way, anxiety can be crippling or just a sign of awareness of being on the edge of a new experience. Try applying the stress questions to anxiety. Being able to look at a feeling and explore it sometimes enables us to shift our view of it, from threat to challenge, even if it is only the challenge of managing it rather than being controlled by it.

Imagine you have a set of old-fashioned weighing scales. In one pan is the problem or cause of anxiety and at the moment it is heavily down on that side. To begin to change the balance you could either remove some of the weights on the problem side or you could outweigh the problem by putting more helpful things into the other pan. You could even do both.

Imagine that the causes of your problem or the contributing factors are weights: how heavy is each? Can you get rid of or reduce any of them? Now think of all the resources you have: skills, friends, abilities, attitudes, willingness to change—how heavy are they? How many of them are in the pan on the positive side? Can you increase them? What practical steps would you need to take to make this happen?

For example, Sally wants to train as a counsellor, but . . .

In the negative pan, she doesn't know how or what she needs to be accepted for training. She is unsure of herself and has little money.

In the positive pan, she is really keen, she is a warm, friendly, caring person and she is currently on benefits which would allow her to study.

What does she need to do to change the balance?

Getting more information would help in two ways: she would have a clearer idea of what was needed, and she would feel increased confidence after having acted. So at a stroke she would have removed the 'I don't know' weight and lightened the 'lack of confidence' weight.

She could continue in this way, taking small steps, building on small successes. Finally the weights would tilt the scales onto the positive side, and she could achieve her goal.

Dealing with feelings of unease

Sometimes, after a counselling session, I am left with a vague sense of discomfort, an unease. I deal with it by first writing my notes, perhaps in more detail than usual, and going over the meeting in my mind. This may be all that is needed to identify what is troubling me. If not, I look closer at the feeling that worries me—something my client has said or done or not said. Is my discomfort related to a risk to the client (suicide or other self-harm, for example)? If yes, then what action do I need to take? Should I consult colleagues, inform other professionals? Can it wait until the next meeting to be discussed with the client? If no, I must take action. If the risk is to a vulnerable person connected with the client, the same steps apply. Is the risk to my safety? What must I do to guarantee this? Again, I must take action. Is the problem in the counselling relationship? I note this for supervision and possibly to explore with the client at our next meeting when I shall have thought it through.

Is the discomfort an emotional one, personal to me, a reaction to distressing material discussed during the meeting? If yes, what do I need to do for me? Phone a friend, go for a walk, go out for a drink? Is the distress more profound? If yes, do I need to book an earlier supervision? Is it bringing up old, unfinished business? If yes, then do I need to see a counsellor?

As you can see, a whole range of possibilities is opened up when you begin to look more closely at a vague discomfort. It is well worth listening to your feelings and acting on them when necessary.

10 How Do You Deal with Endings?

When you see someone off on a journey, do you stay on the platform waving until the train is out of sight? Do you wait to see the 'plane take off? Or do you say a brisk goodbye and leave smartly?

Do you keep mementoes, save old door keys, never throw anything away? Or do you keep only what you are currently using, and avoid clutter? There is a fine balance between holding on and letting go, between valuing your past and having so much of it around there is no room for your present.

The way you are about keepsakes and goodbyes may give an insight into your attitudes to change and endings.

Do you hate goodbyes and avoid them?

How do you feel about change? Have there been too many changes in your life?

Do you welcome change, and charge eagerly ahead, never looking back?

Have you allowed yourself space for regrets?

Do you get involved in regular reunions, keep in touch with all your old friends and your family?

These questions are just starting points for you to think about your attitudes to change. Ignore them if you prefer and just write directly about the topic in your journal.

How do you end your counselling sessions?

Do you always finish to the minute or regularly overrun? It is useful to monitor your performance, and if you are regularly overrunning it would be worth considering why. Is your overrunning confined to a single individual or a certain communication style, for example, the very talkative? If so, you might find it helpful to work through some of the ideas outlined in Chapter Eight (pp. 93–5) on working with talkative clients. If the difficulty is more general, you might need to consider whether you are taking sufficient responsibility for the work you are doing. Maintaining the boundaries is the counsellor's responsibility, and this includes starting and finishing on time.

Does it really matter, or am I just being pernickety? After all, we are humans not robots, and an occasional overrun, a response to a genuine crisis which needs more time, is only natural. However, a regular disregard for agreed boundaries is something else.

One of the ways of offering security to your client is consistency, and this means being there as agreed, starting and finishing on time. It means respecting your own needs and commitments and those of other clients and colleagues. This firm boundary also helps give security when a client is feeling very needy and acting in ways that feel very demanding of your attention. Some needy clients may try to prolong the interview, testing limits and boundaries, and in these circumstances the boundaries need to be reliable, clear and firm.

Some clients drop a little bomb on leaving: they introduce some alarming new piece of information which very often is not intended for immediate attention. They want to move gradually into talking about it.

If your difficulty is more general, perhaps you need to consider what is going on inside you. Do you hesitate to take responsibility for ending the session? Are you concerned about being seen as hard? Do you hesitate because you are worried about being in control, concerned about abusing your power?

Here is fruitful material for personal work or group discussion.

Owning power, taking responsibility

Remember, you have both power and responsibility in this relationship, and to deny them by refusing to exercise them is irresponsible. Your power is there for you to use in maintaining the boundaries, keeping both of you safe, and in ensuring that you can contain your client's pain.

Think of it as learning to drive in a dual-control car. Initially the learner (client) relies more on the skill of the instructor (counsellor) who occasionally takes control of the car, but not of the learner. The aim is to share power and knowledge so that the learner will acquire skills and control and use the power of the car responsibly. There are rules, guidelines—boundaries, if you like—which the instructor is responsible for explaining and ensuring that they are carried out. He is not abusing his power in setting safety limits, but he would be abusing his power and knowledge if he failed to do so, in a potentially dangerous situation.

If this is an issue for you, it is good that you are sensitive to the responsibility you have. I hope that what I have written will help you to feel more comfortable with owning your power.

Endings: a necessary evil or a natural process?

Every counselling relationship has to end, and this ending must be built in to the whole cycle of your work together. Endings and losses of many kinds are also a central theme in many of the problems that bring people to counselling.

EXERCISE: IDENTIFY TYPES OF LOSS
List those problems which have an element of loss in them. Here are some that you might include:

- Bereavement.
- Miscarriage.

- Abortion.
- Amputation, mastectomy or any major surgery which changes body appearance or function.
- Serious long-term ill health or life-threatening disease.
- Job loss after long-term employment.
- Loss of role or status. Parents can feel this when children leave home, or newly retired people can experience retirement as loss.
- Loss of trust, the least visible yet perhaps one of the most painful. This is experienced by an abused child or someone let down or deceived by a friend or partner, or by victims of random violence.
- Loss of something in potential. The loss of never having had something can be incredibly painful and is hard for others to empathise with. The happy childhood that one never had and never can have is one example. This kind of invisible loss gives the lie to the old saying that what you've never had you don't miss! What unwillingly childless couple would agree?

Think about the sort of issues that people might bring to counselling. How many can you think of which do *not* include an element of loss?

Loss in itself is not harmful, although it may be painful. It helps to understand and work with the process. Every change involves a loss or a letting go; every choice we make involves a loss, if only of an alternative experience.

Draw a life map

Think over the course of your life up until now. How many changes have you experienced? Draw a map of your life journey from your birth, when you lost a warm, safe haven where oxygen, food and all services were provided, to the present. Note the changes, the endings and the beginnings. Were there any gains? Could the gains have come without any change? This may bring up memories or feelings that you could usefully talk about with a colleague. You might need to work on a little unfinished business. If a memory is causing you a lot of pain, if you have wanted just to shut it away, now could be a time to begin to ease that pain.

Good endings

You will have noted some endings that felt better than others. What do you feel these had in common? Think about the endings that did not feel so good: what made them different from the better endings?

A major theme in good endings is that they feel right. There are no loose ends. People are given time to prepare to say goodbye and feel part of what is happening—they have choices and some understanding of what is happening. This does not mean that there is no pain or sadness, but even in the most difficult circumstances, it is more like the choice between a clean, skilled, planned amputation to which you give consent, understanding the reasons, and losing a limb through gangrene or injury, without the option of treatment.

Knowing and understanding what is happening does not make things all right; it just helps us to feel less powerless. It gives us the option of working with what is happening and making the best choices possible.

Unsatisfactory endings

Whereas good endings leave no sense of unfinished business, most people feel that bad endings leave them full of regrets—if only I had known that was the last time we would see each other . . . if only we had not had that stupid row . . . if only . . . An unsatisfactory ending has far more might-have-beens than a good ending. Often there has been no warning, no time to prepare, and there is a sense of being helpless, of having no real choice or opportunity to exercise choice. How far do your negative experiences of losses and endings fit this picture?

Ending a counselling relationship
How could you apply the principles of a good ending to this situation? What would a good ending be like in a counselling situation?

Planned
A good ending is not abrupt or unexpected. You have been working towards it all through the counselling sessions. There have been explicit goals whose achievement would signal the end of counselling.

No unfinished business
Both client and counsellor have agreed that their work together is over; there may or may not be an agreement about further work together in the future.

Goodbyes
Both parties take time to acknowledge what they have done together and perhaps look back at their joint journey. They may look at how the client has changed and how those changes happened. They may celebrate new skills and capacities. And there may be some sadness at the ending of a special and important relationship.

Power
I think it is very important that the client should be actively involved in choosing when and how to end the counselling—a final reinforcement of his power, choice and autonomy. How well would he be if he had to wait for you to tell him that he was ready to finish? Surely he came to counselling to gain in confidence, to make his own choices, to take responsibility for himself. Sometimes I raise the subject during a review: 'How much more do you feel we have to do together?' or, 'Do you feel you need to see me any more now that you have (achieved this or worked through that)?
      Sometimes a client will suggest a time-scale or a fixed

number of meetings, or perhaps a short break followed by a session to 'see how I get on', a sort of weaning-off process.

I am always happy when we come to a good ending together, even though there is some sadness at the ending of what we have shared. I do not attempt to hide these feelings. I have a happy memory of a colleague on my counselling course who came in one day to report that his first and so far only client had just finished working with him. He said: 'After my client had gone I was so happy for him (the client) that I was singing and bopping round the house all night.' There might have been selfish reasons not to rejoice, since to stay on the course it was necessary to have clients and he now had none. Money was also an issue for him, and this had been a paying client. But he was joyful. I have always remembered that loving and generous response; it remains my gold standard.

For me a good ending is one where I can rejoice with my client that we have come to the end of our journey together. That he is going, in his own time and his own way, hopefully taking new skills and abilities with him.

The final ending: death
This seems a suitable place to consider the biggest loss and ending of all. What image symbolises death for you? Is it a skeleton, the grim reaper, the old person's friend, a terminal illness? For me the image that comes to mind is a letting go, a sort of freedom, a lightness that floats upwards . . .

Take a little time to think, write and draw around this subject. It would be most helpful if you could share your work with a listening partner.

If you have suffered a recent bereavement, you might prefer not to do this work at present. Or you might welcome the opportunity, and use it as a stepping stone to seeking further help and support if you feel you need it.

I think it is important that we look at what we feel, think and believe about death, before trying to help any client going through a bereavement. By now I am sure you realise how vital it is to know your own feelings and reactions well enough to get them out of the client's way, and also to discover whether you have any unfinished business of your own, which you may want to deal with, any attitudes or beliefs that you might find unhelpful in your counselling work. I am not suggesting that you do specialist 'bereavement counselling' but that you feel able to listen to people's experience of it and if you think that more than basic support is needed you can make a referral.

Some of the concerns you might have about the expression of strong feelings have already been covered in Chapter Five. But death is different: it is the big change, the inevitable challenge. It is also a very natural process and so is the recovery from an important death, the mourning process. In the earlier part of this chapter you looked at what made for good endings and how those that were less satisfying differed. How far do you think the same applies to death, both for the person dying and those close to him or her?

In my experience the same elements are present in all good endings, including death, but *your* answers are what matter here.

Responses to loss

The natural reactions to loss follow a general pattern within which there are many individual variations. In the initial, or impact stage there is shock, numbness, denial, anger, confusion, pain—all in varying proportions. How might these feelings be expressed in behaviour, in speech, in bodily reactions?

Disorganisation

The next stage is one of disorganisation, where the distress, confusion and pain increase, sometimes to agonising proportions. Can you imagine how these feelings are expressed in actions—speech, thinking, behaviour?

Reorganisation

The final stage is one of slow reorganisation, with some slipping back to earlier stages. The bereaved person begins to feel less 'shattered', more in control, perhaps more ready to be involved in life again. How might this reorganisation be expressed in actions and feelings?

The way people react to this major event mirrors all that they are, all that they believe, and reflects their life experience and emotional history. The kind of death and the circumstances in which it takes place, as well as the quality of the relationships involved and the number and value of the connections between those involved, have an influence on how someone reacts and responds to the death. It is quite simple, really: the closer and more important the person was, the greater the loss; the more losses you have previously sustained and the fewer the support systems you have available to you, the greater the likelihood of your needing support. The more unexpected the death, the more traumatic it will be and the greater the impact. Yet people are not fully predictable. These are only general trends and they cannot tell us how any individual will act.

As you would expect, reactions vary greatly and judging them is not likely to be helpful. However, if reactions and behaviour are causing concern to the individual or those close to her, then extra help and support would be a good idea. Remember, it is a natural process and most people get through their losses without counselling support. Some, however, for varying reasons, get 'stuck' or have unusual difficulty and need help.

I have not attempted to cover the special skills required for bereavement counselling in this introductory book, but feel that it might help you to look at your own attitudes to this experience.

In general terms, what helps is good, accepting listening, being non-judgemental, knowing that feelings can be many-coloured. It is possible to love and resent someone, to feel relief and loss, with either of these feelings cancelling out the other. It is important to be able to feel comfortable with the expression of anger as well as grief. In fact, all the skills and attitudes we have been working on throughout this book will be of use to you in supporting someone through a bereavement. If you think this work might appeal to you, seek out further training. You might also like to read some of the books listed in the Book List under bereavement.

11   Supervision and Support

Throughout this part of the book I have referred to the need
for supervision and a support system for counsellors. Some
of you may not have had any experience of this type of
supervision and it may seem a daunting and unpleasant
prospect. Before my first encounter with positive, supportive supervision I felt scared and unwilling to say anything
that might expose my ignorance. I went prepared to defend,
deny or explain away any mistakes. I was working as a
house parent in a residential school for children with emotional and behavioural difficulties. I had been a nurse and
had memories of 'supervision', both as a student nurse and
from the other side, as a ward sister. It had seemed to be
about being 'put right' or 'told off', of making sure that
people did what they were supposed to do. As a student I
had never found it supportive and as a ward sister it had
never occured to me that it could be. I was in for a culture
shock! No recriminations, just a mutual acceptance that I
had made a mistake (to which I had confessed in the
expectation of being berated). Then my supervisor asked
me:
    'What do you feel you have learned from this incident?
How would you handle things differently another time?'
    I was taken by surprise. This felt like a very new idea.
Where was the blame and shame I had been expecting?
Although my work at the school sometimes included a
'listening' element, this was not a counselling supervision. I
have mentioned it because I think it illustrates how positive
it is to be listened to helpfully in supervision. Feeling free
from being judged, I was able to own my mistake and be

helped to learn from it, which I could not have done if Renee had not helped me to feel secure. She left me with a lasting feeling of how supportive good supervision can be. It becomes a resource, a challenge, not a threat, similar in many ways to a good counselling relationship.

EXERCISE: THINKING ABOUT SUPERVISION
Write down your thoughts on the subject of supervision, perhaps answering some of these questions:

What is supervision?
Why do counsellors need supervision?
Do more experienced counsellors still need supervision?
What do you need from a supervisor?
Could someone without counselling training and experience offer you supervision for counselling?

Here are some of my thoughts on these questions. I have deliberately not called them answers because, except for certain BAC guidelines, I am offering suggestions from my own and other colleagues' experience rather than a set of rules.

What is supervision?
Supervision is the opportunity to reflect, with a more experienced colleague, on the process and content of your work. It enables you to explore what is being said and done by you and the client and the expressed and unexpressed feelings and meanings of what you are doing. It can offer technical and moral support and increase your skills and confidence. It can act like a dental mirror, showing you what is happening just outside your awareness. It is a safety net for you and your client and a form of quality assurance. Since regular supervision is written into the BAC code of ethics, you will need access to regular supervision if you are working to these standards.

Who pays?

If you are employed as a counsellor, or are about to be, it is worth asking about arrangements for supervision. If you are extending your skills within your existing work, your employer may not be aware of this need, so you should raise the matter as soon as possible. If you have to pay for it yourself you may find yourself out of pocket. Supervision costs from £25 to £35 per hour upwards, depending on where you live. It is also worth finding out whether you will be 'given' the time off to get your supervision. The recommended minimum is one-and-a-half hours a month and, as you can imagine, the costs mount up.

Why we need supervision

We need supervision for professional and personal reasons. Professionally, we need it to monitor, maintain and improve the standard of our work and for the protection of our clients. Without supervision you cannot be a member of BAC and might well have difficulty in obtaining professional insurance cover. Personally, the benefits of supervision are as a source of support and comfort (in the sense of not being alone in handling difficult situations). Your supervisor can also offer you a technical resource. She can suggest different ways of approaching a problem and help you extend the range of your skills. Her support can make it possible for you to be a more effective counsellor. If you feel supported in your pain and confusion as a counsellor by the quality of your relationship with your supervisor you are better able to support your clients and help them contain their pain. In the same way, a new mother functions better with the loving support of her partner and her own mother. Their care for her helps her care for her baby. I think all counsellors can benefit from such a sense of being supported in their work.

Do more experienced counsellors need supervision?
Yes.

What do you need from a supervisor?

In general terms, I think it is important to have a supervisor who understands the work you do and has a training and orientation similar to yours, and if you do your counselling as part of other tasks, that he or she understands its difficulties and demands. It is also important to have a good fit—by that I mean a sense of being able to work safely with your supervisor in a relationship of mutual trust and respect. Not every counsellor would answer the question in this way. Your requirements may be very different and would reflect your own needs and perceptions.

Could someone without counselling training and experience offer you effective supervision?

No. It is important for your counselling supervisor to be more experienced in counselling than you are. You will need her expertise and competence. If you are adding counselling to other work tasks your supervisor should ideally have some skills and experience in that area also. For example, a nurse using counselling skills would benefit from a counselling supervisor with a nursing background.

Finding a supervisor

Many counselling courses have a list of approved supervisors, and voluntary agencies which provide counselling usually include supervision for their volunteers. There may be a more experienced colleague from whom you could seek supervision, or you could approach a practising counsellor and make a private arrangement. As this is likely to be expensive, you may prefer to enquire whether they run a supervision group you could join. If you are aware of two or three colleagues who also require supervision, you could approach your potential supervisor as a ready-made group. Not only would the cost be reduced, but you would benefit from hearing about other counsellors' work and listening to their supervision. There is also the possibility of 'peer supervision', either in a pair or as a group, but I would strongly recommend that you do not use this as your only form of supervision until you have had some experience both of counselling and of more formal, contracted supervision.

Support systems

Counselling is demanding work and it is vital to take care of yourself. One element in this self-care is building a good support system. You probably already have good personal support systems; now you need to think about building professional support.

What form you would like that support to take?

Can you build on any existing contacts?

Are you aware of colleagues who share your interest in counselling, who might like to become involved in setting up a support system?

If you are currently on a counselling course, have you raised this with the other students?

Are you aware that BAC has local groups which hold regular meetings? In some areas, others interested in counselling have been getting together for mutual professional and personal support.

As a counsellor, I find that some difficulties are easier to work through with other counsellors, however loving friends and family may be. I have been part of a supervision and personal growth group for over five-and-a-half years now. I find it vital and nourishing. We meet monthly in each other's houses.

The addition of a 'growth' element means that we have to continue to work on our self-development, and we divide the time between supervision work and personal work.

We also have informal arrangements between ourselves that allow us to phone a colleague to debrief immediately after an exceptionally heavy session—this is in addition to whatever one-to-one supervision we have arranged individually and varies with our work practice. Some of us are in private practice and some combine our counselling with other work.

My view is that of a counsellor with some experience and I know that my senior colleagues still use and value supervision. I have included the following statement to represent the voice of the new counsellor. The writer is currently a student on a counselling course, seeing clients and, naturally, having supervision. I can echo many of her feelings about the experience:

Counselling can be a lonely road to travel. The majority of your time is spent in isolation. I see supervision in terms of a fellow traveller coming alongside, someone who perhaps passed by this route some time back, someone who may be more experienced in reading the signs.

Although there are those who would say that a supervisor has distinct responsibilities regarding the standard of work and the ongoing assessment of the counsellor, which may be appropriate in a working environment, I see supervision more in terms of a support role.

Yes, the counsellor is encouraged to present her case work, in whatever form is appropriate—written, verbatim, audio recordings and so on. This is a negotiable part of the working alliance.

For me an invaluable part of supervision is the 'here and now' relationship and the openness to explore my own feelings and reactions. Frequently my feelings are all tangled together: client relationships, family relationships, friendships, all intertwined. Supervision helps to begin the process of unravelling them.

It has often been said that counsellors learn from experience. I believe for myself this is true. How often do I agonise over the session that just didn't seem to go right. How much more constructive it is to take my agonising to supervision. Perhaps supervision could be likened to calling out the pilot to direct the ship into a safe harbour where the necessary assessment of damage can be made.

Several important points are made in this statement. Often the relationship between counsellor and supervisor reflects difficulties the counsellor (supervisee) is having with his client. I may find myself being vague and defensive, imagining that my supervisor will not understand the difficulty or will perhaps feel that I am at fault. When I can own this anxiety or am challenged about my vagueness or asked to reflect on how my behaviour is mirroring that of my client, a whole new range of possibilities opens up. I can use the session to explore my feelings; I can have help to plan other ways of working. I can use the time to understand better how my behaviour and beliefs and feelings are affecting my work with my client. I can try to explore with my client the possibility that her vagueness is an attempt to protect herself from a fear of being judged. Without supervision providing trust, support and challenge, I might never pick up the problem or I might fail to confront it.

Some supervisors confine their work with supervisees to client material only; some will look at the impact of the supervisee's feelings and life on his counselling. Personally, I prefer the latter, as it can be very helpful to have parallels pointed out, to be helped to make connections between my life and the client's. This is not a constant theme, but on those occasions when I have felt confused about my reactions to a client or his situation, this ability to look at my own life has been very helpful. This is not my having a therapy session with my supervisor but simply using the extra information to shed new light on a counselling difficulty. If I needed to do some more personal work as a result of issues that came up in supervision, it would be my responsibility to arrange it.

What mix of support and supervision will best fit your needs? Please give a lot of time, thought and effort to answering this for yourself and creating the right balance of these elements for your situation. It might be useful to make an action plan, working out what you want and the steps you will need to take to achieve it. Would it help to make an informal 'contract' with a colleague, to encourage and support you in carrying out your plan?

This exercise will give you valuable experience in action planning and how it feels to be supported in working through one.

If necessary, you could repeat the process to help you establish your professional support.

How did it feel making a contract?

Did the contract make it easier or harder to reach your target?

How aware were you of the skills your partner used to help you in your planning?

Have you gained any insights into how this exercise might feel to a client?

Were the 'steps' you used to break up your task the right size for you—not too hard or too easy?

Referral

This is a skill, not a sign of incompetence. Do you know who you could refer your clients to if they needed more specialist help? It is useful to have some information on this before the occasion arises. Does your workplace have a policy on this, can you refer to senior colleagues? What skills and special expertise are available locally? Do other agencies accept referrals from your workplace directly?

Remember that the more positively your client feels about the referral, the more likely it is to be successful. Choosing an appropriately skilled and experienced and competent colleague is therefore an important responsibility. Your confidence in the quality of the referral will be reassuring to your client.

As I stressed in Chapter Eight when discussing special problems, do suggest referral sensitively. One unfortunate client, who overwhelmed a very new listener with a painful and detailed story of sexual abuse, was further bruised by the listener's response. The unspoken rather than the spoken message was, 'Oh no, this is too much for me. Where can I send her?' Clients are excellent readers of the unspoken language. Her new counsellor had a great deal of repair work to do before being able to work on the original difficulty.

It is hard sometimes to contain your distress when hearing horrendous details, but please remember the client's pain and vulnerability, too. Focusing on her pain while being aware of your own is difficult, yet it is so easy for a vulnerable person to feel rejected, to sense their worst fears about confiding in someone coming true.

Offer your continuing support while finding a more experienced helper, and be available until the new relationship is established.

You might like to think through how you would handle such a situation. How would you feel? How would you broach the idea of referral? Who could you refer your client to?

The skills covered in this part of the book are only basic and need to be practised under supervision, as part of a learning group. Being videoed is very useful, so do embrace the opportunity if this is available to you. I hope that you feel interested enough in counselling to want to continue. I hope you feel, as I do, that the core conditions and helpful assumptions outlined in Chapter Two could usefully apply in any and all relationships.

PART TWO
COMBINING COUNSELLING
WITH OTHER SKILLS

Introduction

This part of the book offers the personal views and experiences of a number of people using counselling or counselling skills. They come from a variety of disciplines and the counselling component of their work varies in depth, intensity and proportion to their main work.

Names and identifying details, such as location, have been changed to protect the privacy and confidentiality of clients and colleagues of the contributors.

The aim of this part is to show how counselling can be used in the context of another profession, to share dilemmas and to raise questions for you to consider. Some contributors simply sent me written material; others were able to have taped discussions with me. I have tried to obtrude as little as possible. The same basic questions were put to all:

- What do you think counselling is?
- Do you follow any particular theory?
- What is your main task and how does counselling fit into it?
- Are there any ethical dilemmas or practical problems that are peculiar to your situation?
- Do you have any advice to offer a colleague who may be considering counselling training in order to add that skill to his or her work?

The answers and the way they are presented are as individual as the contributors who have so generously given their time and effort. We hope that you will find the information interesting and stimulating in itself, that it will give you food for thought and that it will perhaps help in deciding how to add counselling to your work.

There are two other ways that you can use these contributions. In Part One we looked at the skills of summary and the search for themes. Reading through these contributions could offer you practice in these skills. Another possible use is to consider how each contributor uses language, how he or she describes feelings and concerns. Consider their verbal style—is it short and sharp or more relaxed and exploratory?

Since they are all concerned with the same topics, comparison should be easier.

12 Counselling in Further Education

Zelda works in further education: I'll leave her to explain the exact nature of her duties. What we are going to discuss here is her understanding of counselling and how it fits, or does not fit, into her other roles and responsibilities, and perhaps where some of the difficulties lie. For example, if she is going to talk to a colleague or set up a counselling service within work, what boundaries would she want to establish, what support, what supervision? What are the ethical dilemmas she faces when wearing more than one hat, and one of them a counselling hat?

* * *

My contracted job is to teach information technology—in fact I run the department. Some three years ago it was decided that there would be a counselling service and this was written in to the so-called 'mission statement' of the institution. Then they looked round for people who could do it, and since, the year before the reorganisation, the college as it then was had funded me to go on a university certificate course, it became my responsibility, despite the fact that I said repeatedly that, although I was prepared to do some counselling, I was not prepared to be responsible for its organisation. I have never had an official title, and they have respected my request in that sense, but, on the other hand, if anything crops up or if there is organisation to be done, at the moment, I do it.

Did they say how you were to do it—when and how?

It wasn't anything like as organised as that. We'll go back to the reorganisation three years ago. I was a tutor in the old technical college, and I originally went on the certificate course because I felt I needed more skills than I had. There was no thought at that time of setting up a counselling service. We underwent reorganisation, and right from the beginning a group of people, some of whom were just interested, some of whom had a sort of elementary training, got together and talked about how we could possibly set up a skeleton service, which would be a temporary thing until a college counsellor was appointed. And there was agreement from the management, from the beginning, that eventually this would be done. That group met for about a year, and at the end of that time produced a report, and we moved on what we thought was a minimum.

I'm trying to think whether that year we were given any time—I rather suspect that we were not—but in later years we have been given an hour or two hours off work, plus contact time, to do the counselling. I have two hours a week at the moment and I see up to eight clients. Sometimes I've got eight clients, all of whom take at least an hour—not 50 minutes—an hour, so it overruns by a long way. (Fifty minutes are the classic therapy hour.) On the other hand, there are people, because this is spread quite widely, who have that hour or two hours on their timetable but who do very little counselling. The institution probably provides enough time, but there isn't enough in the right place.

When we set out there was no physical space to do this in, and as we stand at the moment it has been a constant battle because the college is short of space and we have no headquarters or recognised place that this is where counselling happens. We are a two-site institution and on one of the sites there is still literally nowhere. For example, last week I saw a student in a little space partitioned off the staff room, where the partition didn't reach the ceiling, and the people she was trying to talk about—the staff she was having problems with—were sitting behind a flimsy, thin partition. And you could hear them talking, making their brews and so on.

On the other site we use a room that doubles up as a staff room for student services staff, and they are very sympathetic: when they know I am booked in with a client, that room is mine and I can shut the door. It is an upstairs room, so there are no interruptions from people walking past on the ground floor, and I can make a drink for the student if I want to. Whilst that room is not ideal, inasmuch as it is not my room and I can't put things in and expect them to stay there, at least I have somewhere that I can go. The boundaries are more intangible and haven't been discussed and written down as policy, the reason being that there has been no one person taking responsibility for this service—it is still, after three years, a temporary thing.

Things like advertising—how we make ourselves known to the students—are done on a very *ad hoc* basis, when someone remembers it and thinks it a good idea. A lot of the staff, and even more of the students, are not fully aware of what the service can offer. This last week there have been problems of whether the service is just for students or whether staff can use it. If it is for staff, that of course raises horrendous problems of confidentiality because the people who would be their counsellors are also their peers in the organisation. There are issues around whether, if you have a student and that student leaves college, you can still continue. Does the counselling have to stop when they go? For example, I have one student who is under disciplinary and may well be asked to leave the college and I'm not sure what my role would then be, whether I stop abruptly or whether I could continue.

And then the other big boundary issues are the other hats you wear.

Because, of course, I am seen around college and identified as a teacher, and quite a lot of students will have problems, part of which belong to the college. And there are issues as to how much can they trust someone who is also a part of that organisation. But the boundaries aren't clarified because there isn't anybody within the institution to clarify them with. I suppose, of all the people within the institution, I have more training than most—of any, I think. But I have no supervision within the institution. I am supervised, but I go outside and pay for my own. And so what I tend to do is think through for myself these issues of boundaries; I make up my own guidelines, but there aren't institutional guidelines because, as I say, the structure is not there.

Do you feel the lack of that?

There is a lack of support, but there is also a lot of freedom. And I have to say that some of the best work I have done has been on those boundaries. I once had a supervisor who was very boundary conscious, and was appalled if you ran five minutes over the time. I do strongly suspect that sometimes the boundaries are there for the protection of the counsellor as much as for the protection of the client. And I can use as much flexibility as I choose, because there isn't anybody there looking over my shoulder very much, or protecting me. As I say, I do have a very good supervisor at the moment. There is the fact that I am having to pay for that, and the hope is that when the counsellor, who is currently advertised for, is appointed, one of her prime jobs will be supervision.

There is the issue of whether you counsel people you teach. OK, do you counsel people you might once have taught? If you don't do that, do you counsel people who are in your division? In other words, people who are perhaps doing A level and see you around very much with that hat on? What I do at the moment is decide case by case. But there is no screening: most students are there and I have to make a decision on the hoof: is it appropriate or is it not?

I have one student I can think of at the moment—literally she was in a crisis state. I happened to run into her and said, 'Come on, I'll make you a brew.' It wasn't, 'Come on, I'll give you counselling.' And if I had had time, I think, to sit back and think 'hang on', she might have been better seeing somebody else, because there are a lot of issues about who she sees me as. On the other hand there is a lot of work done on those issues—it's a very fertile field to be working in. You work with what you've got, don't you? Whatever it is, it's material that can be used.

More and more with student counselling, I feel, the traditional view is that it isn't advice giving. And I suppose I tend to the less directed end of the spectrum. When I look at what students actually ask for, they are wanting advice, and I have a feeling that maybe if it was less pure, if the person who was doing the counselling was also involved within the institution, in things like financial services and advice on housing and stuff like that, then you would get an opportunity to pick up stuff that later could be used. You meet that student in a very informal way and you can then take up some counselling, or use some counselling skills, whichever is more appropriate. Whereas if you wait for that student to refer himself to counselling as such, you never get there.

I think that is the most productive way forward and that is a change for me over the last three years. I would have said no—settle for counselling service, where students come for the 50 minutes, referred by themselves preferably. What I actually see is what a student will experience as problems: 'can't meet deadlines, been thrown out of the family house'. Now if they've been thrown out, what they need is how to get advice on housing aid—counselling can come later if you have built up a relationship and you get the chance to start to build up that relationship.

And there are very practical, nitty-gritty things. A lot of students at 16 years old are frightened to death of what is going to happen to them if they walk into this thing called counselling. They think you've got to be mad to go there. Or if you're not mad when you go, you will be when you've finished. So it's much more acceptable for their own self-esteem to go and seek help on financial matters or whatever, than it is actually for them to refer themselves to counselling.

Counselling is working with a relationship. It's building up by whatever means, and I would use all sorts of means, dependent on the student or the client, to build what will hopefully be a healing relationship. And all the skills, like listening and attending and all the other things we learn about, are for me the tools by which I try to build this healing relationship. And I don't think I'd like to define it any more than that. I would try to be skilled in as many approaches as I could.

My prime job when somebody comes in is the building of a relationship, and if I can get that the rest will follow. And to be honest I can start that with, 'How do you move your furniture out?' and that sort of thing. And that's part of the richness of where I am in that the student will see me in three dimensions. I am not just there for those 50 minutes. If it was purely psycho-dynamic I would have a hard time of it, because there is no way I'm going to remain a neutral screen on which they can project things. I will have a reputation within the institution, they will see me around, so even if I wanted to I can't operate in that way.

And if they were to go back these last three years and get someone in there from the beginning whose prime task it was—who wouldn't be diverted by also running another department, or having to teach lessons or whatever it is— once you've got that one person in there, the rest of the people involved have a focus, have a person through whom they refer, and that would overcome what I think is a big issue for a lot of us—isolation. Because of our timetable, because of the split site, because we are all busy people, we don't get together and meet. Because we don't get together and meet, we don't know what the others are doing, so there is not a coherent service offered to the college. I think that is bad. You go to one person and you get something completely different from what you might get if you came to me.

The other big issue about not having anybody seen as responsible is that the service itself doesn't have status. It is seen in the way that women's work is seen, as 'a nice person, offering a helping hand'. It isn't seen as a professional thing in any way. So you want someone in who is within the management scale if possible, someone who has status within the organisation—who has organisational status—and gives the service a status. And if that person can also be connected with the courses, I think that would help. Not just student services, because student services tend to be the Cinderella service in FE at the moment. If they could be seen to have academic input I have to say that I think the snob value would pay off. I don't think it is essential, but I think it helps.

There is a lot of resistance from staff who feel that this is not something that rightly belongs within a college; that if students need this odd help they should be getting it outside; that we are there to teach, not to wipe their noses. The attitude is seen to be soft, as student-manipulated, whereas they should be kicked out. There is a lot of consciousness-raising, if you like, and education has to go on with staff, particularly tutorial staff.

Having said that, there are an awful lot of staff who are extremely supportive, way beyond what they need to be, and I've had that experience and wouldn't like it to be felt that I haven't been supported within the organisation, but it's been a personal support and goodwill rather than institutional support.

This issue with my own colleagues as opposed to students is the trickiest one of the lot. I have had a couple of colleagues who have come to see me. I suspect that those colleagues would have come anyway, rather than that they have used it because it was a counselling service. But there is one person in the pipeline at the moment, and I don't know who he or she is, who has made enquiries through a third person. What I did with that was say to this third person, 'Go back, talk it through with this person, make sure they are absolutely clear about whether they really do want to see another member of the staff.' This is because, although I know that I will respect confidentiality, I think it might take a considerable amount of time to build trust. Also, once that relationship has been entered into, we cannot easily go back to colleague/colleague, and that could be very sticky. Both of us will have been involved in a relationship that is not a colleague/colleague relationship, and you don't forget that. I've no idea whether this person is a colleague on the same level as myself or higher up in the hierarchy—I don't know who it is. There are lots of issues around that.

When you have a counselling service like the university has, which is quite separate from the academic side of things, where the staff who counsel are not academic, then you've got a different kettle of fish, but if you are not careful an almost incestuous relationship can happen and you have to be very wary. As I say, with someone who knows what they are doing, full of confidence, those tangled issues in themselves can be extremely productive. They can also strangle you. It's not something that I think I would be happy to do.

*   *   *

Have you noticed how positively Zelda feels about working on boundaries? Would you feel the same?

Have you considered the problems of counselling a colleague, perhaps one senior to you? Would it make it easier or harder if they were on your level?

How would you feel about working together afterwards?

Does the status of the counsellor make a difference to her work, or just to how others see her?

What did you think of Zelda's point about combining her counselling with practical help, or using the offer of such help to make it easier for the student to ask for counselling?

Do you find that you, too, are isolated because few people at work share, or understand, or value the task of counselling?

How far do you think her task could be eased by changes within the organisation, by simple measures such as the provision of a counselling room?

Would any of her difficulties apply in your workplace?

How would you go about getting referrals? Would or could you advertise your service within your institution?

Have you gained an impression of Zelda's style of counselling and the theory or theories that she finds important?

How does her practice and understanding of counselling differ from your own?

Would you also have to find time and money to pay for supervision?

Would you prefer to have more clarity in your working boundaries? Or would you also relish the freedom and challenge?

13 Counselling with Speech and Language Therapy

Kay is a speech and language therapist with counselling training and experience. Like the other contributors, she offers her personal view and experiences; she does not claim to speak for all speech therapists or for her profession as a whole. She has also made available some material she has collected and worked on, which contains the views of some of her colleagues.

Feel free to discuss and disagree, to assess and discard. Take only what is useful for you. If this contribution gives you food for thoughtful discussion, Kay will be well pleased.

*　　*　　*

The value of counselling within speech and language therapy has been recognised for many years and our professional body has named advisers in this field. Our role has become more and more holistic. We have recognised the need to focus on the individual and the communication problem, since communication is too intimately linked with personality and human development for us to treat the communication disorder effectively *per se*.

The boundaries of our respective roles are very different. Our remit is not the same as that of the counsellor, and patients/clients come to speech therapy with very different expectations from those they bring to counselling. In terms of clarifying problems and goal-setting, the three introductory stages, as set out by G. Egan (*The Skilled Helper*,

Brookes and Cole, 1982), can easily be 'lifted' as an effective approach in speech therapy. The core values listed by Nelson Jones (*Practical Counselling and Helping Skills*, Cassell, 1988), help pave the way to more effective therapy through active listening and creating.

I do not personally believe, however, that speech and language therapists should be expected or asked to counsel in their work. Confusion may arise when references to counselling are made in training or articles. This is because many perceive this as yet something else to 'learn' and 'use'. In fact the very skills we gain through our training and experience are essentially the same as those needed in counselling.

To quote a colleague: 'Whilst the focus of speech therapy is on the person who does not communicate, offering this focus is used to make changes in the whole of his environment—that is, those involved with him. They need to understand concepts of good communication, how sounds are formed and also something about developmental changes (in children). This must involve movement and change, and a strand of therapy must therefore be counselling.'

Three of my colleagues are quite clear that counselling is part of their work and use the term confidently. One, describing her work with psychogenic voice disorders, pointed out that initial sessions must be structured in such a way as to enable patients to explore and recognise for themselves the underlying factors, and to explore their feelings about this. Once understood, direct voice work may be needed. She described the case of a woman on her first visit, who appeared to appreciate fully the need to explore root causes, but could come up with no definite answer. It was only as she got up to leave that she was able to open up sufficiently to mention her suspicions that her husband was having an affair. Follow-up sessions explored her feelings about this hitherto unadmitted hurt in her life, and how her voice problems linked in. Her voice came back of its own accord. Clearly, counselling skills were required for both therapist and patient to take this journey together.

Another colleague sees her work as 'a way of helping people make the best use of what they know', while a third feels that she does not necessarily need to counsel but she does need to listen. 'It's not what they are saying that's always the most important, it's what's behind the words that you need to listen to, and watch for.' So said one therapist of her initial meetings with the parents of language delayed children.

Two further colleagues with considerable skills and experience both work, with very different approaches, primarily with the parents of pre-school children with language delay. Both stress that they do not counsel; they feel they do not have the qualifications to make such a claim, nor do they see it as part of their role. The nature of their work means that they must be 'more directive' than they would perceive counsellors as being, but they do see their primary goal as establishing a good working relationship with the parents, if therapy is to be successful. Without that it might perhaps be inappropriate to continue.

Why is this so important? 'Because they know the child and I don't . . . Because their concerns and perceptions about the problem may be different from mine.' By listening and observing first, one says, she can 'tune in to the parents' language without imposing her own aim. She feels body posture and movement can tell her far more about how the parent may be really feeling, than what is being expressed in words. Both want to make parents feel comfortable and informed, to take away the mystery of what therapy is about. Both want to be able to open up and explore unspoken fears, anxieties and guilt. Only then can one colleague begin her modelling programme and the other expect parents to take responsibility for what will happen next in therapy. Both use words such as 'listening', 'enabling', 'clarifying', 'reflecting back'.

Since a communication problem within a system causes

imbalance and creates 'stuckness', counselling is the best way of moving out of this situation. This does not mean we as speech therapists must 'counsel', it means that as we gain confidence and experience we can begin to step down off our professional pedestal and share our skills.

Studies show that people respond more to professionals who are recalled as being 'warm, interested, and understanding' than to those who present themselves as 'businesslike'. These qualities are seen as more important than experience or professional efficiency.

When a colleague offered the definition of counselling as 'enabling people to perceive more clearly their problems and how they choose to deal with them', another said, 'Yes, that's it, that is exactly what I do!' She was, however, hesitant to use the term 'counselling' in her work with stammerers. This is because her work is often directive and she may be 'teaching' parents, for instance, about management. Her counselling skills are needed to enable her to break down any resistance to taking responsibility because they want their child to be treated. Unless this is worked through, speech therapy cannot be effective.

Another colleague who also sees counselling as a strand of her work, both with voice and stroke patients, acknowledges that teaching management is an integral part of her task. She is not a counsellor, but she has developed her skills as an enabler and facilitator. Her patients therefore have enough trust in her and themselves to explore their feelings and their emotional blocks in coming to terms with their communication breakdown.

We would not be professional speech and language therapists if we did not ourselves believe that we can bring about change and work alongside people. It is our choice, however, how we define our own boundaries, and to what extent we choose and feel able to 'give away' our skills and work alongside or through our patients.

*   *   *

How does the way Kay uses counselling differ from the way you might use it in your work?

What do you think is meant by the term 'giving away skills'?

Have you got a professional pedestal? Do you spend much time on it? Is it important to you? (I take it to mean professional dignity, distance, a sort of 'white coat barrier'.)

How does Kay's understanding of the counselling tasks differ from your own?

Do you agree or disagree with her ideas?

How do the definitions of counselling given by her colleagues compare to yours?

14   Counselling in School

Judy is a very senior and experienced teacher. She is a
faculty and year head and her specialist subject is English.
She has an infectious and continuing delight in literature,
poetry and the beauty of words which she shares successfully with many of her students. Her other specialist subject, though she would never say so, is 'stroppy' teenagers.
No matter how revolting in any sense, Judy can see the
potential in them as well as the pain. Her ducklings do not
always become swans, but more often than not they become
better ducks!

She is loath to describe what she does as 'pure counselling'. She offers her personal viewpoint as just that: her
views and experiences, a starting point for discussion and
thought. When I asked her what she would say to a young
colleague thinking of offering counselling, she said, 'Don't!
Or only for the personal development.'

Her very individual contribution was in the form of short
notes, vivid sentences, more a series of jottings. I have tried
to preserve the flavour of her work.

*   *   *

Define counselling? Just Carl Rogers.

Record keeping. A terrible dilemma, I do not feel safe to
record (counselling notes), I keep them in my head. I am not
happy with this. I am a head of year/counsellor; if there was
a full-time counsellor who could also help staff . . . (*sigh*).

English teaching is compatible with counselling. The
kids are used to me discussing feelings in poetry, drama and

novels. General counselling ideas get floated in assembly—
Eric Berne's *Transactional Analysis*, the kids know the
terminology. It is a way in to communication.

Supervision. Only from the group (Judy belongs to a
supervision and support group, a private initiative which
she attends in her own time). Occasionally there is a social
worker around who I can talk to. People, colleagues, tend to
unload on me. I just hold it. It has never been long term.

Practical difficulties. These are of course privacy and
freedom from interruption, time and timetabling.

Recognising priorities. If a child says, 'I must see you, I
can't wait,' I say, 'I'll see you at such and such a time.' If he
says, 'It's okay, I won't bother you, don't worry, it doesn't
matter . . .' I say, 'Come in, I can spare you a few minutes.'
There is an ethical problem of priorities here if I should
be teaching another class. There is very little time allowed.

No magic wands. My office door, which I keep unlocked,
is a bolt-hole for kids in trouble, even if I am not in there.
This can be abused/misunderstood by colleagues.

Teachers need support too, need their self-esteem boost-
ing. Children coming to me can be seen as a threat to a
colleague's position. Also there is the practical problem of
kids missing time in their subject.

Children want . . . Most children do not want to be badly
behaved. It is a response to something amiss in their lives.
Change is often imposed on them without discussion. They
are helpless and play up to call out for help or to prove that
they at least have some power. There are limits to my power
to help. Damage is sometimes identified, and before the
child can be helped, governors add to the distress by
permanently excluding a pupil.

In loco parentis. I feel this suggests a love of children,
a need for unconditional, positive regard. Tough love, a
tender toughness.

Counselling. There are increasing pressures on kids,
large comprehensive schools, with a wide variety of backgrounds and ability, increasing stress from broken families,

unemployment, difficult home situations. Sometimes the parents need counselling. There is a need to build up confidence and self-esteem. There is a need for help with relationships between teacher and student and student and student. I have become more aware of these tasks which could be seen as counselling.

It can be difficult to be congruent. Can you be Rogerian in an authoritarian school? There is a conflict of insisting on basic rules, e.g. uniform, of there being no discussion possible in some situations, and at other times allowing kids to say anything.

I am concerned that empathy can be used as a manipulative tool, coercive empathy?

I make an eclectic use of techniques. I fit them into the educational context. My main aim is to help students achieve their full potential.

Trust/confidentiality. I say sometimes I might need to consult others, but I would never do it without first discussing it with you (the child). I would check on the timing of it and the methods.

Counselling on the hoof. I do it while walking down corridors—ten minutes at registration, maybe . . .

The human social functioning type of approach can be very successful—it ends with a sort of plan for the future, which they like to check up on with me. I start with an appraisal of where they are and how they hope to get to where they want to be. I have this typed and we both sign it. Strictly confidential. Sometimes we discuss telling another member of staff that it has been done.

Unhelpful responses. Some staff have an unprofessional attitude to counselling. 'Have you been for your cosy little chat with Mrs Kenny, then?' There is a need to be assertive with teachers like that.

Training colleagues obliquely. I felt a real growth point when I stumbled across the idea of giving a less than subtle colleague my chair in my office as he tried to 'get through to a kid'. Miraculously he went into counsellor mode and started listening! For the first time kid and teacher 'heard' each other and made great strides in their relationship. I sat silent, watching it happen. This student had been drifting, unaware of his potential. His difficulties at home meant he did not always complete his work. Both parties were given a boost which kick-started the kid's academic progress.

Ethical dilemmas. Pregnancy is a major dilemma. How best to help the girl, how to support her in disclosing who and when?

Trusting kids when they say they can deal with it. Awareness of trouble stored should a kid not cope. Kids often wish to protect parents.

One girl, who was sexually abused by a female baby-sitter, just needed to talk. The danger of a repeat performance was gone. She (the girl) knew that her mum and dad would feel shame and guilt if they knew. The girl felt that now I had heard it, it was 'finished business'. So far I have had no regrets.

No guidelines. The whole business of my counselling is left very unstructured. No policy. I fear strict guidelines. Increasingly teachers are prescribed their roles and not allowed to be trusted professionals. Once structures are introduced kids will lose out—for example, Mrs Gillick's outrage that some doctors were putting young girls on the pill without insisting parents knew. They'd tried to persuade girls to confide in their parents but respected confidentiality if this failed. Once this was declared unethical girls stopped consulting their GPs.

Ignorance is bliss. It is painful to discover a child's need for regular counselling and not be able to offer it. This is how counselling on the hoof developed. Kids are so used to not being listened to that even ten minutes' intense 'grunt therapy' is a luxury they respond to (I guess that Judy is referring to encouraging noises, minimal prompts, ums and ahs).

Head of year role. In my role as head of year, encouraging academic success is helped by my using counselling skills. I can pick up danger signs early.

Kimberly (not real name) was getting into trouble with her teachers. We met in my office to discuss this. She was appalled when I suggested she was acting like a 'bimbo'. Was this what she wanted? She realised she was bright and wanted to be educated. She had been trying to discuss this issue with her parents, but got nowhere. She asked to be put on report, wondered if it would be seen as punishment. When I suggested it might help her pass muster with her friends, she was relieved that she could blame it for the fact that she had to work. She would not be called a swot. I had put in the boundaries.

*   *   *

What do you feel about the load Judy carries?

Would you feel as she does about the lack of guidelines?

Should the school provide support and supervision for her valuable work?

How do you think you would work with some of the issues mentioned? You might like to choose one and explore it, research it if you like, look for organisational guidelines, legal obligations and so on.

15 Counselling with Arts-Based Therapies

Lesley works using arts-based therapies and combines this with counselling skills.

*   *   *

How do you define counselling?

I use counselling as a way to help people tell me things that they might find it hard to talk about with family and friends. People often have a lot of emotional overload in their relationships. In the counselling relationship this overload isn't there. People know that they are going to get listened to.

Listening is the important part. The clients know that not only will they get a fair crack of the whip, but the whip is in their own hands all the time. They do not have to carry the counsellor's load, the counsellor is there entirely to help them, to listen to them. The thing about counselling is, because you are listening, you are standing back slightly. So it is possible for you to see a larger part of the picture they are painting for you, and to describe it back to them. And in that way they see parts of themselves that they weren't aware of.

Could you describe your work?

A large part of my work is involved in using art and music with groups of people: a lot of elderly people in residential homes, people with learning disabilities and a lot of communication difficulties; also people with psychiatric problems—a wide variety, really. In using my skills with these groups, counselling has helped me to become much more aware of the dynamics of the group. By watching and listening, by observing more closely what is going on, I can judge more finely how I initiate activities in the group. Music in particular is a means of communication by itself, but in addition to listening to the sounds people are making, by using my counselling skills and watching their body language I can pick up and respond to their underlying feelings. Sometimes they are surprised that I have picked things up, they are not aware of having made that communication. So this can expand their awareness of what they can use to communicate with.

Music is a very emotive language, it has a tremendous emotional charge in it. Quite often very elderly people are particularly moved by it and do not know why, sometimes they even burst into tears. It is very important. I feel that through my counselling skills I have increased my ability to help them with this. It is a very essential discharge of emotion, but it can be very distressing for the people around them who do not understand. And it is 'There there, dear, wipe up those tears . . .' And that doesn't really answer it, because the music may have brought up memory which has provoked what appears to be distress but is a treasure; it is sad and important to them, even when they cannot put a name to the memory.

When I work with individuals, as I am doing increasingly, counselling or counselling techniques are a very important part of the introduction stage of a session. It is necessary before I can use my art techniques for the nub of the work, so to speak, that I understand as clearly as possible where my client is at, what she is feeling, how she has moved since the last time we met. I need a range of observational techniques, very carefully phrased questions, to find out what I need to know in order to apply the art technique I am going to use in her therapy. I actually ask the

questions that will give me the information. That may
sound as if I am manipulating the answers. Far from it: the
questions must be such that she will realise what she is
feeling and what she needs from the session. They are not
so much diagnostic, much more exploratory. You have to
explore the area the client has brought to you, the areas you
have been dealing with (in previous sessions) and the life
that has been lived between sessions. So it is exploratory in
order for me to formulate how we proceed.

At the end of a session I again use similar techniques
because the client will have felt and experienced a great
deal and will need to integrate this. This is called process-
ing, and it needs to be looked at throughout the session. I
must be alert, then, in the talking that closes the session,
bring feelings and experiences out and help the client to see
and question these points and begin to see what relevance
these have in her life.

*   *   *

I asked Lesley if she encountered any ethical dilemmas in
using counselling skills in her work.

She replied that she found no dilemmas in using counselling skills with her primarily arts-based work as they
simply enhance her work and do not conflict with it.

Lesley has found ways to fit her counselling skills into
her work, so smoothly that there are no rough edges. How
far would it be possible to do this in your work situation?
For her there would be no conflict about which code of
ethics to use. She would be able to work within the BAC
code for using counselling skills. Would you consider that
her counselling skills are used primarily to enhance communication and to enable her clients to get the maximum benefits from her art- and music-based therapies? Or
would you describe the quality of her listening, observing
and non-verbal communication as 'therapeutic', helpful in
itself?

16 Counselling in Community Work

Marie has done a basic counselling skills course and now finds herself using these skills both in her everyday life and to some extent in her part-time work.

*   *   *

I took part in a basic counselling skills course about a year ago. Until then I felt I knew a fair bit about counselling but I realised from that course that in fact I had a lot more to learn, and what I had been putting into effect was probably more listening skills. Taking part in the course has made me think more about what I am doing. A lot of the time I find myself adapting skills of counselling to the situation, but it is still helpful to know about the basics and I use as many of the principles as I feel are appropriate at the time.

Counselling to me is a relationship between two people, whereby one is counselling the other and there is a definite contract, not necessarily written, but both parties are aware of what they are undertaking and the differing roles they have. Within that relationship the counsellor listens to the person who has asked for counselling—and that would be part of the contract, that he had asked for it; listens to him and uses various principles and methods that are recognised in counselling, to enable him to come to his own resolution of the problem as he sees it. To my mind the counsellor would not act in any directive way, but more in a challenging way.

This relationship may be over quite a long time and

things within the person, within his life, may change, or he may see underlying causes more clearly. But there has to be choice, so he may choose to opt out, not to continue. The counsellor does not prevent this, she is not directive. This is based on the belief which I see as increasingly valid—that for anyone to make changes in his life, or lifestyle or relationships, it needs to be his decision. So then he himself—OK, with help and professional skill from the counsellor—makes the decision about what to change and how to do it. Because then he has got his own force behind what he is doing.

It may be helpful for you to realise my situation and how I came to use counselling skills as much as I can. I am trained and experienced as a community worker. For the last ten years I have been based at home, bringing up our family, and have been involved in various types of community work on a voluntary basis. This has meant that our house has all sorts of people coming in and out. I also visit elderly people in the community, and I am involved with the local volunteer group, providing transport and helping in lots of other ways. More recently my partner and I have become registered childminders, and over the last few months I have been doing a job on a casual basis in a local old people's home. I come across people in varying situations and have varying relationships with them—friendships going back years or a few months, or people I have just met.

If they seem to be approaching me in that way, I put into practice what I have learnt of counselling skills. I think increasingly I see the value of listening as an important element in relationships. I was brought up in a family where the opposite was the norm. Talking and getting your point across, that was the important thing; if you were being quiet or listening there was not so much value in that.

As time has gone on, from personal experience, from friends who have been supportive and from training, I have come to feel that listening is as important as speaking. In listening you learn as much as if not more than you do when you are doing the speaking. In my general experience of life and with my basic belief in the principles of Christianity, I find that many people have a great need to be listened to, to have personal attention, to be valued for what they have to offer. These people may never have had this earlier in their lives or they might be going through difficulties in their relationships now.

How do you use counselling?

I find myself counselling people at any time, really, certainly using the principles in any relationship I may be in and most often when I feel—it's a gut reaction, really—that they need some particular attention or have a particular concern. Then I have an alert in my head, to focus my attention on them. I say as little as possible about my needs, then try to put some counselling skills in action. These situations are varied—from meeting someone in the centre of town to a neighbour popping in with a young child she is having difficulties with, or an older person in the home where I work . . .

These situations seem to have one thing in common: in all of them you are describing your assessment of people as needing to have this help from you. You do not mention them asking or actively seeking it. You earlier defined counselling as something both parties knew was happening. Is what you are describing nearer to using counselling skills rather than counselling?

It has become part of me to do this (said with a vigorous nod of the head) even though quite often there is a sort of trigger in the head realising what I am doing. Sometimes that trigger means that I quite deliberately shut off what may be my needs in a relationship. In using the skills, certain of them are difficult to put into practice. The important one of making a contract is an example of this difficulty. To stop the flow to say, 'Hang on, let's make a contract', would probably stop what was happening. It would be too formal. Also, they might see me as setting myself up as an expert, they might not feel they want that sort of help. There are certainly a lot of limits and frustrations to working like this. I hope it is still valuable.

Because my home is also my workplace for fostering and elder care, I do most of my listening there. Interruptions are a frustration—a knock at the door, the telephone ringing or needing to attend to children or anyone else who is around. There is also the need to carry on with running our life, like cooking a meal. I am developing ways to help myself with this. For instance, if I see someone needs to talk I will as discreetly as possible take the phone off the hook. I position myself in the room in such a way as to stop anyone coming in, or where I can see if somebody is coming to the door.

My partner is increasingly helpful. I have tried to explain what I am trying to do. Now, without saying anything about an individual, I can drop a hint that someone needs me in this way and he tries to provide a cocoon for the work, protecting us from interruption and taking over other tasks.

What about the issue of counselling family and friends?

There certainly are difficulties about counselling family and friends, probably family even more than friends—with family it is very difficult to stay separate, just to stay quiet and not make any value judgements when you may be part of whatever difficulty they may be relating. I have come to accept, with regret, that in many ways it is just not appropriate for me to be that person (their counsellor).

With counselling friends, the difficulty is that for friendship to flourish it has to be a mutual thing. Usually in any meeting there is an equal amount of talking on both sides. Sometimes, in a counselling situation with a friend, I find that I am trying to find comparable experiences or problems of my own to match hers. I tell her about these, sometimes enlarge on them, make them sound worse than they are or were. This is to try to make her feel that she is not so very different from me, to make us more equal. I am not happy with this. It feels dishonest. I do not want to see her as a victim. This is the real disadvantage in counselling a friend.

*   *   *

Marie raises many interesting points. Her concerns and frustrations with using counselling skills in her home setting, and her understanding of the limits of counselling with family and friends, offer us food for thought.

How would you approach or solve similar dilemmas?

Have you noticed how Marie's life is full of experiences and situations that melt into each other? Home and workplace, family and friends, listening and cooking, voluntary and paid work all flow through her days, linked by her awareness of the needs and concerns of others. One vital thread that is woven through it all is her Christianity.

What support would you seek or feel necessary for yourself if you listened or used counselling skills in a similar range of situations?

She demonstrates that listening can enhance any relationship, while counselling has more limited uses.

Have you experienced the dilemmas she describes in listening to friends with a counselling head on? What conclusions did you come to about counselling family and friends?

17   Counselling in a Health Service Trust

Brian is a staff development manager for a Health Service Trust. His responsibilities lie within the learning disabilities branch of the Community Directorate.

*   *   *

There are 280 staff within our service, with a large number of 'unqualified' staff. They may have a lot of experience or other training but no nursing qualifications. This is why the post was created—I have a training responsibility. I have to make an annual training plan, identify training needs and take a large part in delivering that training. Sixty per cent of my time is spent delivering training, with the remainder planning, co-ordinating and administrating. Another role which is built into my job description is that of staff counsellor. I can allocate up to one afternoon a week to provide a theoretically confidential service. This is for staff, clients, their families—anyone who is involved with our service.

How does this translate into what you do, counselling on a day-to-day basis?

I pick up a lot of concerns during training sessions. Because I am not in the line management, I can be seen as more approachable than a person's own line manager. However, using listening or counselling skills in training is different from using them in a formal counselling setting. I keep a fairly low profile about the counselling that I do, or I could get swamped. If word spread outside my service I could be overwhelmed, because there are very few counsellors available in human services.

Could you tell us more about how you use counselling skills in training?

A lot of the work is experiential, attempting to get people to analyse their own moral values and beliefs. I use a lot of reflective questions to help people look at where their beliefs come from. I listen to people reflect what they are saying and sometimes use challenging skills. I give people the opportunity to share their prejudices and their distorted, maybe mythical beliefs about disability, to get them to explore their feelings about disabled individuals.

Do you challenge their beliefs?

I am asking them to look at their beliefs and how those beliefs affect the people who use the service. It is not saying, this belief is wrong don't have it; it is saying, this is the effect your belief has on the individuals involved. It is asking them to reflect on the consequences of their beliefs. If, for example, you believe that a person with learning disability can't learn, then your attitude to that person will be one that doesn't encourage development.

It seems to me that there is quite a large Rogerian element in your training, that you are trying to create an atmosphere where it is safe to look at attitudes and explore them.

Yes. It is difficult in a large group with many different expectations and levels of experience. Sometimes people are sent for training because their manager is concerned about their attitude. Now I don't believe you can teach somebody to have a different attitude. You can ask them to confront where that belief comes from. They can choose to look for evidence to the contrary and then no longer believe it, and then their attitude will change. But very often it is a matter of raising their awareness and sending them back out into the workplace to make a decision. They might decide to perform in a different way or try a different approach.

So your attitude is very respectful of the individual trainee?

It attempts to be, yes.

Are you trying to model with them what they could do with their clients?

Yes, although the communication skills of some people with learning disabilities can be quite limited. The listening process is certainly something that could be developed. The biggest handicap of all, in my experience, is the way you are treated by other people. Many of our workers have come from backgrounds where they have experienced some sad social conditions, losses of their own. Actually to listen to them, to give them the space to grow and develop, to model how we can listen, is setting the example for how they could work with clients.

So the way you train reflects the way you counsel?

Yes, I don't have any major power to make changes in how people work. I am not expected to come up with any easy answers about how we can change the lives of people with learning disabilities. What I can do, what I see as my role, is raising the awareness that how you are, how you are treated by others, has a major impact on the quality of your life. Then the staff have to go away and see if they want to change anything. I feel under pressure sometimes to come up with answers, but I am quite convinced that there are no easy ones. There are some simple things, skills you can teach, but the overall attitude is a personal commitment. This is something you have to change for yourself, I cannot change your attitude for you. I can offer you reasons and evidence for why you should change, but only you can decide to change.

So somehow you are doing less so that they can do more?

Yes, I am doing less in order to empower them to make decisions of their own. This is geared around attitudinal work, not the practical skills that are taught in a more structured way. When people are finding a difficulty in their workplace, with attitudes of other staff, perhaps, or with conditions that are far from ideal, I cannot change that unless it is a major problem. What I can do is reflect that it is a real dilemma, that things are frustrating, not ideal, and that they will have to struggle with this.

So you are accepting this painful reality rather than trying to deny it or smooth it over?

Yes. Often, if there is a problem in a workplace, it is turned back on the worker. How are you solving this? And where people have felt they have done all they can and it has been demonstrated, then they need to be heard. Yes, you have done all you can, you have not found the magic solution. It is about coping with the situation as it is now, not feeling that you are a failure as a carer because you have not solved it.

There is a big element of support in your teaching, then?

Yes, support, listening, challenging with ideals, theories— we have something to aim for. Challenging what they are doing against the ideals, looking for blind spots; to bring those blind spots to their awareness is a form of prevention.

There seems to be a sort of congruence between your counselling and what you teach, how you teach and what you feel and believe.

It is more my style as a communicator, whether it is teaching a skill, raising awareness, challenging a belief, listening or formally counselling, it is a way I have developed over the years, through experience, successes and failures.

So when you are counselling, are you just being you in that setting?

Yes, I am being me, using formal counselling skills in a formal counselling setting, so in that sense I am being a counsellor. I am being me, I am not being anybody else. I might be using somebody's ideals but if I am not committed to them I won't use them. Whether I am counselling, reading, teaching, driving a car or cleaning my teeth, I am the same person doing different things.

Could you say something about how you see counselling, what you think it is?

Counselling is a bit like gardening, really; you are setting the environment, both the external surroundings and the internal environment of a person's thoughts, feelings and behaviour. You are allowing her the right conditions in which to grow and develop. It is an enabling process, it is managing the boundaries of the environment. But it is very firmly back with them to make decisions and to use me as a sort of sounding board.

Do you have any particular theory you work from?

I used to be behavioural. With a nursing background and a behaviourist training, I used to work with a very Egan-type three-stage model. That has modified itself over the years, there is a large element of Rogerian stuff in what I do now. And I will pick up on certain aspects of other theories, such as HSF (human social functioning) and TA (transactional analysis). I could not say I subscribe closely to one model; I use bits of those I have developed skills in over the years, they seem to work for me.

Do you find that your counselling work ever conflicts with your other duties?

Yes, very much so. I am seen as part of the management team with responsibilities not just for counselling but for training general human resource development. That involves a degree of loyalty to senior management. There are times in a counselling setting when the boundaries, though I make them clear at the outset, become blurred or grey or I feel under pressure.

I follow as closely as I can BAC guidelines on confidentiality. The statement on supervision stands; the statement on only disclosing if you believe severe harm to client or others may be involved, that stands and is made clear to the client at the beginning.

However, people may disclose information which, while not coming into the severe harm category, is of importance to how the service is running. My managers would need to know that information, it would influence their decisions about the service. Withholding that, I feel quite comfortable in the counselling shoes, but there have been occasions when an individual has disclosed that she has told me something; my manager has then come back and said, 'Did you know about this?' That placed me in a dilemma because I couldn't state whether I knew it or not, because it was disclosed under a confidential umbrella.

A lot of referrals are to do with individuals experiencing work problems. Knowing those situations, knowing those individuals who are contributing to the problem, knowing there could be a solution yet not being in a position to take action or make decisions, causes me personal frustration because it could be related to a certain individual's management style, or a certain client group, or a certain workplace. Although as a manager I know how it could be resolved, I cannot take action, I have to empower them to take action or decide to live with it because there is nothing they can do to change it.

What about any ethical dilemmas in combining counselling with your other roles?

There are practical issues about my supervision. As a nurse manager I am supervised by my manager, and she is entitled to know where I am and how I spend my time. There are issues of breaking confidentiality of clients, in order to justify my existence as a counsellor. For example, I have to say I am going to do a home visit to someone who lives in Brighton this weekend; she would know how many of her staff lived there, and it would not take much to guess who I was seeing. If people have to come up to the office and sit outside my room or queue round the building, waiting to see Brian, then it is clear to others that they are entering into a counselling setting, their confidentiality boundaries are at risk.

What about situations where you might have a supervisory responsibility for someone you have counselled previously?

That could happen where I was on call for managers. In our service we all take turns to carry a pager or mobile tele-phone to provide a twenty-four-hour management cover. There might be times when, in the absence of someone's line manager, I would have to go out and make a decision. Then I would see someone very clearly as a service worker rather than as a counselling client. She might not see me that way. I may have spent a long time working with that person on matters which I know influence her job. Then I arrive with my manager's head on; I might have to make decisions which conflict with what I know as a counsellor. I actually have to make that statement to people. I have arrived now and I have got my manager's head on, I am not counselling here.

And you are not influenced by what you know as a counsellor?

Well, I would like to think I am not influenced, but I am sure I am because I know the person as a whole.

So that is difficult. Do you have to try not to be influenced?

It is difficult. I have to try not to be influenced because I have to justify my management decisions. If justifying my decision means disclosing information from counselling, then I cannot justify my decision as this would break confidentiality.

Very hard! It is a tightrope you are walking.

There is no easy answer on that one. Fortunately such conflicts are relatively rare, but it has arisen.

You mentioned supervision from your manager. Does she give you counselling supervision?

No, that is obtained through a completely different source, through a counselling support group which is entirely independent of the service. It is built into my job description that I can have a certain amount of time each month for external counselling supervision. It is not paid for, but at the moment there is no cost involved as it is peer supervision.

Is there any advice you would give to a colleague about to embark on a counselling course with a similar service background to yours?

If they were going to take on the responsibility of being a workforce counsellor, I would recommend they develop a code of practice in agreement with their manager. They should do this before they circulated the news of their availability for counselling. They might look at frequency, duration and number of appointments, boundaries of confidentiality, where they would work, referral—those sorts of issues would need to be set out clearly as the service was being set up. In terms of its impact on you as a person, be prepared: it will change your outlook on life. It won't change you, I don't believe it will change you. It will change the way you see things and maybe the way you feel about them.

* * *

How far would similar ethical dilemmas arise in your workplace situation?

You might care to use some of the issues raised as the basis of group discussion or journal work.

How far do you feel that you are the same person undertaking different tasks? ('I am the same person when I am counselling or brushing my teeth . . .')

Do you feel that this would be a comfortable or uncomfortable way to be?

Could you connect this attitude to any counselling or personality development theory?

18 Counselling and Social Work

Jen is a social worker who has sought further training in counselling. She offers her personal experience and views of the dilemmas of combining counselling and social work.

* * *

I am employed as an adult services social worker. I work primarily with elderly people, most of whom require a service from the social services department. Many of them are in danger of losing their independence through physical or mental frailty, or both.

Some social workers and some employers appear to believe that their training automatically equips them to fulfil the counselling role. But I have always felt that my training in this was somewhat lacking—a quick skip through Virginia Satir's *Conjoint Family Therapy* never did seem sufficient. In-service training in bereavement counselling helped.

I had always thought I was a good listener, but there were many times when this seemed far from enough. I therefore decided to do further training. This began to define the counselling process very differently and to move it away from what I perceive to be the role of a social worker. This has been especially noticeable since the changes brought about by the implementation of Care in the Community. I was never very good at the short, pithy definition; someone once said that no social worker will use two words when twenty-two will do!

As a result, I find it difficult to define what I understand by counselling, but I think it is the attempt by two people to consider the life problems and difficulties being experienced by one of them. This is done within an atmosphere of respect and confidentiality, in an attempt to redefine or reconsider those areas of concern so that the individual can make some choices about how to live that life. It allows the individual to define what these difficulties are and to choose how he or she wishes to respond. This has to be done within the framework of an agreement about the time to be spent and over what period.

I find it difficult to argue that I do this in my job. For one thing, my role is now to assess people's need for services and to attempt to buy in these services wherever possible. This immediately influences how people see me. It automatically narrows the range of problems which they present to me to the practical difficulties they have coping with daily living. My clients want practical help and they rightly perceive me as the gatekeeper. Under these circumstances they are understandably distrustful of attempts to move into a consideration of, for instance, the frustrations that their physical frailties cause. We have moved away from an open consideration of areas of concern to one that is bounded by their need to convince me of their suitability for a particular service.

In the past I have attempted to get round this by agreeing the service provision with them and then attempting to move into the offer of a counselling contract as something separate. Sometimes this was accepted, sometimes not. Recently, though, I have found my room for manoeuvre on this restricted by time considerations. I am increasingly expected to manage the fine details of people's care, and choices about priorities and time management have to be made.

The transition from social worker to care manager shifts the emphasis of the job we do and defines even more how we are perceived.

I would now say that I use skills of active listening to help people define the life problems they are experiencing. I use negotiating skills to arrive at agreement on a package of care which they find acceptable and for which my employing authority can afford to pay. I use the same skills to ensure that the care provided progresses smoothly and to deal with any problems which may arise in its implementation.

I continue to offer bereavement counselling on a limited scale to clients who have lost a significant relationship (generally through the death of a spouse, occasionally through the death of an adult child) and sometimes to their families on their death, but only if I have developed a relationship with the family in the course of my work. So I feel it is fair to say I use counselling skills in my job but that I do not act as a counsellor.

When assessing the importance of Care in the Community, the authority for which I work did consider briefly how it would provide a counselling service. The social service provision was being split into purchasers—care managers who would assess the need for a service and then arrange to buy in that service—and service providers like residential homes, home helps and so on. One possible choice was to include within the range of providers a number of people who would operate a counselling service. The authority decided against it and chose instead to argue that its social workers, now also acting as care managers, could provide a counselling service as well.

In the year since implementation of community care, this decision has proved flawed and may eventually be reconsidered, but the wheels of local authorities grind exceeding slow and we may be overtaken by events. One projection, for instance, involves hiving off care management to the Health Authorities or even into private agencies. Either way, the trend may be for counselling to be recognised as a service which will be bought in, just like the provision of private care. This may be good news for counsellors struggling to maintain private practices; it may not be so beneficial if care managers continue to believe that this is an area of work which they should be doing and so refuse to pay anyone else to do it on their behalf.

My limited knowledge of current social work training gives me the impression that social work educators are not moving quickly enough and may still be trying to lead students to believe that they are equipped—and will be able in their jobs—to fulfil the counselling role. It may be that a number of newly qualified workers will find themselves rapidly disillusioned.

If you are hoping to use counselling in social work, please consider:

1 What supervision can your employing authority offer? It may be that the qualified social worker who is your line manager (or has supervisory responsibilities) has limited counselling training and expertise.

2 If this is the case, what alternative is the authority willing to provide, or will you have to pay for your own supervision?

3 Will your authority recognise the implications for your time and protect your caseload in some way, or will you be expected to work overtime to meet your commitments? If so, you are likely to experience great stress and are unlikely to get paid for the additional hours.

4 What facilities can your employers offer? Is there a room which can be set aside for your uninterrupted use, or would you be expected to see people in their own homes?

   The latter is not, in my experience, conducive to uninterrupted and concentrated work, as the demands of offering hospitality, friends and neighbours dropping in, telephones ringing, children needing attention, *always* impinge.

5 Do you feel your training has equipped you to take on the task you have set yourself, or will you need further training?

6 What are the boundaries of confidentiality? This is an area taken for granted in social work and rarely fully explored. When I have done this in a counselling setting the boundaries have been very clearly defined and tend to

be counsellor, client and supervisor, with a rider about serious concerns regarding self-harm or the abuse of others. The boundaries of social work confidentiality, when honestly explored, are much wider and generally rest within the organisation. So not only the supervisor may know, but also anyone with line management responsibility if need arises. Not only that, but clerks who type reports, help maintain files and answer phones may potentially be included. As a result, you need to establish what boundaries your employer will accept and think about whether your employer's boundaries are acceptable to you.

Many authorities are currently producing guidelines for adult services workers, which cover the expected response to suspected or established abuse of adults. These guidelines may, for instance, expect that you will report your suspicions to the police, regardless of whether your client, abused or abuser, wishes it. What dilemmas will this pose for you?

7 What understanding do your fellow workers have of what you propose to do? I was once asked if I had 'counselled someone into accepting an admission into residential care', in tones that suggested I might as easily have used thumbscrews to convince her of the need to accept this solution.

8 Do consider how you will fit together all the components of your role. A CAB organiser once told me that social workers made lousy advice agency workers because they spent far too long exploring all the implications of the presenting problem and were always looking for the hidden agenda. Advice-giving is a function of social work and often sits uneasily with the counselling ethos of moving at the client's pace and enabling her to make her own decisions.

*   *   *

No need for further questions here: Jen has provided plenty!

19 Counselling in General Practice

Nothing in my professional experience has equalled the satisfaction I have derived from using counselling skills to improve and extend the consultation and from offering counselling to an admittedly small number of patients/clients.

It is difficult to convey the difference between working as the knowledgeable expert with responsibility for, and answers to, another person's problem, and working to help someone find the strength and resources to face, define and own her difficulties, work through them and find her own personal way of coming to terms with them.

Counselling is not an easy option for counsellor or client and, with all the personal and social implications of the position, may be particularly difficult for a doctor who sometimes finds it very hard to grasp the concepts of counselling or their validity. I therefore want to try to address some of the issues peculiar to the general practitioner who wishes to offer counselling.

Our practice is non-fundholding, with an approximate list size of 1,400 patients per doctor, compared to the area average of 2,100. We also employ the maximum possible staff under the reimbursements scheme, with additional funding granted this year for a part-time counsellor.

These are conscious decisions but have serious financial implications for the practice. My partners have accepted the shortfall of about 30 per cent in the income from capitation fees and the additional shortfall due to the funding of staff, in return for the benefit in protected time for personal education and development of special interests, and for the facility to book patients at intervals of ten minutes; many partners in many practices will not.

I have completed a course in counselling and now offer one session per week (four hours) protected counselling time. I also have professional supervision fortnightly, which I fund personally. I am completing a personal counselling contract, to a significant extent dealing with issues identified during training and highlighted in supervision.

How counselling is defined is important to me because I still hear and read statements from doctors like 'I counselled him to give up smoking after his heart attack.' I cannot expect my colleagues to understand the need for me to have protected, uninterrupted time with a patient (which includes them covering for emergencies when it is my turn) in order to tell patients to stop smoking and drinking. It also suggests to me that some health workers, who may actually advocate counselling, have a very limited or even erroneous idea of its nature, the process, concepts and skills involved.

I believe that unless doctors have a very clear idea of the definition, aims and goals of counselling, and continually review them, they will be unable to identify the patients who would benefit and thereby be unable to make appropriate referrals. This potentially denies their patients the help they need or, in the case of inappropriate referrals, may put an already distressed patient in a difficult and unhelpful position. Doctors may also be unable to communicate or co-operate with the counsellor on problems such as the prescribing and potential effects of psychoactive drugs, and concerns on the part of the counsellor about whether a client's complaints might have an organic basis. If the patient/client is to receive the very best care, I believe doctors need to be able to communicate with their counsellors on these points (if no other) in an atmosphere of mutual understanding and respect.

My working definition is that the aim of counselling is for the client to help himself, to clarify his difficulties and to resolve them. Rather than giving advice, reassurance or medication, the counsellor uses the relationship in a skilled and principled way to develop self-knowledge, emotional acceptance and growth, respecting the client's values, personal resources and capacity for self-determination, and systematically attempting to avoid long-term dependency. The offer of counselling and temporary acceptance of the role of client must be clearly stated.

There appears to be basic agreement that professions other than counselling may use the counselling skills of listening, reflecting and empathy in the course of their work and that some may also use the more advanced skills of problem clarification, accurate understanding, summarising and confrontation. I do not feel that practitioners using these skills within the setting of a medical consultation, desirable and legitimate as that is, should refer to this as 'counselling', but should reserve the word 'counselling' to describe an explicit agreement with a client to work within the term of the definition above.

When a patient consults me there is an almost unconscious pattern to the process which fits very closely with a model of consultation known as the hypothetico-deductive model. Often within seconds I shall establish a working guess as to the nature of the presenting problem, perhaps with a number of alternative possibilities. I use the next minute or two to evaluate the information offered, to determine the validity of my first guess, and I may follow this with specific questioning and relevant physical examination where appropriate, to test the validity of my initial hypothesis further. Hopefully I shall have completed this stage in about six to seven minutes. If the initial hypothesis cannot be validated, I substitute another and start the process again. If the initial guess appears valid, I now have three or four minutes to:

- explain what I feel the nature of the problem is;
- describe what I feel should be done about it;

- elicit the patient's own feelings and ideas about the nature of the problem and how it might be resolved;
- explain how these relate to mine (hopefully);
- agree a plan to deal with the problem;
- make the necessary arrangements for what has been agreed;
- write prescriptions where appropriate and record everything in detail in the case records.

Secondary requirements of the consultation are:

- active review of co-existing chronic disease;
- health education on a variety of matters;
- case-finding, for example checking blood pressure even where this was not indicated in the presenting problem;
- dealing with additional presenting problems;
- eliciting and dealing with hidden agendas.

I don't achieve this in most of my ten-minute appointments, I have yet to achieve it in five minutes although I have watched a video of my partner who manages to achieve this with the utmost skill within the ten-minute time-scale.

This is not an exhaustive analysis of medical consultation which is well outside my scope and expertise, but I hope it offers some insight into the routine of general practice thinking.

Many doctors have an intense drive to minister to as many patients as humanly possible, at times to the brink of self-destruction. This, I feel, is fuelled by the current terms and conditions of service under which we work and the current political exhortations to the public to demand more and more while politicians provide less funding for practical care, although apparently unlimited supplies can be found for 'management'.

It is important to remember, however, that a general practitioner is solely responsible for the number of patients he or she chooses to take on. For many complex reasons there are currently vocationally trained practitioners who can find no practice to join, but irrespective of these, a grossly overworked general practitioner is in that situation from choice.

There is a generally held belief that family doctors cannot cope with the number and range of counselling problems that face them, and that those who try find themselves working overlong hours to the detriment of their family life and their own health. I can endorse this and at times it certainly has been true, but thanks to my sympathetic partners I am able to allocate a reasonable amount of time, and I still have this even though we now also employ a counsellor.

A factor that I have found very potent in the debate on the stress produced on doctors when they offer counselling, but which I have not seen acknowledged, is the stress produced when a real and pressing need is perceived and possibly acknowledged by patient and doctor but there is nothing to offer. There is effectively no private counselling in my area—and very few of my patients could think of affording it if it were—and waiting times for clinical psychology may be as much as nine months. Efforts to reduce this time have put the psychologists under great pressure to offer short-term intervention. Employing a counsellor does not necessarily relieve the problem, since a small piece of research (unpublished) which I carried out suggests that counselling referrals come from a pool of previously unmet and unacknowledged need. When there is no counsellor the door to this pool remains firmly closed.

Under these circumstances I have found it less stressful to offer a small number of patients supportive counselling than to wish them good morning, or offer a prescription for mood-altering drugs.

There is no doubt in my mind that a doctor who wishes to offer counselling must accept regular, ongoing supervision. I think this needs to be on a formal contractual basis, possibly more frequently than the minimum recommended by the BAC. It is not always easy to accept this when in other aspects of general practice one is used to confident, autonomous decision-making. Moreover, coming from a background of passionate belief in a free National Health Service and an intense distaste for private medicine, I still find it difficult to come to terms with having to pay for supervision on a regular basis so that I can offer free counselling to my patients. There is no question, however, that it is an essential prerequisite.

Some schools of counselling, particularly perhaps the psychodynamic school, place considerable emphasis on the work needed to terminate the counselling process. General practitioners, however, find it difficult to achieve this successfully when the two parties are quite likely to meet as doctor and patient the following day at the surgery, or possibly even at the client/patient's home. The very nature of the relationship between counsellor and client conflicts so radically with that between doctor and patient that I have found it impossible, as a counsellor, to work towards autonomous decision-making while being responsible for giving advice, performing physical examination, prescribing and monitoring medication. Attempting to do so led to considerable problems for me personally and also for my patient/client. All clients accepted for counselling therefore agree to see a partner for all their medical requirements for the duration of the contract, and some have chosen to continue to do so once the contract has terminated.

Offering medical services to the close family of a client has occasionally proved more difficult than it would otherwise be. A relationship of the nature encountered in counselling generally leaves the doctor with intimate knowledge not only of the client but also of how he or she experiences the immediate family. This may influence the doctor's behaviour towards the husband, wife or child, but it may also lead the client to expect the doctor to behave in a specific way and this may be in conflict with professional judgement. At the moment I have no set way of dealing with this.

At present I am aware of no comparative study of

counselling in primary care which can show a convincing, reproducible, and sustained improvement in the client. I firmly believe, however, that the benefits are self-evident and can recall that, some 12 to 15 years ago, it was likewise impossible to show that treatment of diabetes with insulin prevented the onset of organ and tissue damage due to this disease. Thankfully treatment continued, and as more sophisticated treatment schedules were developed and more sophisticated ways of measuring the effects of the disease and the effects of the treatment were developed, it became very clear that treatment did prevent or slow the onset of the potentially disabling or life-threatening damage that untreated diabetes can cause.

I am sure that this process will be repeated with counselling, but at the moment this remains a matter of belief. Counselling is slow and expensive in terms of doctor time and can only be offered to a very few select patients who can make the transition from patient to client and back. It can be difficult for partners who may not share this belief to accept three-and-a-half hours being devoted to three patients on a regular basis, while they see twenty or more people in that time and when no convincing evidence of the efficacy of the process can be produced.

In conclusion, I would like to offer some positive suggestions as a focus for consideration of some of the problems I have encountered, which may be common to most general practitioners offering counselling and which I could perhaps have avoided had I been less ignorant and naïve.

1 Do get adequate training.
2 Do get regular contracted supervision with an experienced supervisor who has some knowledge of the medical setting and is reasonably sympathetic to the idea of a doctor counselling.
3 Do try to discuss counselling fully and carefully with your partners: why you are doing it; who you are likely to see; who is likely to benefit; and what practice arrangements

you need. An ideal might be protected time within the working day. Doctors do run into trouble with stress if they try to fit counselling in as an extra in their own time.

4 Do think very carefully before offering counselling to a patient. Can you make the jump to counsellor in his case? Can he make the jump to client? Are there any complicating factors, such as previous knowledge of your client or a previous close professional relationship with the family? Does his problem require special expertise? Does the client have the ability and insight to benefit from your method of counselling? Is he embracing counselling for himself or to please you? Are there any other factors which might indicate a tendency towards dependency?

5 Think very carefully about your views on patients requiring medication. If there is any suggestion of psychosis, is counselling the correct therapy for this patient and, if so, are you the right person to offer it?

It may be an idea to discuss these issues in supervision before deciding to offer a counselling contract.

6 Do set yourself a limit for your counselling caseload and do try to keep to it.

7 Do make a definite contract with your client. Explain clearly what counselling and the contract entail, and what the arrangements are for provision of general medical services during the contract.

8 Do think about contacting other doctors in your area who offer counselling. It can be very comforting to know you are not alone, especially if partners are not particularly enthusiastic or supportive.

9 Think about how you will keep records of your counselling. This is a medico-legal hot potato at present. Terms and conditions of service require adequate contemporaneous records to be kept. Do you consider your counselling to be part of your NHS activities, and will a lawyer agree? I personally record the offer of a counselling contract, the patient's response and the termination of that contract in the NHS records. I keep additional

personal records of the counselling sessions separate from the notes in my folder and written on my own paper. The client is aware of the existence of these notes and that they will not follow the NHS records should the client leave the practice.

Whether you decide to offer formal counselling or not, as doctors we all need to improve our ability to listen to our patients, to hear their stories and to respond to them empathetically and appropriately in a human context at the very least. I suggest we all have an obligation to work towards this goal.

*   *   *

Dr Gap has offered a comprehensive and deeply personal picture of his experiences and concerns as a general practitioner using counselling skills.

How far could you identify with his dilemmas?

Is the way you listen in your main role or work function very different from counselling listening?

Could you identify these differences?

Could your counselling involve changing relationships not only with clients but with their families?

How would you handle this?

How important would you consider continuing supervision and personal development?

Would adding a counselling function to your workload increase your stress or change the type of stress you experience, or would it reduce it?

Would there be financial, workload or management implications if you added counselling to your tasks?

PART THREE
THE CLIENTS' EXPERIENCE OF COUNSELLING

Introduction

The experiences that follow are the client's own although some details have been changed to preserve their privacy and that of their families. It was very interesting to talk again with Pauline, Ann and Kim. I usually do a review at the end of counselling but rarely have a follow-up contact so much later.

Some of the comments they made have led me to think more deeply on familiar topics. An example of this is the difference between the warmth of a counselling relationship and a friendship, an issue that Pauline raised. A comment of Ann's has led me to make a change in how I approach an initial interview. Pauline's comment on a similar topic also caused some heart-searching. I am now more aware of how setting boundaries can sometimes be perceived as negative or uncaring when someone is feeling vulnerable. Kim's very acute perception and awareness of her counsellor and the counselling process have given me a lot to think about.

Rereading, thinking and talking about these clients' counselling reminded me just how committed they were and how very hard they worked. I was also stimulated by the questions they raised and the comments they made in their contributions to this book.

The gains and changes that they describe after counselling are those that can be expected as a side-effect. In addition to coming to an individual conclusion about how to respond to their problems, clients may well gain increased coping skills, greater confidence in themselves and a stronger sense of themselves as worthwhile individuals, able to rely and act on their own judgement and have confidence in their own values and standards.

These after-effects of counselling offer a wonderful illustration of Carl Rogers' theories about people's growth brought to life. He believed that we all have within us a lifelong potential for healthy growth and development. This is always present, if not always active. It may be held down or distorted by circumstances, or buried almost too deep to be remembered. Often this burying process begins in childhood. In order to feel loved and accepted we might feel we have to behave in certain ways or, worse still, try to be what we are not. In these circumstances we build a protective self, a false front that starts as armour and can end up as a prison with only one inmate.

One of the major disadvantages of this survival strategy is that the more effectively the false, protective self pleases others, the worse the real person inside feels. If she is offered love or praise she feels sure she does not deserve it. She feels very different inside, not really loved or lovable at all, not really the person that other people see.

Sometimes, as in Ann's situation, people feel that they have been given a rule book which they must live by in order to feel good enough. These rules may feel very important, even vital to keep. Breaking or even questioning them may be quite terrifying. It can take time, persistence and courage to challenge, question, change and rewrite a rule book you have been given long ago. The ability to make your own judgements and have confidence in them is therefore a vital stage in human development and growth.

Carl Rogers calls this a shift from an external locus of evaluation to an internal locus of evaluation. I understand it as a change from receiving the values and judgements of others, and accepting and acting on them without question, to relying on the judgement of your own heart, mind and spirit. Sounds important, an internal locus of evaluation? Well it is, and a wonderful and special achievement; when it happens I always rejoice, as I did when I saw it happen for Ann. If it was written into a fairy tale this event would be like the heroine returning home in triumph at the end of her quest, the rightful heir coming into his kingdom, a discovery of buried treasure that was always yours.

Ann speaks of returning briefly and becoming aware earlier of slipping back. Changing thinking and behaviour is sometimes a long, slow and demanding process. First there is a new awareness operating only after we have made the same old, ineffective responses. Gradually we notice quicker, change our course earlier until, almost without realising, the new ways become natural and instinctive.

Eventually we are able to move on and work on another area of ourselves. Another area? I hear you ask. Well yes, I think so, because I believe that personal and spiritual growth is a lifelong job. But it is optional.

Do I ever expect to be finished? I have a picture of myself on my deathbed, surrounded by people I love, suddenly fitting the last piece of the puzzle into place and giving a great delighted 'Aha!' as my final breath.

Ann feels that it is particularly important for the counsellor and client to be right for each other. I agree that both have to feel that they can work together. The creation of the core conditions (see p. 30) is, I think, the first vital step. Please, however hard it is as a client to take care of yourself in this way, trust yourself enough to listen to your feelings. Opt out of any counselling relationship in which you do not feel respected, valued and safe. Do not stay in a counselling relationship where you do not feel 'heard' or where you suspect the counsellor is not genuine. A counselling relationship in which you feel unable to question what is going on may not be healthy. If you do not feel able to ask, do you feel that you could write your questions? If you cannot bring yourself to do this, are you with the right counsellor for you?

When we reviewed our work together for this book, Ann raised two very interesting questions. We both felt they could usefully be addressed here.

1 *How did I feel being asked to help with a problem which had no solution (her daughter's disability)?*

To hear about and contain the pain of a problem that has no solution is painful. But however painful it is to hear, it is far more painful to live with. I find it helpful to remember that, by offering to hear, *really* hear, how it feels, I am initially giving genuine support and comfort. Then by continuing to accept the client's pain and all her feelings, I am offering not only relief, but space to begin to adjust to the burden she is carrying. As a colleague describes it, 'you can't always lighten the load, but you can help people develop better posture and stronger muscles to carry it' (David Bowker, 1990).

The sense of having a companion, a supportive witness to your pain and struggles, can be very precious. It may not appear to be a very active part but is in fact quite demanding and needs discipline, stamina and sometimes courage. To be present with someone in this way, and also hold an overall awareness of the process that can help your client to be clearer about her options is a skill well worth developing and very rewarding to practise.

2 *How had I felt hearing about her increasingly violent feelings and her fears of losing control and acting on them?*

This potentially violent situation developed due to Ann's increasing frustration, helplessness, pain and near despair in the face of her child's almost hellishly difficult behaviour. (Obviously an actually violent situation would need a more rapid response.) Knowing that it was not the child's fault, and loving her devotedly, did not help; it only made the situation more agonising.

Hearing this and monitoring the developing risks was certainly a difficult task. My job was to offer a safe container for her pain, to let her feel able to speak about her worst fear: that she might break under the incredible pressure and hurt her child. Once she could own the feelings she was having we could assess the risks together. We could decide on the action to take.

This does not mean that I was not assessing the risks myself or that I would not have taken action alone if it had been necessary. I would always prefer to work with a client, but when the safety of another vulnerable person is concerned I would take and indeed have taken whatever steps were necessary to keep them safe, with or without the client's co-operation.

Check your code of ethics. What would you do? What would you be expected to do? Are these the same?

Ann has said that she found safety and reassurance in knowing that, once she had told me, something would be done about the situation, whether by her or me or both of us together. Something would be done. I was glad that we both had a clear understanding about such a situation long before it arose.

Remember my banging on about boundaries in the earlier parts of this book? It really is important, vital even. Imagine having to say, after weeks of listening and building trust, 'Sorry, I cannot keep what you have just told me confidential.' What possible trust would your client have left in you? How difficult it would be to work together and take action together for the safety and well-being of all concerned.

Since you cannot know in advance who might need this warning about the boundaries of confidentiality, everyone needs to hear and clearly understand it before you begin to work with them.

20 Personal Experiences of Counselling

ANN'S CONTRIBUTION

In her comments about what in general terms brought her to counselling Ann is fairly typical: long-standing difficulties and confusions, which she felt unable to sort out, led her to seek help. This did not, and for most people does not, mean a lack of concerned friends or family or of personal resources, by which I mean integrity, courage, reasoning and reflecting ability, and the general ability to manage one's life. However, some combinations of events and feelings are so overwhelming that people temporarily lose access to their skills, strengths and resources.

Ann's anxieties about being judged are also almost universal and reflect the common concerns that most people have about counselling. I have felt this initially on the occasions when I have begun work with a new therapist. It might also be worth mentioning that I have felt this sort of anxiety with certain clients, other very experienced counsellors, for example.

The gains Ann was aware of reflect the depth and quality of the work she herself did in counselling.

Ann's experience
My experience of counselling was that of rediscovering my sense of self. It was one of the most important experiences of my life—perhaps *the* most important.

I went to counselling at a time in my life when I was totally confused. I knew everything had gone wrong in my life and I felt totally unable to take any action to save myself. I felt walled in and that whatever I did would be 'wrong' as judged by others. I had good friends offering me conflicting advice, a dead relationship, a small child with severe behavioural difficulties, a boring ill-paid office job, dreams unfulfilled, and I was entering my late thirties.

My first session gave me an enormous sense of relief. My counsellor did not judge me in any way, She gave me no 'shoulds' or 'oughts', just space to explore what I felt about my life. She had no agenda for me. She began by validating and exploring my own feelings which I had felt were so 'wrong'. Of course the sessions, which went on for over a year, gave me support during specific crises, particularly during my 'descent into hell' when I had cleared all the shelves and was trying to cope alone (twelve months into counselling). Here was someone to be with me when I wept over my child, someone to listen to my fears when I left my job and had no income, someone to understand the agony of splitting up with the father of my child.

She could also tease out the actual choices available to me in any situation, so that I realised I did have choices and could make them, with a growing sense of confidence in my own ability to shape my life.

During the year or more that I received counselling, I came to understand myself much better, and saw my life up to that point in a new light. And not only my life, but the lives of others who had shaped my beliefs and patterns of behaviour, particularly my mother who had died some years previously. The light that counselling threw on her unhappy life shone also on my own, and I perceived that rather than repeat the rules for living that she gave me, I could fashion my own, without guilt.

Since ending my weekly sessions I have been back two or three times, and always my sense of unhappiness has been because I was slipping back into my old ways of doing things. Now, however, it no longer takes so long to redis-cover myself—just a session or two—and more importantly,

I now recognise when I am losing my sense of direction and know how vital it is to recapture it.

Some of the things I did because of counselling, I knew at the start I wanted to do but did not have the will—such as breaking up my relationship. Other things came as a complete surprise. For example, after months of agonising and misery I was able to give my notice at the office with surprising ease. My counsellor worked specifically on my lack of assertiveness. She worked on the beliefs and life patterns I had inherited from my family. I read books she loaned me. I wrote pieces on topics she suggested. I never shared what we talked about in our sessions with anyone else, and I know she did not either, except anonymously and with permission.

Gradually I moved closer to living my own life, with me in control, answerable only to myself, with all the joy, sorrow and responsibility that entails.

Finally I told her that I no longer needed to see her on a regular basis. It felt like saying goodbye to the best friend I ever had. She, of course, was delighted and cheered me on my way.

How far do you think Ann's description of the counselling relationship she formed describes the counselling relationships you have, or would like to have, with your clients?

How would you have worked differently with the issues she presented? The fact that her problems are only sketchily described may make this easier or harder for you, depending on how you approach the question. For example, how would you define a 'dead relationship'? Work on this definition. The fact that we have not been specific about the nature of her daughter's disability should make it easier for you to work from your own experience, so long as you accept that the behaviour was a source of extreme stress and distress to Ann. I think it would not be an exaggeration to call it torture.

How would you feel facing the challenges and dilemmas that Ann offered me?

Books and dreams

Ann mentioned my lending her books. I do this for any client who is interested in learning more about counselling or any aspect of our work together. This is for two reasons—one as part of being as open as possible, giving away my 'power'. It is hard to be accountable to someone who has no opportunity to understand what you are trying to do. It is harder to feel you are a partner in your own recovery if you do not understand what is meant to be going on. The books I have are often specialised and expensive; people who want to read them might not feel able to afford a book that they would read only once, but not all of them would be readily available in the public library. Not every client wants or needs to read these books and I am careful not to push them, but they can be really useful for some. I have told you about this because it illustrates something I think important. I try to be consistent in small actions as well as large ones; to build an equal relationship takes attention to detail, from seating to sharing information, it is about actions as well as attitudes.

PAULINE'S CONTRIBUTION

These are Pauline's thoughts on the process of counselling, some ten or eleven months after we finished working together. She is willing to share the good work we did and especially hopes that it will be helpful to would-be counsellors. Pauline is in her fifth decade, and this is significant because her stage in life raised particular issues for her to work through. These were in addition to her depression although to some extent they contributed to it.

Pauline's experience

It is now eighteen months since my depression started. I have been off medication for four months and stopped being counselled eleven months ago. I realise I have omitted to say when the depression went. As anybody who has ever had depression will know, for a long time afterwards, rather as I imagine someone feels after a heart attack, you are waiting for it to strike again. For me personally it has had a profound effect.

When reflecting on how it feels to be counselled, I am not sure how accurate my recall will be now that I am no longer experiencing the intense pain I was feeling at the time. However, I can certainly look back on that period with more logic than I had then. As a social worker I regard myself as a good listener, perceptive and understanding. I have undertaken level one RSA counselling training, but during my depression I was first and foremost a client. Even though at times a part of me was aware of what the counsellor was doing, it was always on reflection, not while it was happening. Our sessions were definitely centred on me and my pain. This was probably the most crucial part of the whole process: I felt safe, valued, believed and cared about unconditionally.

Even in the depths of my depression I was aware how vulnerable I was and how easily I could be exploited by well-intentioned counsellors. In my first week of counselling I went for a session of aromatherapy, and although the aromatherapy was all right, the amateur counselling of the therapist frightened me considerably. I was told baldly all that was wrong with my life and that I would have to make drastic changes, including possibly giving up work. After that I realised that qualified counselling could help me the most. During our sessions I felt that I had not been disempowered. I felt that my counsellor was helping me to see within myself, reach my own conclusions and ultimately make my own decisions.

There were sessions when I was floundering, when I knew the counsellor was trying to lead me somewhere and I either wouldn't or couldn't go. At times like this she realised that for me analogies were enormously helpful. I felt I was always being told the truth about the present and what lay ahead but it was always done gently and sensitively. Our sessions were a lifeline. There were bad times when I felt the urge to get in touch in between, but even in the early days I had been given or had acquired the coping mechanisms to see me from week to week. I felt secure in the knowledge that, if needed, the counsellor would respond and would never see my increased need as a failure on my part.

On reflection all the sessions were a learning process, but there were three in particular that were revelations of biblical proportions.

1 I realised that my depression had been self-induced inasmuch as my inner hurt, discontent and dissatisfaction had grown over the years. I had ignored it, and this was the only way I could stop myself in my tracks and begin to address it. To do this I had inflicted my own worst nightmare on myself. As you can imagine, this came as quite a shock.

2 I recognised that a long-term deepseated low self-esteem had compounded all the other factors which had contributed to the depression. As someone who is always described as very confident, this realisation had quite an effect on me.

3 This leads me to the final and most difficult revelation. It took many sessions to unearth and at times made me feel as though I was plaiting fog. Simply put, it was the difference between head and heart. In the early days I poured out all my innermost thoughts, going back over many years. I aired every problem and felt confident enough to discuss problems I had never discussed with anyone else. I acknowledged all this and thought that having done so would eliminate the problems and consequently the depression. What I didn't realise was that I wasn't feeling these problems, merely giving them intellectual house room. Once I 'felt' them the floodgates opened. I indulged in long periods of wallowing in self-pity and floods of tears, something I have denied myself for most of my life. I felt my counsellor had

recognised this as a necessary part of my recovery, but it was anathema to me and six months earlier I could never have envisaged it happening.

My own experience of counselling training had made me realise the value of counselling but also that it was not a career I wished to pursue myself. However, it had alerted me to the vital necessity for rapport between counsellor and client as it is such an intimate, albeit transitory relationship. I have great difficulty in putting this into words. Your counsellor does not have to be your friend, even though you may well be sharing thoughts and feelings you have never shared with anybody else. She has to give you confidence in her skills, as does your GP or dentist. But she needs to be closer personally than your doctor. She needs to give you enormous support, a lifeline in many cases, without making you dependent on her. Obviously the reason I am having difficulty expressing this is because it is by its very nature a unique relationship. Its quality is vital to the success of counselling.

Early on in the depression I was convinced my whole lifestyle, both at home and at work, needed to be radically altered. This was a terrifying thought. As the counselling progressed I realised that any changes that were needed were within myself, and after fifty-three years *in situ* this would be no easy matter.

Outwardly many people will see very little difference in me other than that I am more laid back. I say 'No' more often and I physically do not run around ministering to people and their needs as much as I used to.

Inwardly, however, things are very different. The long-standing feeling of restlessness is rarely there these days. Instead of feeling constantly 'up' I now fluctuate between 'up' and 'down' more often. I recognise the areas that cause me problems—low self-esteem and lack of assertiveness. If things do not go as I would wish I can reason them out not just in my head but in how they make me feel. I tell people how I feel rather than coping with it myself. I can do all these things without feeling inadequate or a fraud. It does not work all the time: I have had several anxious situations since counselling ended and I shall undoubtedly continue to do so. But I now have the coping mechanisms within myself and when the situation is resolved I get a real sense of achievement. If the situation is proving difficult to resolve, I talk about it and seek advice and reassurance until it is resolved or until I can accept in my heart as well as my head that it is insoluble. There have been times when I have been tempted to ring my counsellor, but instead I have sat back and thought, 'How would she help me to see this situation?' So far that has been enough. However, I would see seeking counselling again as a positive, not a negative, which indicates how far I have progressed.

On good days I feel reborn and I secretly smile at the new me inside, living happily alongside the best of the old me. On bad days I feel the worst of the old me is flexing its fifty-three-year-old muscles and saying, 'I'm not going down without a fight'. I recognise what is happening and know that the bad days will go and the good ones return. It's not Nirvana but it is the closest I have ever been and hopefully it will continue to improve. I would like to be more assertive and have more self-esteem but the answers are within me; I just have to keep working at it. Sometimes it works, sometimes it doesn't, so what!

I have always thought how difficult and distressing it must be for the people close to anyone suffering from depression. We live in a society where there is still a stigma attached to any mental health problem: I feel this is through fear caused by ignorance. Consequently close family and friends do not have many people to whom they can express their fears and anxieties. I learned through counselling that I should ask people how they feel rather than assume that I know. I have often made this assumption in the past— frequently, it turned out, being hopelessly off the mark. I have done this to such a degree that more than once I have transferred my deepest feelings to others and convinced myself that the feelings were theirs. What follows is a summary of the views expressed by those who were closest to me during this period.

Jason (26) and Nick (31) are my two sons, both of whom live some twenty miles away with their respective partners. As both of them work full time and have no transport, we do not see one another on a daily basis. Because of this physical distance they feel somewhat detached, but not uncaring about my depression. I only contacted or visited them when I was well and able to, although it was obvious I was generally unwell because I was unable to have my granddaughter to stay as often as they expected. As to my having counselling, Jason freely admits it was something to which he had given no previous thought as he has never been in need of it himself. Like Nick he feels that I should pursue whatever I feel would be of use to me. Neither of them feels it is for them to try to influence me but that I should do what is best for me.

Glenys is a work colleague who has worked as a Samaritan and also does volunteer work at a hospice. She has completed an intermediary counselling course and is very enthusiastic about the benefits of counselling. She displays great skills in this area and would like to pursue it further. She has identified five key areas of significance for her:

1 As I am her manager she found herself in a difficult position when I instinctively started to contact her. I gave this a very perfunctory thought and then dismissed it as I realised my needs took priority. When I returned to work it presented no problems, partly due to Glenys' skills and partly due to our sharing intense feelings.

2 Despite her varied experience, she felt she gained an insight into depression that she had not previously experienced. She found this valuable and it also made her realise what an intensely lonely position you are in when you are depressed.

3 It made her feel privileged that I trusted her enough to confide in her and seek her help. She was not surprised that I contacted her initially but was surprised that I continued to do so once I was receiving professional counselling.

4 On my return to work I was aware that the rest of the team treated me very gently and were wary of approaching me with problems, often going first to Glenys before involving me. This was to ascertain whether I should be approached, and if I was, how I would react. Of course Glenys herself did not answer these questions.

5 Glenys said she felt pride in the way I coped on returning to work and in how I have progressed from strength to strength since. She has been aware of setbacks, some of which I have confided to her and some I have worked out for myself.

I found Glenys' involvement a key factor in my recovery, not just because of her undoubted skills but also because she was the only person involved who had first-hand experience of me in the workplace and as a manager. Thank you, Glenys.

My husband and I have been together for fifteen-and-a-half years and married for the past eighteen months. He went through a whole range of emotions: fear that I would harm myself (I did in fact give him all my antidepressants and he gave me two days' medication at a time); worry because although he did not understand depression, he could see the effect it was having on me; uncertainty as no one was able to say whether I would improve and how long it would take; powerlessness, because no matter what he did or was prepared to do, he could not help me improve the situation. He initially felt that counselling was a waste of time; he is a very pragmatic man who believes you should be able to sort yourself out. Knowing this, I am amazed at how tolerant, sympathetic and understanding he has been. As time went on he began to recognise the valuable effect

that counselling was having on me and he now acknowledges that there are some people for whom counselling is
very beneficial. My husband bore the brunt on a daily basis,
saw me at my very worst, then saw me improve only to
slide downward again. I am thankful for his love and
unending support.

My daughter Justine (29) lives on the Wirral with her
husband and our main contact was by telephone. She became
cautious about ringing me because she did not know what to
expect. If I was down it made her feel helpless. She would
choose her words carefully, not wanting to say anything that
might make me feel worse. At the other end of the scale she
did not want to appear too happy in case it made me realise
what I was missing. She felt she could not offload or discuss
any problems she might be experiencing—she had lost a
shoulder to cry on. She had mixed feelings about counselling: she could not understand why I needed outside help, yet
on reflection she realised the value of impartiality. No matter
how old your parents are, they are the strong ones, invincible,
and it comes as a shock when they appear unable to cope and
are in need themselves.

KIM'S CONTRIBUTION

This contribution by a young person shows, from the client's
point of view, what works and what doesn't. It also gives an
insight into the awareness of clients and how they perceive
their counsellor's attitudes. Kim is a thoughtful, sensitive
observer, well able to put her feelings and experiences into
words, and her contribution is given as she wrote it.

Kim's experience
My first experience of counselling was with a school counsellor during school hours in an office belonging to two male
teachers. The first problem was that it was in school. This
meant that people wanted to know where I was going, and as
I could think up no reasonable excuse, I told the truth.

This exposed me to all their prejudice against 'shrinks' and 'lunatics'.

The office was small, crowded and very unprivate. A constant stream of interruptions flowed through, beginning with one of the teachers coming for paper and continuing with telephone calls, stares from interested pupils and visits to see if I was all right. My counsellor did nothing to prevent them, but sat smiling serenely, encouraging me to talk with questions which required one-word answers, and a very 'you're all right, dear' air.

I didn't know what to expect when I first agreed to counselling, but because both my parents are counsellors I had the vague idea that I would be in control and that no one would be judging or investigating me. I also expected to come to my own conclusions about what to do and that I could decide when I had finished. I found myself lying about what I felt because of the way she asked me about my feelings. It was always obvious how she felt. Oddly enough I did like her, and during the time I was being counselled I was unable to admit to feeling judged.

All the time I was being counselled by her I felt it was very important she didn't dislike me. I was on trial and it was important that I never expressed an opinion she didn't agree with. This left me very vulnerable and open to attack, so that any face she made or tactless word she used to show that she disagreed with me made me feel humiliated and dashed down.

In the end it was definitely she who decided I was well again. I was never open with her for fear of her censure, so we got through my troubles, to her satisfaction, within a few weeks. I came in for my appointment, sat down and she asked me whether I still felt I needed to come. I explained that I was worried about money at home, and instead of helping me talk out this worry she ridiculed and laughed at me, saying, 'I can't help you with that, what do you expect me to do? Pull ten pounds out of the air?'

It didn't feel like she counselled from the point of view of most counsellors. It feels to me now as if she had to have been through something similar to her client so that she could tell them everything would be fine and maybe offer advice. She always seemed well off, so I suppose she couldn't understand poverty. But in that one sentence she had shaken my trust in her and I couldn't work with her again because she judged me!

My second counselling experience was altogether different. Even in the preliminary meeting I got more out than in all my sessions with my first counsellor. In my first proper session with my new counsellor I established a relationship with her different from the one I had with Jenny (I have called her Jenny because I have to call her something. It is not her real name). I was expressing my own emotions this time. My new counsellor got me to draw a picture of my family as I saw it and I said some horrid things about them, things I would never have dared to say to Jenny, but my new counsellor took my side in any argument I had and never once asked me if I could understand their point of view, or wanted to know if I was sure I was being reasonable.

I am sure it helped a great deal to know that I wasn't being judged by anyone, and to know that I had her support in whatever I chose to do.

At the end of the session we discussed what I had drawn with my mother and at the end of that one hour I felt like a whole weight had been lifted off my mind.

The room we work in is large and well spaced and there are no interruptions. The atmosphere is much more relaxed and so I am able to talk more easily. Apart from not feeling judged, the other most important thing to me is the way she asks questions. Her questions are always open, so I can say as much as I want in answer and sometimes lead on to other things.

When *I* (heavily underlined several times) decided to finish counselling it was totally my decision, not anyone else's, and the relationship broke off in such a way that I knew I could come back.

With the new counsellor I felt special, important, whereas Jenny was working to a schedule, always rushing off after three quarters of an hour whether I needed to carry on or not. With my new counsellor I felt like a person she could take interest in; sometimes we could even talk about things, like what I want to do when I grow up and counselling ethics, but to Jenny it was as if I was just another part of her job.

I have only recently admitted this to myself, as when I met Jenny she seemed such a motherly person (in a fairy tale book sort of way) that I couldn't bring myself to admit that the counselling wasn't doing any good.

How do you feel reading this?

Do you think counselling young people needs special skills?

Do the core conditions still apply?

Do you find Kim's observations disconcertingly sharp?

What did you notice about the basic conditions we have talked about in this book in her description of her first counselling situation?

Kim makes the vulnerability a client feels crystal clear. How could things have been handled differently in the first situation to help her feel less threatened?

The British Association for Counselling

Throughout this book I have referred from time to time to this Association, and if you are interested in training as a counsellor you would be well advised to get in touch with BAC. They can recommend courses that meet their own high standards, and they publish directories that provide information about training and counselling services. They have also developed a Code of Ethics and Practice which any reputable counsellor will abide by in work and training.

BAC publishes its own quarterly journal, *Counselling*, as well as a number of books, and its library holds a stock of useful films and videos on counselling. Apart from its national headquarters in Rugby, it has a network of local branches and contact groups. To find out if there is one in your area, and for further information about the Association, contact the following address:

British Association for Counselling, 1 Regent Place, Rugby, Warwickshire CV21 2PJ.

Tel: (information) 01788 578328; (office) 01788 550899. Fax: 01788 562189.

Book List

This is a very individual book list. It is not about 'shoulds' or 'oughts' or required reading. Any counselling course will give you a well-chosen, well-balanced reading list, reflecting the course content. This list is for *fun*, full of books that I have found not only helpful but inspiring. If you have found my approach to this book interesting, or want to follow up any topics, these books will help.

Transactional Analysis

T.A. Today, Ian Stewart and Vann Joines. Lifespace Publishing, Nottingham, 1987.

If you want to learn more about Strokes or Victim, Rescuer and Persecutor—in fact anything about transactional analysis, this is the best book I know. It is clear and detailed and easy to work through.

Born to Win, M. James and D. Jongeward. Addison-Wesley, 1987.

Another good book on transactional analysis, with some gestalt. Helpful, clear and simple to use, with lots to teach us. Has a very positive and optimistic tone.

Women as Winners, D. Jongeward and D Scott. Addison-Wesley, 1976.

Also worth trying. Not only useful to women or those working with them. Lots of helpful exercises and clear explanations on using transactional analysis for personal growth.

Carl Rogers

What can I say? I am a convicted Rogers fan! If you want to read more about the man and his ideas, try:

On becoming a Person. Constable, 1967.
Client-Centered Therapy. Houghton Mifflin, 1954.
  Still worth reading. It is also interesting to compare with later work and see ideas developing and the writer expanding.
On Personal Power. Constable, 1967.

Not TA, but compatible with it . . .
Self Therapy, Muriel Shiffman. Wingbow Press, 1967.
  Do not be misled by the title. This can be used to help both you and your clients understand how old, unfinished business can get tangled up with present life. A light approach, even light-hearted at times, but full of really useful information and a simple system for tracking old feelings—detective work is how she describes it. If it has a disadvantage it is that it can be a little 'wife and mother' in tone, but if this does not get in your way it can be a very helpful tool.

Journal Writing
Life's Companion, Christina Baldwin. Bantam, 1991.
  This is so full of interesting and inspiring ideas for writing, it should be twice the size. Has a strong spiritual element. Wonderful exercises. If these don't get you writing, I don't know what will.

Sexual Abuse
The Courage to Heal, Ellen Bass and Laura Davis. Cedar, 1990.
  A big book, needs to be worked through slowly. Excellent step-by-step guide for client and counsellor. Written in partnership by survivor and counsellor. Not an easy read but a very useful resource. Now there is also a workbook and a book for partners of survivors. I haven't read these but if they are as good as the 'parent' book they should be well worth getting. The voice of survivors is strongly represented in this book.

More personal are:

I Know Why the Caged Bird Sings, Maya Angelou. Virago, 1983.

> Very moving autobiography, not easy to forget. Both sad and beautiful to read.

Cry Hard and Swim, Jacqueline Spring. Virago, 1987.

> I especially like the way the therapeutic relationship is described, the awareness of the need for the client to be able to go back into her ordinary life and family between intense sessions.

The Drama of Being a Child, Alice Miller. Virago, 1987.

For Your Own Good, Alice Miller. Virago, 1987.

Thou Shalt Not be Aware, Alice Miller. Pluto Press, 1985.

> Alice Miller's books are excellent but can be very emotionally challenging. Distressing reading for parents. Not recommended when you are feeling low or vulnerable. Choose your time and they have a lot to offer.

Abuse by Therapists

Sex in the Forbidden Zone, Peter Rutter, M.D. Mandala, 1989.

Mind and Body

Dreambody, Arnold Mindell. Arkana, 1990.

> A real shake up and wake and think book. I think it makes the links between mind and body very clear. I find the idea that illness is a dream of the body really fascinating.

Illness and Healing

From a more medical slant, but with a very positive message for counsellors are:

Getting Well Again, O. Carl Simonton, M.D., Stephanie Matthews Simonton and James L. Creighton. Bantam, 1984.

Teach Only Love, Gerald G. Jampolsky. Bantam, 1983.

Making Miracles, P. C. Raid. Thorsons, 1989.
This is a really amazing book, good to read if you need reminding of the courage and power of ordinary people. I find reading it encouraging and cheering. It looks at the stories of people who have made extraordinary recoveries in spite of all the medical opinions and advice. It looks at what these very different people may have in common.

Depression

Choosing Not Losing, Dorothy Rowe. Fontana, 1988.
Anything by Dorothy Rowe is going to be good, clear, positive and helpful. Good exercise for the mental muscles, lots to think over, plenty to stimulate you and challenge you.

Something Different

What We May Be, Piero Ferrucci. Turnstone Press, 1982.
This is a wonderful book on psychosynthesis, full of exercises and visualisations. If you like the book, consider taking the training or attending workshops, or you may be lucky enough to have a practitioner near enough for you to go to. Contact the Institute of Psychosynthesis, Highwood Park, Nan Clark's Lane, Mill Hill, London NW7.

More Off Beat

If You Meet the Buddha on the Road Kill Him, Sheldon Kop. Bantam, 1983.
A surprising read, very stimulating. It puzzled me when I first read it; now, years later, I think I know what he was getting at when he talked of 'playing' in therapy. If it irritates you it is useful, I found, to work out why.

You Can Heal Your Life, Louise Hay. Eden Grove, 1990.
This very definite, positive approach either hits the spot for you or brings you out in hives. I find it raises my spirits and is full of useful techniques for raising self-esteem. It does stress self-responsibility and owning our power. It works for me.

The Road Less Travelled, M. Scott Peck. Hutchinson, 1983.

Another that you will either be pressing on your friends or losing in an airport lounge. A Christian perspective on psychological and spiritual growth. Easy to read, lots to think about and/or disagree with. Shares with us his working and thinking and growing as a psychotherapist. Warm and honest, human.

Assertion

Ann Dickson has written these two (more by now, I hope!) lively, friendly, approachable books to help with problems of sexuality and assertiveness for women. *The Mirror Within* (1985) looks at sexuality and *A Woman in Your Own Right* (1982) covers assertiveness. Both published by Quartet.

Communication

Making Contact, Virginia Satir. Celestial Arts, 1976.

If you never get another book on communication, get this one.

Meditation

Meditation: A Treasury of Techniques, Pam and Gordon Smith. C. W. Daniel, 1989.

This book is rightly called a treasury. Big, full of wonderful photographs which are a meditation just to contemplate, and gentle, beautifully crafted meditations. Treat yourself. You don't have to eat brown rice to enjoy it, you can just do it.

Adult Development

Passages, Gail Sheehy. Corgi, 1979.

About the predictable crises of adult life, not focusing on the problems, more about how people find their way through, the attitudes and thinking that seems most helpful.

Pathfinders, Gail Sheehy. William Morrow, 1981.
   This looks at outstanding individuals whose response to risk and challenge in their lives has resulted in exceptional solutions to exceptional problems.

Fantastic Journeys
If you are attracted by myth and imagery you may find the following books as inspiring, useful and informative as I do:
The Hero Within, Carol Pearson. HarperCollins, 1986.
   This book describes itself as being about 'the stories that help us make meaning of our lives'. I can't do better than that at giving you a flavour of it. Fun, full of exercises and a good way to understand yourself better, and with ideas to dwell on and be enriched by.
The Heroine's Journey, Maureen Murdock. Shambhala, 1990.
   For women to answer the question, What is this all for? Wonderful source for personal work, as is the book above.

And finally . . .
Healers on Healing, Richard Carlson and Benjamin Shield (eds.). Rider, 1988.
   This book describes itself as being about healers, but I think it could be as applicable to counsellors. See what you think. A wide variety of practitioners give their views on what makes for healing and recovery.

*   *   *

Bereavement
The following are not part of my personal, special selection, but they are marvellous books for anyone wanting to study bereavement counselling:
Bereavement, Colin Murray Parkes. Tavistock, 1972.
On Death and Dying, Elisabeth Kübler-Ross. Tavistock, 1970.
Grief Counselling and Grief Therapy, W. Worden. Tavistock, 1983.

Index